The Philosophy and Science of
Predictive Processing

Also available from Bloomsbury

Advances in Experimental Philosophy of Mind,
edited by Justin Sytsma
Advances in Experimental Philosophy of Science,
edited by Daniel A. Wilkenfeld, Richard Samuels
Arguing from Cognitive Science of Religion,
by Hans Van Eyghen
Great Philosophical Objections to Artificial Intelligence,
by Eric Dietrich, John P. Sullins, Bram van Heuveln,
Chris Fields, Robin Zebrowski
Methodological Advances in Experimental Philosophy,
edited by Eugen Fischer, Mark Curtis
Philosophy in a Technological World,
by James Tartaglia

The Philosophy and Science of Predictive Processing

Edited by Dina Mendonça, Manuel Curado, and Steven S. Gouveia

BLOOMSBURY ACADEMIC

LONDON • NEW YORK • OXFORD • NEW DELHI • SYDNEY

BLOOMSBURY ACADEMIC
Bloomsbury Publishing Plc
50 Bedford Square, London, WC1B 3DP, UK
1385 Broadway, New York, NY 10018, USA
29 Earlsfort Terrace, Dublin 2, Ireland

BLOOMSBURY, BLOOMSBURY ACADEMIC and the Diana logo
are trademarks of Bloomsbury Publishing Plc

First published in Great Britain 2021
This paperback edition published in 2022

Cover design by Charlotte Daniels
Cover image © 4X-image / iStock

A catalogue record for this book is available from the British Library.

Library of Congress Cataloging-in-Publication Data
Names: Mendonça, Dina, editor. | Curado, Manuel, 1967- editor. | Gouveia, Steven S., editor.
Title: The philosophy and science of predictive processing / edited by
Dina Mendonça, Manuel Curado and Steven S. Gouveia.
Description: New York, NY : Bloomsbury Academic, 2020. | Includes bibliographical
references and index.
Identifiers: LCCN 2020033552 (print) | LCCN 2020033553 (ebook) |
ISBN 9781350099753 (hardback) | ISBN 9781350197299 (paperback) |
ISBN 9781350099760 (ePDF) | ISBN 9781350099777 (eBook)
Subjects: LCSH: Psychology–Methodology. | Prediction (Psychology) |
Cognitive science. | Neurosciences.
Classification: LCC BF38.5 .P478 2020 (print) | LCC BF38.5 (ebook) | DDC 150.1/12–dc23
LC record available at https://lccn.loc.gov/2020033552
LC ebook record available at https://lccn.loc.gov/2020033553

ISBN: HB: 978-1-3500-9975-3
         PB: 978-1-3501-9729-9
         ePDF: 978-1-3500-9976-0
         eBook: 978-1-3500-9977-7

Typeset by Integra Software Services Pvt. Ltd.,

To find out more about our authors and books visit www.bloomsbury.com
and sign up for our newsletters.

Contents

List of Figures

Notes on Contributors

Anil Seth is Professor of Cognitive and Computational Neuroscience and Founding Co-Director of the Sackler Centre for Consciousness Science at the University of Sussex. He is also Co-Director of the Canadian Institute for Advanced Research (CIFAR) Azrieli Program on Brain, Mind, and Consciousness; Editor-in-Chief of Neuroscience of Consciousness (Oxford University Press); and a Wellcome Trust Engagement Fellow. He holds degrees in Natural Sciences (MA, Cambridge, 1996), Knowledge-Based Systems (M.Sc., Sussex, 1996), and Computer Science and Artificial Intelligence (Ph.D., Sussex, 2001). From 2001 until 2006 he worked at The Neurosciences Institute in San Diego as a Postdoctoral and then Associate Fellow, after which he returned to Sussex. He has published more than 180 research papers, his 2017 TED talk on consciousness has been viewed more than nine million times, and his first full-length book—*Being You: Consciousness and the Beast Machine*—will be published by Faber & Faber/Penguin in 2021.

Thomas van Es is a doctoral researcher at the University of Antwerp under supervision of Erik Myin. He has published on non-representational approaches to the Embedded View of vision and predictive processing. Financed by an FWO grant, studies Prediction Error Minimization theories, in particular the use of representational contents, and its intersection with Sensorimotor Theory. He did both his BA and Research Master's at the University of Groningen. The BA thesis delved into the infinite regress problem in epistemology, supervised by Jeanne Peijnenburg. The topic of his Research Master's thesis was the intersection of Predictive Coding and Sensorimotor Theory, in particular on perceptual experience and attention, supervised by Fred Keijzer and Catarina Dutilh Novaes. Further scientific interests include the free will problem, determinism in physics, epistemology and philosophy of science in general.

Erik Myin is currently Senior Full Professor at the Department of Philosophy at the University of Antwerp. He defended his Ph.D. on naturalistic approaches to perception and meaning at the Vrije Universiteit Brussel in February 1993. He took up a fulltime position at the Department of Philosophy at the University of Antwerp in 2004. He has published on the philosophy of mind and philosophical psychology in philosophical, interdisciplinary, and scientific journals. Besides authoring solo pieces, he has collaborated with both philosophers and scientists. He has organized many conferences and workshops, and he has participated as invited speaker in conferences and workshops worldwide—the last two in February 2018 in Wollongong, Australia, and in March 2018 in Memphis, United States. Erik Myin has a continuing collaboration with fellow philosopher Daniel Hutto, first at the University of Hertfordshire, now at the University of Wollongong, Australia. Together they have written two monographs published by MIT Press, and a number—still counting—of papers in which they defend their Radical Enactivist approach to perception and cognition.

Colin Klein is Associate Professor in the School of Philosophy at the Australian National University. He works on philosophy of science and philosophy of mind, especially in methodological issues around philosophy of neuroscience and computational theories of mind. His recent research involves developing an interventionist account of explanation in cognitive neuroscience. He has published widely, including in *Philosophy of Science, The British Journal for the Philosophy of Science, Proceedings of the National Academy of Sciences*, and *NeuroImage*. His 2015 book *What the Body Commands: The Imperative Theory of Pain* won the David Harold Tribe Prize.

Richard Menary is an Australian Research Council Future Fellow at Macquarie University, Sydney. He holds an M.Sc. in Cognitive Science from the University of Birmingham and a Ph.D. in Philosophy from King's College London. He has written and edited books for Palgrave Macmillan and MIT Press and has published many articles on the philosophy of mind and cognitive science with journals such as *Mind and Language, Synthese*, and *Philosophical Psychology*. He has developed a conceptual framework for understanding cognition called Cognitive Integration. It is a contribution to the embodied, embedded, and extended cognition movement in philosophy and cognitive science and the extended synthesis movement in evolutionary biology—particularly cultural evolution and niche construction. It is a framework for understanding and studying cognition and the mind that draws on several sources: empirical research in embodied cognition, arguments for extended cognition, distributed cognition, niche construction and cultural inheritance, developmental psychology, social learning, and cognitive neuroscience.

Alexander James Gillett is Lecturer in the Philosophy department at Macquarie University. He completed a Ph.D. in Philosophy of Cognitive Science at Macquarie University in 2018. His thesis examines the conceptual foundations of the distributed cognition framework in cognitive science. His current research focuses on how human spatial cognition is shaped by ontogenetic and phylogenetic factors relating to the acquisition of cultural practices (i.e., encultured). He has additional interests in the philosophy of science, especially pertaining to the nature of interdisciplinary research.

Klaus Gärtner studied Philosophy at the University of Regensburg (Germany). Before joining the Center for Philosophy of Sciences of the University of Lisbon, he obtained his Ph.D.—funded by the Foundation of Science and Technology—at the Faculty of Social and Human Sciences of the New University of Lisbon as a collaborator of the Institute of Philosophy of the NOVA (IFILNOVA) in 2014, with his dissertation entitled *From Consciousness to Knowledge: The Explanatory Power of Revelation*. In 2010 he was a visiting Ph.D. student at the Centre for Consciousness at the Australian National University (ANU) in Canberra, Australia, under the supervision of David Chalmers. He mostly works on contemporary Philosophy of Mind and Cognition. At the moment, his focus includes topics in the area of Conscious Experience and trends in 4E Cognition. Klaus is a founding member of the Lisbon Mind and Reasoning Group.

Robert Clowes is Researcher and Invited Auxiliary Professor at the New University of Lisbon, Portugal. He also directs the Lisbon Mind & Reasoning Group at the New University of Lisbon, which specializes in research devoted to mind, cognition, and human reasoning. Robert's research interests span a range of topics in philosophy and cognitive science, including the philosophy of technology, memory, agency, and the implications of embodiment and cognitive extension for our understanding of the mind and conscious experience. He is particularly interested in the philosophical and cognitive scientific significance of new technologies, especially those that are built on top of global digital networks, such as the Internet and Web. His work has appeared in a variety of journals, including *Review of Philosophy and Psychology, AI & Society, New Ideas in Psychology, Phenomenology and the Cognitive Sciences, Philosophy and Technology*, and the *Journal of Consciousness Studies*.

Dina Mendonça (Ph.D. University of South Carolina, United States, 2003) is a research member of IFILNOVA and works on Philosophy of Emotions and Philosophy for Children at the New University of Lisbon, FCSH NOVA (Universidade Nova de Lisboa). Her current research is focused on the application the Situated Approach to Emotions, which takes emotions as dynamic and active situational occurrences (Mendonça 2012) to Ethics and Decision-Making. This research of Deweyan inspiration aims at elaborating a critical interpretation of the philosophy of emotions clarifying different methodological and philosophical approaches to emotions, as well as identifying the key issues and problems for emotion and further complexities of our emotional world (Mendonça 2013, 2014, 2017). She is the author of several papers on emotion theory and, in addition, promotes and creates original material for application of philosophy to all schooling stages, and as an aid in the creative processes.

Manuel Curado is a professor at the University of Minho, National Defense Auditor, Doctor cum laude from the University of Salamanca, MA from the Nova University of Lisbon, graduate from the Universidade Católica Portuguesa (Lisbon), and holder of the Top Management Course for Public Administration (CADAP). He was visiting professor in the universities of Moscow, Russia (MGIMO and MGLU), and professor Erasmus in the University of Padova (Italy); he collaborated with the universities of Porto, Coimbra, Universidade Católica Portuguesa and Vigo. Moreover, he is the author of various books, all in Portuguese: *As Viríadas do Doutor Samuda* (Coimbra, Imprensa da Universidade de Coimbra, 2014), *Um Génio Português: Edmundo Curvelo* (Coimbra, Imprensa da Universidade de Coimbra, 2013), *Porquê Deus se Temos a Ciência?* (Porto, Fronteira do Caos, 2009), *Direito Biomédico: A Legislação Portuguesa* (Lisboa, Quid Juris, 2008), *Luz Misteriosa: A Consciência no Mundo Físico* (Famalicão, Quasi, 2007), and *O Mito da Tradução Automática* (Braga, Universidade do Minho/Cehum, 2000). Finally, he is also the editor of several books: *Obras Completas de Edmundo Curvelo* (Lisboa, Fundação Calouste Gulbenkian, 2013), *Deus na Universidade: O que Pensam* *os Universitários Portugueses sobre Deus?* (Porto, Fronteira do Caos, 2011), *Cartas Italianas de Verney* (Lisboa, Sílabo, 2008), *Pessoas Transparentes: Questões Actuais de Bioética* (Coimbra, Almedina, 2008), and two titles in collaboration with Alfredo Dinis, SJ, *Mente, Self e Consciência* (Braga, Universidade Católica Portuguesa, 2007) and *Consciência e Cognição* (Braga, Universidade Católica Portuguesa, 2004). He co-edited (with Steven S. Gouveia) *Philosophy of Mind: Contemporary Perspectives* (Cambridge Scholars Publishing, 2017) and *Perception, Cognition, and Aesthetics* with (Routledge, 2019).

Laurent Perrinet (Researcher, CNRS) is Computational Neuroscientist specialized in large-scale neural network models of low-level vision, perception, and action. He co-authored more than thirty-five articles in computational neuroscience and computer vision. He graduated from the aeronautics engineering school SUPAERO, in Toulouse (France), with a signal processing and stochastic modeling degree. He received a Ph.D. in Cognitive Science in 2003 on the mathematical analysis on temporal spike coding in multi-scale and adaptive representation of natural scenes. His research program is focusing in bridging the complex dynamics of realistic, large-scale models of spiking neurons with functional models of low-level vision. In particular, as part of the FACETS and BrainScaleS consortia, he has developed experimental protocols in collaboration with neurophysiologists to characterize the response of population of neurons. Recently, he extended models of visual processing in the framework of predictive processing in collaboration with the team of Karl Friston at the University College of London. This method aims at characterizing the processing of dynamical flow of information as an active inference process. His current challenge is to link this mathematical formalism with the event-based nature of neural information.

Steven S. Gouveia is a Ph.D. candidate researcher at the University of Minho (funded by FCT: SFRH/BD/128863/2017), supervised by the philosopher Manuel Curado and the neuroscientist Georg Northoff. He is a visiting researcher at Minds, Brain Imaging and Neuroethics Unit at the Royal Institute of Mental Health at the University of Ottawa. He is a researcher at Mind, Language and Action Group, Institute of Philosophy at the University of Porto, and at the Lisbon Mind & Reasoning Group, IFILNOVA—Universidade Nova de Lisboa. He has published eight books on various topics such as Philosophy of Mind, Bioethics, Democracy or Artificial Intelligence, with prefaces by Noam Chomsky and Peter Singer. He will soon publish his new book *Homo Ignarus: Rational Ethics for an Irrational World* and he is the host of the international documentary *The Age of Artificial Intelligence*. More information: www. stevensgouveia.weebly.com.

Sina Fazelpour is Social Sciences and Humanities Research Council Postdoctoral Fellow at the Philosophy Department of Carnegie Mellon University. His research focuses on issues of fairness and transparency in machine learning–based decision support systems. His work has been published in journals such as *Synthese, European Journal for Philosophy of Science, Consciousness and Cognition*, and *Current Opinion in Neurobiology*. He holds a Ph.D. in Philosophy from the University of British Columbia, a M.Sc. in medical biophysics from the University of Toronto, and a B.Eng. in electrical and biomedical engineering from McMaster University.

Madeleine Ransom is a Ph.D. candidate at the Philosophy Department of the University of British Columbia. Her research is centered on how empirical work in perceptual learning can inform the philosophy of perception. She has published papers in journals such as Philosophy and Phenomenological Research, and Consciousness and Cognition. She is currently a fellow at the W. Maurice Young Centre for Applied Ethics at UBC, where she is working on the ethical implications of varieties of perceptual bias.

Chris Thornton is Lecturer in Informatics at the University of Sussex. His research is concerned with development and use of information theory in cognitive science and psychology. He is both an enthusiast for and a critic of the paradigm of predictive processing, and has written several articles that aim to clarify the computational details of what is proposed.

Lisa Feldman Barrett, Ph.D., is University Distinguished Professor of Psychology and Director of the Interdisciplinary Affective Science Laboratory (IASLab) at Northeastern University, with research appointments at Harvard Medical School and Massachusetts General Hospital. Her research focuses on the nature of emotion from both psychological and neuroscience perspectives. Dr. Barrett is the recipient of numerous research awards, including the 2018 APS Lifetime Mentor Award and a 2007 NIH Director's Pioneer Award for transformative research. She is an elected fellow of the Royal Society of Canada, the American Academy of Arts and Sciences, and several other scientific societies. Her research has been continuously funded by NIH and NSF for over twenty years. Dr. Barrett also educates lawyers, judges, and other legal actors about emotion, neuroscience, and the law as part of her work for the Center for Law, Brain and Behavior. In addition to publishing over 230 peer-reviewed papers and 50 book chapters, Dr. Barrett has testified before US Congress in support of basic behavioral research funding and has edited five volumes, including the 4th edition of the *Handbook of Emotion*, published by Guilford Press. Her book, *How Emotions Are Made: The Secret Life of the Brain*, is published by Houghton Mifflin Harcourt, and features a discussion of predictive processing in the brain.

Lorena Chanes, Ph.D., is Assistant Professor of the Department of Clinical and Health Psychology-Serra Húnter Programme at Universitat Autònoma de Barcelona. Her research focuses on cognitive and affective processes that ultimately lead to conscious experience, with a special emphasis on their underlying neural bases and disruptions in neuropsychiatric conditions. She is also interested in ethical considerations and cultural implications related to mental health. She has authored several papers in high-impact journals and a chapter in a major handbook of psychobiology (*Fundamentos de Psicobiología*), published by Panamericana. Since her early career, her research and training have been continuously funded by public agencies and non-profit foundations.

Karl Friston is a theoretical neuroscientist and authority on brain imaging. He invented statistical parametric mapping (SPM), voxel-based morphometry (VBM), and dynamic causal modeling (DCM). These contributions were motivated by schizophrenia research and theoretical studies of value learning, formulated as the dysconnection hypothesis of schizophrenia. Mathematical contributions include variational Laplacian procedures and generalized filtering for hierarchical Bayesian model inversion. Friston currently works on models of functional integration in the human brain and the principles that underlie neuronal interactions. His main contribution to theoretical neurobiology is a free-energy principle for action and perception (active inference). Friston received the first Young Investigators Award in Human Brain Mapping (1996) and was elected a Fellow of the Academy of Medical Sciences (1999). In 2000 he was President of the international Organization of Human Brain Mapping. In 2003 he was awarded the Minerva Golden Brain Award and was elected a Fellow of the Royal Society in 2006. In 2008 he received a Medal, College de France and an Honorary Doctorate from the University of York in 2011. He became of Fellow of the Royal Society of Biology in 2012, received the Weldon Memorial prize and Medal in 2013 for contributions to mathematical biology, and was elected as a member of EMBO (excellence in the life sciences) in 2014 and the Academia Europaea in (2015). He was the 2016 recipient of the Charles Branch Award for unparalleled breakthroughs in Brain Research and the Glass Brain Award, a lifetime achievement award in the field of human brain mapping. He holds Honorary Doctorates from the University of Zurich and Radboud University.

Thomas Parr began his academic career at University College London (UCL) medical school. After completing an undergraduate degree in Medical Sciences with Neuroscience, he enrolled on the UCL MBPhD program, combining his Ph.D. with clinical studies. He works in the theoretical neurobiology group, led by Professor Karl Friston, at the Wellcome Centre for Human Neuroimaging at the UCL Institute of Neurology. His research interests include active inference, computational neurology, and the oculomotor system.

Shaun Gallagher is the Lillian and Morrie Moss Chair of Excellence in Philosophy at the University of Memphis (2011–). He holds a secondary appointment as Professorial Fellow on the Faculty of Law, Humanities and the Arts, at the University of Wollongong (Australia). He is the recipient of the Humboldt Foundation's first Anneliese Maier Research Award (2012–2018). He is also Honorary Professor of Health Sciences at the University of Tromsø in Norway. From 2007 to 2015, he held a secondary appointment as Research Professor of Philosophy and Cognitive Science at the University of Hertfordshire (UK). He was Honorary Professor of Philosophy at the University of Copenhagen (2010–2015), and Honorary Professor of Philosophy at the University of Durham (UK) (2013–2016). He has held visiting positions at the Medical Research Council's Cognitive and Brain Science Unit at Cambridge University, the Danish National Research Foundation Center for Subjectivity Research at the University of Copenhagen, the Ecole Normale Supériure in Lyon, the Centre de Recherche en Epistémelogie Appliquée (CREA), Paris, Die Kolleg-Forschergruppe Bildakt und

Verkörperung, Humboldt University in Berlin, and most recently at Keble College, University of Oxford (2016). He is also a founding editor, and continues as a co-editor-in-chief of *Phenomenology and the Cognitive Sciences*, an interdisciplinary journal published by Springer (Google Metrics). His research interests include phenomenology and the philosophy of mind, philosophical psychology, embodiment, intersubjectivity, hermeneutics, and the philosophy of time.

Zachariah A. Neemeh is a Ph.D. student in philosophy at the University of Memphis. He is also a graduate student affiliate of the Institute for Intelligent Systems. He was a 2019 fellow of the Kavli Summer Institute in Cognitive Neuroscience. His research interests include 4E cognition, phenomenology, psychopathology, consciousness, perceptual experience, and artificial intelligence.

Jakob Hohwy is Professor of Philosophy at Monash University, Melbourne, Australia. He was trained in Aarhus, Denmark, St. Andrews in Scotland, and at the Australian National University. Hohwy has established the Cognition & Philosophy lab in the Philosophy department at Monash and conducts interdisciplinary experiments in philosophy, psychiatry, and neuroscience. Hohwy's research focuses on contemporary theories in theoretical neurobiology and their implications for consciousness, self, and belief. He is deputy editor of *Neuroscience of Consciousness* and is the author of *The Predictive Mind* (OUP, 2013).

Stephen Gadsby is a Ph.D. candidate in the Cognition and Philosophy lab at Monash University, Melbourne, Australia, supervised by Professor Jakob Hohwy. He holds a MRes from Macquarie University, where he was supervised by Associate Professor Colin Klein. Gadsby conducts interdisciplinary research related to philosophy, psychiatry, and psychology and has published on a number of topics including *anorexia nervosa*, body representation, delusional beliefs, psychiatric taxonomy, and the sense of bodily ownership.

Preface:
The Brain as a Prediction Machine

Anil Seth

Sackler Centre for Consciousness Science, Department of Informatics, University of Sussex, UK. Email: a.k.seth@sussex.ac.uk.

How does the brain work? Gather enough philosophers, psychologists, and neuroscientists together (ideally with a few mathematicians and clinicians added to the mix) and I guarantee that a group will rapidly form to advocate for one answer in particular: that the brain is a *prediction machine*. This is an idea with a long history, many current variations—the Bayesian brain, predictive coding, predictive processing, the free energy principle, active inference, to name a few—and, if the advocates are to be believed, a bright future. At times, it seems that the prediction machine view—let's call it the "PM view" for short—can explain everything and anything. At other times it seems hard to isolate any empirical data points that unambiguously support the PM view over alternative theories. This is why this impressive and enlightening collection—"The philosophy and science of predictive processing"—is both timely and valuable. Its chapters cover three main topic areas that are each central to the PM view of mind and brain: the philosophy, the neuroscience, and applications to clinical disorders. Importantly, the divisions are not strict: many lines of argument and evidence reverberate among the sections. Equally important is that there are contributions from both supporters and critics of the PM view, providing a balanced perspective and allowing the reader the opportunity to draw his or her own conclusions.

The essence of the PM view is that the brain is continually engaged in formulating predictions, or hypotheses, about the causes of its sensory inputs, and in testing these predictions against incoming streams of sensory signals—thereby shaping perceptual content, guiding action, and driving learning. On most interpretations, the brain accomplishes this by implementing some approximate form of Bayesian inference, wherein sensory signals are combined with "prior" expectations or beliefs, to form "posterior" representations. Whether neural systems actually perform Bayesian computations, or whether they merely behave as if they do, is one of many intriguing questions that permeate the PM dialogue and which are explored in the chapters of this collection. (See in particular the chapters by Erik Myin and Thomas van Es, and Colin Klein.)

The historical roots of the PM view are rich and varied. For me, they trace most directly to earlier theories of human perception. These theories reach all the way back to Plato with his Allegory of the Cave; they have prominent echoes in Kantian theories of perception, but perhaps the most relevant historical anchors are found in Hermann von Helmholtz's notion of perception as "unconscious inference" and in Richard

Gregory's description of perception as brain-based hypothesis testing (Gregory 1980, von Helmholtz 1867). Both Helmholtz and Gregory recognized that perception must involve a process of active interpretation—or "best guessing"—in which noisy and ambiguous sensory signals are combined with prior expectations about the way the world is, to form the contents of what we perceive. Yet their insights went rather against the grain, at least in the latter part of the twentieth century. The standard view of perception in this period was as a process of hierarchical feature detection, in which the perceptual content is "read out" from incoming sensory signals in a bottom-up or "outside-in" direction. The dominance of this view was not surprising, given its (at least superficial) match to experimental data, and since to many people it "seems as though" perception happens in this outside-in direction: a brain-based window onto an external world.

Things started to change at the turn of the century, and the PM view has now gained considerable visibility and momentum. This ascendancy has been driven by many factors, one of the more significant being the development of mechanistic (process) theories which describe how neural systems might actually implement predictive perception and control. The central idea here is that the brain implements approximate Bayesian inference through a process of "prediction error minimization." In this picture, top-down signals within perceptual hierarchies convey predictions, while bottom-up signals report "prediction errors"—differences between what the brain expects and what it gets—at each level in the hierarchy. Perception becomes a process of continual minimization of prediction error, with the consequence that the top-down predictions settle on an approximate Bayesian posterior, this being the "best guess" of the hidden causes of sensory inputs. Intuitively, predictive perception happens from the inside-out, just as much—if not more—than from the outside-in.

In the neuroscience of perception, mechanistic proposals of this sort first came to prominence in an influential paper about "predictive coding" in the visual system (Rao and Ballard 1999). They achieved bandwagon status a decade later through the extraordinarily impactful work of two neuroscientifically oriented philosophers, Jakob Hohwy (2013) and Andy Clark (2013), who each articulated persuasive—though somewhat conflicting—views of how the brain uses predictions to shape perception, cognition, and action. At the same time, steadily gaining momentum in the background was another and at first glance distinct line of work which has since become equally influential. Karl Friston's "free energy principle" starts not with the challenge of inferring a perceptual world from a barrage of ambiguous sensory signals, but from an insight about what it means for a biological system (or on some readings, *any* system) to exist (Friston 2010). For Friston, predictive perception is a consequence of a more fundamental imperative for living systems to minimize (information-theoretically) surprising events. An exploration of the synergies and tensions between these alternative versions of the PM view, and other perspectives too, is one of more valuable gifts of the present collection (see, for example, the chapter by Richard Menary and Alexander Gillett).

Having followed and in small ways contributed to the PM view for a number of years, I am convinced that its insights readily justify its current prominence, fuel enthusiasm for its future trajectory, and demand the sort of incisive analysis that this book provides. I'll summarize just a few of these insights, as they appear to me.

The PM view of perception is transformational because it reveals perception to be an active, constructive process, rather than a passive registration of an external, objective reality. This amounts to a kind of "Copernican inversion" in the way we think about perception. Even though it may "seem as though" we perceive the world from the outside-in, it is in fact the other way around, and recognizing this both changes everything, and leaves everything seeming the same way it always did. Practically, the PM view helps explain subjective features both of normal, neurotypical perception, and of aberrant perception in psychiatric conditions such as schizophrenia—where there is now a lively debate about the brain basis of hallucinations (see, for example, A. R. Powers et al. 2017 as well as the excellent chapters in Part III of this book).

The PM view also reframes how we think about "attention" in perception. The now standard story is that attention becomes a process of adaptive "weighting" of sensory prediction errors (Feldman and Friston 2010) through optimization of the inferred precision of sensory signals (though see the challenging chapter by Sina Fazelpour and Madelaine Ransom). The PM perspective also helps reunite perception with action under a single process, since prediction errors can be quashed both by updating predictions and by performing actions that (are predicted to) furnish the anticipated sensory data. The suppression of prediction error through action is called "active inference" (Friston et al. 2010)—an idea which reanimates both the unfairly neglected "perceptual control theory" of William Powers (W. T. Powers 1973) and ideomotor theories of action proposed by William James and others, long ago. The chapter by Laurent Perrinet cover much of this terrain, exploring predictive processing accounts of perception all the way from the retina to the expression of action, while the chapter by Thomas Parr and Karl Friston applies the concept of active inference to shed new light on disconnection syndromes in neuropsychology.

Then there's the relevance for how we conceive of the "self." A straw-man view might conceive the "self" as "that which does the perceiving," perched behind the windows of the eyes (or the ears)—the recipient of wave-upon-wave of incoming sensory data. On the PM view, the self itself is a perception, another active interpretation of sensory data—but this time the data comes from the body as well as from the world. In my own work I've considered how emotion and embodied experiences of selfhood might depend on predictive perception of interoceptive signals (Seth 2013, Seth and Tsakiris 2018, Seth et al. 2011) [see also Barrett and Simmons 2015 and the chapter by Lisa Feldman Barrett and Lorena Chanes in this book], but there is much more to be said here. In particular, the role of predictive control in prospectively regulating self-related processes may go a long way toward explaining why perceptions of selfhood "feel" different, phenomenologically speaking, from perceptions of the world around us. The philosophical relevance of the PM view for selfhood is insightfully explored in the chapter by Robert Clowes and Klaus Gartner, and its applications to psychopathology in the chapters by Jakob Hohwy and Stephen Gadsby, and Zachariah Neemeh and Shaun Gallagher, as well as in the other chapters in Part III.

The mechanistic basis of predictive perception in approximate Bayesian inference has also led to new synergies with artificial intelligence and machine learning. While much of current machine learning remains dominated by powerful feedforward "deep learning" architectures trained by backpropagation (LeCun et al. 2015), increasing attention is being paid to neural networks that incorporate "generative models" of the sort implicated in prediction error minimization schemes. These generative models—which are able to "generate" sensory signals corresponding to predicted causes—in fact have a long history in artificial intelligence, extending back at least as far as the appropriately named "Helmholtz machines" first described by Geoffrey Hinton and Peter Dayan in the 1990s (Hinton and Dayan 1996). Today, algorithms based on generative models are being explored for their potential to learn from smaller quantities of data, to generalize effectively to new situations, and even to autonomously select what new data to learn from, in order to improve. In this collection, the chapter by Chris Thornton expertly examines the computational aspects of predictive processing, arguing that predictive processing can in principle accomplish any computational task.

Finally, there is the ever-present question of consciousness. If the PM view is indeed a comprehensive theory of mind and brain, what does it have to say about this most central but most relcalcitrant of phenomena? Here, I see a difference in the remit of the PM view as compared to theories such as global workspace theory (Baars 1988, Dehaene and Changeux 2011), integrated information theory (Tononi et al. 2016), and higher-order thought theory (Lau and Rosenthal 2011). These theories offer themselves first and foremost as theories of consciousness—in other words, they have subjective experience, in one form or another, as their primary explanatory target. In contrast, the PM view may be better understood as a theory *for* consciousness science, rather than as a theory *of* consciousness. It provides a potent set of concepts and experimental methods for mapping neural mechanisms to the subjective, phenomenological properties of conscious perception—but it does not (at least not obviously) explain how or why consciousness happens in the first place. Perhaps, though, the piece-by-piece building of explanatory bridges between the physical and the phenomenological will turn out to be the most productive objective for any science of consciousness (Seth 2016). The contentious subject of consciousness is insightfully discussed in the pages of this book, most directly in the chapters by Steven S. Gouveia, and by Lisa Feldman Barrett and Lorena Chanes—but in many other places too.

More than any other contemporary perspective on brain and mind, the PM view is exercising both philosophers and scientists, and in doing so creating new spaces in which ideas from each tradition come into direct contact. This close interaction presents new challenges and opens new opportunities, both of which take the stage under the expert curation of the Editors of this collection. Within its pages you will find a great deal to ponder about the ways in which the brain is, or is not—or both is and is not—a prediction machine.

Acknowledgments

I am grateful to the Dr. Mortimer and Theresa Sackler Foundation, which supports the Sackler Centre for Consciousness Science, and to the Canadian Institute for Advanced Research (CIFAR Azrieli Program on Brain, Mind, and Consciousness).

References

Baars, B. J. (1988), *A Cognitive Theory of Consciousness*, New York: Cambridge University Press.

Barrett, L. F., & Simmons, W. K. (2015), "Interoceptive Predictions in the Brain," *Nature Reviews Neuroscience*, 16 (7): 419–29. doi.org/10.1038/nrn3950.

Clark, A. (2013), "Whatever Next? Predictive Brains, Situated Agents, and the Future of Cognitive Science," *Behavioral and Brain Sciences*, 36 (3): 181–204. doi.org/10.1017/S0140525X12000477.

Dehaene, S. and Changeux, J. P. (2011), "Experimental and Theoretical Approaches to Conscious Processing," *Neuron*, 70 (2): 200–27. doi.org/S0896-6273(11)00258-3.

Feldman, H. and Friston, K. J. (2010), "Attention, Uncertainty, and Free-energy," *Frontiers in Integrative Neuroscience*, 4 (215). doi.org/10.3389/fnhum.2010.00215.

Friston, K. J. (2010), "The Free-Energy Principle: A Unified Brain Theory?," *Nature Reviews Neuroscience*, 11 (2): 127–138.

Friston, K. J., Daunizeau, J., Kilner, J. and Kiebel, S. J. (2010), "Action and Behavior: A Free-energy Formulation," *Biological Cybernetics*, 102 (3): 227–60. doi.org/10.1007/s00422-010-0364-z.

Gregory, R. L. (1980), "Perceptions as Hypotheses," *Philosophical Transactions of the Royal Society B Biological Sciences*, 290 (1038): 181–97.

Hinton, G. E. and Dayan, P. (1996), "Varieties of Helmholtz Machine," *Neural Networks*, 9 (8): 1385–403. doi.org/S0893608096000093.

Hohwy, J. (2013), *The Predictive Mind*, Oxford: Oxford University Press.

Lau, H. and Rosenthal, D. (2011), "Empirical Support for Higher-Order Theories of Conscious Awareness," *Trends in Cognitive Sciences*, 15 (8): 365–73. doi.org/10.1016/j.tics.2011.05.009.

LeCun, Y., Bengio, Y. and Hinton, G. (2015), "Deep Learning," *Nature*, 521 (7553): 436–44. doi.org/10.1038/nature14539.

Powers, A. R., Mathys, C. and Corlett, P. R. (2017), "Pavlovian Conditioning-induced Hallucinations Result from Overweighting of Perceptual Priors," *Science*, 357 (6351): 596–600. doi.org/10.1126/science.aan3458.

Powers, W. T. (1973), *Behavior: The Control of Perception*, Hawthorne, NY: Aldine de Gruyter.

Rao, R. P. and Ballard, D. H. (1999), "Predictive Coding in the Visual Cortex: A Functional Interpretation of Some Extra-classical Receptive-field Effects," *Nature Neuroscience*, 2 (1): 79–87. doi.org/10.1038/4580.

Seth, A. K. (2013), "Interoceptive Inference, Emotion, and the Embodied Self," *Trends in Cognitive Sciences*, 17 (11): 565–73. doi.org/10.1016/j.tics.2013.09.007.

Seth, A. K. (2016), "The Real Problem," *Aeon*. https://aeon.co/essays/the-hard-problem-of-consciousness-is-a-distraction-from-the-real-one.

Seth, A. K. (2019), "From Unconscious Inference to the Beholder's Share: Predictive Perception and Human Experience," *European Review*, 273 (3): 378–410.

Seth, A. K., Suzuki, K., & Critchley, H. D. (2011), "An Interoceptive Predictive Coding Model of Conscious Presence," *Frontiers in Psychology*, 2 (395). doi: 10.3389/fpsyg.2011.00395.

Seth, A. K. and Tsakiris, M. (2018), "Being a Beast Machine: The Somatic Basis of Selfhood," *Trends in Cognitive Sciences*, 22 (11): 969–81. doi.org/10.1016/j.tics.2018.08.008.

Tononi, G., Boly, M., Massimini, M. and Koch, C. (2016), "Integrated Information Theory: From Consciousness to Its Physical Substrate," *Nature Reviews Neuroscience*, 17 (7): 450–61. doi: 10.1038/nrn.2016.44.

von Helmholtz, H. (1867), *Handuch der physiologischen Optik*, Leipzig: Voss.

List of Abbreviations

ABC	Affective, Bodily, and Cognitive Symptoms.
AI	Active Inference
AN	Anorexia Nervosa
ANN	Artificial Neural Network
APA	American Psychological Association
CAPTCHA	Completely Automated Public Turing Test to Tell Computers and Humans Apart
CBT	Cognitive Behavioral Therapy
CS	Conditioned Stimulus
CPU	Central Processing Unit
DAB	Desire-as-Belief
DACB	Desire-as-Conditional-Belief
DL	Deep Learning
DSM–5	Diagnostic and Statistical Manual of Mental Disorders (5th edition)
DNA	Deoxyribonucleic Acid
EEG	Electroencephalography
EV	Embedded View
FEP	Free Energy Principle
fMRI	functional Magnetic Resonance Imaging
FFA	Fusiform Face Area
FLE	Flash-lag Effect
GPU	Graphics Processing Unit
HMB	Heuristic Markov Blankets
ICD-10	International Classification of Diseases (10th revision)
IoC	Illusion of Control

lrAM	long-range Apparent Motion
IND	Independence
LDWs	Losses Disguised as Wins
MDD	Major Depressive Disorder
MDP	Markov Decision Process
NCC	Neural Correlates of Consciousness
NCCcon	Neural Consequences of Consciousness
NPC	Neural Predisposition of Consciousness
preNPC	Neural Prerequisite of Consciousness
OMB	Ontological Markov Blankets
PC	Predictive Coding Theories
PEM	Prediction Error Minimization
PF	Prediction Fallacy
PM	Prediction Machine view
PP	Predictive Processing
PTSD	Posttraumatic Stress Disorder
RF	Receptive Fields (of a neuron)
SNNs	Spiking Neural Networks
SOC	Self-organized Criticality
SPEM	Smooth Pursuit Eye Movements
SPM	Statistical Parametric Mapping
STA	Spatiotemporal Alignment
STE	Spatiotemporal Expansion
STG	Spatiotemporal Globalization
STN	Spatiotemporal Nestedness
UCS	Unconditioned Stimulus
V1	Primary Visual Cortex
VSDI	Voltage-sensitive Dyes
WHO	World Health Organization

Introduction

Dina Mendonça, Manuel Curado, and Steven S. Gouveia

Predictive processing (PP) is the focus of this edited collection. This approach can be seen as the last conceptual effort to understand and explain everything related to the human mind. In this way it stands as a promise for a unique theoretical background that will unify the various sciences that study the brain, the mind, and its psychology into one systematic framework. In sum, PP is announced as being the final revolution needed to achieve a full explanation of our complex mental life standing as a sort of Holy Grail for the conscious brain. Is this claim exaggerated? This volume will debate that and other relevant questions.

While the theoretical framework is being progressively elaborated to attain its ambitious unifying goal, it works as a wonderful way to revise and identify central problematic issues concerning understanding the mind and the functioning of the brain. It offers a new philosophical conceptual notation to reevaluate longstanding problems of a variety of research areas that are being reconceptualized due to the impact of the novel approach.

PP overcomes the model of passive conception of the brain and, turning the perceptive process upside down, shows how minds are complex engines of prediction constantly anticipating the bottom flow of information. Though PP is often taken as an outcome of the Bayesian brain theory, it can also be seen as deriving from information theory and using the predictive payoff as an organizing concept (Thornton 2017), and its philosophical roots can be traced back to Immanuel Kant (Swanson 2016, Wiese and Metzinger 2017: 2).

PP proposal offers to be a unifying overarching theory of the mind, which may ultimately serve as a general framework for the psychological phenomenon and the neuronal activity of the brain. The proposal has been decisively adopted by cognitive science because it can be applied to perception, action, cognition and emotion and their relationships (Wiese and Metzinger 2017: 2) and, more importantly, it shows that there is a way to conceive the mind that could be adopted by a wide variety of disciplines. Given the certainty that PP could be applied to a wide variety of phenomena and fields, the understanding of its core conceptual theory is crucially important. Therefore, it is fundamental to grasp how it emphasizes the active role of the mind, its dynamical function, and how it offers a set of ideas capable of being understood by experts of various areas of research.

The present anthology offers an interdisciplinary array of essays from scholars and researchers of cognitive science from a variety of disciplines, both from well-recognized scholars as well as promising younger researchers, and hopes to be a unique contribution focusing on critically examining PP and its promises. In addition to showing the wide range of application of this novel intellectual proposal, it includes a critical examination of some of the problematic issues surrounding the new approach, and can be used both as a thorough introduction to PP framework, as well as an insightful collection for a more detailed and critical reading.

The book has three parts that cover different aspects of PP theory. It begins with the first part that focuses on Predictive Processing and philosophical approaches, including four chapters. The first is a chapter by Thomas van Es and Erik Myin entitled "Predictive Processing and Representation: How Less Can Be More" that analyses the connection between PP and the representational foundations arguing that the theoretical framework is most coherent and strong in its nonrepresentational version, and consequently that the research efforts will be most fruitful by furthering exploring it under its non-representational version.

It is followed by a chapter by Colin Klein, "A Humean Challenge to Predictive Coding," which argues that the PP coding is best understood within a Humean philosophical outlook. Despite the fact that some authors have argued that the philosophical roots of PP are Kantian (e.g., Swanson 2016), Klein's chapter shows that when its Humean strike is highlighted it demonstrates how predictive coding reveals an interesting issue about value learning.

Then, in the chapter "Are Markov Blankets Real and Does It Matter?" Richard Menary and Alexander James Gillett show how a reevaluation of the concept of Markov Blankets could provide a way to see in a new light several questions concerning PP philosophical commitments. Among other things they point out how certain descriptions of the framework emphasize the role of embodied action while others stress the internal brain processes more in isolation, revealing how internalism and externalism about the mind are at stake in this different philosophical emphasis.

The last chapter of this section was written Klaus Gärtner and Robert Clowes. With the title "Predictive Processing and Metaphysical Views of the Self," they show how PP can be seen to endorse different accounts of the self; moreover, the authors argue that further critical reflection identifies the pre-reflective view of the situational self as the most adequate to fit the PP framework.

The second part of the collection covers the connection of Predictive Processing with approaches in Cognitive Sciences and Neuroscience. In the first chapter of this part, Laurent Perrinet explains in "From the Retina to Action: Dynamics of Predictive Processing in the Visual System" how PP offers a unified theory to explain a variety of visual mechanisms, and what future directions are required to provide the complete design of the generic PP circuit.

The following chapter, "Predictive Processing and Consciousness: Prediction Fallacy and Its Spatiotemporal Resolution", by Steven S. Gouveia, discusses the PP framework and its explanatory power regarding consciousness, if any at all. Building upon how spatiotemporal dynamic account suggests that consciousness can be traced to the spatiotemporal dynamics of the brain's neuronal activity, the chapter concludes that PP requires a wider context of dynamic spatiotemporal mechanisms to account for both contents and their association with consciousness.

The seventh chapter, "The Many Faces of Attention: Why Precision Optimization Is Not Attention," by Madeleine Ransom and Sina Fazelpour, focuses on the connection of PP with attention. The authors argue that PP needs to go beyond the precision weighting of prediction error to accommodate the full range of attentional phenomena.

The section concludes with a chapter by Chris Thornton entitled "Predictive Processing: Does It Compute?" which considers PP from a computational and engineering perspective, and, after identifying a number of technical problems, advances a number of ways in which PP could successfully eliminate them.

The third and final part of the book unfolds the not easily understood connection of Predictive Processing with Mental Health. The first chapter of this section by Lorena Chanes and Lisa Feldman Barrett further elaborates how PP could help to understand the ways the brain works both in healthy and in dysfunctional conditions. In their chapter, "The Predictive Brain, Conscious Experience and Brain-related Conditions", they describe how PP contributes to understand the precise way the global structure of the information flow is disrupted and the unified field of experience altered in mental disorders and brain damage.

The following chapter on "Disconnection and Diaschisis: Active Inference in Neuropsychology" by Thomas Parr & Karl J. Friston outlines a discrete formulation of active inference and shows how it can improve our understanding of neurological disease enabling the rewriting of the notion of functional diaschisis.

Right after this, the chapter "The Phenomenology and Predictive Processing of Time in Depression" by Zachariah A. Neemeh and Shaun Gallagher describes how recent analyses in PP complement the phenomenological approach to intrinsic time and reinforces understanding how the alterations in the intrinsic temporal structure of the experience of time occur in depression.

Finally, to close the section, "Why Use Predictive Processing to Explain Psychopathology? The Case of *Anorexia Nervosa*," a chapter written by Stephen Gadsby and Jakob Hohwy, applies the PP framework for mental disorder by applying it to *anorexia nervosa*, an eating disorder that is characterized by a complex set of symptoms. The authors defend that this framework can valuably contribute for future better explanations in the field of psychopathology.

As claimed by Anil Seth in the preface to this book, the PP approach has a long history and a bright future. Hopefully, this anthology will leave the reader with the intellectual desire to continue reading about PP and its promising outcomes while it will also help to set an agenda for future research on this valuable theoretical evidence-based framework.

References

Swanson, Link R. (2016), "The Predictive Processing Paradigm Has Roots in Kant," *Frontiers in Systems Neuroscience*, 10: 79.

Thornton, Chris. (2017), "Predictive Processing Simplified: The Infotropic Machine," *Brain and Cognition*, 112: 13–24.

Wiese, W. and Metzinger, T. (2017), "Vanilla PP for Philosophers: A Primer on Predictive Processing," in T. Metzinger and W. Wiese (eds.), *Philosophy and Predictive Processing*, Frankfurt am Main: MIND Group, pp. 8–25.

Part One

Predictive Processing: Philosophical Approaches

Predictive Processing and Representation: How Less Can Be More

Thomas van Es
University of Antwerp
Erik Myin
University of Antwerp

1. Introduction

Attempts to explain cognitive phenomena can be representational or non-representational. Representationalist approaches to all or some cognitive phenomena have been criticized for a few decades (see for example Di Paolo et al. 2017, Gibson 1979, Hutto and Myin 2013, 2017, Varela et al. 1991). Nonetheless, wide-ranging representationalism continues to thrive as the mainstream position in cognitive science. In this chapter, we investigate whether this is because the issues have been solved, with particular focus on predictive processing (PP). We argue that, despite significant effort, PP still can't have the representations it lays claim on. Further, we will defend that the relevant explanatory work can be done without representations. This shows that PP gains from a non-representational interpretation.

PP, in short, is a theoretical framework that places cognition, action, and perception under a single banner of prediction error minimization (Clark 2016, Hohwy 2013). The standard interpretation is as follows. In order to maintain the system's homeostasis, the brain is thought to actively predict the barrage of stimuli entering the system. These predictions are tested against the actual stimuli, and the brain's primary (or only) function is to minimize the prediction errors that result from this testing. This prediction error minimization system is optimized using representational models that mirror the causal-probabilistic structure of the world. These models are continuously updated and fine-tuned as the brain detects prediction errors. Representations here are thought to perform their causal role because of their representational status (Clark 2016, Gładziejewski 2016, Hohwy 2013).

Whether it is legitimate to understand PP in a representational way is contested (Bruineberg et al. 2018, Hutto 2017, Kirchhoff and Robertson 2018). Central to the notion of representation is that it has *content.* On a standard understanding, contentful representation is for a representation to have a target which it represents in a way as being such that it may not be so (Travis 2004). In having a target the contentful representation is intentional; in representing this target *in a way*, it is intensional. Supposing contents in a naturalistic framework require being able to tell a naturalistically credible story of how both of the representational properties, intentionality and intensionality, can be natural properties. This requires being able to account for how these properties of intentionality and intensionality originate: how some naturally occurring properties genuinely *are* the representational properties. Moreover, it needs to show that the representations play a causal role *qua* representations—a causal role which derives from the fact that they are bona fide representations.

Many have argued that standard representational understandings of cognitive systems are inflated because they cannot provide an answer to these challenges about the natural origin and causal efficacy of contents (Hutto and Myin 2013, 2017, Rosenberg 2015). Nonetheless, some theorists have attempted to argue that these challenges can be met in the case of PP. According to a recent idea, representations in PP are analogous to cartographic maps, and attain their representational status by analogy to this prototype. This involves relating to the target by way of structural similarity, and further requires action guidance, decouplability, and misrepresentation (Gładziejewski 2016, Gładziejewski and Miłkowski 2017). As it seems Gładziejewski's proposal has gained significant traction in the literature, we will take this particular proposal of representations in PP to be representative (Kiefer and Hohwy 2018, Lee 2018, Pezzulo et al. 2017, Wiese 2017, Wiese and Metzinger 2017, Williams 2018, Williams and Colling 2018, but see also Dołega 2017).

Here we will argue that this recent attempt to rescue the representational paradigm is not up to the job. Furthermore, we will argue that any explanatory advantages PP might have can be retained without representations. First, we will discuss general objections against representationalism. Second, we will discuss Gładziejewski's (2016) account of representation and analyze whether it solves those issues. Third, we will offer a sketch of an alternative approach to PP, to show that we can move forward without mental representations. Finally, we will conclude that PP is best understood in a non-representational way.

2. General Objections against Representationalism

The account of representation endorsed by philosophers and cognitive scientists alike is one according to which representing involves describing, characterizing, picturing "things as being thus and so—where, for all that, things need not be that way" (Travis 2004: 58). In other ways, representation involves specifying in a way which can be true or false, accurate or inaccurate, or something akin. Something that is specified in some way can be compared to the world, and it can either be correct or not correct, aligned or misaligned. Moreover, representation requires some form or medium of specification, that is description, characterization, or picture—something which has "saying power." As this characterization of representation resonates with the way representation is widely understood philosophically, we will take it as offering legitimate criteria that any candidate representation in PP should minimally meet. Further, due to the causal/explanatory context in which representations are invoked in PP, defenders of representational PP need to establish that representations play a role *qua* representation: contents need to be causally efficacious.

Let's call "structural accounts of representation," all those that construe representation as a relation between some domain of reality and some distinct structured entity, where representation is construed in terms of some mapping, causal or other, between elements and or relations in the domain of reality, and elements or relations in the structure. A minimalistic structural account would count causal covariation between some worldly entity and some other entity as representational, while a cartographical map of a terrain would be an example of a more complicated form of structural representing. Pure structural accounts of representation face some well-known difficulties for meeting the criteria of our characterization (see for example de Oliveira 2018 for more, and further references). A prominent issue is that they over-generate representations, as structural similarities are widespread. This applies not just to the most minimal, correlational, reading of similarity, but also to more complex readings. That is, there seems to be no principled limit on what can be seen as structurally similar to something else—and there seems to be no principled distinction between what can be seen to be structurally similar, and what genuinely *is* structurally similar. Moreover, and independent of this, structural accounts of representation should provide an explication of why the structural relations amount to being representational relations, over and above being *just* structural relations.

A way to accommodate these two concerns is to add a functional component to a structural basis. Such has become standard practice (see again de Oliveira 2018). That is, most accounts of representation, while including a structural component, require that the structural elements and/or relations play some role in the functioning of the system of which they are a part. They should be a *"fuel for success"* (Godfrey-Smith 1996, Miłkowski and Gładziejewski 2017: 339, Shea 2007, 2014). Adding function constrains the class of relations that could count as representational with respect to a pure structural account—representation is only to be found where there is function. Moreover, by introducing function, causal roles come into play, to potentially offer a solution to demand that representations be causally efficacious.

In order to assess whether structural-plus-functional theories of representation can successfully meet the challenge of showing that candidate representations meet the appropriate criteria for being a representation, the question should first be answered what is doing the representing in such accounts. Or: where are the candidate representations located in such an account?

Of course, the representation cannot just be identified with the structures, because then the allegedly different combined structural/functional view inherits all the problems of a pure structural account. That is, if the structural elements represent by themselves, all the questions raised with respect to structural representations can be raised again. So the function has to play a constitutive role for representation in a combined account. This leads to two problems, however. First, the need for adding function arises because structural similarities are cheap, and ubiquitous. Let us see whether a function plus structural similarities account sufficiently constrains the notion of representation.

Consider some examples. There are many structural similarities that will, *prima facie*, be excluded with this requirement of functionality. Think for example of the structural similarities between the dimensions of a countertop and that of a cardboard box. The relation is certainly not representational, and indeed, without further context, the structural similarities are not a fuel for success of an action. But what if we decide to place the box on the countertop? The structural similarities are now a *fuel for success* in the action of placing the box. It is because of the structural similarities between the countertop and the box that the action is successful. Had the countertop been convex, the cardboard box most likely would have slid off. In much the same way the structural similarities are a fuel for success in socks and our sliding them on our feet, door knobs and our turning of them to open doors, and our sitting on chairs. Yet none of these exploitable structural similarities are representations.

This over-generation of representation extends further and encompasses any sort of adaptive behavior. Any behavior that is adapted to the world contains structural similarities to whatever aspects of the world it is adapted to. These structural similarities, further, are, *prima facie*, a fuel for success. We are able to walk so easily due at least in part to the structural similarities that hold between the shape of our feet and the surface of the world. The same story can be told for any adaptive behavior.

Second, any combined structural/functional account will struggle with ascribing a causal role to representation. The move to include function, or use, in the definition of representation is *prima facie* convincing: if a representation is only the type of relation that enables usage, it has to have causal effect. There are now, however, two ways in which "use" is employed in representations. This invites a circle that is difficult to escape from. A representation is defined by its *use*. Only when a composition of driftwood is *used* as a map can the composition count as a representation for the structure of the terrain it is used for (Ramsey 2007). However, as representations figure in an explanatory context, the *usefulness* of a representation, in turn, is defined in terms of the representational relation it bears onto the target. In other words, the way the relations are used are what make them representational, and their representational status is what makes them useful. Put differently,

(A) a structural similarity is used, *because* of
(B) its representational relation to the world.
Further, a structural similarity is said to have
(B) a representational relation to the world, *because* of
(A) the way it is used.

This clearly shows the circularity of the argument. We ground (A) in (B), and, conversely, ground (B) in (A). The representational status of the structural similarities is thus grounded in our use, and our use of the structural similarities is grounded in their representational status. If representational status is to be grounded in use, then use cannot in turn be grounded in its representational status. This is viciously circular.

If the use of a relation is what grants the relation representational status, then there are two options. Either the use of the representation is based in something non-representational, or it is based in something representational. The representationalist thus faces a dilemma. She may attempt to ground the use of representations into something non-representational. One option would be to ground its usefulness in, say, covariance (or some other characteristic of the relation). Yet this means that it is not the representational relation, but the covariational relation that actually figures in the causal explanation. The representational status of the relation has become causally irrelevant. There would be no point to ascribe representational status to a relation in which only its covariation is causally relevant. The same goes for any other characteristic invoked here—structural similarity instead of covariance, for example. The representationalist may then opt for the second horn, and attempt to ground the use of representations in their representational relation to the world. This ensures a position in the explanatory causal chain for the representation, but now the account of representation can no longer be use-based. If it remains use-based, this comes at the cost of confusing explanandum and explanans: the representational status and use now serve to explain one another circularly.[1]

This does not mean that we argue representational status cannot ever be grounded in use. On the contrary, public representations attain their representational status by way of social norms under which particular objects are used as stand-ins for others, and are thus grounded in our practices, our use (Hutto and Myin 2017, Van Fraassen 2008). Yet the cognitive system's reliance on representations cannot be grounded in social norms in the same way (Tonneau 2012: 339). Mental representations in PP are thought to precede social activity, instead of being a product thereof. There is thus a clear disanalogy between a cognitive agent's activity and our personal level use of public representations. Thus, for our current purposes, grounding representations in use is insufficient to qualify for full representational status.

3. Can PP Have Its Representations?

Standardly, PP is viewed as a representational theory of cognition (Clark 2016, Hohwy 2013). Though most theorists working on PP take this as a background assumption, few people have attempted to unearth the foundations of this supposed representational character. There has, however, been one proposal that seems to have gained traction in the field (Kiefer and Hohwy 2018). This is Gładziejewski's (2016) proposal, in which he uses Ramsey's (2007) *compare-to-prototype* strategy to attempt to answer the job description challenge.[2] His prototype of choice is a cartographic map, to which he claims PP's models are analogous to. These models recapitulate the causal-probabilistic structure of the world. He argues that these models are structural representations that relate to what they represent by way of structural similarity, a broader category than, say, pictorial similarity. He acknowledges that structural similarity in itself is not enough to warrant representational status, and therefore gives a set of four distinct conditions for anything to count as a structural representation. Conjoinedly, he argues these conditions are what make cartographic maps representational, and by the compare-to-prototype strategy, the same should go for PP's models (2016: 570). Summing them up: structural representations (1) represent by way of structural similarity, "(2) guide the action of their users, (3) do so in a detachable way, and (4) allow their users to detect representational errors" (Gładziejewski 2016: 566). To cover all bases, we will discuss the four conditions separately and analyze whether they solve the problems mentioned above, or work toward a solution. Consequently, we can conclude whether the proposal has succeeded in naturalizing representations, thus countering the general concerns regarding the kind of representationalist account endorsed by Gładziejewski, or not.

The first condition is that structural representations represent their target by way of structural similarity. In particular, the structure that the brain trades in is thought to be the causal-probabilistic structure of the world (Gładziejewski 2016). This is intended to define the type of representations relevant here. As we have seen above, rather than excluding unwanted types of representation, however, structural similarities are "cheap"; they are ubiquitous. This is acknowledged by Gładziejewski (2016) and the further conditions are intended to constrain the class of relevant relations.

The second condition is that the representation guides the actions of the user (Gładziejewski 2016). As we have seen above, the role of the addition of function is twofold. The first role is to emphasize the role of a representation's use, as opposed to being merely passive "mirrors of nature" (Gładziejewski and Miłkowski 2017: 338). The second role is to avoid with the problem of over-generating representations, by limiting "the class of representation-relevant similarities to *exploitable* similarities" (Gładziejewski and Miłkowski 2017: 338, emphasis in original). To recapitulate our earlier discussion, function does not fulfill either role. Action guidance does little to constrain "the class of representation-relevant similarities," because exploitable similarities are still nearly everywhere. It also cannot serve to ensure the causal efficacy of representations. This produces a vicious circle in which the representational status of a similarity is grounded in the similarity being used, and the use of the similarity is grounded in its representational status. This means that the remaining two conditions, detachability and representational error detection, need to do all the necessary lifting to secure representational status.

The third condition to qualify for representational status is detachability (Gładziejewski 2016). This covers the notion that representations represent their target, regardless of the presence of that target. A cartographic map, for example, is thought to represent the terrain it is a map of, regardless of whether this terrain is actually present to the user or not. Put differently, a representation is required to be usable *off-line*.

Presence is however not a simple unitary phenomenon. In any given room, the people that are in that room can be said to be present. Anyone counting as absent would be a person that isn't in the room. Some of these people may stand behind others, leaving some people obscured from a particular perspective. From that perspective, then, the stimuli pertaining to that person are absent. Presence in PP is of the latter sort: the presence of stimuli pertaining to the target. Because of this, according to PP, engagement with the obscured person requires the use of an internal representation to stand in for the lacking stimuli. Thus, for anything to be a representation, it needs to be capable of being used in the absence (of the stimuli) of the target.

The requirement to be able to use the representation off-line is intended to be a mark of distinction between representations and mere detectors or causal mediators (Gładziejewski and Miłkowski 2017). After all, a detector can only detect that which is *present*, whereas an internal representation should be available even in the absence of the target. The thought is thus as follows. Any behavior that is thought to require off-line cognition so that the stimuli of the target are absent requires representation. Any representation, in turn, involves the possibility of off-line use. This creates a circularity, so that off-line cognition is defined in terms of requiring representation, and representation is defined in terms of being available for off-line cognition. Perhaps this problem could be lived with if there were additional justification for the representationalist position. However, the only justification given seems to be an argument by default, resting on the idea that representationalism is *the only game in town*. Non-representationalism is thought not to be able to account for off-line cognition.

Though not a strong argumentative strategy, it is reasonable to accept the stipulative definition above if representationalism is indeed the only possible explanation. There have however been a few non-representational proposals for what is termed off-line cognition that warrant discussion (e.g., Bruineberg et al. 2018, Bruineberg and Rietveld 2014, Di Paolo et al. 2017: ch. 8, Kirchhoff 2018a, b, Van Dijk and Withagen 2016; see also Degenaar and Myin 2014). At the very least, the existence of non-representationalist alternatives requires the representationalist to put in more work to explain why the alternatives fall short and why representations only fit the bill. Due to this, the circular stipulation defining representations in terms of off-line availability and off-line availability in terms of requiring representation lacks the further justification that is needed. This means that the condition of off-line use, detachability, without further support, does not solve nor work toward a solution for the arguments against representationalism.

Moreover, consider that a cardboard box and a counter top fit the bill here as well. The map, Gładziejewski's prototypical exemplar, is thought to be detachable in the sense that we can use the map for planning ahead in the absence of the terrain it represents. This is possible because the structural similarities between the map and the terrain hold in such way that we can exploit them, even for future planning. The same holds for the cardboard box and the counter top, the structural similarities of which we can exploit to place the former on the latter. Because of this, we can also exploit this structural similarity in the absence of the counter top, say, when you are walking home with the box in your hands, pondering where to place it in your home, and realizing the counter top is a good fit. Yet the cardboard box does not represent the counter top. This drives the point home that detachability in this sense need not be exclusively a feature of a representation.

The fourth condition is that representation can go wrong; in particular, that such an error should be detectable. In the case of cartographic maps, for example, an error will be detected when a pathway planned with the map does not lead to the intended destination. According to Gładziejewski, error detection in PP comes in the form of practical use (2016: 577–9). If an action is recruited on the basis of a particular prediction of the brain, yet the predicted outcome of the action *increases* prediction error rather than minimizes it, an error is detected. If one, for example, moves one's head about to get a cup of tea behind a laptop in view, and the cup of tea remains missing, the prediction that the cup was behind the laptop is detected to be erroneous.

The possibility of misrepresentation is crucial to the notion of representation. However, anything that meets only the first three conditions—structural similarity, action guidance, and detachability—can be described in non-representational terms (Gładziejewski 2016: 570). And there is nothing intrinsically representational about error detection, unless the error is supposed to be representational error from the start. There is nothing intrinsically representational about failure to grasp a cup, nor is there anything intrinsically representational about detecting that failure. A non-representational relation indeed does not necessarily become representational if one is to add in error detection as a fourth ingredient. Indeed, it is unclear from Gładziejewski's proposal when and how error detection, a sensitivity for reacting to misalignment, turns into mis*representation*. Consider again the cardboard box and the counter top. If the structural similarity is successfully exploited, the cardboard box can rest on the counter top. Yet if the structural similarity does not hold in such a way as to support the action, the cardboard box will slide off. The falling off the box is a way to detect this error. Yet none of this entails that the cardboard box *represents* the counter top.

More work has been done, however, on misrepresentation in PP. Kiefer and Hohwy (2018) recently argued for a naturalistic measure of misrepresentation in PP. This measure has been analyzed and shown to bottom out in Shannon-informational covariance by Kirchhoff and Robertson (2018). Shannon-information is not inherently representational, and covariance is insufficient to ground content (Hutto and Myin 2013). The discussion cited is rather technical, leaving a full exposition out of the scope of this chapter. Essentially, it is as follows. Kiefer and Hohwy (2018) argue that the brain's continuous effort to minimize long-term prediction error can be cast in models of Bayesian statistics. The brain approximates a probability distribution of the possible states of the world. The extent to which the brain's *approximation* of the prior probability distribution *diverges* from the *actual* posterior probability distribution is captured by the Kullback-Leibler divergence. This is thus the degree to which the brain's *approximate* model diverges from the *actual* posterior model, and is thought to stand for the degree of misrepresentation. Kirchhoff and Robertson (2018) display that this divergence in itself is but a measure of the divergence of a covariational relation. In this sense, if A reliably covaries with system B, then information about system A will be information about system B. The divergence, in short, is "a measure of informational covariance," but falls short of providing a measure of misrepresentation (Kirchhoff and Robertson 2018: 277).

It thus seems that none of the four conditions actually help the representationalist to secure the status of representation. Yet there are two remaining questions to be answered. First, Gładziejewski's argument was not that the conditions separately would suffice for representational status, but only conjoinedly. As we have shown above, however, not a single condition seems to actually do the work it is intended to do by Gładziejewski (2016). It is reasonable to assume that, without additional argumentation to the contrary, if all the parts of a system do not work as intended, the whole will not work as intended either. Crucially, no reason is given in Gładziejewski (2016) *how* precisely the conjoining of the four conditions representational status engenders representational status where there avowedly is none before the conjoining. Moreover, recall the cardboard box and its structural similarities with the counter top. As discussed above, the relation between the box and the counter top checks all the conditions, yet is clearly not representational. In justifying representational status, all the weight is carried by the analogy to maps. But maps are *found to be* representational. The representational status of maps is taken as a given. This brings us to our second point: what about the compare-to-prototype strategy employed by Gładziejewski? Should we subscribe to this strategy, and agree on the analysis of the features of a cartographic map that make it representational? If so, how can it be that these features do not seem to secure representational status for cardboard boxes or models in PP while they do for maps? Is this not incoherent?

No it isn't, because not all use is equal. Some sociocultural practices are representational, because the aim of these practices is to describe the world in a certain way that is evaluable for truth or falsity, accuracy or inaccuracy. Truth-telling practices, practices in which people offer description which can literally be true or false, are the paradigm of such. There is no point in justifying whether moves in truth-telling practices have truth conditions, because by definition, they have. Other social practices, such as those for making maps whose use can be shared, are analogous to truth-telling practices. A map-making practice prescribes how representers should go about to represent whatever can be represented in that practice, and how end-users should act based on what is represented. Because of a shared representational practice, bus stops will be represented by *this* item on the map, and distances in *that* way. Because the practice determines ways of representing, users will be able to get to the bus stop from a distance by relying on the map.

Clearly there are different uses of representations within a representational practice. Some uses create, or change representations, and other uses rely on existing representational practices, for example, when deciding which route to take on the basis of a map. Crucially, however, both of these are uses *within* a representational practice. Some uses within a practice are not representation-creating, but some are. Both uses, however, are representational, and what makes them representational is their embeddedness in a practice that is a representational one.

The concept of functional "use" in the literature on representation in the way of Gładziejewski (2016) is a different one than use-within-a-representational practice. Even if it is analogous, even if it can be said to share features with use within a practice, this doesn't mean that it thereby shares all its features. Such is the nature of analogy. To begin with, there's a serious issue concerning whether the kind of within-practice use the functional notion of use is most analogous to, is appropriate, because that kind of "consuming" use relies on there being existing representations and representational norms, rather than engendering such. More importantly, the reason why use in a representational practice constitutes representation is because the practice is a representational one. The existence of such representational practices gives us the idea of representation, just like the existence of truth telling-practices gives us the idea of truth evaluability.

Analogies might be drawn between functional use and use in representational practice, and between biological norms of adaptivity and sociocultural norms of accurate representation, yet there remains "a root mismatch between representational error and failure of biological function" (Burge 2010: 301). Nothing in Gładziejewski (2016) shows that this idea of a mismatch is mistaken. To illustrate: because of a shared representational practice, bus stops will be represented by *this* item on the map, and distances in *that* way. Genuine misrepresentation, over and above malfunction, becomes possible, as when one misrepresents a crossing as a bus stop. Mislocating a bus stop is a representational mistake, if it goes against the norms of the practice. In contrast, tampering with the neural antecedents of action might or might not lead to malfunction, but it doesn't violate representational norms—note that an unusual pattern of neural activation, one that goes against the "structural similarity" one can project on previous activations, might *add* functionality. Also, drawing the bus stop at the wrong place will be a misrepresentation from the moment it is drawn, while it will have to be found out whether an anomalous pattern of activation is functional or its opposite.

In short, the representational status of any object is attained in virtue of its use by agents, embedded in a social practice of using particular sorts of objects as representations for particular targets (Hutto and Myin 2017, Tonneau 2012, Van Fraassen 2008). If social practices are what lend objects their representational status, it is clear neural models do not qualify. After all, neural models are thought to precede the practices that representations are a product of. This marks a clear difference between cartographic maps and neural models, and it is due to this disanalogy that cartographic maps may be said to represent a target terrain when being used in the relevant social practices, yet neural models may not lay claim to the same representational status.

The challenge for Gładziejewski (2016) was to provide a notion of representation that could solve the known issues with representations described in the previous section. These issues were that structural similarity is too broad, and if use is to be the grounding for representations, representations cannot also serve to ground use. We have seen that the first two conditions fall victim to exactly these objections. Gładziejewski (2016) anticipated this, and prepared two more conditions to cover the missing ground. We have shown above that neither detachability nor misrepresentation is up to the task that had been laid out. This means that, not only is PP's current notion of representation insufficient to warrant representational status, it also has not done well to solve the problems that were already known.

4. Does PP Need Representations Anyway?

Despite the aforementioned worries, we need to take care not to throw the baby out with the bathwater. The question is whether we can keep the explanatory appeal of PP while resisting the representational pull, the enticement to invoke representations (Di Paolo et al. 2017). If we believe the bulk of the PP literature, this issue is insurmountable (Clark 2015, 2016, Hohwy 2016, Seth 2013). There has been, however, an effort to bring PP and non-representationalism closer together than initially seemed possible (Anderson 2017, Fabry 2017, Kirchhoff 2018a, 2018b, Kirchhoff and Robertson 2018).

The primary explanatory appeal of PP is that it can account for our sensitivity to statistical regularities in the environment. The ongoing barrage of stimuli unfolds rapidly and dynamically, yet we seem to navigate the environment fluidly and skillfully, even when things don't always go as could be expected. PP's main explanatory resource is the internal model in which the statistical regularities are encoded. However, we have shown that the appeal to representations is unwarranted. This means that internal models and their purported explanatory power meet a similar fate. How can we account for our sensitivity to such regularities if not by invoking internally encoded representations?

One option is to explain our sensitivity to statistical regularities in the environment by appealing to the environment that the organism is, and its ancestors have been, embedded in. Orlandi (2012, 2013, 2014) proposes the Embedded View (EV) to explain visual perception in particular, though it can reasonably be extended to cover other sensory modalities. EV explains visual processing by relying on the facts of the environment instead of internal representations of those facts (see also Myin and Degenaar 2014). There is a caveat: Orlandi (2014) argues we still need to invoke representations further down the line. We will argue that this is unnecessary with the explanatory tools EV offers. This puts us on the right track to understand how to continue without internal representation.

EV explains the visual system's sensitivity to statistical regularities by relying on the facts of the environment themselves without encoding them internally. Orlandi states: "Relying on a fact means acting in accordance with a fact, and with a corresponding principle, without representing either" (Orlandi 2014: 3). This means that the organism can rely on particular statistical regularities, say the co-occurrence of particular patterns of stimulation and a particular object, without representing this. An example she gives is the detection of edges in the environment. It is a fact that particular strong changes in light intensity are typically caused by edges. Historically, these changes in light intensity have been encountered so often in co-occurrence with the presence of edges that "it would be surprising if evolution did not take care of this." She continues, "in this explanation, external facts account for why we pick up on edges rather than on something else. No additional representational resources are needed" (Orlandi 2014: 154). Thus, instead of representations, we appeal to the rich ancestral interactional history with the world to pick up on edges when confronted with particular changes in light intensity. We thus appeal to the environment the organism is embedded in to explain the organism's sensitivity to statistical regularities, rather than merely to a subpersonal part of the organism-environment system.

This may serve well to explain evolutionarily developed sensitivities, but PP accounts for regularities that the organism can become sensitive to ontogenetically even within an hour (Mole and Zhao 2015). Indeed, one of the features of modeling in PP is continuous updating to reflect newfound evidence, allowing for a flexible approach to a dynamically unfolding world. The model is thus highly malleable. As we will show, EV is well equipped to account for the flexibility of our sensitivity to statistical regularities.

The central idea, developed in Orlandi (2014), is that the system is *wired* to be sensitive. This means that the perceptual system has many features that "developed, and continue to develop under evolutionary and environmental pressure" (Orlandi 2014: 3). In particular, Orlandi likens the wiring of the perceptual system to the manner in which a connectionist network is wired. She states:

> We can imagine (…) a connectionist network trained to detect something by being repeatedly exposed to it. Such training causes the network to display characteristic patterns of activation where low-level configurations are associated with high-level ones and *vice versa*. We can then think of a high-level state as "checking" the pattern of activation at the lower, sensory level where this ultimately just means that the high-level state activates in a way that is more or less compatible with the lower-level pattern of activation.
>
> (Orlandi 2014: 88)

This means that a connectionist network can be trained by repeated exposure to become sensitive to particular patterns of activation. The "high-level states" come to co-vary reliably with lower-level patterns of activation, such that it reliably detects particular features. We can see that, in this case, the interactional history of the system allows it to develop a sensitivity to particular patterns, without encoding these sensitivities internally (Orlandi 2014, Ramsey 2007). Yet the system does require a training signal in the first place. Yet much like PP, for a connectionist network "the world itself (…) provide[s] the 'training signal' you need" (Clark 2016:18). Contrary to PP, it should be noted that the connectionist network's transition between lower-level and high-level states is not regulated by a representation. It is a transition afforded by a strong connection between the two levels (Orlandi 2014: 153).

It is important here to distinguish a wired system from a *hardwired* system. A hardwired system would be wired for a particular task without allowing for this particular configuration to be *re*wired, adapting to a new situation. There is nothing in the notion of a wired system, however, that necessarily constrains the system's malleability. In fact, connectionist networks seem to be a particularly good example of how this could work. Orlandi states that connection networks "come to be sensitive to the presence of mine echoes by simply adjusting their connections. Similarly, pigeons may stop pecking on a key as a result of extinction or counterconditioning without following any rules" (Orlandi 2014: 147). What this means is that *repeated exposure* to the training signal is how the system comes to detect the relevant features of the environment in the first place. It also shows that the network's sensitivities are "updated," or, rather, that they adapt to a dynamically unfolding world so that the "high-level states" that detect, say, eatability, do not co-activate anymore in the presence of the patterns of stimulation pertaining to a set of keys. In the perceptual system, this means that the organism's interactional history with the world itself can account for its sensitivity to the encountered regularities. These regularities, again, need not be encoded internally (similar ideas have been expressed by many authors disagreeing with representationalism, including Gibson (1979) and Skinner (1953)).

We can now also see how it can be that the perceptual system can sometimes be misaligned with the world. This happens when a "high-level state" co-activates with a particular pattern of stimulation that is not caused by the same feature in the world it typically co-activates with. Think of the occurrence of edges, a robust statistical regularity. Realistically drawn scenes in street art, for example, may be drawn so as to give the illusion of depth from a particular perspective. What happens here is that the pattern of stimulation has the changes in light intensity that typically co-occur with edges, causing the "high-level states" that track edges to activate. Upon closer inspection, by moving about, changing our perspective or touching the surface on which it is painted, we notice that these new patterns of stimulation are actually quite different from those pertaining to edges. Here we detect the error in our perception without requiring matching an internal representation with a world that is out of reach. It is mis*perception* without mis*representation*.

In sum, by relying on the facts of the world we can explain how we become sensitive to particular statistical regularities in the world, both phylo- and ontogenetically as well as how sometimes we are misaligned with respect to the environment. Nonetheless, Orlandi argues that we still need to invoke representations. Specifically, representations are needed to account for two distinct features of the visual system: (1) completion, in which an organism interacts with a whole object despite only its (sometimes partially occluded) perspectival front side impinging on its senses (Orlandi 2014: 127), and (2) taking as, in which we *take* the light reflected off a cow that impinges on our senses *as* coming from a cow (Orlandi 2014: 150).

To account for completion, Orlandi argues, there are parts of the object that are not currently present to the organism, that the system needs to represent internally (2014: 127). The idea is that, because these parts of the object are *absent*, there is no feature of the system that could *detect* those parts of the object for the relevant high-level state to co-activate. However, as we have argued elsewhere this need not be an issue (Hutto and Myin 2017: Ch. 7, van Es 2019). The signal with which the system was trained to co-activate with was always a pattern of stimulation that only ever involved a perspectival front side of an object, and oftentimes these objects were partially occluded. The interactional history with an object that allows for the sensitivity to the particular regularities is based on widely varying sorts of interactions with the particular object, so that a "high-level state" that detects, say, cups, co-activates with patterns of stimulation that are caused by mere front sides of cups, partially occluded cups, upside down cups, etc. This means that we can rely on the fact that we are only confronted with a perspectival front side of 3D objects and that regularly these objects are partially occluded to explain why, nonetheless, the relevant "high-level state" still picks up on the presence of the object. Just as we do not need to encode the rule that "specific changes in light intensity pertain to edges," we also do not need to encode a rule that "partially occluded front sides pertain to full objects." Instead, we can rely on the facts of the environment that the rigidity of objects is statistically robust.[3]

Our capacity to take a particular pattern of stimulation as coming from, say, a cow, also requires representation, according to Orlandi (2014: 150). The idea is that, for this to occur, there needs to be an internal representation of COWness with which the pattern of stimulation can be matched so as to count as a token of that type. Yet here too our interactional history with the world seems to cover all that is needed to account for what happens in the perceptual system. For whenever we have encountered patterns of stimulation that pertained to cows, they co-occurred with the presence of cows, or images of cows. This allows us to perceive a cow, and interact with the cow as we have interacted with previously met cows. All of this does not, however, cover the categorization of individual cows as tokens of a type. But, we argue, though such ability to apply a category is representational, it is not part of the visual system. Instead, this representational ability is part of a larger sociocultural and lingual practice in which particular objects, features, and scenes are given particular names or labels. This means that we do not need to invoke internal representations for our categorizing a cow as a particular instantiation of COWness; we need only invoke public, lingual representational practices, similar to cartographic maps.

In sum, we provide a non-representational alternative to account for our sensitivity to statistical regularities. We have shown that this can account for malleability, misperception, completion, and "taking as" to the extent that it involves the perceptual system. This means that we do not need to invoke representational models. However, there is a sense in which an organism would *be* a model, if it is responsive to statistical regularities in the way described. Locating models in PP at the organism level is not uncommon (Friston 2013: 213). But this claim is only distinctive if it is asserted that the organism *embodies* a model, in contrast to it *containing* a model that the organism uses, or that in some way guides its actions. Rather, in the unfolding of action, the state of the world could be read off, or inferred, by an external observer. In fact, such inferring of how the world is could probably take place by observing aspects of the organism's brain activity. Hutto describes such an external perspective in which the brain can *be* a model through the lens of PP as follows:

> The brain might be used as [a] model by scientists in the sense that they could use brain activity to make reliable predictions and claims about how things stand with the world on the basis of their background knowledge. But if REC is right that is not what the brain itself does in supporting basic cognition.
>
> (Hutto 2017: 13)[4]

There might be more to invoking this perspective than making a philosophical point about the relation between organism and model. Focusing on which variables in the environment are systematically tracked by the organism, where such tracking is enabled by systematic correlation between environmental variables and brain processes, can teach observers a lot about what the relevant environmental properties are for the organism, and about the phylogenetic and ontogenetic causes of its current activity. If some property is systematically tracked, it might have been selected to be tracked, or a tendency to track properties of that kind might have been selected, for example. By investigating the correlational or tracking structure of the environment/ brain relations, it might be possible to separate what genuinely matters for this organism from what only looks to matter.

It is further possible to interpret some of the most celebrated work in cognitive science as at least partly clinging to this methodology. Marr's (1982) theory of vision, for example, might be given a correlational reading, so that the various stages of visual processing it describes are not about building up more complex representations, but about tracking more complex properties, much like the connectionist networks we have seen above (Orlandi 2014: Note 3). The search for environmental variables organisms are sensitive to is of course an integral part of much ecological psychology already—paying increased attention to the brain as enabling this sensitivity is complementary, not contrary to such research (Gibson 1979). Though Marr's approach and ecological psychology are standardly seen in contrastive terms, the proposed perspective forms a unifying umbrella covering both of them. That is, abandoning the commitment to universal representationalism holds integrative potential.

Rosa Cao has argued against a common interpretation of single neuron activity in the following way:

> It seems more reasonable to … give up the common interpretation that a single neuron is doing something like representing "a very small piece of the world outside the organism" though indeed its activity may be well correlated with the structure of that small piece of the world. Instead, the role of the single neuron is more like that of the man inside Searle's Chinese Room—taking inputs and systematically producing outputs in total ignorance of their meaning and of the world outside. The single cell responds to local regularities and rewards, which as a result of evolution have become coordinated (in some complicated fashion) with external regularities and distal rewards for the whole organism.
>
> (2012: 66)[5]

What is said here regarding single cells applies to collections of cells, and to neural processes on multiple scales. They too are in the business of enabling coordination between what happens at various levels of coordination with "external regularities and distal awards for the whole organism." In fact, depending on contingencies of empirical support, a modified, that is non-representational, PP might allow us to learn much about how such multi-scale organism-environment coordination is possible.[6]

5. Conclusion

In this chapter we have reviewed whether PP's use of representations is warranted. We have first outlined general objections against representationalism, focusing particularly on the structure plus function account of representation. Second, we analyzed Gładziejewski's (2016) account of representations in PP as it has gained significant traction in the literature. Here we argued that his account does not do the necessary explanatory lifting to combat the general objections. In particular, the first two conditions for representation, structural similarity, and action guidance struggled with the general difficulties, and the further two conditions, off-line use and misrepresentation, were not found to suffice to carry the additional weight necessary for representation. Finally, we argued that the pivotal analogy with an allegedly prototypical representation, cartographic maps, goes awry. It leaves out the social environment in which representational practices come to be and give them representational status: a dimension not available to justify the representational status of neural models. In the final section we have outlined a positive alternative, with particular focus on why PP does not *need* its representations. Drawing on Orlandi's work on the Embedded View (2012, 2013, 2014) we argue that sensitivity to statistical regularities can be explained by relying on the environmental facts without encoding them internally. Further, we have argued that there may be a place for models in a non-representational approach to cognition, but only as used by scientists, external observers, in their investigation of the organism. Finally, we have proposed that stepping away from representationalism offers potential for unifying approaches to perception.

Notes

1   A similar objection is present in Di Paolo et al. (2017: 25). Oliveira (2018) argues with the same argumentative structure applied to the debate on the representational status of models in science.
2   Lee (2018) argues that a structural account of representation can naturalize content. In this, he relies heavily on the notion of representation from Gładziejewski (2016) discussed here. Because of this, our criticism on Gładziejewski's proposal extends to Lee's reliance on it.
3   Interestingly, Orlandi (2012) argues that the rigidity of objects is one example of the visual system's reliance on statistical regularities, which would presumably make invoking representations redundant. It seems that if we can rely on objects typically being rigid, we can also rely on the front sides we are confronted with to be caused by a rigid object: it pertains to the same feature of the visual system.
4   REC is a radically non-representational approach to basic cognition expounded in Hutto and Myin (2013, 2017).
5   This passage is cited in a related context in Hutto and Myin (2017: 238–9).
6   See Flament-Fultot (2016, 2019) for reasons to remain cautious about the prospects of any version of PP.

References

Anderson, M. L. (2017), "Of Bayes and Bullets: An Embodied, Situated, Targeting-based Account of Predictive Processing" in T. Metzinger and W. Wiese (eds.), *Philosophy and Predictive Processing*, Frankfurt am Main: MIND Group.

Bruineberg, J. and Rietveld, E. (2014), "Self-organization, Free Energy Minimization, and Optimal Grip on a Field of Affordances," *Frontiers in Human Neuroscience*, 8 (599): 1–14.

Bruineberg, J., Kiverstein, J. D. and Rietveld, E. (2018), "The Anticipating Brain Is Not A Scientist: The Free-energy Principle from an Ecological-enactive Perspective," *Synthese*, 195 (6): 2417–44. doi.org/10.1007/s11229-016-1239-1.

Burge, T. (2010). *Origins of Objectivity*. Oxford University Press.

Clark, A. (2015), "Predicting Peace: The End of the Representation Wars—A Reply to Michael Madary" in T. Metzinger and J. M. Windt (eds.), *Open MIND*: 7(R), Frankfurt am Main: MIND Group. doi.org/10.15502/9783958570979.

Clark, A. (2016), *Surfing Uncertainty: Prediction, Action and the Embodied Mind*, New York: Oxford University Press.

Cao, R. (2012), "A Teleosemantic Approach to Information in the Brain," *Biology & Philosophy*, 27 (1): 49–71.

Degenaar, J. and Myin, E. (2014), "Representation-hunger reconsidered," *Synthese*, 191 (15): 3639–48.

Di Paolo, E., Buhrmann, T. and Barandiaran, X. (2017), *Sensorimotor Life: An Enactive Proposal*, New York: Oxford University Press.

Dołega, K. (2017), "Moderate Predictive Processing" in T. Metzinger and W. Wiese (eds.), *Philosophy and Predictive* Processing, Frankfurt am Main: MIND Group.

Fabry, R. (2017), "Transcending the Evidentiary Boundary: Prediction Error Minimization, Embodied Interaction, and Explanatory Pluralism," *Philosophical Psychology*, 30 (4): 395–414.

Flament-Fultot, M. (2016), "Counterfactuals versus Constraints: Towards an Implementation Theory of Sensorimotor Mastery," *Journal of Consciousness Studies*, 23 (5–6): 153–76.

Flament-Fultot, M. (2019), "Versatilité et infaisabilité. Vers la fin des théories computationnelles du comportement moteur," PhD Thesis, Sorbonne Université, Ecole Doctorale V, Paris.

Friston, K. (2013), "Active Inference and Free Energy," *Behavioral and Brain Sciences*, 36: 212–13.

Gibson, J. J. (1979), *The Perception of the Visual World*, New Jersey: Lawrence Erlbaum.

Gładziejewski, P. (2016), "Predictive coding and representationalism," *Synthese*, 193 (2): 559–82.

Gładziejewski, P. and Miłkowski, M. (2017), "Structural Representations: Causally Relevant and Different from Detectors," *Biology & Philosophy*, 32 (3), 337–55.

Godfrey-Smith, P. (1996), *Complexity and the Function of Mind in Nature*, Cambridge: Cambridge University Press.

Hohwy, J. (2013), *The Predictive Mind*, New York: Oxford University Press.

Hohwy, J. (2016), "The Self-evidencing Brain," *Noûs*, 50 (2): 259–85.

Hutto, D. D. (2017), "Getting Into Predictive Processing's Great Guessing Game: Bootstrap Heaven or Hell?," *Synthese*, 1–14. doi.org/10.1007/s11229-017-1385-0.

Hutto, D. D. and Myin, E. (2013), *Radicalizing Enactivism: Basic Minds without Content*, Cambridge MA: MIT Press.

Hutto, D. D. and Myin, E. (2017), *Evolving Enactivism: Basic Minds Meet Content*, Cambridge MA: MIT Press.

Kiefer, A. and Hohwy, J. (2018), "Content and Misrepresentation in Hierarchical Generative Models," *Synthese*, 195: 2387–415.

Kirchhoff, M. (2018a), "The Body in Action: Predictive Processing and the Embodiment Thesis" in A. Newen, L. De Bruin, and S. Gallaghe (eds.), *Oxford Handbook of Cognition: Embodied, Extended and Enactive*, New York: Oxford University Press.

Kirchhoff, M. (2018b), "Predictive Processing, Perceiving and Imagining: Is to Perceive to Imagine, or Something Close to It?," *Philosophical Studies*, 175: 751–67.

Kirchhoff, M. and Robertson, I. (2018), "Enactivism and Predictive Processing: A Non-representational View," *Philosophical Explorations*, 21 (2): 264–81.

Lee, J. (2018), "Structural Representation and The Two Problems of Content," *Mind and Language*, 2019;34: 606–26.

Marr, D. (1982), *Vision: A Computational Investigation into the Human Representation and Processing of Visual Information*, San Francisco, CA: W. H. Freeman.

Mole, C. and Zhao, J. (2015), "Vision and Abstraction: An Empirical Refutation of Nico Orlandi's non-cognitivism," *Philosophical Psychology*, 29 (3): 365–73.

Myin, E. and Degenaar, J. (2014), "Enactive Vision" in L. Shapiro (eds.), *The Routledge Handbook of Embodied Cognition*, New York: Routledge, pp. 90–8.

de Oliveira, G.S. (2018), "Representationalism Is a Dead End," *Synthese*. https://doi.org/10.1007/s11229-018-01995-9.

Orlandi, N. (2012), "Embedded Seeing-as: Multi-stable Visual Perception without Interpretation," *Philosophical Psychology*, 25 (4): 555–73.

Orlandi, N. (2013), "Embedded Seeing: Vision in the Natural World," *Noûs*, 47 (4): 727–47.

Orlandi, N. (2014), *The Innocent Eye: Vision Is Not a Cognitive Process*, New York: Oxford University Press.

Pezzulo, G., Donnarumma, F., Iodice, P., Maisto, D. and Stoianov, I. (2017), "Model-Based Approaches to Active Perception and Control," *Entropy*, 19 (6): 266.

Ramsey, W. M. (2007), *Representation Reconsidered*, Cambridge: Cambridge University Press.

Rosenberg, A. (2015), "The Genealogy of Content or the Future of an Illusion," *Philosophia*, 43: 537–47.

Seth, A. (2013), "Interoceptive Inference, Emotion and the Embodied Self," *Trends in Cognitive Sciences*, 11: 565–73.

Shea, N. (2007), "Consumers Need Information: Supplementing Teleosemantics with an Input Condition," *Philosophy and Phenomenological Research*, 75: 404–35. doi.org/10.1111/j.1933-1592.2007.00082.x.

Shea, N. (2014), "Exploitable Isomorphism and Structural Representation," *Proc Aristotelian Society*, XIV: 77–92. doi.org/10.1111/j.1467-9264.2014.00367.x.

Skinner, B. F. (1953), *Science and Human Behavior* (No. 92904), New York: Simon and Schuster.

Tonneau, F. (2012), "Metaphor and Truth: A Review of Representation Reconsidered by W. M. Ramsey," *Behavior and Philosophy*, 39/40: 331–43.

Travis, C. (2004), "The Silence of the Senses," *Mind*, 113 (449): 57–94.

van Dijk, L. and Withagen, R. (2016), "Temporalizing Agency: Moving Beyond On-and Offline Cognition," *Theory & Psychology*, 26 (1): 5–26.

van Es. (2019), "The Embedded View, Its Critics, and a Radically Non-representational Solution," *Synthese*, 1–17. doi.org/10.1007/s11229-019-02385-5.

van Fraassen, B. C. (2008), *Scientific Representation: Paradoxes of Perspective*, Oxford: Oxford University Press.

Varela, F., Thompson, E. and Rosch, E. (1991), *The Embodied Mind: Cognitive Science and Human Experience*, Cambridge MA: MIT Press.

Wiese, W. (2017), "What Are the Contents of Representations in Predictive Processing?," *Phenomenology and the Cognitive Sciences*, 16 (4): 715–36.

Wiese, W. and Metzinger, T. (2017), "Vanilla PP for Philosophers: A Primer on Predictive Processing" in T. Metzinger and W. Wiese (eds.), *Philosophy and Predictive Processing*, Frankfurt am Main: MIND Group. doi.org/10.15502/9783958573024.

Williams, D. (2018), "Predictive Processing and the Representation Wars," *Minds and Machines*, 28 (1): 141–72.

Williams, D. and Colling, L. (2018), "From Symbols to Icons: The Return of Resemblance in the Cognitive Neuroscience Revolution," *Synthese*, 195 (5): 1941–67.

2

A Humean Challenge to Predictive Coding

Colin Klein

The Australian National University

1. Predictive Coding versus Humeanism

1.1. Humeanism

Humeanism, broadly speaking, is the thesis that belief and desire are distinct psychological entities with distinct but complementary roles in causing action. Desires motivate you to make the world a certain way. Beliefs tell you the way the world actually is. Belief and desires work together to drive action. But beliefs and desires are fundamentally *orthogonal*. As Smith (1984: 7) puts it, "For any belief and desire pair that we imagine, we can always imagine someone having the desire but lacking the belief, and vice-versa." Since there are no necessary connections between Belief and Desire, neither can be reduced to the other. Our psychology thus always needs two kinds of states to explain action.

Humeanism has primarily been defended in the context of moral psychology. Moral beliefs provide an interesting test case: anti-Humeans think there's no gap between believing an action to be good and being motivated to do it. Humeans leave open the possibility of being unmoved by the mere belief that some action is good (as, indeed, often seems to be the case).

Within philosophy of mind, Humeanism is often taken as a commonplace of folk psychology (Dennett 1987). That is not (just) tradition. There are good theoretical reasons to separate out beliefs and desires. Beliefs and desires are often taken to have different direction of fit, and so are responsive in different ways to the world. Beliefs and desires also seem to have different dynamics. Beliefs change on the basis of evidence and deliberation. Desires change by being satisfied, and perhaps by other (often obscure) routes. Our beliefs about our desires don't seem to affect our desires. I believe that eating crisps is bad for you. That, on its own, doesn't affect my desire for a pack of crisps (alas!). Conversely, functioning grown-ups don't let what they want affect their estimation of what is true: however much I desire that crisps be healthy, I know that this is no evidence in favor of them being healthy.

Distinguishing belief and desire also brings straightforward *explanatory* advantages that are difficult to get with just one entity. Because beliefs and desires are orthogonal, we can trivially explain why two people with the same beliefs act differently (their differing desires), and *mutis mutandis* for identical desires. Separating belief and desire gives us combinatorial resources: the complex set of actions we observe gets explained by a relatively smaller, tidier set of beliefs and desires plus laws of combination.

As an example, consider the hoops that old-fashioned behaviorism had to jump through to try to reduce belief/desire talk down to talk of observable behavioral patterns (Putnam 1967). What does it mean to say that someone is thirsty? That they are disposed to drink if there is water available. But that can't be right: they are disposed to drink if water is available *and* there is no lion between them and the water *and* there is not lemonade nearby *or* their past encounter with that particular lemonade has not produced the utterance "this lemonade is really far too sour" *and* …. Even if you think you *could* get by just talking about behavior in this way, every explanatory law ends up sounding impossibly complex and *ad hoc*. Whereas by talking about the desire for water and how it interacts with other beliefs and desires, one gets a lot of explanation for cheap.

I've given only a crude sketch of Humeanism. The broad division is really between doxastic and motivational states, and beliefs and desires might not be the only members of those categories—one might want to include emotions or bodily sensations (Klein 2015) as among the intrinsically motivating states, for example. One might also want a theory with more mathematical sophistication. Decision theory, broadly construed, shows how to combine belief-like and desire-like states in optimal ways (Buchak 2016). When considering changes among belief-like states themselves, Bayesianism is an attractive formulation about how an agent should change their degree of belief, consistent with the laws of probability.

Humeanism and Bayesianism work well together. David Lewis, for example, defended a version of Humeanism couched in terms of credences and values. As he puts it:

> Desires are contingent. It is not contrary to reason—still less is it downright impossible!—to have peculiar and unusual desires, or to lack commonplace ones. It may be contrary to the laws of human nature, but those laws themselves are contingent regularities. Likewise there are no necessary connections between desire and belief. Any values can go with any credence.
>
> (Lewis 1996: 304)

The result combines the plausibility of traditional Humeanism with the power of Bayesianism. It's a nice package, and has worked well.

Yet within the heart of every philosopher is a tiny Ockham. He urges parsimony. Bayesianism has struck some as *such* a powerful theory that we might be able to get by with it alone. That is, with sufficient cleverness we might be able to do with credences only, rather than credences plus values.

This chapter is about one such story, and how it fails.

1.2. Predictive Coding

Consider a simple homing missile. It has a sensor array which can track an infrared source. The steering fins are driven by the angle between the observed position of the source and the center of the field. This tends to bring the source back to the center, thereby eliminating deviations from its course to the target. Constant adjustments, combined with the missile's forward motion and a bit of luck, will lead the missile to impact.

We can fit the Humean story (if we are so inclined) to the missile's behavior. The missile has a *desire* to hit the target. It also has a *belief* about where the target currently is, and conditional on that some beliefs about the best actions to take to get to the target.

However, there's a wholly different way of explaining the homing missile, one closer to the cybernetic roots of its design (Ashby 1976). We could say that the missile *expects* or *predicts* that the heat source will be in the center of its array. The deviation results in a certain *prediction error*. It steers so as to *minimize* prediction error, which eventually brings it to its target.

This second way of describing the missile, note, only appeals to *one* state-type (predictions) and *one* sort of process (error minimization). The state-type looks much closer to belief than to desire, and works with more complex cases just as well. A more sophisticated missile (e.g.) models the shape of its target too; we could picture it as starting with a guess and then updating its model in response to error. That looks a lot like updating credences in various potential models. So from this perspective, we can unify what looks like two different state-types into one, *contra* Humeanism.

This potential unification is at the heart of *predictive coding* approaches to cognition. Predictive coding (PC) theories claim that the brain is a mechanism for updating models of the world via minimizing prediction error (Clark 2013, 2015, Hohwy 2013). In its most ambitious form, PC also claims that this is *all* that the brain does.[1]

A key part of predictive coding is *active inference*. Many models of motor control are fundamentally predictive, and use prediction error to guide skilled action; as Clark puts it, "Motor control is just more top-down sensory prediction" (Clark 2015: 21). We guide our actions in part by utilizing predictions about what will happen, and minimizing the mismatch.

This strategy generalizes. A mismatch between prediction and the world can be fixed either by updating beliefs or by changing the world. So in Clark's formulation:

> My desire to drink a glass of water now is cast as a prediction that I am drinking a glass of water now—a prediction that will yield streams of error signals that may be resolved by bringing the drinking about, thus making the world conform to my prediction. Desires are here re-cast as predictions apt to be made true by action.
>
> (Clark 2017: 115)

To act, then, you predict that you've *already* obtained the goal state, and then use the mismatch between that and the world to drive adaptive action. As Wiese puts it, "Loosely speaking, this entails a suspension of disbelief in the evidence for an absence of movement …. In other words, we attend away from evidence that we are not moving to enable our predictions to be fulfilled." (2017: 1240)

By doing so, we bring the world in line with our predictions. And, *contra* the Humean, we do so with just one thing.

1.3. What This Needs to Work

So far we have considered toy examples of a single desire and a single action, and set up the details the way we'd like. For PC to upend Humeanism, we'd have to show that this is possible for the complex set of beliefs and desires that we appear to have.

This means that PC theories must give a systematic, or at least non-*ad hoc*, way of translating between putative desires and some corresponding credences that can do the same work. The typical way this is done is via appeal to credences about the evolutionarily typical states of organisms (see, for example, Hohwy 2013: 85–6). I have argued (Klein 2018) that this strategy is a non-starter. Very crudely, there are a great number of evolutionarily advantageous states that are atypical for individuals (most male elephant seals never mate, but that is not an argument against it), and a great number of evolutionarily bad states that are typical for individuals (most fish end up eaten by bigger fish). This pattern holds across various ways of carving up the reference class for "typical."

Dubious evolutionary links are an optional feature of PC, however. PC is anti-Humean, and one might just appeal to various placeholder notions familiar from the anti-Humeanism literature. Perhaps all PC needs is, for example, a translation scheme which takes us from "I desire X with degree P" to "I believe with credence P that X *is good/is valuable/is worth pursuing*." Cash out the details as seems fit. The upshot is that we get a special class of credences with the right sorts of *bona fides* to be inserted into the Bayesian story. In any case, PC needs *something* along those lines if it is to work. Our question, then, is whether one can find a suitable translation scheme between desires and the right sorts of beliefs.

1.4. The Structure of the Argument

I'll argue for no. The argument of the paper is conditional: *if* you want PC to be a mechanistic story, *and* you want to be a thoroughgoing Bayesian, *then* you should be a Humean. Most predictive coders agree with the antecedent and deny the consequent. If the conditional holds, they have to give up at least one thing: either PC isn't really a mechanistic story, or it's not a good Bayesian theory, or its anti-Humean ambitions are misplaced.

The conditional uses a few terms of art. By *mechanistic story*, I mean that the models PC presents are meant to be taken as roughly literal descriptions of the causal-mechanical processes that give rise to perception and action. Given that PC has grown out of cognitive neuroscience and empirically oriented philosophy of mind, this should not raise any eyebrows. Further, as Colombo and Hartmann (2015) argue, Bayesian cognitive theories (of which PC is an instance) are too weak unless read as constraining causal-mechanical models.

I take the requirement for a mechanistic story to be a low bar, but it does imply two important constraints.

First, insofar as PC gives a story about *transitions* between states, that ought to imply a story about the causal mechanisms that underlie those transitions. Second, insofar as PC posits explanatory entities (like beliefs or models or whatnot), it is not allowed to posit infinitely many of them. Entities have to be instantiated, and there's only so much room in the skull.

Second, by a *thoroughgoing Bayesian*, I mean that insofar as your credences get updated, they get updated only by conditionalization on the available evidence. We can allow for some wiggle room (cognitive science is messy) and for complex, compartmentalized systems of belief and whatnot. The point is just that if you have some credences and you have to posit some additional way to update them that doesn't at least approximate conditionalization, then you're no longer being a good Bayesian. Updating by conditionalization is typically taken to be the core requirement for rational belief change on Bayesian frameworks: any other rule leaves one open to various kinds of exploitation. Conversely, optimality arguments in favor of Bayesianism (whether epistemic or evolutionary) place conditionalization at their core (for a nice review, see Okasha 2013).

The conjunction of these two constraints is clearly important to Predictive coders. Here's Hohwy motivating his project:

> In many ways, this broad line of reasoning is the impetus for this book: there is converging evidence that the brain is a Bayesian mechanism. This evidence comes from our conception of perception, from empirical studies of perception and cognition, from computational theory, from epistemology, and increasingly from neuroanatomy and neuroimaging. The best explanation of the occurrence of this evidence is that the brain is a Bayesian mechanism.
>
> (Hohwy 2013: 25)

Similarly, Clark presents PC as a mechanism for implementing ideal Bayesian updating to the best approximation we can muster (see esp. 2015 Appendix 1).

The link to Bayes is also important for the grand unifying ambitions of PC. For if PC is right, you can give a theory of mind with a single explanatory bit of ontology (models with credences) *and* a single transition rule (conditionalization). There may be a bit of complexity added by the connections between bits, but in general the grand, unifying ambitions of PC are supported precisely by its link to a relatively austere version of Bayesianism.

There is a very general argument, due to David Lewis (1988, 1996), that a Bayesian should be a Humean. The point of the chapter, then, is to spell out this argument in a way that makes it clear that it is a problem for the predictive coder. I'll first go through and give an informal sketch of what motivates the argument. I will then turn to Lewis's more formal version and some of the secondary literature around it. The formalities are important, because they show that the issue is not (just) with particular formulations of PC—the project as a whole faces a serious challenge. Finally, I'll conclude with some reflections on learning, which is at the heart of the problem.

2. The Informal Version

2.1. Setup

Any organism faces a trade-off between avoiding the bad and learning about the good. A new path might be more efficient or more dangerous. A new mushroom may lead to an awesome Saturday night or an agonizing death. While some basic actions may be hard-wired, a lot needs to be learned from experience. Worse, sometimes things change: the formerly good path becomes home to a hungry lion.

This learning process must take into account two distinct sorts of information: objective, non-relational information about the way the world actually is, and subjective, relational information about the value that different states have for you. Humeans, who separate credence and value, can handle this naturally by positing two different sorts of learning processes, each fit for purpose in its relevant domain. So, for example, one might appeal to Bayesian conditionalization for the credence end of things, and reinforcement learning for the value end. Other combinations are possible. The point is just that the orthogonality of credences and values permits wholly distinct learning processes.

Predictive coding, on the other hand, must make do with just credences, and just conditionalization. That creates a fundamental tension: an adequate account of action doesn't permit learning, and vice-versa.

2.2. The Necessary Stickiness of Desire

Take Clark's case of drinking water. Let's assume that the relevant proposition is something like

D: When I am thirsty, I drink water;

I have an appropriately high credence in **D**. If I am thirsty and I am not drinking, the mismatch between **D** and the world drives me to drink some water.

A few remarks about **D**. It is formulated conditionally because drinking is not unconditionally good. This gives a nice story about the cessation of action. Drinking eventually slakes my thirst, which makes **D** irrelevant.[2] **D** is formulated in terms of what *I* do, because it's only a mismatch between my own actions and the world that can drive my action. What makes it the case that I have a high credence in **D** in the first place might be (e.g.) evolutionary considerations about what things like me do, but my atypicality with respect to my conspecifics isn't enough to drive action. I've put the conditional in terms of actions, but the point should generalize to (e.g.) variational Bayes formulations that talk of internal control states rather than actions (Friston et al. 2012a). Finally, I've made **D** as simple as possible for exposition. More complication will not help.

D is meant to drive action. However, this comes with an important caveat. At first glance, if I am thirsty and not drinking, I could do two things to reduce the mismatch with **D**. I could drink water, *or* I could lower my credence in **D**.[3] That is, when I get thirsty, I could just decide that I am not the sort of thing that drinks when I'm thirsty; indeed, my current lack of drinking would seem to provide powerful ongoing evidence against **D**.

However, updating your beliefs is always going to be an easier solution than taking action. On the predictive coding story, changing your belief to "I don't drink when I'm thirsty and will die of dehydration" isn't obviously wrong—that model is just as accurate, and probably more certain.

This is the nub of what is known as the "dark room problem." An organism which enters a dark room and stays very still would appear to minimize prediction error, even though it eventually dies of thirst. That's obviously maladaptive, and the problem for PC is to say why actual organisms don't do this. The standard response is that our internal model doesn't predict dying in a dark room—that, in Clark's formulation, "animals like us live and forage in a changing and challenging world and hence 'expect' to deploy ... complex strategies" (2013: 193).

Yet this standard response is confusing. The deep mystery is not figuring out the reasons that organisms have to avoid pointless death: everyone agrees on those. Rather, the mystery is that *given* these reasons, it's not clear why a predictive coder should be motivated by them. Properly understood, the Dark room problem is just a vivid illustration of the fact that, of two ways to make **D** true, we only ever do one of them. It's not clear, given PC, why that should be (Klein 2018).

The only way I can see to avoid this bad outcome is if **D** somehow ends up *sticky*: that is, if it is effectively impossible to update **D** itself. Note that this means there must be a difference between predictions: some of them get updated (the belief-like ones) and some don't (the desire-like ones). In my earlier (2018) critique, I suggested that this breaks the fundamental simplicity of the PC model. Put that to one side. Also put aside worries about how the two states are reliably distinguished; presuppose for now whatever magic you'd like. Perhaps **D** gets arbitrarily high credence, or precision, or whatever you need to make it sticky. Assume whatever is necessary, so long as it is consistent with a mechanistic, thorough Bayesian story.

2.3. A Sticky Problem

Now comes the problem: If **D** can't be updated, *D can't be updated*. That means my experiences can't actually change what I value. That seems wrong.

Suppose the water in my area becomes contaminated—enough to make me a little sick, and that previously unattractive pineapple juice now becomes a better option to quench my thirst. It is unclear how this fact alone would even come to bear on **D**, but ignore that.

D is sticky, which means that it is resistant to evidence. So whatever evidence is supposed to be a valid reason to change **D** won't do the job. Indeed, note that the evidence that the water is bad—which is ultimately supposed to bear on **D**—is surely going to be somewhat imprecise and inconsistent. In terms of evidence against **D**, then, it will be much weaker than the extremely strong sensory evidence I have that I am not drinking water when I am not drinking water. Which means that if **D** is sticky enough to drive action, it's too sticky to revise.

There are two tempting ways to get out of this, neither of which PC can actually endorse. First, you could think that **D** is just too simple: that in fact, the right analogue is something like "When I am thirsty *and* I do not have previous evidence that the water is bad *and* .... I drink." Now, that's a super weird response. It wriggles out of the problem by denying that you actually learn anything about what's good (you always know all the relevant conditionals, and all you ever learn is which antecedent to apply). But even if you're one of the rare philosophers of cognitive science who have a fondness for the Platonic Doctrine of Recollection, it still won't do. That ellipses hides a lot. The possible combinations of states that count for or against drinking are effectively infinite, which means in turn that the number of distinct specific states in which I drink will be infinite. So while complicating **D** might result in a good *description* of how I act, it can't specify the *mechanism* by which I act. But that's what PC needed.

Second, it's tempting to think of more elaborate schemes about how to update **D**. Why not (say) just add a rule that lets you update **D** in case you get evidence that the water is bad? The problem is generated because of the inflexibility of the updating rule, after all. But remember, the inflexibility is a feature, not a bug. Add a rule that doesn't involve updating by conditionalization, and you're no longer a thorough Bayesian. But that's what PC needed.

So it's not that there aren't solutions. It's just that the obvious solutions involve either giving up on PC being a mechanistic story or else giving up on the thoroughgoing Bayesianism. That secures the conditional argument.

2.4. A Further Perspective

Before moving to Lewis, I want to offer a further perspective on the informal argument. One of the standard arguments in favor of Humeanism is supposed to be that beliefs (and the like) just aren't the sort of thing that can motivate. That is, there is a *synchronic* problem getting things with a belief-like direction of fit to do the job they need to do. That's arguably a piece of folk psychology, and PC abandons it in the course of showing how a belief-like state can be made to do the right kind of work. I think that's fine: good models can trump folk psychology.

But what the above shows is that there is a much stickier *diachronic* problem that the anti-Humean faces, one that bites PC especially hard. It's not just that credences and values appear to do different things. They also require being updated in different, often orthogonal, ways. This is related to direction of fit worries: one should update a belief when it becomes false, and a value when it becomes bad for you. Yet diachronic updating is a distinct, and arguably more difficult, problem that predictive coders must solve. For one, the attraction of PC rests on the unificatory power of a single, austere, learning rule; that leaves them with fewer resources. For another, PC's standard solution to the synchronic problem appears to make the diachronic problem intractable, because it requires making the value-like credences too sticky to change.

Finally, and again, it's worth reiterating that the Humean has a lot easier time here. For the Humean already has two distinct state-types, which means they can easily appeal to two distinct rules. Neither the synchronic nor the diachronic problem get much purchase; what the Humean loses in ontological parsimony, they more than gain back in simplicity of the overall dynamics.

3. Lewis's General Argument

3.1. The Setup

The above argument was linked to a particular way of cashing out things like **D**. PC is a broad tent, and perhaps you favor some other way of linking up value and credence.

There is a very general argument by Lewis (1988, 1996) that appears to weigh against *any* attempt to reduce values to credences. This has received surprisingly little attention in the PC literature (Ransom, Fazelpour, and Mole (2017: footnote 11) is the only mention I've found). That's a pity. I think that, properly understood, Lewis's argument shows that the informal argument in section 2 will hold regardless of how you cash out the particulars.

I'll start with Lewis's argument, then look at some responses to tie it all together. I follow the presentation in Lewis 1996. First, let's suppose each individual can be described as having two functions: V, which takes propositions to their value to the individual; and C, which takes propositions to an individual's credence in the proposition. The Humean thinks that this description holds because there are distinct desires (that ground V) and beliefs (that ground C).

The job for the non-Humean is to show a principled way to translate from V to C. That is, for any proposition A, we want a mapping function that takes us from $V(A)$ to a belief that has the right motivational role. We did that in an ad hoc way above when we went from "I desire to drink water when I'm thirsty" to "When I'm thirsty, I drink water." But that translation could take any number of forms, so long as it is consistent— we might posit a high credence in "Drinking water is good" or "Drinking water is the thing to do" or whatever. I'll cash this out as "A is good" below, but that's shorthand for a bunch of different possibilities.

Using Lewis's terms, PC must posit a *halo function* that maps any proposition A onto a corresponding A^0 such that $V(A) = C(A^0)$. What Lewis terms the *Desire-as-Belief* (DAB) thesis is just the claim that some such function exists. This is not yet to give a mechanism, but merely to posit a systematic mapping; conversely, the Humean *denial* of DAB is the claim that there is no such systematic mapping.

Now, this is something of an odd setup by many lights. DAB as stated collapses goodness into two states—good or bad, halo-on or halo-off—and altering this to allow for degrees of goodness and badness requires a more complex account (See Hájek 2015 for an excellent discussion).

While these may be difficulties for Lewis's account considered quite generally, I submit that they are *also* issues for PC. That is, it is also unclear quite how the PC framework deals with degrees of value, given that most of the framework is spelled out in terms of the *optimal* action for the agent in question (see, for example, Friston et al. 2012b). I think DAB is actually a relatively good picture of how PC envisions the translation from value to credence; let's assume, for the sake of argument, that it is fit for purpose.

3.2. The Argument

As a logical matter, DAB is equivalent to the conjunction of two other propositions:

Desire as conditional belief (DACB): $V(A) = C(A^0/A)$
Independence (*IND*): $C(A^0/A) = C(A^0)$

DACB says, roughly, that your values should link up to the credences that something is good conditional on you actually having that thing. Put that to one side; IND is where the action will be. IND says that your belief that A is good should be independent of whether A is actually the case. That seems like a good general rule of thumb. IND is also necessary for the predictive coder. It is the mismatch between A^0 and A that drives action, so that mismatch needs to be preserved in the face of evidence that what is good does not (yet) obtain.

Yet as Lewis notes, IND does not generally hold. Indeed, there are clear counterexamples. Suppose A and $A^0 > 0$, and that I learn that $\sim(A \ \& \ A^0)$. Then $C(A^0|A) = 0$, but $C(A^0) > 0$. IND fails.

To make the case concrete, suppose I've heard that sit-ups are good for you (and I want to do anything that's good for me). I don't really know what I'm doing, but I dutifully attempt some. I pull my back. I conclude that either sit-ups aren't good for you, or else I wasn't actually doing sit-ups. In that case, the value I place on sit-ups conditional on me having done them is zero: I tried, and I got hurt. But I am unsure whether I really did sit-ups, and so I'm unsure of whether sit-ups are as bad as they seem. So my value on sit-ups *tout court* remains nonzero. Which means that the credences doing value-like work are not independent of the credences that are supposed to drive action, which is what the predictive coder needs.

DAB says that there's a mapping from (apparent) values to credences. That's the halo function. That mapping needs to be specified independently of what's actually the case, so that value-like credences can drive actions. But then updating by conditionalization will, in many cases, break that mapping. So contra DAB, we can't map values to credences after all.

3.3. A Refinement

There has been considerable discussion of Lewis's result. As Hájek and Pettit (2004) note, an important class of responses can be captured in terms of quantifier scope. Making the quantifiers more explicit, Hájek and Pettit contrast two versions of DAB:

> Lewisian DAB: There is a halo function such that for any pair of C and V and any proposition A, $V(A) = C(A^0)$

In other words, there is a single, fixed halo function that holds across shifts in credence. This is arguably how PC actually sets things up (or, at least, this is the most plausible way to read predictive coders' frequent appeal to an organism's evolutionary history). Hájek and Pettit agree that Lewisian DAB is untenable. However, they note that by re-ordering the quantifiers, we get the much more plausible:

> Indexical DAB: For any pair of C and V and any proposition A, there is a halo function such that $V(A) = C(A^0)$

Indexical DAB is much easier to satisfy, because it allows A-halo to vary as a function of circumstance. Intuitively, this allows for the possibility that an agent may (e.g.) learn that they were wrong about what is good (2004: 83). The most plausible way of cashing this out in the ethical case involves "indexicalist" formulations, on which the halo function tracks something indexed to the agent.[4]

Lewis himself seems to think that letting the halo function vary would be a cheap victory. Hájek (2015) notes that this is only if the halo function is allowed to vary arbitrarily, so long as there is an interpretation on which the halo over a proposition is "genuinely earned" (p. 440). I take this to mean that the halo function and its dynamics need to reflect something about how we think the corresponding predicate (like "is good") behaves.

But here we come to the crux of the problem for PC. The debate around Lewis is primarily about *whether* an appropriate mapping from *V* to *C* can be found. PC needs something more: it needs to tell us *how* that updating can take place. The lesson of either form of DAB, I take it, is that however this works, conditionalization is out of the question. So if there's a mechanistic story, it's not a thoroughly Bayesian one: something other than conditionalization has to be in place to keep the halo function happy.

But that's just to say that the predictive coder can't have a mechanistic story that's also fully Bayesian about change in credences—unless, of course, they want to posit some other states (like desires) that underwrite the remapping of the halo function across updates in credences. Which is, again, to secure our conditional.

4. Conclusion: Change Matters

I suggested at the end of section 2 that the deep problem for the predictive coder has to do with diachronic change in values. If you want to give a mechanistic story (and PC should), and you don't want to give up on thorough Bayesianism about credence change (and doing so would make PC unattractive), then you need to posit other processes to keep this running. You need to do this, note, *even* if you think that action in the particular case is driven entirely by mismatch with credence-y things. In section 2, I argued that this mismatch only works if you can keep the value-like credences fixed, which means you need some other mechanism for them to change when they need to change. In section 3, I gave Lewis's argument that no matter how you set this up, you can't get by with just conditionalization on one's credences. Something has to give. And that, you might think, is a good place to return to desires, or values, or something old-fashioned—not because you need them for action, but because you need them to learn which actions are best.

These problems with PC have remained obscure, I think, because of the belief that certain modeling results show that the PC framework can operate without a formal value function. So, for example, in criticizing Ransom et al. (2017), Clark claims that objectors who focus on the initiation of action fail "to recognize the true scope of the formal demonstration that any set of behaviors prescribed by reward, cost, or utility functions can be prescribed by an apt set of systemic beliefs or priors" (2017: 117). Yet the "apt" part does more work than it might seem, and more work than it should.

The modeling results that Clark refers to (such as Friston et al. 2012a) typically start by fixing the value function, and then showing that optimal policies with respect to the value function can be learned. These are usual quite sparse problems as well: in the case of Friston, Samothrakis, and Montague, for example, they consider a mountain car problem that has a single, fixed goal and in which the agent has already "learned the constraints afforded by the world it operates in" (2012a: 533).

Here's one way to interpret such claims: if you give me an initial credence function C and a non-updating value function V, along with complete flexibility about how to set the actual credences (interpreted as a lack of constraints on the halo function), I can find a total set of credences C^* that allows an agent performing active inference to act as if they were behaving in accordance with the initial C and V.

Yet what the above has shown is that even if we can do this, and even if we are convinced that this is not mere description but picks mechanisms, we're *still* missing a story about how the valued propositions change. The mountain car doesn't have to deliberate about what's good in life: it has to get to its spot, and that's it. Keeping that fixed, learning about what *means* will get it to its end is unproblematic.

Our lives are not so simple. We must learn about what is good, and we must re-learn what are good changes when the world changes. A very natural way to model this is to separate out learning about the world and learning about value, and to treat these as distinct but co-equal processes that fruitfully interact. PC can remain an interesting and valuable part of the story about how beliefs are updated if you'd like—there's just more work to do too.

Humeanism is not without its flaws. However, positing two independent state-types—with different evolutionary demands, different directions of fit, and different combinatorial resources—brings along a host of explanatory resources. Whatever marks of simplicity Humeanism loses by having two state-types rather than one, it gains back and more on the simplicity and empirical plausibility of the resulting explanations it can give.[5]

Notes

1   I will speak about predictive coding very broadly, to include (for example) accounts that talk about the Free Energy Principle (Friston 2010) or Active Inference (Kirchoff et al. 2018). While there are important differences within this family, all are committed to a single state-type and Bayesian updating, and so will be vulnerable to the critique below.

2   Here I assume that it is the underlying physiological change rather than the action which slakes thirst; see my (2015: 20ff) for discussion and defense.

3   Strictly speaking, there are also two more options: I could revise my belief that I'm thirsty, or I could revise my belief that I am not drinking water. I take it that both of these would result in high-error situations and so aren't viable. By contrast, revising **D** is a way of minimizing prediction error, since it is only the conflict with **D** that gives rise to any error in the first place.

4   An alternative response involves separating evaluative and non-evaluative propositions (Bradley and List 2008), and then restricting update to the non-evaluative ones. As Bradley and List note, this would be controversial even in the home domain

of metaethics, as it would require denying supervenience of the evaluative on the non-evaluative. In the cognitive case it would be equivalent to the unattractive claim, discussed in section 2.3, that we have innate fine-grained knowledge about the good and bad states of the world. (See Klein 2018 for further discussion.)

5 Thanks to Peter Clutton, Ben Henke, Julia Haas, Ross Pain, and the editors of the present volume for helpful comments on a previous draft, and to an audience at Macquarie University for useful feedback in the early stages of the project. This chapter was supported by Australian Research Council grant FT140100422.

References

Ashby, W. R. (1976), *Design for a Brain; the Origin of Adaptive Behavior*, London: Chapman and Hall.

Bradley, R. and List, C. (2008), "Desire-as-belief Revisited," *Analysis*, 69 (1): 31–7.

Buchak, L. (2016), "Decision Theory" in C. Hitchcock and A. Hájek (eds.), *Oxford Handbook of Probability and Philosophy*, Oxford: Oxford University Press.

Clark, A. (2013), "Whatever Next? Predictive Brains, Situated Agents, and the Future of Cognitive Science," *Behavioral and Brain Sciences*, 36 (3): 181–253.

Clark, A. (2015), *Surfing Uncertainty: Prediction, Action, and the Embodied Mind*, New York: Oxford University Press.

Clark, A. (2017), "Predictions, Precision, and Agentive Attention," *Consciousness and Cognition*, 56: 115–19.

Colombo, Matteo and Hartmann, Stephan. (2015), "Bayesian Cognitive Science, Unification, and Explanation," *The British Journal for the Philosophy of Science* 68 (2): 451–84.

Dennett, D. (1987), *The Intentional Stance*, Cambridge: MIT Press.

Friston, K. (2010), "The Free-energy Principle: A Unified Brain Theory?," *Nature Reviews Neuroscience*, 11 (2): 127–38.

Friston, K., Samothrakis, S. and Montague, R. (2012a), "Active Inference and Agency: Optimal Control without Cost Functions," *Biological Cybernetics*, 106 (8–9): 523–41.

Friston, K., Thornton, C. and Clark, A. (2012b), "Free-energy Minimization and the Dark-room Problem," *Frontiers in Psychology*, 3: 1–7.

Hájek, A. (2015), "On the Plurality of Lewis's Triviality Results" in B. Loewer and J. Schaffer (eds.), *A Companion to David* Lewis, New York: John Wiley & Sons.

Hájek, A. and Pettit, P. (2004), "Desire Beyond Belief," *The Australasian Journal of Philosophy*, 82 (1): 77–92.

Hohwy, J. (2013), *The Predictive Mind*, New York: Oxford University Press.

Kirchoff, M. et al. (2018), "The Markov Blankets of Life: Autonomy, Active Inference and the Free Energy Principle," *Journal of the Royal Society Interface*, 15 (138): 20170792.

Klein C. (2015), *What the Body Commands: The Imperative Theory of Pain*, Cambridge: MIT Press.

Klein, C. (2018), "What Do Predictive Coders Want?," *Synthese*, 195 (6): 2541–57.

Lewis, D. (1988), "Desire as Belief," *Mind*, 97 (387): 323–32.

Lewis, D. (1996), "Desire as Belief II," *Mind*, 105 (418): 303–13.

Okasha, S. (2013), "The Evolution of Bayesian Updating," *Philosophy of Science*, 80 (5): 745–57.

Putnam, H. (1967), "The Nature of Mental States" Reprinted in *Philosophical Papers v2: Mind, Language, and Reality*, pp. 429–40.

Ransom, M., Fazelpour, S. and Mole, C. (2017), "Attention in the Predictive Mind," *Consciousness and Cognition*, 47: 99–112.

Smith, M. (1984), *The Moral Problem*, Cambridge: Blackwell.

Wiese, W. (2017), "Action Is Enabled by Systematic Misrepresentations," *Erkenntnis*, 82 (6): 1233–52.

3

Are Markov Blankets Real and Does It Matter?

Richard Menary and Alexander James Gillett

Macquarie University, Australia

1. Introduction

Philosophers of mind and cognition are warming up to the consequences of the predictive processing framework. The unique selling point of the framework is that it will unify perception, cognition, and action within a single explanatory framework (Clark 2016, Friston 2010, Hohwy 2013, 2015). Even more astonishing is the claim that a single principle, the free energy principle, is the ultimate explanation for all of the above (Friston 2010). In amongst the empirical of predictive processing in cognitive neuroscience, a diverging set of philosophical accounts of the framework have recently emerged. In particular, Andy Clark's (2013, 2016, 2015, 2017a) *action-oriented account* of the framework which gives more emphasis to the role of embodied action and Jakob Hohwy's (2013) account of the framework as largely a matter of internal predictive processes in the brain—*the isolated brain interpretation* (Fabry 2017, Hohwy 2015). These are important statements that frame predictive processing and the free energy principle in the clothing of externalism and internalism about the mind (positions that have a long history in the philosophy of mind).

There are several intriguing problems and conceptual issues that require working through in the emerging philosophical approaches to the predictive framework, but one of the central issues is an old one: Where do the boundaries of the mind lie? (e.g. Clark and Chalmers 1998). The primary issue that we will address is the role of Markov blankets in this debate, where a Markov blanket is a set of nodes or states that partition those states into those that comprise the blanket, those that are internal to it and those that are external to it. In so doing, the Markov blanket determines the boundary of a system (comprising the blanket and internal states).[1] We will consider the philosophical ramifications of taking Markov blankets to be a real ontological category: a class of entity with genuine causal powers. The alternative is to consider Markov blankets as a convenient fiction. A heuristic device that aids in modeling real, complex systems;

The research for this chapter was made possible by ARC Future Fellowship FT 130100960. Thanks to feedback from audiences at the Australasian Association of Philosophy and the University of Wollongong. Thanks also to Chris Whyte and Chris Hewitson for useful comments on an earlier draft of this chapter.

an instrumentalist approach that makes no ontological commitment. The former does appear to have important consequences for the boundaries of the mind debate, but the exact status of Markov blankets and hierarchies of blankets within blankets is ontologically costly.

We consider examples of the deployment of Markov blankets in the broader literature, but we think that Friston's work is having a profound effect on philosophical argument and that this requires some reflection and analysis. We will not, primarily, be considering the mathematical basis of the Markov blanket literature or provide any detailed formal analysis. Quite enough has already been written here; by contrast, too little has been written providing a conceptual interpretation of the Markov blanket idea and its consequences for philosophical arguments concerning the boundaries of the mind.[2]

Markov blankets are a methodological tool first devised in the machine learning literature for statistically separating a node in a Bayesian network from other nodes in the network; the Markov blanket for a node closes off the node from the rest of the network and consists in the node's parents, its children, and its children's other parents (Pearl 1988). Markov blankets have subsequently been adopted and leveraged into the debates about how to understand predictive processing, and whether they bound the system at the brain or at some larger unit of analysis (Clark 2017, Fabry 2017, Hohwy 2016, Kirchhoff et al. 2018, Ramstead et al. 2019). However, they have been used in much broader discussions of the origins of life and biological self-organization (Friston 2013), evolution, and even social/cultural organization.

We shall argue that the debate about the boundary of the mind is based on some assumptions about Markov blankets that both sides need to examine more carefully. In particular, given that Markov blankets were originally a methodological heuristic and not an ontological category with causal powers, it is not clear how they can properly demarcate the boundaries of cognition. To be clear, by ontology we are referring to the standard formulation of this notion as a claim about reality or existence, and a capacity to bring about particular effects. In other words: are Markov blankets a modeling technique or are they real physical entities? As has recently been noted by Colombo and Wright (2018) in their discussion of the free energy principle in general, these are important questions that practitioners cannot overlook. The current problem is that many of the central proponents of the boundaries of the mind debate jump between a heuristic and ontological account, sometimes holding both constant at the same time.

In this chapter we propose that until this issue is resolved the Markov blanket concept cannot be used to demarcate the boundaries of mind and world. This is because the original concept of a Markov blanket, as introduced by Judea Pearl, does not have the resources to make a decisive contribution to the boundaries of the mind debate, because it is simply a heuristic used in Bayesian graphs. The concept of a Markov blanket that derives from Friston's work is an extension of the original concept, but, as yet, there has been limited discussion of the warrant of this extension. Pearl's original formulation was a mathematical idealization that enabled researchers to resolve problems in machine learning. Such modeling techniques are standard practices throughout the sciences but are not held to have an accurate representational warrant. Friston's usage treats Markov blankets as causal features of the world and thus overlooks the idealization involved in this modeling technique. Not only does this issue need addressing, but there are also a range of related philosophical issues about the sort of metaphysical position that is endorsed in this formal ontology.

We first outline the origins of Markov blankets in machine learning before then turning to how they have been used in the debate between externalism and internalism. In particular, we will focus on the costs and consequences to philosophers and cognitive scientists working within the embodied and extended tradition. Both interpretations of predictive processing[3] have exactly the same presuppositions about the Bayesian brain making guesses about hidden environmental variables—which are occluded by the Markov blanket. For the brain-bound interpretation this is a standard, if extreme, formulation of internalism but, for action-orientated views there is a tension here. One putative resolution of this tension is to emphasize the role of active inference in overcoming the seclusion of the Markov blanket to integrate the brain, body, and world in a manner that is at least consistent with the various strands of the 4E tradition (see Clark 2017, Kirchhoff and Kiverstein 2019, Ramstead et al. 2019). However, as we shall argue in more detail below, the active inference interpretation still has the same problem concerning the heuristic or ontological status of Markov blankets. We conclude the chapter by reiterating the remaining challenges for both sides in the internalist-externalist debate who wish to use the Markov blanket concept to bound cognitive systems.

2. What Is a Markov Blanket?

The term "Markov blanket" was introduced by Judea Pearl (1988, see also Clark 2017), in a discussion of probabilistic reasoning in machine learning. The Markov blanket was introduced as a way of separating a node in a Bayesian network from other nodes in the network (that are not its offspring or its parents). Bayesian networks, also defined by Pearl, "consist of a set of nodes, representing random variables. Together with a set of directed edges from one node to another, which can be used to identify statistical dependencies between variables (e.g. Pearl 1988)" (Griffiths and Yuille 2008: 43).

Bayesian networks are simply graphical representations of conditional dependencies and independencies, which show the direct causal relations between a set of variables of a system. The network functions as a model of the domain in question and allows for algorithms that can be used to make probabilistic inferences. Below is a diagram depicting a simple Bayesian network.[4] The top two panels are sets of variables that denote states external to a system across two time periods *t–1* and *t*. The bottom panel shows a set of evidence variables at time *t* based on the available sensory information. A model of evidence variables at time steps *t–1* and *t* then encodes for the conditional probabilities of the observable variables. Keeping track of these observable states involves calculating the probabilities of past states. This involves a Markov blanket (Figure 3.1):

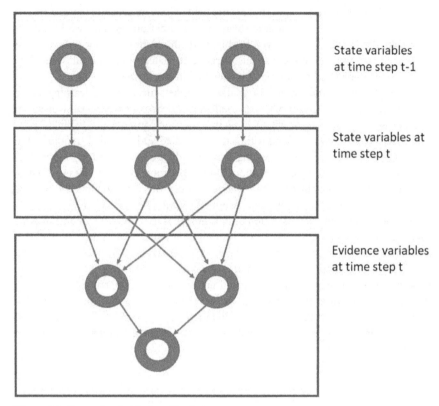

State variables at time step t-1

State variables at time step t

Evidence variables at time step t

Figure 3.1 Example of a Markov Blanket

A Markov blanket can be simply described as follows: "the *Markov Blanket* of a variable *X* is the smallest set Mb(*X*) containing all variables carrying information about *X* that cannot be obtained from any other variable .... In a causal graph this is the set of all parents, children and spouses of *X*" (Pellett and Elisseeff 2008: 1296). A concrete example can be seen in how Zhu and colleagues (2007) utilize Markov blankets to predict the expression of thousands of genes. Gene expression is a complex physical process in which there are large degrees of freedom and multiple interacting causal pathways. By using Markov blankets in their model of the target system, the experimenters are able to bracket the irrelevant features and focus on the crucial aspects of the data set that the algorithms in their model need to operate over. Zhu and colleagues state clearly that the Markov blanket formalization enables their algorithm to compute a solution that would not otherwise be effective (3241). We return to this example below. We note at this point that Markov blankets are a heuristic device for modeling a far more complex target system, by isolating only those parts of the system that are relevant for statistical analysis. There are no ontological claims made by the authors concerning Markov blankets.

However, Friston's description of a Markov blanket is an ontological notion that plays an important causal role in the self-organization of a complex system. This is not a heuristic construct which is useful for data analysis. Rather than acting as a heuristic for tracking certain variables, the Markov blanket now actually maintains the separation of internal and external states (Friston 2013):

> The existence of a Markov blanket induces a partition of states into internal states and external states that are hidden (insulated) from the internal (insular) states by the Markov blanket. In other words, the external states can only be seen vicariously by the internal states, through the Markov blanket.
>
> (Friston 2013: 2)

Second, the Markov blanket determines the integrity of the system such that it can obey the free energy principle.[5] In Friston's Free energy framework, if there are no Markov blankets, there can be no distinction between internal states and hidden external variables and, therefore, no motivation for the need to make predictions about those hidden variables.

Third, the Markov blanket idea can be applied at different scales such that "the Markov blanket of an animal encloses the Markov blankets of its organs, which enclose Markov blankets of cells, which enclose Markov blankets of nuclei and so on" (Friston 2013: 10).

As we have already seen, the original idea of a Markov blanket was simply to determine the distinction between a node and its offspring (that are causally connected) from other nodes in the same network, thereby facilitating more accurate forms of Bayesian inference. It does not, *at all*, sponsor the idea that Markov blankets actually determine boundaries of organisms and their environments, such that internal states (nodes) of an organism are hidden from external states of an environment in an ontological or causal sense. If one wishes to endorse the Fristonian conception, then one has moved far beyond the simple concept introduced in the machine learning literature.

The question then becomes what warrants this extension of the concept? There is a distinct gap in the literature concerning this warrant (also see Colombo and Wright 2019 for similar points). Indeed, it is a hidden variable about which limited inferences have been made. We propose that to avoid confusion on the matter we should distinguish between *heuristic Markov Blankets* and *ontological Markov Blankets* (or HMBs and OMBs for short). One of the most important aspects of the extension is that OMBs are now an ontological category to be found in nature. They are no longer a heuristic for partitioning nodes in a network—an HMB. The application of OMBs is often argued to be the result of a system acting in accordance with the free energy principle. In other words, any system that seeks to minimize free energy spontaneously partitions itself into internal, sensory, and active states; which separate it from external, or environmental states (Friston 2013). There has been a rush to extend further and wider to almost every level of organization in nature, from cells to brains and beyond to populations and even entire societies (Clark 2017, Kirchhoff et al. 2018, Ramstead et al. 2019).

To summarize:

Heuristic Markov blanket	A heuristic for determining the parents, siblings, and offspring of a variable in a causal graph. It performs a useful function in artificial Bayesian networks.
Ontological Markov blanket	An ontological category determining the boundaries of self-organizing systems that minimize free energy, that is their function. They do so at multiple scales of organization from individual cells, to cell assemblies, brains, organisms, groups, and even populations.

We think that getting clearer on this distinction would be of general benefit to the debate. Namely, which concept is being used and how it is being used.

In a forthcoming paper the justification for using the Markov blanket construct to determine the boundaries of a self-organizing system is that it provides a formal definition of what we mean by the internal states of a structure, or system, being independent of the external states (Palacios et al. 2020). The definition is clear: "A Markov blanket is a set of states that separates the internal or intrinsic states of a structure from extrinsic or external states" (Palacios et al. 2020: 1). However, this simple definition is elaborated through several stages:

The boundary comprises "sensory and active states, as is the case for biological systems, like membrane receptors and the cytoskeleton underneath them. In other words, a (biological) physical boundary is a Markov blanket (with sensory and active states)" (Palacios et al. 2020: 1–2). This can be formally defined in such a way that for any structure its internal states will be conditionally independent of its external states. Importantly, the definition "precludes a (spatially dependent) direct coupling between internal and external states, such that they only influence each other vicariously through the Markov blanket" (Palacios et al. 2020: 2). Therefore, a Markov blanket, in the extended sense, is just this collection of active and sensory states that partitions external states from internal states and thereby determines the boundary of (in this case) a physical system. There are several things to note about this: first, any system that self-organizes must have sensory and active states (at least functionally). This might be obvious when talking of organisms, but if we are talking of cells it is not obvious at all. We have to extend the concept of sensory states and active states to include the kind of signaling that a cell might engage in with its local environs. A cell membrane would form a Markov blanket between the internal intracellular states and external states and, as such, would form the sensory states that would mediate the electrochemical signals with external (hidden) states of the environment (Friston 2013). What we then have to imagine is that the internal intracellular states are making inferences about the external states on the basis of the mediating sensory states comprised by the cell membrane and that those inferences are equivalent to approximate Bayesian inference: "Put simply, this proof says that if one interprets internal states as parametrizing a variational density encoding Bayesian beliefs about external states, then the dynamics of internal and active states can be described as a gradient descent on a variational free energy function of internal states and their Markov blanket" (Friston 2013: 4).[6]

Step two moves from the "the existence of a Markov blanket S x A implies a partition of states into external, sensory, active and internal states" (Friston 2013: 2) to a set of statements that are crucial for the understanding of a Markov blanket as having causal powers: "External states cause sensory states that influence—but are not influenced by—internal states, while internal states cause active states that influence—but are not influenced by—external states" (Friston 2013: 2). These dependencies are said to cause a circular causality that resembles the action-perception cycle in so far as external states cause changes to internal states via sensory states and internal states cause changes to external states via active states. The entire interpretation depends upon an interpretation of internal states as "encoding Bayesian beliefs about external states" (Friston 2013: 4). Given a variational free energy formulation, the details of which need not concern us here, "the internal states will appear to have solved the problem of Bayesian inference by encoding posterior beliefs about hidden (external) states, under a generative model" (Friston 2013: 4). This may sound reasonable when we are talking about organisms and their environments, but now remember that there are Markov blankets of Markov blankets; so although we might be inclined to argue that the sensory and active states of an organism set the boundaries of its cognitive system (e.g., the brain), it is less obvious how the concept of a Markov blanket can be used to determine a hierarchy of organizational structures (such as genes, cells, organs, bodies, ecosystems, etc.).

Palacios and colleagues illustrate the hierarchical self-assembly of Markov blankets of Markov blankets with computational simulations of the self-organization of simple ensembles of synthetic cells: "Crucially, these simulations use simple generative models, embodying the prior 'belief' that each member can play the role of an internal, active or sensory state within the ensemble. In other words, Markov blankets at one level of organisation possess prior beliefs there is a Markov blanket partition at the level above" (2020: 6). However, cells don't have "beliefs" about what role they will play in the higher-level blanket, but they can make inferences about the "hidden state"—what role they will play in the higher-level Markov blanket (remember that Markov blankets are composed of sensory and active states). Effectively each cell must already encode a belief or model of what role it plays and by communicating with other cells it can form part of a higher-level organization (a conglomerate of cells) that differentiates itself from the external milieu. Palacios and colleagues speculate that the prior beliefs or generative models might be specified by genes (2020: 12). These priors would determine what a cell would expect to receive as a signal from its neighbors.

What should we make of all this? Mathematical specifications and computational simulations are idealizations. The question is whether they are supposed to be realistic models of actual natural processes. If they are, then we need more realistic scaled-up models. If they are not, then they are simple heuristics. Idealizations of this kind cannot decide the boundaries of the mind debate without further work. One solution is to adopt the HMB model—i.e., Markov blankets are thought of as heuristic models of self-organizing systems where states are partitioned into sensory, active, and internal on the basis of prior generative models which determine the expected signals that the state will receive depending upon which role it will play.

However, the arguments of Friston (2013), Palacios et al. (2020), Kirchhoff and Kiverstein (2019), and Ramstead et al. (2019) that we are discussing assume the OMB interpretation. In biological and adaptive systems, the self-organizing partition of states (the formation of a Markov blanket) is determined by the prior generative model which must be a result of genetic encoding and evolution. Ultimately all of this bottoms out in the free energy principle, but the inferences that are made by internal states about hidden external states are Bayesian, even if only by approximating Bayesian inference. Without Bayes's theorem none of this account would make any sense, nor would it be tractable, but the problem this raises is the nature of the prior beliefs for small-scale (cells or cell assemblies) and large-scale systems (populations of organisms), which must encode prior beliefs or generative models.

There are various ways of attempting to ameliorate the reduction, but Bayes's theorem applies to beliefs as we standardly understand them—states that are more or less probable on the basis of their propositional content. Why is this the case? Because in Bayes's theorem we update the posterior probability of a belief on the basis of new evidence and we understand both the belief and the evidence propositionally. Palacios and colleagues recognize this worry:

> Here we associate biochemical structures, gradient flows and kinetics with Bayesian priors and belief propagation or updating—as opposed to propositional or representational beliefs .... However, this is an "as if" interpretation; in the same sense that the folding of macromolecule to minimise its thermodynamic free energy in computational chemistry—e.g., Lammert et al. (2012)—looks "as if" it is trying to minimise (thermodynamic) free energy.
>
> (Palacios et al. 2020: 11)

Here there is an immediate jump from an OMB interpretation to an HMB interpretation. This seems entirely obvious to us, but there is a suppressed inference which could be made: Although cells might only look as if they are performing Bayesian inferences, brains and organisms proper are performing those inferences, in which case Bayesian priors and belief updating are accurate explanations of what the brain/organism is actually doing, even if they are only "as-if" explanations of what cells are doing.

Even as an HMB interpretation, the application of the Markov blanket construct to organisms requires us to think of those organism's states as being organized like a Bayesian network. Remember that Bayesian networks, in computer science, where they were first developed, are graphs that represent concepts—usually propositions—and the connections (edges) between the nodes indicate a relationship—usually statistical/causal.[7] Algorithms—like the Markov chain casino algorithm—are then applied to the graphs to calculate various probabilistic outcomes based upon the nodes and edges in the network. Bayesian networks are not supposed to be accurate models of the way that organisms work. Nor are they supposed to be accurate models of the way that brains work.

However, they do have their uses. Bayesian networks can be used as abstract models of gene regulatory networks, by modeling the causal and statistical relationships between genes, but nobody thinks that gene regulatory networks are actually Bayesian networks. The potential for confusion between the *structure* of a way of representing causal dependencies and the *nature* of physical systems themselves cannot be underestimated here. One can see this confusion more clearly when one considers what scientific models are, and what relationship they bear to a target system.

3. Models in Science

In the extensive literature on scientific models, there is a distinction between dyadic accounts, which focus on the representational relationship between the model and the target system, and more complex views which do not see the representational relationship as exhausting how scientific models operate in scientific practice. For instance, Giere (2004) sees the relationship of a scientific model and its target system as a quaternary relationship of: $S \to M \to W \to P$. Namely, a scientist or scientific community (S) use a model or set of models (M) to represent a target system in the world (W) for a particular purpose (P). As Morrison and Morgan (1999) have extensively shown, a realistic representation is only one of many reasons why a scientist or scientific community might design, build, and manipulate a model. A non-exhaustive list collected by Morrison and Morgan shows that models can be used for pedagogical reasons, for measurement, for gaining explanatory leverage, to explore imprecise or ill-specified aspects of a theory, to facilitate theory and hypothesis generation, and to function as a means of experimentation (1999: 18–25).

Importantly, whether or not the model is a realistic representation of the target system is often irrelevant to these concerns. Indeed, in many cases a realistic representational relationship is actually detrimental to the purposes to which the model is put. Indeed, as Glennan has recently stated, there is a general consensus among philosophers of science that "models that are idealized, heuristic, and often clearly false are key tools for representing and intervening in nature" (2017: 8; also see Cartwright 1999, Giere 2004, Morgan and Morrison 1999, Weisberg 2007, Wimsatt 2007). For instance, if one is trying to ascertain what is the most important difference-making variable in a putative system, then there is a utility in idealizing or eliminating the degrees of freedom of other variables, such that one can more easily determine the role of that variable (Humphreys 2004).

In this context the question of whether Markov blankets are useful methodological tools becomes a matter of their explanatory power. They have clear use in the original field of adoption, machine learning, and have been imported with successful gains in other fields (e.g., genetics, economics, and bioinformatics). Indeed, their abstract and idealized nature has made them an easily portable tool. Whether or not they are accurate realistic representations of their target system and why various scientific communities are adopting them are more complex issues. For example, Zhu and colleagues (2007)[8] apply a Markov blanket genetic algorithm to help with a problem of sorting and classifying data sets about the activity and interaction of large numbers of genes from microarray technology. The main classificatory problem is that the gene expression data is noisy and high dimensional; standard feature selection algorithms face problems of "intractable computational time" (2007: 3237). The solution imports "a cross-entropy based technique, known as Markov Blanket for identifying redundant and irrelevant features" (2007: 3237). This is the HMB technique imported from machine learning to improve modeling techniques for better classifying and sorting large data sets on genes, gene expression, and gene regulation. It is not an OMB—that is, not an ontological claim about the real nature of genes.

This is the point at issue and the potential for confusion is evident in the recent literature. Take the following definition of a Markov blanket from Ramstead and colleagues (2019: 5):

> A Markov blanket is a set of states that enshrouds or statistically isolates internal states from external or hidden states. This figure depicts the partition of the states into internal and external states. In the parlance of graph theory, the Markov blanket is a set of nodes that shields the internal states (or nodes) from the influence of external states; in the sense that internal states can only be affected by external states indirectly, via the blanket states (Friston et al. 2017b). Internal and external states are therefore separated, in a statistical sense, by the Markov blanket (b), which itself comprises sensory (s) and active states (a)—defined as blanket states that are and are not influenced by external states respectively. The top panel schematises the relations of reciprocal causation that couple the organism to its ecological niche, and back again.

The move is from HMBs as taken from Bayesian graphs directly to an OMB interpretation of the relationship between an organism and its environment.

A further example is from Kirchhoff (2018: 2527):

> A Markov blanket constitutes a set of states that separates internal and environmental states. Markov blankets *depend for their existence on reciprocal coupling between constituent processes*. It can be shown that *Markov blankets operate in much the same way as a cell boundary* (Friston 2013). This is because the states comprising the blanket are functionally and dynamically dependent upon each other. Markov blankets can thus be understood as *the statistical definition of operational closure*, demarcating internal from external states, which, at the same time, establish the dynamics required to define the system as a unity. [Our italics]

Kirchhoff is citing Friston as aiming to show that any self-organizing system will behave in such a way that it *appears* to be minimizing free energy (or maximizing Bayesian model evidence). Cells that don't minimize free energy (maximize Bayesian model evidence) will die.[9] There is an important move made from [1] an "as if" or an appearance of free energy minimization, from behavior that is consistent with this description to [2] Markov blankets as actual entities with causal powers (i.e., from HMB to OMB).

In Kirchhoff's definition quoted above, Markov blankets are both statistical definitions (HMBs) and things that exist (OMBs) because of (real) reciprocal causal relations and operate (causally) in a way that is similar to cell boundaries. The shift is clear: in the original definition that we began the chapter with, HMBs are simply a modeling technique for making inferences less cumbersome in Bayesian networks, but now they are an ontological category that does causal work in maintaining boundaries and the integrity of cells and organisms (or other complex systems). Either a Markov blanket is a real causal structure in nature, like a cell boundary (OMB), or it is a statistical concept that *may* be used to simplify and understand the (real) complex causal relationships between organisms and their environments, by simplifying those relationships as an abstraction, as being akin to a Bayesian graph or network (HMB).[10] But it cannot be both, because the OMB involves a claim about the real nature of physical entities and the HMB does not. Resolving this issue is crucial if we are to properly understand the role that Markov blankets are supposed to play in the debate between internalists and externalists.

To summarize, Markov blankets are a means of statistically bounding a set of related states from a set of hidden external states. This concept began in machine learning, but as a portable methodological tool has found use in other fields. Markov blankets, as abstractions, do not have causal powers and are not ontological categories. Their introduction into the debate between internalism and externalism appears to have rushed past this important distinction without considering its implications.

In the remainder of this chapter we will consider how the concept of a Markov blanket has been used in the internalism-externalism debate. The question in the background is as follows: if Markov blankets are not ontological entities, then can they still play a useful role by enabling some explanatory leverage? In addition, in this more modest guise, we must also ask whether the benefits gained here are able to overcome the evident confusions that we have begun to list. The following argument will make it clear that it is an uphill struggle for advocates of their use in this debate, and that until the challenges are met, this concept will appear to be a red herring distracting, rather than aiding, our exploration of the major issues.

4. Fabry, Clark, and Kirchhoff on Markov Blankets and Boundaries

The concept of Markov blanket in play is the extended Fristonian concept. All of the discussion of the boundaries of the mind that we evaluate below simply assume that Markov blankets are OMB blankets. However, there are two ways in which the boundaries get drawn in the discussion. The first is an evidentiary boundary: Markov blankets determine which variables play the role of the internal informational models and which the external evidence (information). In other words, one set of variables play the role of the Bayesian model and the other the hidden environmental variables about which predictions are made. The evidentiary boundary may cleanly follow the ontological boundary between mind and world, but it does not follow that it must. Where the ontological boundary between mind and world lies and where the epistemic boundary between model and evidence lies may not be the same. The second boundary is more obvious; it is ontological: Markov blankets determine the boundary between internal states of a system and external, or environmental, states of a system. Indeed, more powerfully, Markov blankets maintain the boundary between any self-organizing complex system and its environment, including cells, brains, organisms, and even populations. We summarize these differences in a table at the end of this section. We now discuss examples of how the Markov blanket concept is used in differing ways by prominent thinkers in the externalist-internalist debate.

Fabry and Clark both deny that Markov blankets can mark an important boundary between mind and world. Fabry (2017) argues that Markov blankets are compatible with a more traditional dynamic conception of the interaction between an organism and its environment. Invoking both Friston and Beer she makes the following claim:

> However, this kind of circular causality leaves plenty of room for the idea that the organism is continuously interacting with its local environment in virtue of the direct causal relation between sensory and active states.
>
> (Fabry 2017: 404)

The claim here is that continuous reciprocal causation between organism and environment shows that the Markov blanket is not a fixed boundary between mind and world. Clark (2017) takes a similar position. Markov blankets are dynamical and shifting boundaries not fixed and static ones.

> So even once we fix on some Markov blanket organization of interest, that organization will itself be realized as a process undergoing constant change. Any Markov blanket bounded organizational form can be changed, re-deployed, or re-configured through interaction with the inner and outer environment.
>
> (Clark 2017: 14)

However, as has been pointed out to Fabry by one of the authors,[11] and as Anderson (2017) has recently pointed out, if one takes a Helmholtzian inferential starting point then it does not sit happily with a dynamical conception of Predictive Processing. To be clear, if one follows the Helmholtzian/Fristonian line that the brain is constantly making predictions about hidden variables, then it seems obvious that the evidential boundary marked by a Markov blanket is required to make sense of why there would need to be predictions in the first place. Top-down predictions (in the brain) make sense of bottom-up sensory signals from the world. The bottom-up signals are error signals that correct the weightings for the top-down predictions. As Anderson puts it:

> One key aspect of the problem of perception as sketched above is that there is insufficient information delivered by the senses to specify the world. Another is the notion that the immediate function of perception is the veridical, objective representation of the external world. These two suppositions work together to support an inferential, reconstructive account of perception that centrally features the maintenance of world models. The core of Hohwy's account of predictive processing is an explanation of how Bayesian updating enables the construction and maintenance of such models.
>
> (Anderson 2017: 14)

However, there is a question here about whether Clark is committed to the same picture. Anderson thinks that there are strong echoes to be found in Clark's approach:

> And yet we also have, on the other hand, the persistence of the model of perception not as attunement, but as inference from effects to causes, which leads to metaphors of cognitive confinement, of perception as hallucination ([Clark 2016: 14]), as

an *Ender's Game*-style simulation in which our access to reality is mediated by a virtualization of it ([ibid.,] 135).

(Anderson 2017: 9)

According to Anderson, Clark is caught between his endorsement of action-oriented direct engagement with the world and perception as modeling the environment and making predictions about incoming sensory signals. If Anderson is right, then it is even worse for 4E proponents; the brain creates an internal model—a kind of simulation, or hallucination—of the external environment and it is only to this model that it has direct access (Metzinger 2004 [2003], Wiese and Metzinger 2017).[12]

Returning to Markov blankets, this is where things get tricky. Hohwy's seclusionism makes sense of the inferential account of perception. The brain must make predictions, because the environment is "hidden" (Hohwy 2013, also see Wiese and Metzinger 2017 who refer to this as the "environmental seclusion" postulate). Clark and Fabry, by contrast, argue that the evidentiary boundary marked by the Markov blanket shifts to include tools, representations, and the like, such that they are part of the internal system that makes predictions about the hidden external variables. But then, the objection may go; when we make inferences about the iPhone we do so from behind a Markov blanket, so sometimes the iPhone is inside the blanket—presumably when we use it to make inferences about hidden environmental variables—and sometimes it is not—when we need to make inferences about the iPhone from inside the blanket. This fits with Clark's notion of shifting boundaries, growing and shrinking to incorporate tools and external representations at need.

However, there is a caveat that Hohwy can fall back on. The precision estimation functions of the brain are always behind a Markov blanket relative to the environment. The brain is continuously making predictions (inferences) about incoming sensory signals about hidden environmental variables. This is a constant, unlike the shifting boundaries approach of Clark. Consequently, we have a principled boundary, even if there is some shifting at some point. This still seems to be consistent with Hohwy's internalist focus on the neural processes that constitute precision estimations as our only genuine cognitive resources. This is where the nuts and bolts of cognition reside. Everything else outside of the brain is just a mere input into the system and is not constitutive of cognitive processing.

If this is correct, then it follows that there is no real way—no causal way—to distinguish between Clark and Hohwy's position. The evidentiary boundary does not appear to sponsor a stronger ontological boundary between mind and world. Remember that OMB blankets determine the boundary between a self-organizing system that minimizes free energy and the environment and thereby maintains its physical integrity—its boundaries. Therefore, we need a stronger, Fristonian-ontological-style concept of Markov blanket to make any progress on the question of the boundary between mind and world. However, we should continue to bear in mind that there is a lack of warrant—from argument or evidence, or on purely methodological/operational grounds—for the move from HMBs to OMBs. In the rest of this section we examine the most recent efforts to deploy OMBs in the debate about the boundaries of the mind.

4.1. "Blankets of Blankets of Blankets … "

As we discussed above in section 2, recent papers by Kirchhoff and colleagues have made it clear that there are complexities in trying to articulate an externalist ontology using predictive processing and Markov blankets (Kirchhoff et al. 2018, Palacios et al. 2020, Ramstead et al. 2019). Their central claim is that the boundaries of cognition are plural—both methodologically and ontologically. In itself this is not a wild claim and fits with a range of other views in scientifically motivated metaphysics. Glennan (2017) has labeled them "pluralist-realist" views (e.g., Ladyman and Ross's (2007) "rainforest realism," Giere's (2004) "perspectival realism", and Wimsatt's (2007) "rainforest ontology"—as opposed to Quinean deserts). The core link between these views is that there are multiple correct ways to carve nature at the joints, and that this is dependent on both the causal structure of nature and the interests of the investigator (Glennan 2017: 93). Kirchhoff and colleagues' interesting claim is that one can use the Fristonian OMB concept to organize how one goes about discerning the boundaries of the mind (and life) at multiple levels. The OMB concept is said to operate from DNA, nerve cells, neural populations, and the entire brain; up to brain-body-world hybrid systems; and even over entire environmental niches (Clark 2017, Kirchhoff et al. 2018, Ramstead et al. 2019). Furthermore, Ramstead and colleagues claim that an action-orientated position is not contradicted by the manner in which Markov blankets render external states hidden because active inference is able to integrate all layers of the hierarchy.

As we see it there are several controversial claims here that require more detailed exposition, argumentation, and empirical demonstration.

Ramstead and colleagues (and others) are putting forward what Hutchins (2014) refers to as a "fractal ontology." The same formal properties of their ontology are postulated to be recapitulated at multiple levels of the putative metaphysical and methodological hierarchies that compose *all* cognitive systems and living systems. This universal claim, if true, would prove to be of huge benefit to the investigation of cognitive systems since we would now have an underlying principle that not only cashes out our ontology but also provides us with a methodological tool for how to go about identifying and investigating these systems.

However, as stated above, the formal ontology of Ramstead and colleagues' proposal sees Markov blankets as both methodological heuristic and core component of their formal ontology. To be clear, on our formulation, this entails that they are utilizing Markov blankets as both HMBs and OMBs. But, as we raised in Sections 2 and 3, it is far from clear that one can claim that Markov blankets are the core constituent of a formal ontology. Using HMBs as a methodological tool to identify and investigate cognitive systems is a neat proposal, but one that requires more concrete empirical examples to support this universalist claim. But to further claim that they are also an ontological category (OMBs) requires significantly more justification. As we argued above, many models in scientific practice lack any realistic representational qualities and are highly idealized fictions. On what grounds can Ramstead and colleagues justify that the structure of cognition has the properties of their formal ontology? More is required to overcome the more deflationary instrumental interpretation and refashion the concept as carrying genuine ontological weight.

Indeed, it is noteworthy that if Ramstead and colleagues continue with this goal then this leads their position into debates in philosophy that have a lineage stretching back to Bertrand Russell's reflections on the structure of mind and matter (1927). In the philosophy of science, a strong position defending realism—and the correspondence of our best theories and their mathematical entities to the real structure of the world—is structural realism. Russell held the view that the mathematical structures of our best scientific theories represented the real structure of the universe but not objects themselves.

This Kantian view was also supported by a range of other philosophers and scientists at the time, such as Henri Poincaré, Sir Arthur Eddington, and Ernst Cassirer (see Frigg and Votsis 2011, Ladyman 2014 for overviews). But others, such as Ladyman and colleagues (French and Ladyman 2003, Ladyman and Ross 2007), have rejected this more epistemic position and claimed that an ontological claim is justified. One of the authors (Gillett 2012) has noted that this bridges into an ongoing debate in the philosophy of mathematics and the "remarkable success of our mathematical theories" (Wigner 1960; also see Bangu 2012, Colyvan 2001b). The predictive capacities of many scientific theories utilizing mathematical techniques have struck many theorists as nigh on miraculous. Although attempts have been made to dismiss the issue (see Bangu 2012 for an overview), the puzzle—and what it implies—remains. Should we take mathematical entities of our best current theories to be real? And if they are real, what relationship do they have to nature? A common naturalistic position in philosophy going back to Quine and Putnam is to accept these states of affairs and advocate a form of Platonism (see Colyvan 2001a). And some structural realists have also adopted Platonism and Pythagorean metaphysical positions (see Gillett 2012 for an overview). Our point here in drawing these connections is to highlight the strong Platonist and Pythagorean metaphysical attitudes that are implicit in Ramstead and colleagues' formal ontology approach: "to use a mathematical formalism to answer the questions traditionally posed by metaphysics; i.e., what does it mean to be a thing that exists, what is existence, etc." (2019: 3). Determining what is and what is not utilizing mathematics is to adopt a Pythagorean metaphysical position (unless further defined). So, once one takes the path that they have advocated toward OMBs—as the central piece of their formal ontology—then one needs to take very seriously the ontological implications.

As we have stated, the current reasonable position is that Markov blankets are a methodological tool (i.e., an HMB)—whether they have the scope that Ramstead and colleagues' claim is a matter for empirical investigation. To claim more than this requires demonstration—both theoretical and empirical—and this will inevitably lead to tackling the wide range of other concerns for realists that philosophers in other fields have been grappling with for centuries. Indeed, these issues about whether abstract entities exist or have causal powers go back to Plato's dialogue the *Sophist* in which the Eleatic stranger declares that to exist is to have causal powers—what is now known as "the Eleatic Principle" (Colyvan 2001a). All these questions raised here cannot simply be eschewed by claiming that one has a formal ontology. One must present an argument as to why a mathematical formalism here is appropriate for articulating one's ontology and what kind of representational relationship it has to the target phenomena (in terms of scientific modeling, not mental representation). Arguably, such a position could be formulated based upon the success of the predictions that the predictive processing and free energy models give us in a range of domains. But until such evidence is forthcoming this claim is mere supposition. And furthermore, it is up to the defenders of this position to show how the Fristonian OMB-based formal ontology responds to these long-standing problems of Pythagorean metaphysical positions (as in physics and mathematics).

The challenges here are not intended as a knockdown against the positions of Fabry, Clark, or Kirchhoff and colleagues. Instead, our aim has merely been to demonstrate that cashing out the internalist-externalist debate in terms of Markov blankets leads us into much troubled philosophical waters. Far from moving the debate forward, there is a very real danger that the Markov blanket concept is a red herring that distracts effort away from the real issues at hand.

5. Conclusion: The Markov Blanket Is a Potential Red Herring in the Externalism-Internalism Debate

We conclude that there are several important philosophical questions that need to be considered in more detail if one wishes to use Markov blankets as a central feature of a Predictive Processing or an Active Inference approach to tackling the internalist-externalist debates.

First, theorists need to be clearer about when and whether they are using Markov blankets as either methodological heuristics (HMBs) to gain explanatory leverage or an ontological category (OMBs) to describe the genuine structure of mental systems. Furthermore, theorists also need to be careful of what inferences they are drawing from the use of Markov blankets as either a methodological tool or an ontological category. As our discussion has highlighted, in too many places there is an ambiguity in what roles Markov blankets play. It is crucial that this is clarified because whether Markov blankets operate as methodological heuristics or ontological entities entails subsequent philosophical challenges that must also be resolved.

Second, for proponents of the ontological view, more argumentation and justification must be provided for the notion that OMBs demarcate an ontological boundary. At present, as we have demonstrated above, given the fact that Markov blankets do not have causal powers (because they are methodological modeling technique rather than a real thing), it is not clear how they can play the role that some theorists are claiming in the externalist-internalist debate.

Third, although the complexities around OMBs suggest that one might want to limit the use of Markov blankets to a more modest role as explanatory modeling devices (without strong realist representational overtones) as HMBs, there are still a number of difficult issues that must be worked out for the methodological view. As we discussed above, the use of explanatory models that are highly idealistic to the point of being realistically false is standard throughout the sciences (see Cartwright 1999, Giere 2004, Morgan and Morrison 1999, Weisberg 2007, Wimsatt 2007). However, if a Markov blanket is only a methodological tool (HMB), then we still require an argument—for example, inference to the best explanation—as to why it would support either internalism or externalism. Here the difficulties begin. Prima facie it would seem that the stronger position is Hohwy's brain-bound interpretation. However, now that the extended mind hypothesis has been put forward, the internalist must offer a non-question-begging response (Clark and Chalmers 1998). Furthermore, work by Clark (2013, 2017a, 2017) and others, especially Kirchhoff (Kirchhoff et al. 2018, Palacios et al. 2020, Ramstead et al. 2019), has argued that Markov blankets can be applied to supra-individual cognitive systems. This indicates that more detailed argumentation is needed to decide the matter and does not settle the issue as straightforwardly as the internalist would perhaps like.

The issue here hangs on the manner in which Markov blankets work: namely, by isolating a set of co-dependent internal states from a set of hidden external states. If we accept that this is the manner in which the brain as a whole operates, then this entails that external processes and states are hidden to the internal brain states (and this point holds whether one uses Markov blankets to cash out one's ontology or as a heuristic model of cognition). Both Hohwy's brain-bound interpretation and Clark's action-orientated account accept this state of affairs. For Hohwy the matter is now simply one of accepting the Kantian implications of the position and its attendant problems (see Anderson 2017)—what Hohwy (2017) has amusingly labeled the *Nosferatu view*. For Clark, and other externalists such as Fabry and Kirchhoff, the issue now is how to escape the implications of the fact that Markov blankets, by definition, render all external states hidden. We looked at the general claim, by Fabry (2017) and Clark (2017) and Kirchhoff and Kiverstein (2019), that Markov blankets are not stable and instead fluctuate through the dynamic and continuous activity of a cognition system. However, we argued that the evidentiary boundary does not sponsor a stronger metaphysical boundary between mind and world, but this is what is required if one is committed to OMBs. Ramstead and colleagues (2019) use Markov blankets in both the HMB and OMB sense; this we argued is problematic, because it is not clear how they can move from a strictly methodological HMB account to a strongly realist OMB account. There are also particular consequences for their formal ontology. A formal ontology requires a resolution of the issues concerning structural realism and an account of how the formal ontology is an accurate account of the target phenomena.

In general, we conclude that although Markov blankets are *not necessarily* a red herring in the internalism-externalism debate, much more work is required to clarify how Markov blankets move the debate forward without miring it in a wide set of complex philosophical and theoretical issues. Until this clarifying work has been done, arguably, Markov blankets are a red herring because they divert the argument from the real question at hand: where are the boundaries of the mind?

Notes

1   We will give a full definition in the next section. It is important to note that the Markov blanket started out as a purely heuristic construct in machine learning (Pearl 1988).

2   We are aware, of course, that there is a growing literature here and we will discuss a selection of the most prominent contributions.

3   Action oriented and isolated.

4   The following description of the example and diagram are based on http://www. bayesia.com/bayesian-networks-examples.

5   Although we don't consider the free energy principle in detail in this chapter, it is supposed to be the ultimate explanation of self-organization and the formation of Markov blankets in Friston's ontology. The free energy principle can be stated as follows: "This principle states that for organisms to maintain their integrity they must minimize variational free energy. Variational free energy bounds surprise because the former can be shown to be either greater than or equal to the latter. It follows that any organism that minimizes free energy thereby reduces surprise—which is the same as saying that such an organism maximizes evidence for its own model, i.e. its own existence" (Kirchhoff et al. 2018: 3).

6   We shall have more to say about this below.

7   It is important to note that although we are referring to computer science here, that our usage of the term "ontology" throughout the chapter refers to the standard philosophical meaning—as stated in the introduction.

8   As mentioned above.

9   Thanks to Chris Whyte for helping with this point.

10   Such as in the Zhu et al. (2007) paper.

11   Personal communication by Richard Menary.

12   It has been pointed out to us by a reader of a draft of this chapter that Anderson and Chemero (2013) are not opposed to inferential processes in perception per se, just model/representation heavy processes. This may be true, but it is clear from the above that Anderson is warning of the costs of a Helmholtzian view of perception, especially when it leads to a "model heavy" simulation/hallucination account of perceptual consciousness, the kind of account that Clark has recently endorsed.

References

Anderson, M. L. (2017), "Of Bayes and Bullets: An Embodied, Situated, Targeting-Based Account of Predictive Processing" in T. Metzinger and W. Wiese (eds.), *Philosophy and Predictive Processing*, Frankfurt am Main: MIND Group, pp. 1–14.

Anderson, M. L. and Chemero, T. (2013), "The Problem with Brain GUTs: Conflation of Different Senses of 'Prediction' Threatens Metaphysical Disaster," *Behavioral and Brain Sciences*, 36: 204–5.

Bangu, S. (2012), *The Applicability of Mathematics in Science: Indispensability and Ontology*, London: Palgrave Macmillan.

Cartwright, N. (1999), *The Dappled World: A Study of the Boundaries of Science*, Cambridge: Cambridge University Press.

Clark, A. (2013), "Whatever Next? Predictive Brains, Situated Agents, and the Future of Cognitive science," *Behavioral and Brain Sciences*, 36: 181–204.

Clark, A. (2015), "Embodied Prediction" in T. Metzinger and J. M. Windt (eds.), *Open MIND*, Frankfurt am Main: MIND Group, pp. 1–19.

Clark, A. (2016), *Surfing Uncertainty: Prediction, Action, and the Embodied Mind*, New York: Oxford University Press.

Clark, A. (2017a), "Busting Out: Predictive Brains, Embodied Minds, and the Puzzle of the Evidentiary Veil," *NOUS*, 51 (4): 727–53. doi.org/10.1111/nous.12140.

Clark, A. (2017), "How to Knit Your Own Markov Blanket: Resisting the Second Law with Metamorphic Minds" in T. Metzinger and W. Wiese (eds.), *Philosophy and Predictive Processing*, Frankfurt am Main: MIND Group.

Clark, A. and Chalmers, D. (1998), "The Extended Mind," *Analysis*, 58 (1): 7–19.

Colombo, M. and Wright, C. (2018), "First Principles in the Life Sciences: The Free-energy Principle, Organicism, and Mechanism," *Synthese* [published online]: 1–26.

Colyvan, M. (2001a), *The Indispensability of Mathematics*, Oxford: Oxford University Press.

Colyvan, M. (2001b), "The Miracle of Applied Mathematics," *Synthese*, 127: 265–77.

Fabry, R. (2017), "Transcending the Evidentiary Boundary: Prediction Error Minimization, Embodied Interaction, and Explanator Pluralism." *Philosophical Psychology*, 30 (4): 391–410.

French, S. and Ladyman, J. (2003), "Remodeling Structural Realism: Quantum Physics and the Metaphysics of Structure," *Synthese*, 136: 31–56.

Frigg, R. and Votsis, I. (2011), "Everything You Always Wanted to Know About Structural Realism but Were Afraid to Ask," *European Journal Philosophy of Science*, 1: 227–76.

Friston, K. (2010), "The Free-energy Principle: A Unified Brain Theory?," *Nature Reviews Neuroscience*, 11: 127–38.

Friston, K. (2013), "Life as We Know It," *Journal of the Royal Society Interface*, 10: 1–12.

Friston, K. J., Parr, T. and de Vries, B. (2017b), "The Graphical Brain: Belief Propagation and Active Inference." *Network Neuroscience*, 1 (4): 381–414.

Giere, R. (2004), "How Models Are Used to Represent Reality," *Philosophy of Science*, 71: 742–52.

Gillett, A. J. (2012), "Blurring: Structural Realism and the Wigner Puzzle," *Polish Journal of Philosophy*, 6 (2): 33–52.

Glennan, S. (2017), *The New Mechanical Philosophy*, Oxford: Oxford University Press.

Griffiths, T. L. and Yuille, A. (2008), "A Primer on Probabilistic inference" in N. Chater and M. Oaksford (eds.), *The Probabilistic Mind: Prospects for Bayesian Cognitive Science*, Oxford: Oxford University Press, pp. 33–58.

Hohwy, J. (2013), *The Predictive Mind*, Oxford: Oxford University Press.

Hohwy, J. (2015), "The Neural Organ Explains the Mind" in T. Metzinger and J. M. Windt (eds.), *Open MIND*, Frankfurt am Main: MIND Group.

Hohwy, J. (2016), "The Self-evidencing Brain," *Noûs*, 50: 259–85.

Hohwy, J. (2017), "Prediction Error Minimisation vs. Embodied Cognition," Presentation at *Predictive Engines: Andy Clark and Predictive Processing (workshop at Macquarie University)*. https://www.youtube.com/watch?v=mlP9cHTf8yA&t=, accessed January 5, 2019.

Humphreys, P. (2004), *Extending Ourselves: Computational Science, Empiricism, and the Scientific Method*, Oxford: Oxford University Press.

Hutchins, E. (2014), "The Cultural Ecosystem of Human Cognition." *Philosophical Psychology* 27 (1): 34–49.

Kirchhoff, M. (2018), "Autopoiesis, Free energy, and the Life–mind Continuity Thesis," *Synthese* 195: 2519–40.

Kirchhoff, M. and Kiverstein, J. (2019), "How to Determine the Boundaries of the Mind: A Markov Blanket Proposal," *Synthese*, [published online], 1–20. https://link.springer.com/article/10.1007/s11229-019-02370-y.

Kirchhoff, M., Parr, T., Palacios, E., Friston, K. and Kiverstein, J. (2018), "The Markov Blankets of Life: Autonomy, Active Inference and the Free Energy Principle," *Journal of the Royal Society: Interface*, 15: 20170792.

Ladyman, J. (2014), "Structural Realism" in E. N. Zalta (ed.), *The Stanford Encyclopedia of Philosophy*. https://plato.stanford.edu/archives/win2016/entries/structural-realism, accessed January 2, 2019.

Ladyman, J. and Ross, D. (2013), "The World in the Data" in D. Ross, J. Ladyman and H. Kincaid (eds.), *Scientific Metaphysics*, New York: Oxford University Press, pp. 108–50.

Ladyman, J. and Ross, D., with Spurrett, D. and Collier, J. (2007), *Every Thing Must Go: Metaphysics Naturalised*, New York: Oxford University Press.

Lammert, H., Noel, J. K. and Onuchic, J. N. (2012), "The Dominant Folding Route Minimizes back bone distortion in SH3," *PLoS Computational Biology* 8 (11): e1002776.

Menary, R. (2015a), "Mathematical Cognition: A Case of Enculturation" in T. Metzinger and J. M. Windt (eds.), *Open MIND*, Frankfurt am Main: MIND Group.

Menary, R. (2015b), "What? Now: Predictive Coding and Enculturation—A Reply to Regina E. Fabry" in T. Metzinger and J. M. Windt (eds.), *Open MIND*, Frankfurt am Main: MIND Group.

Metzinger, T. (2004[2003]), *Being No One: The Self-model Theory of Subjectivity*, Cambridge, MA: MIT Press.

Morrison, M. and Morgan, M. S. (1999), "Models as Mediating Instruments" in M. S. Morgan and M. Morrison (eds.), *Models as Mediators: Perspectives on Natural and Social Science*, Cambridge: Cambridge University Press.

Palacios, E. R., Razi, A., Parr, T., Kirchhoff, M. and Friston, K. (2020), "On Markov Blankets and Hierarchical Self-organisation," *Journal of Theoretical Biology*, 486: 110089.

Pearl, J. (1988). *Probabilistic Reasoning in Intelligent Systems: Networks of Plausible Inference*, Morgan-Kaufmann.

Pellet, J. P. and Elisseeff, A. (2008), "Using Markov Blankets for Causal Structure Learning," *Journal of Machine Learning Research* 9: 1295–342.

Ramstead, M., Kirchhoff, M. D., Constant, A. and Friston, K. (2019), "Multiscale Integration: Beyond Internalism and Externalism," *Synthese* (online): doi.org/10.1007/s11229-019-02115-x.

Russell, B. (1927), *The Analysis of Matter*, London: Routledge Kegan Paul.

Weisberg, M. (2007), "Who Is a Modeler?" *British Journal of Philosophy of Science*, 58: 207–33.

Wiese, W. and Metzinger T. (2017), "Vanilla PP for Philosophers: A Primer on Predictive Processing" in T. Metzinger and W. Wiese (eds.), *Philosophy and Predictive Processing*, Frankfurt am Main: MIND Group. doi.org/10.15502/9783958573024.

Wigner, E. (1960), "The Unreasonable Effectiveness of Mathematics in the Natural Sciences," *Communications in Pure and Applied Mathematics*, 13.

Wimsatt, W. (2007), *Re-engineering Philosophy for Limited Beings: Piecewise Approximations to Reality*, Cambridge, MA: Harvard University Press.

Zhu, Z., Ong, Y-S. and Dash, M. (2007), "Markov Blanket-embedded Genetic Algorithm for Gene Selection," *Pattern Recognition*, 40 (11): 3236–48.

4

Predictive Processing and Metaphysical Views of the Self

Klaus Gärtner

Centro de Filosofia das Ciências, Departamento de História e Filosofia das Ciências, Faculdade de Ciências, Universidade de Lisboa, Lisbon, Portugal

Robert Clowes

IFILNOVA, FCSH, New University of Lisbon, Lisbon, Portugal

1. Introduction

Recent years have seen a rise in the discussion about predictive processing (PP) or predictive coding (Clark 2015b, Friston 2010, Hohwy 2013). This framework turns traditional approaches to cognition and perception upside down. While traditional views assume that, for example, perceptual information travels up the cognitive hierarchy, where it is centrally integrated to form a representation about the world, PP argues that information flow is primarily top-down. This means the brain is essentially a prediction machine, which tests its postulated models against incoming (sensory) information. At the same time, notions of the minimal or core self have become very influential. Nowadays, they are widely discussed in Philosophy of Mind, Cognitive (Neuro) Science, Psychology, and Psychiatry. In this context, the metaphysical discussions about the status of the self gained new force. There are several alternatives

We would like to thank Paul Smart, Wanja Wiese, Gloria Andrada and the audience of International Conference on Philosophy of Mind "Minds, Brains and Consciousness" at the University of Minho (Braga, Portugal) for their feedback. We would also like to thank Steven Gouveia, Dina Mendonça, and Manuel Curado for their support. Finally, we would like to extend our gratitude to the Lisbon Mind and Reasoning Group, the ArGLAB, the Instituto de Filosofia da NOVA, the Centro de Filosofia das Ciências da Universidade de Lisboa, a Universidade Nova de Lisboa, the Faculdade de Ciências Sociais e Humanas, the Universidade de Lisboa, the Faculdade de Ciências da Universidade de Lisboa, the Departamento de História e Filosofia das Ciências da Faculdade de Ciências da Universidade de Lisboa, the Fundação para a Ciência e a Tecnologia (FCT), and Fciências.ID.

Klaus Gärtner's work is endorsed by the financial support of FCT, 'Fundação para a Ciência e a Tecnologia, I.P.' under the Stimulus of Scientific Employment (DL57/2016/CP1479/CT0081) and by the Centro de Filosofia das Ciências da Universidade de Lisboa (UIDB/00678/2020).

Robert W. Clowes's work is supported by FCT, 'Fundação para a Ciência e a Tecnologia, I.P.' by the Stimulus of Scientific Employment grant (DL 57/2016/CP1453/CT0021) and personal grant (SFRH/BPD/70440/2010)

available to spell out this idea of the self. The four most prominent views are the *substance view* (e.g., Corabi and Schneider 2014, Lowe 1996, 2001, 2009, Nida-Rümelin 2014), the *standard phenomenological view* (Gallagher and Zahavi 2015, Parnas 2003, Parnas and Sass 2011, Sass and Parnas 2003, Sass et al. 2013, Zahavi 2005, 2014, Zahavi and Kriegel 2015), the *no-self view* (e.g., Krueger 2011, Metzinger 2011), and the *relational view* (Ciaunica and Fotopoulou 2017, Hutto 2018).

The question arises if and how the metaphysical discussion about the sense of self changes in the context of PP. Even though, there are many notions of how the PP framework accounts for the self (Apps and Tsakiris 2014, Gerrans 2015a, 2015b, 2019, Hohwy 2007, Hohwy and Michael 2017, Kiverstein 2018, Letheby and Gerrans 2017, Limanowski and Blankenburg 2013, Lin 2015, Moutoussis et al. 2014, Newen 2018, Wiese 2019, Wiese and Metzinger 2012), it seems that basic metaphysical considerations about the self are seldom broached directly.[1] In this chapter our focus is explicitly upon how and whether PP constrains the metaphysics of the self, what these constraints might be, and, given these constraints, seeks to articulate an account of self which we think fits most adequately with PP.

In section 2 of the chapter we will discuss the idea of PP. We focus upon how this framework offers a new integrated account of perception, imagination, and cognition for agents which is implemented by a cognitive architecture that continuously deploys and develops a multi-scale and multimodal action-oriented model of the world in order to organize its behavior (Clark 2015b). Essentially, the brain and mind are thought of as a prediction machine, which constantly predicts incoming sensory signals. Crucially, in order to predict these incoming signals, higher-level neural systems develop generative models of the systems that pass information to them, and indirectly refer the causal structure of their environment. The resulting neural structure is thus ordered hierarchically, mutually constraining the different prediction models on each level and constantly modeling the world at a variety of temporal and spatial scales. The reason we introduce the philosophical relevant assumptions of the PP framework is to set the stage for the discussion on how to integrate metaphysical self-accounts within this framework and ultimately upon what sort of self we might expect an PP system to have.

In section 3 we turn to what we think are the most relevant metaphysical views about the sense of self and how they are constrained by PP. Section 3.1 is dedicated to outlining some of the most widely held metaphysical interpretations of the minimal or core self, that is, accounts about if and how the self exists. In section 3.1.1, we present the *standard phenomenological view*, the main claim of which is that the minimal self is constituted by pre-reflective self-awareness. According to this idea every conscious experience entails this kind of self-awareness, that is, every conscious experience incorporates a pre-reflective experience of oneself. On this view the notion of the self is metaphysically well-grounded. In section 3.1.2, we introduce the *substance view*. This account holds that selves are basic entities—i.e., entities that are not reducible to other entities—who possess object-like properties such as qualities and relations.

Section 3.1.3 presents the *no-self view*. This account holds that even though the self is, phenomenologically speaking, almost inescapable, this does not amount to metaphysical existence of a self. Strictly on the no-self view the core self does not exist and our phenomenological sense of it is a kind of illusion (Metzinger 2011). Finally, in section 3.1.4, we introduce the *relational view*. The main idea is that any kind of self can only arise in relation to others. Strictly speaking, this is not a single view, but a bundle of views characterized by this principle idea.

Section 3.2 is dedicated to the constraints PP imposes, if true, on metaphysical accounts of self. In section 3.2.1, we discuss the constraints stemming from PP for any metaphysical notion of the self. We conclude that there are two basic constraints. First, that the self, or an illusion of it, cannot be constant, and must be subject to change; we call this the *mutability* constraint. Second that the self forms part of a convolved multi-layered structure of a hierarchically organized mind; we call this the multi-layered constraint. Section 3.2.2 examines each of the four metaphysical self-models in the light of these constraints posed by PP. We think that most proposed self views within the PP framework fall—to some degree—within the four metaphysical categories. We argue that there are good reasons that especially realist self views have more trouble in respecting the PP constraints of requirements. The reason is PP's mutability constraint.

We will show, however, that this does not have to be the case. Therefore, in section 4, we argue that we need a reliable metaphysical self first, which then fits nicely with the constraints implied by PP. In section 4.1, we introduce the *pre-reflective situational self* developed by us elsewhere Clowes and Gärtner (2018)[2] and we will demonstrate why this notion of the sense of self is advantageous in this context. In sections 4.1.1 and 4.1.2 we will show how this notion fits with the basic idea of the PP constraints. First, since a core tenet of the situational self view is that the pre-reflective sense of self undergoes change as we encounter different situations, we claim that it respects the mutability constraint. Second, since this account assumes that the self incorporates processes on the sub-personal level, the pre-reflective conscious level, and the reflective conscious level, it supports a multi-layered account of the self.

Finally, in section 4.2, we will give some indications about how the pre-reflective situational self could be implemented by PP.

2. The PP framework

PP is a recent and innovative way to think about the brain and the mind (Clark 2015b, Friston 2009, 2010, Hohwy 2013). It conceives the brain as constantly predicting sensory information. According to this view, the brain is understood as a prediction machine, where incoming sensory information is interpreted through a hierarchically ordered and mutually constraining set of prediction models. These prediction models are constantly tested against incoming sensory input. Since the same cognitive mechanisms implement both cognition and perception, the PP framework promises a unifying model that deeply integrates perception and cognition; from PP vantage point, perception appears more cognitive and cognition more perceptual. So far, PP has sparked new productive theories in a host of areas in cognitive science starting with ideas about the visual cortex (Rao and Ballard 1999), but quickly encompassing new ideas about the deep integration of imagination, perception and thinking (Clark

2012a, 2012b), the role of interoception in self and bodily presence (Seth et al. 2011, Wiese and Metzinger 2017), emotions (Seth and Critchley 2013), the sense of agency, the role of action in cognition (Clark 2015a) and explanations of mental illness, especially schizophrenia (Fletcher and Frith 2009). Indeed, insofar as it proposes a new integrative understanding of mind (Wiese and Metzinger 2017), it may be the most radical and far-reaching perspective on cognitive science available today.

The notion of generative models is central to PP. The standard interpretation holds that the role of the brain in PP systems is to produce and continually update a set of convolved—or interrelated and mutually constraining—models of the world. These models, as Clark puts it, "capture the statistical structure of some set of observed inputs by inferring a causal matrix able to give rise to that very structure" (Clark 2016: 21). This inferred causal matrix is deployed through continually attempting to produce incoming sensory information which can be viewed as a sort of simulation of what the system "expects" to happen next. Such models are generative, in the sense that the system is continually producing a convolved multidimensional set of expectations of what should happen next.[3] Generative models are—at least on the standard interpretation—constituted by a hierarchically organized set of neural systems tuned to the prediction of incoming sensory information, or, in the case of higher levels of the hierarchy, predictions of the output activity of lower levels of the hierarchy at an ever-more refined set of temporal and spatial scales. By forming predictions from the agent's interactions with the world it is said that the causal structure of the world is progressively revealed (Clark 2015b). Thus, the PP framework describes sensory input not as percepts, but rather as incoming information that already matches either the current best hypotheses of the generative model or else error information that has to be "explained away." Sensory input, therefore, only propagates up the processing hierarchy, when higher-level predictions have failed to correctly predict this information. These so-called error signals are used in the higher-level prediction processes to either refine the existing generative models, or to create new ones.

The lowest level of predictions are concerned only with micro-domains. This means neural models engage in the prediction of errors about, for example, the orientation of a line scanned by the retina. Higher-level prediction systems predict the activities of the lower-level systems, which include indirect and more general predictions about the perceptual field and its dependencies upon the actions of the agent. In essence, while traditional cognitivism assumes that perceptual information travels up the cognitive hierarchy where it is centrally integrated to form a representation about the world, PP argues that information flow is primarily top-down, that is, higher-level systems predicting the activity of lower-level systems. Here information only travels up the hierarchy when it is unexpectedly contradicting the expectations of the ordered hierarchy of brain models. Moreover for PP, models at each layer mutually constrain each other through permanent ongoing interaction. It's also important to note that there are parallel constraints at the same level of the hierarchy. Representations produced by PP should not be understood as atomistic but as highly convolved and existing within an emergent web of mutual constraints (Metzinger 2003, Wiese 2018).

Therefore, PP describes perception, cognition, and the structure of mental representation in ways that are quite different from traditional cognitivism.[4] Another way in which it is different, and here it is more in tune with the enactivist approach to cognition, is that the brain is not to be understood as passively trying to make sense of incoming information to form representations, but rather actively testing its representational media against its ongoing worldly interactions (Adams et al. 2015, Clark 2015c). Acts of perception therefore start with the prediction of how the world is. By using hierarchical generative models, the brain maintains a simulation of the causal structure behind the incoming sensory input. According to Clark (2015a), the mind can be understood as inferring or projecting a virtual model that is constantly tested and refined through incoming sensory information. This sensory information also includes the active exploration of the environment (Gärtner and Clowes 2017). Perception can therefore be seen as "richly world revealing" (Clark 2015b).

PP as integrative theory of mental phenomena can be applied to further domains such as imagination, hallucination, and dreaming (Clark 2012a). Here the predictive models refer to offline simulations—which are similar to perception—but without the sensory input as feedback. Within this unifying theory, sensory integration and models of attention seem to follow directly from PP. This view also seems to allow for new insights into phenomena such as schizophrenia (Clowes 2017, Fletcher and Frith 2009), binocular rivalry (Hohwy et al. 2008), or theories on conscious presence (Seth et al. 2011). As a consequence of its unifying character, it is our objective to apply PP to metaphysical accounts of the self.

3. PP and Metaphysical Self-accounts

Now, for the rest of the chapter we will consider only theories of the self that mirror our phenomenology explicitly. We do this for the sake of space, but also because we think that in most of the literature these models are considered to deal with the most basic sense of self.[5] In this section, we discuss the problem of how to bring together the PP framework and metaphysical ideas of the self. We will argue that some standard metaphysical interpretations of the self do not in fact concord well with PP. Consequently, we will show what kind of self-account we think is appropriate. To do so, we will first introduce what we consider the most important metaphysical notions of the self. Then, we will argue that there are a few constraints for these metaphysical accounts stemming from the PP framework. Finally, we will show why problems arise for certain of these metaphysical views on self from these constraints.

3.1. Type of Self-accounts

We will consider four standard metaphysical views about the self. These accounts seem to fulfill all the necessary conditions laid out in the beginning of the section, namely, they refer to basic notions of the self and are consistent with our phenomenology. The views we will examine include the *standard phenomenological view*, the *substance view*, the *no-self view*, and the *relational view*.

3.1.1. The Standard Phenomenological View

This view goes back to phenomenologists such as Sartre and Merleau-Ponty (1962). Currently championed by Dan Zahavi, this approach is one of the most widely expressed in the recent self debate (Gallagher and Zahavi 2015, Parnas 2003, Parnas and Sass 2011, Zahavi 2005, 2014, Zahavi and Kriegel 2015). On this view, the minimal self is constituted by the pre-reflective self-awareness that is held to be a part of every conscious experience (Gallagher and Zahavi 2015, Gärtner 2018, Zahavi and Kriegel 2015). Gallagher and Zahavi explain it in the following way:

> Experiences are characterized by a quality of *mineness* or *for-me-ness*, the fact that it is *I* who am having these experiences. All the experiences are given (at least tacitly) as *my* experiences, as experiences *I* am undergoing or living through. All of this suggests that first-person experience presents me with an immediate and non-observational access to myself, and that (phenomenal) consciousness consequently entails a (minimal) form of self-consciousness.
>
> (Gallagher and Zahavi 2015: § 1)

In general, we can say that the standard phenomenological view holds that it is only when we are phenomenally pre-reflective aware of the self, then there is a self, and since pre-reflective self-awareness forms part of every experience, it is constant.

3.1.2. The Substance View

The substance view of the self goes back to Descartes (1998). However, there are contemporary philosophers who hold this idea (e.g., Corabi and Schneider 2014, Lowe 1996, 2001, 2009, Nida-Rümelin 2014). The basic idea of the substance view is that selves are real entities which bear object-like properties and extend over time. This means selves have mental properties such as experiences and thoughts (Corabi and Schneider 2014). Therefore, while the standard phenomenological view holds that the minimal self forms part of the experience itself, the substance view insists that selves have experiences.[6] According to Lowe (2009), selves are simple substances, that is, basic entities such as subatomic particles. For him, this stems from the fact that we are not identical to our body. The reason, or so he claims, is that the body consists of body parts, but body parts—for example, the brain—lack the unifying element that selves possess. Only the self as non-dividable substance has the ability to unify our thoughts, experiences, feelings, etc.

In the case of experiences, this idea can be described in the following way: we have experiences with different kinds of phenomenal qualities such as redness and blueness. These phenomenal qualities can be described as object-like properties which extend over time and therefore change—for example, from a red perception to a blue perception. However, there is a persistent entity, namely the self, which is constant and stable that has those experiences. Nida-Rümelin (2014) refers to this as "basic intentionality," that is the fact "that something is *phenomenally given* to some subject" (Nida-Rümelin 2014: 263).

3.1.3. The No-self View

This view is often discussed in opposition to the standard phenomenological view and the substance view and is defended most famously by Thomas Metzinger (2011), but also discussed by Joel Krueger (2011) and is deeply embedded in some strands of the Buddhist tradition. Metzinger claims that being an anti-realist about the self is to deny that (a) the self is a substance; and (b) the self is an intrinsic property.[7] His argument starts with the idea that in folk psychology the no-self possibility strikes us simply as wrong. According to Metzinger, however, this is a mistake. He thinks that phenomenologically speaking the self is an invaluable concept, but this does not mean that there is a metaphysical necessity for it. Metzinger argues that even though we cannot think—in phenomenological terms—of possible worlds where selves do not exist, this does not constitute a metaphysical necessity for their existence. It is simply a functional fact that we, as human beings, cannot think of worlds without selves where a first-person perspective is still possible. For Metzinger, this is only a contingent fact, due to the structural organization of our brain. This means the fact that the self is phenomenologically necessary for us does not constitute a metaphysical necessity for its existence.[8]

3.1.4. The Relational View

Finally, the relational view holds that a self is only possible in relation to others (Ciaunica and Fotopoulou 2017, Hutto 2018). This view stands in opposition to the prior approaches since it holds that the sense of self is not of the individual prior to all social interactions. This view can take quite opposite positions. For instance, on the one hand, Ciaunica and Fotopoulou (2017) defend an account of minimal self based on developmental considerations: they argue for the importance of touch in the development of the minimal self, already in the fetal stage. Hutto (2018), on the other hand, defends a late-developing rationalism, which holds that an idea of the self only arises when we are able to form concepts. The sense of self goes hand in hand with the development of the ability to create self-narratives and is therefore in need of concepts and language.

3.2. PP Framework and the Metaphysics of the Self

In the rest of this section, we will discuss two things: (a) the constraints that we think stem from the PP framework for any kind of metaphysical self-account; and (b) whether or not the above characterized models can fulfill these constraints. So, let us begin with (a).

3.2.1. PP Constraints on Self-accounts

As laid out in the previous section, PP has a strongly unifying character. This means sharp boundaries between perception, cognition, experience, and other mental states may blur. Further, this framework claims that the structure of the brain is composed by different prediction systems which are hierarchically ordered. The overall purpose of the brain is to posit generative prediction models, where higher systems predict what the lower systems are doing and, in the case of perception, only the lowest system predicts energetic changes in the visual receptor field. This means information flow is essentially top-down from higher prediction systems to lower prediction systems. The only information that may travel up the hierarchy are prediction errors based on sensory input. These prediction errors are used to revise the generative models or create new models altogether. This leads many to believe that perception is a sort of "controlled hallucination" (Clark 2015b), where we start out with a prediction model and test it against the incoming sensory information. The difference between perception and imagination is therefore less than usually assumed. That is due to the idea that within the PP framework, imagination also starts with the prediction model. It is, however, not tested against incoming sensory input. It is therefore "offline."

Now, how does this constrain our metaphysical theories about the self? Agreeing with others (Gerrans 2019, Hohwy 2007, Hohwy and Michael 2017, Letheby and Gerrans 2017, Limanowski and Blankenburg 2013, Wiese 2019), it is our view that within the PP framework the self is given through a generative prediction model. We think that this idea has two essential consequences for a metaphysical self-account: first of all, since generative prediction models are undergoing constant change and even structural evolution, we should expect that insofar as the self can be experienced, sensed, or registered in any way it too must be mutable and undergoing change.

Second, according to the PP framework, the brain is an hierarchical multi-layer prediction machine which constantly strives to predict perceptual events at a multitude of temporal and spatial scales. This multi-layered character emerges from the way that hierarchical PP systems model causal impingements on the agent. Mental events should not then be expected to exist as self-contained atoms, but as embedded in a dynamic array of related entities and through a complex web of mereological relations.[9] Insofar as PP implies a single perceptual/cognitive mechanism for perception, we should expect that this character is also respected in all mental events with self-modeling being no exception. If this holds for mental events in general,[10] then it should hold for the self as a particular kind, content, or dimension of mental events (Hohwy and Michael 2017, Letheby and Gerrans 2017, Wiese 2019). We call these two constraints the mutability constraint and the multi-layeredness constraint.

To be clear, we think that these two constraints do not give us any hint about how the self arises. This means whether or not the self or the sense of self is innate—as suggested by the standard phenomenological view, the substance view, and the no-self view—or only arises in relation with others—as suggested by the relational view—is not affected by these constraints. This is the case, because it is not *a priori* clear whether we start out with some sort of minimal self model "offline," or if the self comes into existence only when we perceive the world "online." Also, the question of whether or not we have to be aware of the self to count as self—as suggested by the standard phenomenological view—or a sub-personal model of the self may already constitute a self—as suggested by the substance view—is not touched. The PP framework only demands that selves include the possibility of change and that the self is multi-layered.

One might think, however, that this is not the whole story. For instance, according to Schlicht (2017), PP also constrains the basic nature of the self, namely the self as the subject of experience. He argues that the self as subject does not form part of the representational content of the self-model. Following Recanati (2007), Schlicht thinks that even though the subjective self partly influences the accuracy conditions of perceptual experiences usually determined by the content, it does not form part of the representational content. The self as a subject is rather the way something is presented to me or my perspective, that is the mode in which we perceive, imagine, etc. As a consequence, most representational self-models posited within the PP framework cannot account for this kind of self. In Schlicht's view, it is not clear how the PP framework can deal with this issue.

In a related analysis, Woźniak (2018) argues that PP cannot deal with the self as subject because it is agnostic about theories of phenomenal consciousness. Woźniak thinks that PP has no problems with dealing with the self as phenomenal object—which can be assessed by methods stemming from science and phenomenology. However, he thinks that PP cannot explain the metaphysical self as subject.[11] The reason is the following: for the self as object it is enough to argue that PP is consistent with the idea of an underlying unconscious representational generative self-model that, when entering the stream of consciousness, creates a related conscious content. What is essentially described by PP is the "the structure and dynamics of the underlying representational architecture" (Woźniak 2018: 11). However, PP does not specify which representational content becomes conscious in the first place. According to Woźniak, this has the advantage that PP does not have to commit to a specific theory of consciousness, on the one hand. But, on the other hand, this means that PP is too unspecific of a theory when it comes to explaining topics related to consciousness such as the self as subject.

We agree that there is a problem. In a sense, Schlicht's worry can be dealt with more easily. Schlicht and Venter (2019) give one answer to this problem. In their view, one can adapt the PP framework to account for the self as subject. To do so, we simply have to develop PP in an action-oriented manner. This means, "focusing on agency and all factors involved in the specification and consumption of affordances as relational properties between a particular agent and her environment, it is possible to adequately address the implicit articulation of the subject in the accuracy conditions of perception, construed as action-oriented through and through" (Schlicht and Venter 2019: 203).

An alternative way consists in denying that the self as subject is a mode of presentation. According to self-representationalism (Kriegel 2009a, 2009b, Levine 2006), the self as subject or pre-reflective self-awareness is representational. It is self-representational, where the relevant mental state represents itself in the right manner. Without going into detail, we want to point out that this is an alternative theory about how we can think about the self as subject. Since the self is construed as being representational, we think it may help PP to overcome the problem posed by Schlicht.

Woźniak's claim seems to be more complicated to deal with. He argues that there is a general problem of when PP engages with consciousness and related topics. Even though we agree, we think that this is not a particular problem to PP. The Representational Theory of Mind was initially introduced to explain intentionality and not consciousness (Lycan 2015, Pitt 2018). The Representational Theory of Consciousness is only recent. Since PP in its current form is quite recent, we may suspect that sooner or later there will be new developments regarding its relation with consciousness and related issues. For now, we will therefore focus on the explicit posits of the PP framework and not its shortcomings. As argued in this section, we think that the two constraints PP impresses on metaphysical theories of the self are that we should think about the self as being dynamic and multi-layered.

3.2.2. Self-accounts and the Constraints of PP

It is now time to turn to the question of how the notions of the self introduced in the last section and the constraints posed by the PP framework come together. Let's start with the standard phenomenological self view. The basic claim of this view is that being pre-reflectively self-aware is identical to being a minimal self (Clowes and Gärtner 2018). This means the minimal self is not having experiences, rather it forms part of the experience. When it comes to the multi-layered qualities that, according to PP, a self has to have, this model has a way to comply with this restriction. Even though the self only exists in consciousness, it can take at least two forms. It can be pre-reflective and reflective. One may argue that only the pre-reflective form constitutes the minimal self in which we are interested here and the reflective form is only derivative, but pre-reflective consciousness and reflective consciousness are two different forms of consciousness which may constitute different mental layers. If true—and since the self forms part of consciousness in this view—one could argue that the self is multi-layered.

We do not want to push this point too far and get caught up in this discussion. It is just worth noting that one could develop an account of self that is consistent with PP on this basis. The main reason that we are not interested developing this idea any further is that the standard phenomenological view fails clearly in the other constraint stipulated by PP, namely the fact that a self-model should allow for change. Zahavi and Kriegel (2015) explicitly note that the self "is not a detachable self quale that one could introspect in isolation from any other content of consciousness, but rather an experiential feature of all phenomenal episodes that remains constant across them and constitutes the subjectivity of experience" (Zahavi and Kriegel 2015: 39). This quote alone gives us the direct answer to our question: the phenomenological view does not allow for changes within the minimal self. It is an essential property of the minimal self or pre-reflective self-awareness that it is constant across all experiences. However, many proponents of PP try to accommodate the idea of a phenomenological sense of self in a broad sense (Apps and Taskaris 2014, Gerrans 2019, Hohwy 2007, Hohwy and Michael 2017, Kiverstein 2018, Letheby and Gerrans 2017, Limanowski and Blankenburg 2013, Newen 2018, Wiese 2019). As we will see, there are differences to the here portrayed standard phenomenological view, but the more important divide is whether the self is real or not.

So, what do the realists think? Usually, the substance view of the self holds that selves are basic entities which exhibit object-like properties and extend over time. Now, it could be argued that the substance view does allow for change over time and therefore fulfills the first PP constraint. It is however interesting to note here how change over time is described within the context of this view. Consider for instance how Lowe (2009) refers to it: "[selves] are persisting bearers of qualities and relations, in respect of which [they] continually undergo qualitative and relational change" (Lowe 2009: 79). This is interesting in so far as it shows that the self is the bearer of change but does not change itself; that is, what is changing are the relations and qualities the self bears.

Consider, for instance, the idea that someone has an experience. Now, the self who has the experience stays constant; changes occur only in virtue of changes within the phenomenal qualities. This means that, for example, redness may change to blueness, but the bearer or the self stays constant. If we assume that in the PP framework the self is given through a dynamically changing generative model, then we should also assume that the self is mutable. The reason is that the self is tied to a prediction model in the brain which can be revised or updated due to incoming error information. If we believe, as we do, that mental events mirror this architecture, then the self—being a mental event—should be mutable as well.

A similar conclusion can be drawn about the multi-layeredness of the self. Even though we can become aware of the self, the self does not form part of the stream of consciousness. Nida-Rümelin (2014) states that becoming pre-reflectively aware of the self is due to the fact that the self[12] is having the experience. This does not mean that the self forms part of the experience. In a different context, Lowe (2009) argues that selves are basic non-dividable entities which unify our mental life. Being a basic entity, a fixed point so to say, does not allow for a multi-layer view about the self. This is the case almost by definition: the self is a basic entity. The substance view is a single-layer view which stipulates that the self is a basic entity to our minds.

However, there are recent realist accounts (Hohwy and Michael 2017, Newen 2018) about the self within the PP community. For instance, Hohwy and Michael (2017) defend a type of substance view of the self. They argue in great detail how the internal, multi-layered model of the self arises. Further, they show how this self-model entertains all the right kind of functions to be called a genuine self. The main argument hangs on the idea that their self-conception points to a self as being the "hidden cause" of cognitive states such as thoughts and feelings. This indicates a self-entity. Hohwy and Michael state the following: "Our proposal is to conceive of this internal model of endogenous causes as a representation of *the self*. The suggestion, then, is that agents model the self as a hierarchy of hidden, endogenous causes, and further, that the self is identical to these causes" (Hohwy and Michael 2017: 8). To understand the idea better, Hohwy and Michael give a neat example, namely the representation of seasons. In their example they think that in short-term scenarios it is enough to take an umbrella with you whenever it rains. However, in long-term scenarios it seems better to know how seasons influence the possibility of rainfall. In a sense, seasons are the deeper hidden cause to determine the probability of rain, even though it does not form part of the actual perception of rainfall. The same is true for the self. In short term, a representation of the body is enough to interact with the world, but in long term it is up to the self representation—which for them is a substantial self—to determine what we think and feel.[13] The reason Hohwy's and Michael's self view can account for a phenomenological sense of self is that they assume that the self model is the way we consciously experience our first-person perspective.

There is clearly a question that arises here: is the Hohwy and Michael view a realist account of the self? According to the standard substance view and the standard phenomenological view, it is not. Hohwy and Michael are not willing to give up the mutability constraint posed by PP. Their self-account allows for change. So, in classical terms, this self view does not fulfill the necessary character to be a substantialist view of the self. However, Hohwy and Michael are aware of this tension. So their main argument why the self should be considered as real is that the self-model fulfills most of the functions attributed to the self. In our view, this is a way to go. But based on this idea alone, it seems rather difficult to evaluate whether or not they are really defending a realist view of the self or if they are simply obeying the intuition of a substantial self.

Although Hohwy and Michael (2017) allegedly defend a realist view of the self, some proponents of the PP framework are not only reluctant to endorse this account, but reject it explicitly (Gerrans 2015a, Letheby and Gerrans 2017, Wiese 2019). They defend the no-self view. This approach states that in a phenomenological sense we naturally have a sense of self, but metaphysically it does not exist. This view certainly has several similarities with the standard phenomenological view. The biggest difference consists in the evaluation of the sense of self. While the phenomenologists argue that because we have a self-experience, it must be real, no-selfers argue that having a self-experience does not tell us anything about metaphysics, or as Krueger (2011) puts it: there is not a "resting place for a stable, permanent, or enduring self" (Krueger 2011: 52). As the reader can see in this remark, the no-self view is not committed to a constant, persisting self. Much to the contrary, this view denies this possibility explicitly. *Prima facie* it seems that the PP framework is anti-realist (Gerrans 2015a, Letheby and Gerrans 2017, Wiese 2019) almost by default. The thought is that this kind of self-account gives you all you need, that is, a self-model with an anchoring point for our mentality, without putting up with the restrictions of a realist account, namely a constant entity. Further this view can subscribe to multi-layeredness. Letheby and Gerrans (2017) and Wiese (2019) argue for an anti-realist notion of the self which is both dynamic and present in different levels of the cognitive hierarchy.

The importance of the self in Letheby and Gerrans consists in the idea that the self, as self-representation, is an ordering principle across the cognitive hierarchy tied to the respective goals of the organism; that is, "perceptual representations are organized in an egocentric space; interoceptive representations are interpreted as signals of adaptively relevant events or 'core relational themes' [...]; and narratives are structured around the fortunes and prospects of a protagonist" (Letheby and Gerrans 2017: 9). This view goes along with the idea of Hohwy and Michael (2017) that the self model must be a robust construction, but without postulating a substantial self. The sense of self is explained in terms of binding. Binding means that separate cognitive features from different areas of the brain are combined into a unified representation and can be explained in neural, cognitive, and phenomenal terms. Consequently, "the self-model allows us to feel that the experiences resulting from the interplay of the salience system with other (cognitive, emotional, and affective) systems whose activity it coordinates belong to a consistent unified entity: the self" (Letheby and Gerrans 2017: 4).

Wiese's account is based on Metzinger's idea of attentional agency (Metzinger 2013, 2017). For Wiese, the self is an attentional agent, which reveals itself in "the most fundamental instance of self-experience as a knowing subject and agent" (Wiese 2019: 68). This self as attentional agent (SANTA) is best described in the phenomenal sensation that "I" am controlling what is the focus of my attention. The reason that this self seems to be substantial lies, according to Wiese, in the fact that it is felt as enduring, that is, present at any moment. He thinks, however, that this does not amount to being a self substance, since phenomenology is not metaphysics. Wiese explicitly distinguishes his view from the standard phenomenological view by stating that SANTA is not some phenomenal aspect embedded in the stream of consciousness, but a phenomenal property that conscious creatures do not necessarily entertain. We welcome this clarification, but we think that as far as the phenomenology of the sense of self is concerned, all the PP positions discussed here slightly differ in their interpretation. They all deviate from the standard phenomenological view in some sense, but still try to accommodate the phenomenology of the sense of self.

Finally, the relational account—or better relational accounts—is somewhat difficult to classify in this discussion. All approaches share the assumption that the self arises in relation to others. However, these views are developed in quite different ways. On the one hand, we have accounts that argue that the minimal self is generated within developmental stages of our psychology (Ciaunica and Fotopoulou 2017), while, on the other hand, rational accounts argue for the creation of the self only in self-narrative practices (Hutto 2018). The important objective of the relational accounts is to explain where exactly the self enters the picture. In a sense, these views stand in opposition to the individualistic views—which include the other notions discussed in this and the previous section—which assume that the self is somehow innate. As stated above, at least Hohwy and Michael (2017) can strictly speaking also count as relational account. The fact that those ideas focus on the etiology of the self may provide a valuable explanation of the changes happening within an inconstant, dynamical self within the PP framework, but it does not give us a particular self account.

4. The Pre-reflective Situational Self and the PP Framework

With some effort, possibly, all the previously discussed self-accounts may be bent to fit PP. However, it seems that the constraints stemming from PP favor clearly anti-realism about the self. Given this fact, we suggest we need to go back to the basics. We should not defend any old kind of self-account within the PP framework; we should do the metaphysics. So, the objective of this section is to do exactly that. We will defend our realist view of the sense of self, which we think fits very nicely with the PP framework. This view is called the *pre-reflective situational self*.

Elsewhere we (Clowes and Gärtner 2018) argue for a self-account that is neither invariant nor conceptually single-layered; that is, consistent with the PP implication that all modeled entities or systems exist in a set of convolved relations with each other. Moreover, the same entities are addressed both by the conscious mind and by the cognitive unconscious. We show that if we introduce the possibility of a changing self which forms part of many layers of our cognitive economy, we are in a better position to explain certain phenomena. In the case of schizophrenia, we consider the fact that patients suffering from this illness have troubles in acting appropriately and adaptively within their social environment. Something that has been noted in the literature recently (Fuchs 2015, Krueger 2018, Lysaker and Lysaker 2008, Ratcliff 2017). In our view, pre-reflective self-awareness is functionally oriented toward being situationally adaptive; that is, it must respond appropriately to situations in the social environment. Following Lysaker and Lysaker (2008), we think that we need to flexibly and pre-reflexively incorporate our "self-positions" (Clowes and Gärtner 2018), something that schizophrenic patients find difficult or impossible. These self-positions allow us to manage and navigate our social surroundings. It is only through being adaptive in this sense that we are able to act and think appropriately within the social context. Only then can we fulfill our social roles and the expectations with which we are confronted.

To explain this point, let us consider an everyday situation in a thought experiment. Imagine, for instance, Susan. Susan is a college professor and a Mom, among other things. When she is at the university and teaches—or thinks about giving a class— her sense of self instantaneously and automatically moves to her role as a university professor. This includes many different facets, like responding to her students expectations and knowing her own. She also has to act appropriately to fulfill her duties. At least sometimes, taking up this role does not require her reflection on it. She simply inhabits her role as a professor naturally. Now, the sense of self Susan is having is partly determined by the way she inhabits her role. This means her feelings, attitudes, emotions, etc. depend on her self role. However, when Susan comes home and slips in her role as a Mom, she deals with her son who wants to play video games. To do so, she needs a different set of emotions, dispositions, etc. Without reflection Susan inhabits her role as a mother. She pre-reflectively starts inhabiting a different role that her life asks for. This shows nicely how we often change self-positions without even recognizing it, or at least, only peripherally.

4.1. The Pre-reflective Situational Self and the Constraints of PP

4.1.1. The Pre-reflective Situational Self and Mutability

In this view, the self incorporates two things, namely changes within the self and processes happening, at least, on the sub-personal level, the pre-reflective conscious level, and the reflective conscious level. To see how changes within the self happen, consider normal persons like Susan who fluidly and appropriately change self-positions just as the social situation demands. These transitions include adaption in attitude, the way one acts, and even emotions. However, people do not have to reflect in order to accomplish these changes; they arise, so to say, spontaneously and naturally in the context of managing and coping with everyday life. Of course, self-positions can overlap. We find ourselves sometimes in contradictory social situations. Here, adapting our self-position may lead to inner conflict and we, therefore, need to reflect and make an effort. Generally, however, we smoothly shift into the appropriate social roles without reflection just as the social environment demands. Since changes in self-positions usually do not occur reflectively—we think that it happens in the background of our mind—we usually do not—or only peripherally—detect these changes consciously. This view stipulates a functional approach to pre-reflective self-awareness. The occurring changes in our pre-reflective sense of self allow us to maneuver our thoughts and actions in a situationally flexible, meaningful, and appropriate way.

There is however another important aspect to keep in mind. We cannot attribute changes in self-positions to changes in neither the phenomenal qualities nor to what is called the narrative self, because it is not redness changing to blueness; that is, it is not one quality changing to another quality. Rather, it is the self-perspective that is changing, that is, not some property belonging to the self, but the self itself.

With respect to the relation between pre-reflective situational self and narrative self, the question is whether or not we are considering a minimal or core notion of the self or an already overarching concept. The narrative self is, per theory (Gallagher 2000), characterized by a narrative about the past, present, and future of an individual. It is supposed to account for the coherence of self over time. It is, therefore, a contingent extension to the core notion of self.[14] According to Schechtman (2011), there are two dominant ways of cashing out this idea. Either one thinks that the self is a narrative or one holds that the self is intimately linked to our capacities of invoking a narrative in thinking and explanation. Both notions describe the self over time. We, however, argue that the pre-reflective situational self does not require this temporal dimension or any narrative abilities. This kind of self is pre-reflectively and directly given to us through social interaction. Due to our need to adjust to immediate social requirements of social environments, the pre-reflective situational self has to be functionally individuated. The situational self positions us adequately within the social context. It helps us to navigate these situations and makes it possible to act appropriately.

There remains the question of whether or not the pre-reflective situational self view amounts to an existing self or not. On the one hand, we should not think about the self as a stable and unchanging aspect—such as defended by the substance view and the standard phenomenological view. On the other hand, we do not have to think about the self in terms of the no-self view either. Rather, we might think of the self as a labile aspect of the phenomenal field which while changing continues to play the same role and, very importantly, occupies the same place (Clowes 2018). As we will see next, the self can be found in different layers of our cognitive apparatus.

4.1.2. The Pre-reflective Situational Self and Multi-layeredness

The second constraint PP puts on metaphysical self-accounts is that the self does not only exist in one cognitive layer. In Section 3, we stated that it is particularly hard for the substance view to fulfill this requirement since it is often interpreted as a basic entity (Lowe 2009). The standard phenomenological self-account may do a bit better. Since it allows for a pre-reflective and reflective self (Zahavi and Kriegel 2015), there is the possibility for a multi-layered self. However, since the minimal self is constant and does not allow for change, the multi-layeredness of this account seems quite limited. The best prospects stem from the no-self view. If we interpret this account in phenomenological terms (Krueger 2011, Letheby and Gerrans 2017, Metzinger

2011, Wiese 2019), it can overcome the limits of the standard phenomenological view. Since no-selfers do not argue for a constant metaphysical self, but only for a phenomenological self, they allow explicitly for changes and hierarchies within the sense of self (Metzinger 2003).[15]

We think, however, that the pre-reflective situational self also fits with the multi-layeredness requirement and this has to do with the way this view describes changes in self-positions. Changes in self-position mostly happen on the sub-personal level. Of course, we sometimes become aware of this fact, but mainly only peripherally. This means we become aware of a change but only pre-reflectively. When we become aware of a change reflectively, this usually means that there is a conflict between self-positions or some sort of distortion of the phenomenal field as we find in Depersonalization Disorder or Prodromal Schizophrenia (Clowes 2018, Sass et al. 2013). Now, the main focus of this view is that the self, as self-position, functionally adapts to the social situation. Since we think that the mental architecture reflects the hierarchical architecture of the brain, the multi-layeredness stems from the fact that this view explicitly allows for dynamic changes of the self-position which occur in different parts or layers of the cognitive hierarchy. One way of spelling this out can be found in Hohwy (2013). Hohwy holds that experiential states also have hierarchical architectures. In the context of introspecting one's own experiences, Hohwy argues that the structure of experiential events mirrors the structure of perception. He calls this double bookkeeping. For him, experiential models are also hierarchical and multi-layered prediction models and they usually accompany perception—even if often unconsciously. Models of perception and models of experience, therefore, usually go hand in hand. According to Schwengerer's (2018) interpretation this means that "the brain's model of the world includes a model of experiences that creates experiential expectations" (Schwengerer 2018: 6). And since experiential models accompany perceptual models, both are based on sensory information. Now, Schwengerer (2018) goes a step further and shows that what works for experiences also works for other mental events. This means it is not just experience that should be thought of in terms of PP, but rather that mental events in general consist in a hierarchical and multi-layered structure. We think that if we take PP to be a unifying framework of how the brain and the mind works, the idea that mental events are also hierarchical and multi-layered is reasonable.

Even though we are not explicitly endorsing the double bookkeeping view of mental events, we think it gives some motivation of why we should think about the self in hierarchical, multi-layered terms. Consider what was said in the beginning of the last paragraph, namely that the change in self-positions can happen on a sub-personal, pre-reflectively conscious, and reflectively conscious level. We think that—assuming that mental events consist of a hierarchical, multi-layered architecture—the self must be found in more than one cognitive layer; that is, the self can at least be found in layers corresponding to the sub-personal, pre-reflectively conscious, and reflectively conscious. One important consequence, or so we think, is that the pre-reflective situational self-account is compatible with PP and therefore a realist alternative. In the final section, we will briefly suggest a way of implementing the pre-reflective situational self in the PP framework.

4.2. PP and the Pre-reflective Situational Self: Some Indication for Implementation

So, the pre-reflective situational self seems to fulfill all the necessary conditions for being adapted to the PP framework.[16] The final question then is how PP implements this self-account. In this chapter, we can barely scratch the surface of this problem. What we say is that many theories think that the way to anchor our mental life is by introducing an unifying and stable element and this is often the self. But if what we said here is right then this is not necessary and PP will show why. The predictive mind can recognize itself in these dynamic processes because it can predict the patterns of these processes. Seth (2013) suggests that the minimal self within the PP framework consists of a constant or familiar pattern because changes are based on the organisms need to predict its own dynamics to stay alive. PP can explain why and how organisms develop hierarchically complex models of themselves. According to Seth and Critchley (2013), the fact that an organism acquires the capacity to regulate itself gives it the possibility to predict its own internal bodily states. Also, the organism can predict and generate changes by its own actions (Linson et al. 2018).

This is of course a very brief answer and must be developed further elsewhere. However, we think it is enough to show that PP and the pre-reflective situational self view are not only smoothly going hand in hand in a conceptual setting, there are good reasons to believe that the pre-reflective situational self can fulfill the metaphysical constraints for a self-account posited by PP nicely and can also be implemented by the framework. Of course, further research is necessary. For now, we hope that we have convinced the reader that, when it comes to metaphysical self views within the PP framework, the pre-reflective situational self view is a realist and realistic alternative.

5. Conclusion

In this chapter we have tried to bring together the PP framework and metaphysical views of the self. First, we introduced PP and the relevant metaphysical self-accounts. Then we argued that despite its often held unifying potential PP also motivates certain constraints on our metaphysical conceptions of self: we discussed two of these, namely the mutability and the multi-layeredness constraints. We have shown that the standard accounts of the self come with certain difficulties when applied to the PP framework—the no-self account clearly being able to deal best with those constraints. Nevertheless, we introduced, in a final step, a different kind of metaphysical self view, namely the *pre-reflective situational self* and argued that it is an alternative to be considered. Also, it seems to be the only "realist" version of the self that respects the constraints, that is, without it we seem to be forced toward anti-realism.

Notes

1   For instance, the idea that the self classically fulfills two different roles, namely,
     as forming part of the perceptual content, that is, being an object, or a part of the

perceiver, that is, being the subject. It has been argued that the self as subject is limited by PP (Schlicht 2017, Schlicht and Venter 2019, Woźniak 2018). However, while Schlicht and Venter think that the self as subject cannot form part of the representational content of the self-model, Woźniak argues that PP has troubles to provide a metaphysical account of the self as a metaphysical "I" altogether, since it is agnostic about theories of phenomenal consciousness. We will pick up on these thoughts in section 3.

2   Earlier formulations can be found in Clowes (2015, 2018) and Lysaker and Lysaker (2008).

3   It should be noted however that there is at least one radically different interpretation of what is meant by a generative model. The alternative interpretation is to see the generative model as being realized by the "extended dynamic singularity," produced around the biological core of the agent itself (Kirchhoff and Kiverstein 2019). Discussion of this alternative and highly controversial interpretation goes beyond the scope of this chapter but it essentially sees the agent situated in its ecological niche as itself a generative model.

4   Albeit they echo many aspects of the connectionist approach to cognition.

5   We will therefore avoid as much as possible discussing PP in the context of the narrative self.

6   Nida-Rümelin (2007) discusses in detail the difference between having experiences and being experiences.

7   Actually Metzinger (2011) gives two further conditions for being an anti-realist about the self, namely (c) the claim that no scientific theory to self-consciousness is in need of a "self"; and (d) the negation that an indexical "I" refers to an ontological independent entity.

8   Wiese (2019) discusses this idea in detail.

9   See Metzinger's discussion of the *Convolved Holism of the Phenomenal Self* in section 6.2.4 of his *Being No-One* (Metzinger 2003). Metzinger emphasizes how each part of each whole is experienced as a series of part/whole relations. While fully developing the connections between Metzinger's phenomenological account of the dynamic interrelated character of mental contents goes beyond this discussion, we want to signal here its potential compatibility with what we call the multi-layeredness constraint, and also the need to develop an elaborated version of this constraint, especially a phenomenological level of description.

10   For instance, Hohwy's double bookkeeping account of phenomenality (Hohwy 2013) argues that the model of experience mirrors the model of perception. Clowes (2018) discusses the self as a dimension of experience that can be explained in terms of PP in the context of schizophrenia, and Schwengerer (2018) thinks that we can translate Hohwy's model to all mental states.

11   Following Woźniak (2018), the here presented metaphysical theories of the self count as metaphysical theories of the self as subject.

12   Or someone as Nida-Rümelin (2014) puts it.

13   Since Hohwy's and Michael's account is developmental, it can also count as a PP version of the relational view of self.

14   Although Daniel Dennett (1991) may disagree. For him the self consists only in centers of narrative gravity with no real core behind or beneath them.

15   As stated in section 3, we think that it is difficult to evaluate the relational views. This is the case because they are rather a bundle of views which are especially concerned with when the self arises. We explicitly acknowledged and acknowledge that it is

possible for some of the accounts to tackle both problems, namely mutability and multi-layeredness.

16   It is noteworthy that Moutoussis et al. (2014) also think that PP is well suited to incorporate the self in social interaction. There is however a major difference between the here advocated view and their account. On the one hand, Moutoussis et al. think that the "interpersonal self" is based on a quite complex mechanism of actively inferred social exchanges and add that prior to the interpersonal self-dimension there is already some sort of minimal self. On the other hand, we think that situatedness within the social environment enters the game already on a pre-reflective and even cognitively unconscious level.

References

Adams, R. A., Friston, K. J. and Bastos, A. M. (2015), "Active Inference, Predictive Coding and Cortical Architecture" in M. F. Casanova and I. Opris (eds), *Recent Advances on the Modular Organization of the Cortex*, Berlin: Springer, pp. 97–121.

Apps, M. A. J. and Tsakiris, M. (2013), "The Free-energy Self: A Predictive Coding Account of Self-recognition," *Neuroscience & Biobehavioral Reviews*, 41: 85–97. doi: 10.1016/j.neubiorev.2013.01.029.

Ciaunica, A. and Fotopoulou, A. (2017), "The Touched Self: Psychological and Philosophical Perspectives on Proximal Intersubjectivity and the Self" in C. Durt, T. Fuchs and C. Tewes (eds.), *Embodiment, Enaction, and Culture Investigating the Constitution of the Shared World*, MIT Press, pp. 173–92.

Clark, A. (2012a), "Dreaming the Whole Cat: Generative Models, Predictive Processing, and the Enactivist Conception of Perceptual Experience," *Mind*, 121 (483): 753–71. doi.org/10.1093/mind/fzs106.

Clark, A. (2012b), "Whatever Next? Predictive Brains, Situated Agents, and the Future of Cognitive Science," *Brain and Behavioral Sciences*, 36 (3): 181–253.

Clark, A. (2015a), "Embodied Prediction" in T. Metzinger and J. M. Windt (eds.), *Open MIND*, Frankfurt am Main: MIND Group.

Clark, A. (2015b), *Surfing Uncertainty: Prediction, Action, and the Embodied Mind*, New York: Oxford University Press.

Clark, A. (2015c), "Predicting Peace: The End of the Representation Wars" in T. Metzinger and J. M. Windt (eds.), *Open MIND*, Frankfurt am Main: MIND Group.

Clark, A. (2016), "Busting Out: Predictive Brains, Embodied Minds, and the Puzzle of the Evidentiary Veil," *Noûs*, 51: 727–53. doi.org/10.1111/nous.12140.

Clowes, R. W. (2015), "The Reality of the Virtual Self as Interface to the Social World" in J. Fonseca and J. Gonçalves (eds.), *Philosophical Perspectives on Self*, Lisbon: Peter Lang.

Clowes, R. W. (2017), "The Ipseity Disturbance Theory of Schizophrenia and Predictive Processing" in I. Hipólito, J. Gonçalves and J. G. Pereira (eds.), *Schizophrenia and Common Sense: Explaining Madness and Social Values*, Berlin: Springer Mind Brain Studies.

Clowes, R. W. (2018), "Rethinking the Ipseity Disturbance Theory of Schizophrenia through Predictive Processing" In I. Hipólito, J. Gonçalves and J. G. Pereira (eds.), *Schizophrenia and Common Sense*, Springer, pp. 113–36.

Clowes, R. W. and Gärtner, K. (2018), "The Pre-reflective Situational Self," *Topoi*, 39 (2020): 623–37. https://doi.org/10.1007/s11245-018-9598-5.

Corabi, J. and Schneider, S. (2014), "Metaphysics of Uploading," *Journal of Consciousness Studies*, 19 (7–8): 26–44.

Dennett, D. C. (1991), *Consciousness Explained*, New York: Little Brown.

Descartes, R. (1998), *Discourse on Method*, Translated by D. Cress, Indianapolis: Hackett.

Fletcher, P. and Frith, C. (2009), "Perceiving Is Believing: A Bayesian Approach to Explaining the Positive Symptoms of Schizophrenia," *Nature Reviews: Neuroscience*, 10: 48–58.

Friston, K. (2009), "The Free-energy Principle: A Rough Guide to the Brain?" *Trends in Cognitive Sciences*, 13 (7): 293–301.

Friston, K. (2010), "The Free-energy Principle: A Unified Brain Theory?" *Nature Reviews Neuroscience*, 11 (2): 127–38.

Fuchs, T. (2015), "Pathologies of Intersubjectivity in Autism and Schizophrenia," *Journal of Consciousness Studies*, 22 (1–2): 191–214.

Gallagher, S. (2000), "Philosophical Conceptions of the Self: Implications for Cognitive Science," *Trends in Cognitive Sciences*, 4 (1): 14–21.

Gallagher, S. and Zahavi, D. (2015), "Phenomenological Approaches to Self-Consciousness" in. E. N. Zalta (ed.), *The Stanford Encyclopedia of Philosophy*, Spring 2015 Edition. http://plato.stanford.edu/archives/spr2015/entries/self-consciousness-phenomenological/.

Gärtner, K. (2018), "Conscious Experience and Experience Externalization" in I. Hipólito, J. Gonçalves and J. G. Pereira (eds.), *Schizophrenia and Common Sense: Explaining Madness and Social Values*, Berlin: Springer.

Gärtner, K. and Clowes, R. W. (2017), "Enactivism, Radical Enactivism and Predictive Processing: What Is Radical in Cognitive Science?," *KAIROS*, 18 (1). doi.org/10.1515/kjps-2017-0003.

Gerrans, P. (2015a), "All the Self We Need" in T. Metzinger and J. M. Windt (eds.), *Open MIND*, Frankfurt am Main: MIND Group.

Gerrans, P. (2015b), "Metamisery and Bodily Inexistence" in T. Metzinger and J. M. Windt (eds.), *Open MIND*, Frankfurt am Main: MIND Group.

Gerrans, P. (2019), "Depersonalization Disorder, Affective Processing and Predictive Coding," *Review of Philosophy and Psychology*, 10 (2): 401–18.

Hohwy, J. (2007), "The Sense of Self in the Phenomenology of Agency and Perception," *Psyche*, 13 (1): 1–20.

Hohwy, J. (2013), *The Predictive Mind*, New York: Oxford University Press.

Hohwy, J. and Michael, J. (2017), "Why Should Any Body Have a Self?" in F. de Vignemont and A. J. T. Alsmith (eds.), *The Subject's Matter: Self-Consciousness and the Body*, Cambridge: MIT Press.

Hutto, D. (2018), "Selfless Activity and Experience: Radicalizing Minimal Self-Awareness," *Topoi*. doi.org/10.1007/s11245-018-9573-1

Kirchhoff, M. D. and Kiverstein, J. (2019), *Extended Consciousness and Predictive Processing: A Third Wave View*, London: Routledge.

Kiverstein, J. (2018), "Free Energy and the Self: An Ecological–Enactive Interpretation," *Topoi*. doi.org/10.1007/s11245-018-9561-5.

Kriegel, U. (2009a), *Subjective Consciousness*, Oxford: Oxford University Press.

Kriegel, U. (2009b), "Self-representationalism and phenomenology," *Philosophical Studies*, 143: 357–81.

Krueger, J. W. (2011), "The Who and the How of Experience" in M. Siderits, E. Thompson and D. Zahavi (eds.), *Self, No Self: Perspectives from Analytical. Phenomenological and Indian Traditions*, New York: Oxford University Press, pp. 27–55.

Krueger, J. W. (2018), "Schizophrenia and the Scaffolded Self," *Topoi*, 39 (2020): 597–609. https://doi.org/10.1007/s11245-018-9547-3.

Letheby, C. and Gerrans, P. (2017), "Self Unbound: Ego Dissolution in Psychedelic Experience," *Neuroscience of Consciousness*, 2017 (1): 1–11.

Levine, J. (2006), "Conscious Awareness and (Self-) Representation," in U. Kriegel and K.W. Wiliford (eds.), *Self-Representational Approaches to Consciousness*, Cambridge: MIT Press, pp. 173–98.

Limanowski, J. and Blankenburg, F. (2013), "Minimal Self-Models and the Free Energy Principle," *Frontiers in Human Neuroscience*, 7: 547.

Lin, Y.-T. (2015), "Memory for Prediction Error Minimization: From Depersonalization to the Delusion of Non-Existence" in T. Metzinger and J. M. Windt (eds.), *Open MIND*, Frankfurt am Main: MIND Group.

Linson, A., Clark, A., Ramamoorthy, S. and Friston, K. (2018), "The Active Inference Approach to Ecological Perception: General Information Dynamics for Natural and Artificial Embodied Cognition," *Frontiers in Robotics and AI*, 5 (21). doi.org/10.3389/frobt.2018.00021.

Lowe, E. J. (1996), *Subjects of Experience*, Cambridge: Cambridge University Press.

Lowe, E. J. (2001), "Identity, Composition and the Self" in K. Corcoran (ed.), *Soul, Body and Survival*, Ithaca, NY: Cornell University Press.

Lowe, E. J. (2009), "Serious Endurantism and the Strong Unity of Human Persons" in L. Honnefelder, E. Runggaldier and B. Schlick (eds.), *Unity and Time in Metaphysics*, Berlin: Walter de Gruyter.

Lycan, W. (2015), "Representational Theories of Consciousness" in E. N. Zalta (ed.), *The Stanford Encyclopedia of Philosophy*, Fall 2019 Edition. https://plato.stanford.edu/archives/fall2019/entries/consciousness-representational/.

Lysaker, P. H. and Lysaker, J. T. (2008), *Schizophrenia and the Fate of the Self*, New York: Oxford University Press.

Merleau-Ponty, M. (1962), *Phenomenology of Perception*, London and New York: Routledge & Kegan Paul.

Metzinger, T. (2003), *Being No One: The Self-Model Theory of Subjectivity*, Cambridge: MIT Press.

Metzinger, T. (2011), "The No-Self Alternative" in S. Gallagher (ed.), *The Oxford Handbook of the Self*, Oxford: Oxford University Press.

Metzinger, T. (2013), The Myth of Cognitive Agency: Subpersonal Thinking as a Cyclically Recurring Loss of Mental Autonomy, Frontiers in Psychology, 4, art. 931. doi: 10.3389/fpsyg.2013.00931.

Metzinger, T. (2017), "The Problem of Mental Action: Predictive Control without Sensory Sheets" in T. Metzinger and W. Wiese (eds), *Philosophy and Predictive Processing*, Frankfurt am Main: MIND Group.

Moutoussis, M., Fearon, P., El-Deredy, W., Dolan, R. J. and Friston, K. J. (2014), "Bayesian Inferences about the Self (and Others): A Review," *Consciousness. Cogn*, 25: 67–76. doi: 10.1016/j.concog.2014.01.009.

Newen, A. (2018), "The Embodied Self, the Pattern Theory of Self, and The Predictive Mind," *Frontiers in Psychology*, 9: 2270. https://doi.org/10.3389/fpsyg.2018.02270

Nida-Rümelin, M. (2007), "Grasping Phenomenal Properties" in T. Alter and S. Walter (eds.), *Phenomenal Concepts and Phenomenal Knowledge: New Essays on Consciousness and Physicalism*, Oxford: Oxford University Press.

Nida-Rümelin, M. (2014), "Basic Intentionality, Primitive Awareness and Awareness of Oneself" in A. Reboul (ed.), *Mind, Values, and Metaphysics*, Berlin: Springer.

Parnas, J. (2003), "Self and Schizophrenia: A Phenomenological Perspective," in T. Kircher & A. David (eds.), *The Self in Neuroscience and Psychiatry*, Cambridge: Cambridge University Press, pp. 217–41.

Parnas, J. and Sass, L. (2011), "The Structure of Self-consciousness in Schizophrenia" in S. Gallagher (ed.), *The Oxford Handbook of the Self*, Oxford: Oxford University Press, pp. 521–46.

Pitt, D. (2018), "Mental Representation" in E. N. Zalta (ed.), *The Stanford Encyclopedia of Philosophy*, Winter 2018 Edition. https://plato.stanford.edu/archives/win2018/entries/mental-representation/.

Rao, R. P. and Ballard, D. H. (1999), "Predictive Coding in the Visual Cortex: A Functional Interpretation of Some Extra-Classical Receptive-Field Effects," *Nature Neuroscience*, 2 (1): 79–87.

Ratcliffe, M. (2017), *Real Hallucinations: Psychiatric Illness, Intentionality, and the Interpersonal World*, MIT Press.

Recanati, F. (2007), *Perspectival Thought: A Plea for (Moderate) Relativism*, Oxford: Clarendon Press.

Sass, L. A. and Parnas, J. (2003), "Schizophrenia, Consciousness, and the Self," *Schizophrenia Bulletin*, 29 (3): 427–44.

Sass, L. A., Pienkos, E., Nelson, B. and Medford, N. (2013), "Anomalous Self-experience in Depersonalization and Schizophrenia: A Comparative Investigation," *Consciousness and Cognition*, 22 (2): 430–41.

Schechtman, M. (2011), "The Narrative Self" in S. Gallagher (ed.), *The Oxford Handbook of the Self*, Oxford: Oxford University Press.

Schwengerer, L. (2018), "Self-Knowledge in a Predictive Processing Framework," *Review of Philosophy and Psychology*, first online. https://doi.org/10.1007/s1316.

Seth, A. K. (2013), "Interoceptive Inference, Emotion, and the Embodied Self," *Trends in Cognitive Sciences*, 17 (11): 565–73.

Seth, A. K. and Critchley, H. D. (2013), "Extending Predictive Processing to the Body: Emotion as Interoceptive Inference," *Behavioral and Brain Sciences*, 36 (03): 227–8.

Seth, A. K., Suzuki, K. and Critchley, H. D. (2011), "An Interoceptive Predictive Coding Model of Conscious Presence," *Frontiers in Psychology*, 2: 395.

Schlicht, T. (2017), "Experiencing Organisms: From Mineness to Subject of Experience," *Philosophical Studies*, 175 (10): 2447–74.

Schlicht, T. and Venter, E. (2019), "Getting the World Right: Perceptual Accuracy and the Role of the Perceiver in Predictive Processing Models," *Journal of Consciousness Studies*, 26 (3–4): 181–206.

Wiese, W. (2018), *Experienced Wholeness: Integrating Insights from Gestalt Theory, Cognitive Neuroscience, and Predictive Processing*, Cambridge: MIT Press.

Wiese, W. (2019), "Explaining the Enduring Intuition of Substantiality. The Phenomenal Self as an Abstract 'Salience Object'," *Journal of Consciousness Studies*, 26 (3–4): 64–87.

Wiese, W. and Metzinger, T. (2012), "Desiderata for a Mereotopological Theory of Consciousness: First Steps towards a Formal Model for the Unity of Consciousness" in S. Edelman, T. Fekete and N. Zach (eds.), *Being in Time: Dynamical models of Phenomenal Experience*, Amsterdam: John Benjamins.

Wiese, W. and Metzinger T. (2017), "Vanilla PP for Philosophers: A Primer on Predictive Processing" in T. Metzinger and W. Wiese (eds.), *Philosophy and Predictive Processing*, Frankfurt am Main: MIND Group. doi.org/10.15502/9783958573024

Woźniak, M. (2018), "'I' and 'Me': The Self in the Context of Consciousness," *Frontiers in Psychology*, 9 (1656). https://doi.org/10.3389/fpsyg.2018.01656.

Zahavi, D. (2005), *Subjectivity and Selfhood: Investigating the First-Person Perspective*, Cambridge, MA: MIT Press.

Zahavi, D. (2014), *Self and Other: Exploring Subjectivity, Empathy and Shame*, Oxford: Oxford University Press.

Zahavi, D. and Kriegel, U. (2015), "For-me-ness: What It Is and What It Is Not" in D. Dahlstrom, A. Elpidorou and W. Hopp (eds.), *Philosophy of Mind and Phenomenology*, London: Routledge.

Part Two

Predictive Processing: Cognitive Science and Neuroscientific Approaches

5

From the Retina to Action: Dynamics of Predictive Processing in the Visual System

Laurent Perrinet
Institut de Neurosciences de la Timone (UMR 7289),
Aix Marseille Univ, CNRS, Marseille, France

1. Motivation: Role of Dynamics in the Neural Computations Underlying Visual Processing

Vision, the capacity of making sense of the luminous environment, is traditionally thought as a sequence of processing steps from the retinal input to some higher-level representation. It is often thought that this sequence of independent processing steps, or "pipeline," is implemented by a feedforward process in the visual pathways, through the thalamus and then to the visual areas within the cerebral cortex. Such a model of vision is sufficient to explain the simple detection of the printed character you are currently looking at, and thus for the reading of a full sentence. Indeed, such an ability involves rapid and unconscious low-level processes. Importantly, such ability in humans is also largely immune to changes in luminance (like a shadow on this page) or to geometrical deformations, such as when reading this text from a slanted perspective. More generally, vision will correctly complete the image of a word with missing letters or with ambiguous or incorrect detections due to an overlapping clutter. Such a robustness is characteristic of biological systems, hence it's use as a Turing Test for security algorithms such as CAPTCHAs. In contrast, models of vision as implemented in computers can learn complex categorization tasks on very precise data sets but are easily outperformed by an infant when it comes to a naturalistic, flexible, and generic context. Going even further, human vision is also characterized by higher-level processes and allows for prospective predictions such as those revealed during mental imagery—and is a basic ground stone for one's creativity, or *imagination*. Vision is thus a highly complex process, yet, it is still not completely understood. As a matter of fact, the most surprising fact about vision is the ease with which sighted persons may perform these abilities. To rephrase (Wigner 1990), "the Unreasonable Effectiveness of Vision in the Natural World" invites us to focus on this cognitive ability for a better understanding of the brain in general.

Anatomically, vision is the result of the interplay of neural networks which are organized in a hierarchy of visual areas. Each visual area is itself a dynamical process, from its first stage, the retina, to the efferent visual areas which help in forming a parallel and distributed representation of the visual world. Moreover, this organization is largely self-organized and very efficient metabolic-wise. To make sense of such complex network of visual areas, it has been proposed that this system is organized such that it efficiently *predicts* sensory data (Attneave 1954). This ecological approach (Atick 1992) allows to explain many aspects of vision as predictive processing. Such an approach takes different forms such as redundancy reduction (Barlow 1961), maximization of information transfer (Linsker 1990), or minimization of metabolic energy. Formalizing such optimization strategies in probabilistic language, these may be encompassed by the "Bayesian Brain" framework (Knill and Pouget 2004). More generally, it is possible to link these different theories into a single framework, the Free Energy Principle (FEP) (Friston 2010). This principle constitutes a crucial paradigm shift to study predictive processes at both philosophical and scientific levels. Key to this principle is the notion that, knowing the processes that generated the visual image and the internal generative model that allows its representation, predictive processes will take advantage of *a priori* knowledge to form an optimal representation of the visual scene (Rao and Ballard 1999). This knowledge constitutes an explicit (probabilistic) representation of the structure of the world. For instance, an image which is composed of edges will be understood at a higher level using the a priori knowledge of the link between any individual edges to form a representation of the *contours* of visual objects. In the time domain, the knowledge of geometric transforms such as the motion of visual objects will help predict their future positions and to ultimately track the different bits of motion, but also to represent contours invariantly to this motion.

However, there are limits and constraints to the efficiency of vision. First, luminous information can be noisy and ambiguous, such as in dim light conditions. This constrains the system to be robust to uncertainties. This highlights a key advantage of predictive processing as this involves learning a generative model of sensory data. On the one hand, by explicitly representing the precision of variables (the inverse of the inferred variance of its value), one can optimally integrate distributed information, even in the case that this uncertainty is not uniform and dynamically evolving in the system. On the other hand, a generative model allows to explicitly represent transformations of the data (such as a geometrical transform of the image like a translation or a rotation) and therefore to make predictions about future states. Second, neural networks have limited information transfer capacities and always need some delay to convey and process information. In humans for instance, the delay for the transmission of retinal information to the cortex is approximately 50 milliseconds, while the minimal latency to perform an oculomotor action is approximately an additional 50 milliseconds (Kirchner and Thorpe 2006) (see Lamme and Roelfsema 2000) for equivalent values in monkeys). While this naturally constrains the capacity of the visual system, we will herein take advantage of these delays to dissect the different visual processes. In particular, we will focus in this chapter on the role of these fundamental temporal constraints on the dynamics of predictive processes as they unravel with the passage of time.

To illustrate the challenge of representing a dynamic signal, let's use the example of the recording of a set of neural cells in some visual areas. Let's assume that these recordings are evoked by an analog visual signal (as a luminous signal projected on a population of retinal sensory cells) and that we may extract the analog timings of spiking events for a population of cells. We may then choose to display this data in a "raster plot," that is, showing the timing of the spikes for each of the identified cell. Time is thus relative to that of the experimenter and is given thanks to an external clock: It is shown a posteriori, that is, after the recording. In general, this definition of an absolute time was first formalized by Newton and defines most of the laws of physics, using time as an external parameter. But there is yet no evidence that neurons would have access to a central clock which gives a reference to the absolute, physical time. Rather, neural responses are solely controlled by the *present* distribution of electro-chemical gradients on their membrane, potentially modulated by neighboring cells. Such a notion of time is local to each neuron and its surrounding. As a consequence, the network's dynamics is largely asynchronous, that is, timing is decentralized. Moreover, this local notion of (processing) time is *a priori* disjoint from the external time which is used to represent the visual signal. Such an observation is essential in understanding the principles guiding the organization of visual processes: A neural theory of predictive processes can be only defined in this local (interoceptive) time, using only locally available information at the present instant. In particular, we will propose that neural processes in vision aim at "predicting the present" (Changizi et al. 2008) by using an internal generative model of the visual work and using sensory data to validate this internal representation.

This chapter will review such dynamical predictive processing approaches for vision at different scales of analysis, from the whole system to intermediate representations and finally to neurons (following in a decreasing order the levels of analysis from Marr (1982)). First, we will apply the FEP to vision as a normative approach. Furthermore, visual representations should handle geometrical transformations (such as the motion of a visual object) but also sensory modifications, such as with eye movements. Extending the previous principle with the capacity of actively sampling sensory input, we will define active inference (AI) and illustrate its potential role in understanding vision, and also behaviors such as eye movements (see section 2). Then, we will extend it to understand how such processes may be implemented in retinotopic maps (see section 3). In particular, we will show how such a model may explain a visual illusion, the Flash-lag effect. This will then be compared with neurophysiological data. Finally, we will review possible implementations of such models in spiking neural networks (see section 4). In particular, we will review some models of elementary micro-circuits and detail some potential rules for learning the structure of their connections in an unsupervised manner. We will conclude by synthesizing these results and their limits.

2. Active Inference and the "Optimality" of Vision

Optimization principles seem the only choice to understand "The Unreasonable Effectiveness of Vision in the Natural World." However, trying to understand vision as an emergent process from efficiency principle seems like a teleological principle in which causation would be reversed (Turkheimer et al. 2019). Still, the "use of the teleological principle is but one way, not the whole or the only way, by which we may seek to learn how things came to be, and to take their places in the harmonious complexity of the world" (D'Arcy Thompson 1917: ch. 1). Putting this another way, it is not of scientific importance to know if the brain is using explicitly such a principle (for instance that some of its parts may use Bayes's rule), but rather that such a set of rules offers a simpler explanation for the neural recordings by shedding light on processes occurring in this complex system (Varoquaux and Poldrack 2019). We will follow basic principles of self-organized behavior: namely, the imperative to predict at best sensory data, that is, in technical terms, to minimize the entropy of hidden states of the world and their sensory consequences.

2.1. Perceptions as Hypotheses, Actions as Experiments

For instance, it is not yet known why the fast mechanism that directs our gaze toward any position in (visual) space, the saccadic system, is at the same time fast and flexible. For instance, this system may quickly adapt for contextual cues, for instance when instructing the observer to count faces in a painting. Most theories will explain such mechanisms using sensory or motor control models, yet few theories integrate the system as a whole. In that perspective, the FEP provides with an elegant solution. As a first step, we will consider a simplistic agent that senses a subset of the visual scene as its projection on the retinotopic space. The agent has the ability to direct his gaze using saccades. Equipping the agent with the ability to actively sample the visual world enables us to explore the idea that actions (saccadic eye movements) are optimal experiments, by which the agent seeks to confirm predictive models of the hidden world. This is reminiscent of Helmholtz's definition of perception (Von Helmholtz 1867) as hypothesis testing (Gregory 1980). This provides a plausible model of visual search that can be motivated from the basic principles of self-organized behavior. In mathematical terms, this imperative to maximize the outcome of predicted actions is equivalent to minimizing the entropy of hidden states of the world and their sensory consequences. This imperative is met if agents sample hidden states of the world efficiently. In practice, once the generative model is defined; this efficient sampling of salient information can be derived using approximate Bayesian inference and variational free-energy minimization (Friston 2010). One key ingredient to this process is the (internal) representation of counterfactual predictions, that is, of the probable consequences of possible hypothesis as they would be realized into actions. This augments models of an agent using the FEP such as to define active inference (AI).

Using the SPM simulation environment (*Statistical Parametric Mapping: The Analysis of Functional Brain Images—1st Edition* 2012), Friston et al. (2012) provide simulations of the behavior of such an agent which senses images of faces, and knowing an internal model of their structure. In modeling the agent, they clearly delineate the hidden external state (the visual image, the actual position of the eye or motor command) from the internal state of the agent. Those internal beliefs are linked by a probabilistic dependency graph that is referred to as the generative model. Applying the FEP to this generative model translates (or compiles in computer science terms) to a set of differential equations with respect to the dynamics of internal beliefs and the counterfactual actions. An agent forms expectations over sensory consequences it expects in the future under each possible action. This formulation of active inference forms what is called a Markov decision process (Mirza et al. 2018). As a system following the FEP, this process is predictive. Yet, it extends the classical predictive processing of Rao and Ballard (Rao and Ballard 1999) by including action (and priors related to motor commands) to the overall optimization scheme. The chosen action is the one which is expected to reduce sensory surprise and is ultimately realized by a reflex arc.

Simulations of the resulting AI scheme reproduce sequential eye movements that are reminiscent of empirically observed saccades and provide some counterintuitive insights into the way that sensory evidence is accumulated or assimilated into beliefs about the world. In particular, knowing the localized image sensed on the retina, saccades will explore points of interests (eyes, mouth, nose) until an internal representation of the whole image is made. This AI process allows to bridge the image in intrinsic (retinal) coordinates with extrinsic world coordinates which are prevalent in visual perception but actually hidden to the agent. Interestingly, if one were to only look at the behavior of this agent, this could be encompassed by a set of differential equations, but that would miss the causal relationship with internal variables as defined above. In addition, this model highlights a solution to a common misconception about FEP as surprise minimization. Indeed, if the agent was to close his eyes, the sensory surprise would be minimal as one would then precisely expect a pitch-dark visual scene. However, in the graph of dependencies (i.e., generative model) which defines the agent, such a counterfactual (prospective) hypothesis would be highly penalized as it would also be a priori known that such an action would not yield a minimization of the surprise about the visual scene. Globally, it is therefore more ecological to keep eyes open to explore the different parts of the visual scene.

2.2. Is There a Neural Implementation for Active Inference (AI)?

As we have seen above, once we have resolved the optimization problem given the whole setting (generative model, priors) the agent that we have defined is simply ruled by a set of differential equations governing its dynamics. Technically, these equations are the result of a generic approximation on the form of the internal representation. In particular, the optimization problem is simplified when using the Laplace approximation, that is, when internal beliefs are represented by multidimensional Gaussian probability distribution functions. This holds true in all generality when transforming variables in higher dimensions, such is the case for generalized coordinates (Friston et al. 2010). Such coordinates represent at any (present) time the Taylor expansion of the temporal trajectory of any variable, that is, the vector containing the position, velocity, acceleration, and further motion orders. Consequently, the solution provided by these equations gives a plausible neural implementation as a set of hierarchically organized linear/nonlinear equations (Heeger 2017). In particular these equations are the Kalman-Bucy filtering solution (Kalman 1960) which provides with a Bayes-optimal estimate of hidden states and actions in generalized coordinates of motion. This generalizes the predictive coding framework offered by Rao and Ballard (1999) for explaining the processing mechanisms in the primary visual cortex. Similar to that model, the dynamical evolution of activity at the different levels of the hierarchy is governed by the balance in the integration of internal (past) beliefs with (present) sensory information (Heeger 2017). In particular, the relative weights assigned to the modulation of information passing are proportional to the (inferred) precision of each individual variable in the dependency graph. This allows us to predict the influence of the prior knowledge of precision at any given level on the final outcome.

Practically, the predictive power of AI in modeling such an agent is revealed by studying deviations from the typical behavior within a population of agents. For instance, there are acute differences in the smooth pursuit eye movements (SPEM) between patients from (control) neurotypic or schizophrenic groups. First, SPEM are distinct from the saccades defined above as they are voluntary eye movements which aim at stabilizing the retinal image of a smoothly moving visual object. For a target following the motion of a pendulum for instance, the eye will produce a prototypical response to follow this predictable target. Interestingly, schizophrenic agents tend to produce a different pattern of SPEM in the case that the pendulum is occluded on half cycles (for instance, as it passes behind an opaque cardboard on one side from the midline). In general, SPEM may still follow the target, as it is occluded (behind the cardboard) yet with a lower gain (Barnes and Asselman 1991). As the target reappears from behind the occluder, schizophrenic agents engage more quickly to a SPEM response (Avila et al. 2006). Extending the agent modeled in Friston et al. (2012), an agent which has the capability to smoothly follow such moving object was modeled in Adams et al. (2012). This model allows in particular to understand most prototypical SPEM as a Bayes-optimal solution to minimize surprise in the perception/action loop implemented in the agent's dependency graph.

Especially, by manipulating the *a priori* precision of internal beliefs at the different levels of the hierarchical model, one could reproduce different classes of SPEM behaviors which reproduce classical psychophysical stimuli. For instance, Adams et al. (2012) found for the half-cycle occluded pendulum that manipulating the post-synaptic gain of predictive neurons reproduced behaviors observed in schizophrenia and control populations. Such a difference in the balance of information flow could have for instance a genetic origin in the expression of this gain and vicariously in the behavior of this population. Importantly, such a method thus allows to perform quantitative predictions: Such applications of computational neuroscience seem particularly relevant for a better understanding of the diversity of behaviors in the human population (see for instance Karvelis et al. 2018, Kent et al. 2019).

2.3. Introducing Delays in AI: Dynamics of Predictive Processing

An interesting perspective to study the role of neural dynamics in cognition is to extend this model to a more realistic description of naturalistic constraints faced by the

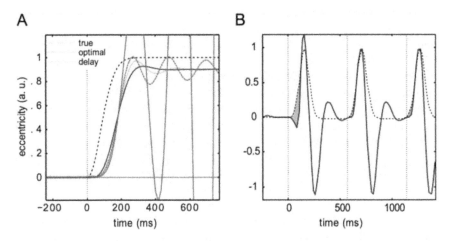

Figure 5.1 (A) This figure reports the response of predictive processing during the simulation of pursuit initiation while compensating for sensory motor delays, using a single sweep of a visual target. Here, we see horizontal excursions of oculomotor angle (dark line). One can see clearly the initial displacement of the target that is suppressed by action after approximately 200 milliseconds, modeling a prototypical pursuit eye movement. In addition, we illustrate the effects of assuming wrong sensorimotor delays on pursuit initiation. Under pure sensory delays (dotted line), one can see clearly the delay in sensory predictions, in relation to the true inputs. With pure motor delays (light dashed line) and with combined sensorimotor delays (light line) there is a failure of optimal control with oscillatory fluctuations in oculomotor trajectories, which may become unstable. **(B)** This figure reports the simulation of smooth pursuit when the target motion is hemi-sinusoidal, as would happen for a pendulum that would be stopped at each half cycle left of the vertical (broken lines). The generative model used here has been equipped with a second hierarchical level that contains hidden states, modeling latent periodic behavior of the (hidden) causes of target motion. With this addition, the improvement in pursuit accuracy apparent at the onset of the second cycle of motion is observed (light shaded area), similar to psychophysical experiments (Barnes and Asselman 1991). (Reproduced from Perrinet et al. (2014) under the terms of the Creative Commons Attribution License, © The Authors 2014.)

visual system. Indeed, the central nervous system has to contend with axonal delays, both at the sensory and at the motor levels. As we saw in the introduction, it takes approximately 50 milliseconds for the retinal image to reach the visual areas implicated in motion detection, and a further 50 milliseconds to reach the oculomotor muscles and actually realize action (Kirchner and Thorpe 2006). One challenge for modeling the human visuo-oculomotor system is to understand eye movements as a problem of optimal motor control under axonal delays. Let's take the example of a tennis player trying to intercept a passing-shot ball at a (conservative) speed of 20 m/s. The position sensed on the retinal space corresponds to the instant when the image was formed on the photoreceptors within the retina, and until it reaches our hypothetical motion perception area. At this instant, the sensed physical position is in fact lagging 1 meter behind, that is, approximately at an eccentricity of 45 degrees. However, the position at the moment of emitting the motor command will be also 45 degrees *ahead* of its present physical position in visual space. As a consequence, if the player's gaze is not directed to the image of the ball on the retina but to the ball at its present (physical) position, this may be because he takes into account, in an anticipatory fashion, the distance the ball travels during the sensory delay. Alternatively, optimal control may direct action (future motion of the eye) to the expected position when motor commands reach the periphery (muscles). Such an example illustrates that even with such relatively short delay, the visual system is faced with significant perturbations leading to ambiguous choices. This ambiguity is obviously an interesting challenge for modeling predictive processing in the visual system. Extending the modeling framework of Adams et al. (2012) for SPEM, it was observed in Perrinet et al. (2014) that representing hidden states in generalized coordinates provides a simple way of compensating for both delays. A novelty of this approach is to include the delays in the dynamics by taking advantage of generalized coordinates. Technically, this defines a linear operator on those variables to travel back and forth in time with arbitrary intervals of time, allowing in particular to represent the state variables in the past (sensory delay) or in the future (motor delay). Note that (1) this representation is active at the present time, (2) it allows for the concomitant representation of precision of state variables, and (3) this allows for the evaluation of counterfactual hypothesis of sensory states (based on past sensory states) and of an action which has to be inferred now, knowing it will be effective after the motor delay. Applying such an operator to the FEP generates a slightly different and more complicated mathematical formulation. However, it is important to note that to compensate for delays, there is no change in the structure of the network but just in how the synaptic weights are tuned (similar to what we had done in the first section of this chapter): "Neurobiologically, the application of delay operators just means changing synaptic connection strengths to take different mixtures of generalized sensations and their prediction errors" (Perrinet et al. 2014: sec. 3.1). In particular, when the agent has some belief about these delays, it can Bayes-optimally integrate internal beliefs. Such a behavior is still regulated by the same type of internal equation.

We illustrated the efficacy of this scheme using neuronal simulations of pursuit initiation responses, with and without compensation. Figure 5.1(A) reports the conditional estimates of hidden states and causes during the simulation of pursuit initiation, using a simple sweep of a visual target, while compensating for sensory motor delays. Here, we see horizontal excursions of oculomotor angle (blue line) and the angular position of the target (dashed black line). One can see clearly the initial displacement of the target that is suppressed after a few hundred milliseconds. This figure also illustrates the effects of sensorimotor delays on pursuit initiation (red lines) in relation to compensated (optimal) active inference. Under pure sensory delays (dotted line), one can see clearly the delay in sensory predictions, in relation to the true inputs. Of note here is the failure of optimal control with oscillatory fluctuations in oculomotor trajectories, which become unstable under combined sensorimotor delays.

Interestingly, this model extends to more complex visual trajectories. In particular, it has been shown that gaze will be directed at the present physical position of the target (thus in an anticipatory fashion) if that target follows a smooth trajectory (such as a pendulum). More striking, this is also true if the trajectory is *predictable*, for instance for a pendulum behind a static occluder (Adams et al. 2012, Barnes and Asselman 1991). Figure 5.1(B) reports the simulation of smooth pursuit when target's motion is hemi-sinusoidal, as would happen for a pendulum that would be stopped at each half cycle, left of the vertical. Note that contrary to the agent modeled in Adams et al. (2012), this agent has the biological constraint that sensory and motor processing is delayed. The generative model has been equipped with a second hierarchical level that contains hidden states that account for the latent periodic behavior of target motion. One can clearly see the initial displacement of the target that is suppressed after a few hundred milliseconds (pink shaded area). The improvement in pursuit accuracy is apparent at the onset of the second cycle of motion, similar to psychophysical experiments (Barnes and Asselman 1991). Indeed, the model has an internal representation of latent causes of target motion that can be called upon even when these causes are not expressed explicitly (occluded) in the target trajectory. A particular advantage of this model is that it provides a solution for the integration of past and future information while still being governed by online differential equations. This therefore implements some form of Bayes-optimal temporal memory.

2.4. Summary

To sum up, we have shown here that a full visual perception/action cycle could be understood as a predictive process under the active inference (AI) framework. In particular, we have shown that such models could reproduce the dynamics observed in eye movements, in particular when introducing realistic constraints such as sensory-motor delays. Further models should allow for the introduction of even more complex structural constraints such as the physical laws governing the motion of visual objects such as an *a priori* bias (Damasse et al. 2018), gravity, or external cues (Kowler et al. 2014). This may help synthesize most laws governing the organization of perception, as formalized in the Gestalt theory.

3. Predictive Processing on Visual Maps

While we have shown the role of predictive processing at a macroscopic scale by designing each neural assembly as a node in a dependency graph, is there any evidence for such processes in visual space?

3.1. The Flash-lag Effect as Evidence for Predictive Processing in Topographic Maps

The flash-lag effect (FLE) is a visual illusion which is popular for its generality and simplicity. In its original form (MacKay 1958), the observer is asked to keep fixating

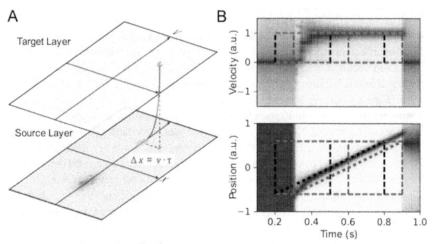

Figure 5.2 In Khoei et al. (2017), we propose a model of predictive processing in a topographic map. **(A)** The model consists of a two-layered map: an input source target integrates information from visual sensors. For simplicity we only display here the horizontal dimension and this map represents on each axis respectively position and velocity. Using this map as a representation of belief (here using a probability distribution function), it is possible to project this information to a second target layer that integrates information knowing a compensation for the delay. In that particular case, speed is positive and thus information of position is transported toward the right. **(B)** Response of a model compensating for a 100 milliseconds delay to a moving dot. Representation of the inferred probability of position and velocity with delay compensation as a function of the iterations of the model (time). Darker colors denote higher probabilities, while a light color corresponds to an unlikely estimation. In particular, we focus on three particular epochs along the trajectory, corresponding to the standard, flash–initiated, and terminated cycles. The timing of these epochs is indicated by dashed vertical lines. In dark, the physical time and in lighter green the delayed input knowing a delay of 100 milliseconds. See text for an interpretation of the results. (Reproduced from Khoei et al. (2017) under the terms of the Creative Commons Attribution License, © The Authors 2017.)

at a central cross on the screen while a dot traverses it with a constant, horizontal motion. As it reaches the center of the screen, another dot is briefly flashed just below the moving dot. While they are vertically perfectly aligned, the flashed dot is perceived as *lagging* the moving dot. This visual illusion saw a resurgence of scientific interest with the motion extrapolation model (Nijhawan 2002, Nijhawan and Wu 2009). However, other models such as differential latency or postdiction were also proposed, such that it is yet not clear what is the neural substrate of the FLE. Here, extending the model compensating for delays (Perrinet et al. 2014), we extend the model of predictive processing on the visual topography using an internal representation of visual motion (Perrinet and Masson 2012) to define an anisotropic diffusion of information Figure 5.2(A). The model that we used for the FLE can be used with any image. In particular, a single flashed dot evokes an expanding then contracting isotropic activity while a moving dot may produce a soliton-like wave which may traverse an occlusion (Khoei et al. 2013). More generally, this model may be described as a simplification of the Navier Stokes equation of fluid dynamics using the advection term. As such, solutions to these equations are typically waves which are traveling on the retinotopic map. A particular feature of these maps is that these include an amplification term for rectilinear motions. As a consequence, once an object begins to be tracked, its position is predicted in the future, such that position and velocity are better estimated. On the contrary, a dot which is moving on an unpredictable trajectory is explained away by the system. This explains some of the nonlinear, switch-like behaviors explained by this model (Perrinet and Masson 2012). It is of particular interest at this point to understand if such a model extends to other stimuli or if we can precise its neural correlate.

Applied to the image of the FLE, activity in the model shows three different phases; see Figure 5.2(B). First, there is a rapid build-up of the precision of the target after the first appearance of the moving dot (at 300 milliseconds). Consistently with the Fröhlich effect (Jancke and Erlhagen 2010), the beginning of the trajectory is seen ahead of its physical position. During the second phase, the moving dot is efficiently tracked as both its velocity and its position are correctly inferred. This is ahead of the delayed trajectory of the dot (green dotted line). Motion extrapolation correctly predicts the position at the present time and the position follows the actual physical position of the dot (black dotted line). Finally, the third phase corresponds to motion termination. The moving dot disappears and the corresponding activity vanishes in the source layer at $t = 900$ milliseconds. However, between $t = 800$ milliseconds and $t = 900$ milliseconds, the dot position was extrapolated and predicted ahead of the terminal position. At $t = 900$ milliseconds, while motion information is absent, the position information is still transiently consistent and extrapolated using a broad, centered prior distribution of speeds: Although it is less precise, this position of the dot at flash termination is therefore, with *hindsight*, not perceived as leading the flash.

3.2. Neural Correlate of Apparent Motion

Let's apply a similar approach to another visual illusion: When two stationary dots are flashed at close successive positions and times, observers may experience a percept of motion. This transforms the presentation of a discrete pattern into a continuous one. This visual illusion is called apparent motion and can persist over a relatively long range (superior to the characteristic size of the RF of a neuron in the primary visual cortex, V1). Similarly to the study above for the FLE, it is believed that this long-range Apparent Motion (lrAM) can be explained by predictive processes. Due to the dynamical characteristics of lrAM, a neural implementation of this illusion may consist in the propagation of visual information through intra-cortical interactions. In particular, these lateral interactions may evoke waves of activity in V1 which may modulate the integration of the sensory information coming from thalamocortical connections. An interesting prospect is thus to record neural activity during the presentation of the lrAM stimulus. This allows to quantitatively assess why the superposition of two dots as in lrAM is "more" than the sum of the two dots in isolation.

In a recent study (Chemla et al. 2019), we used VSDI to record the activity of the primary visual cortex (V1) of awake macaque monkeys. Is there any difference between the response to the single dot and that to the two dots? Indeed, VSDI recordings allow to record the activity of populations of V1 neurons which are approximately at the scale of a cortical column. In addition, the recorded response is rapid enough to capture the dynamics of the lrAM stimulus. Recordings show that as the evoked activity of the second stimulus reaches V1, a cortical suppressive wave propagates toward the retinotopic wave evoked by the first dot. This was put in evidence by statistically comparing the response of the brain to the response of the two dots in isolation. In particular, we found that thanks to this suppressive wave, the activity for the brain stimulus was more precise, suggesting that such suppressive wave could serve as a predictive processing step to be read-out in upstream cortical areas.

In particular, we found that the activity that we recorded fitted well with a mean-field model using a dynamical gain control. Qualitatively, this model reproduced the propagation of activity on the cortex. Importantly, this model allowed to show that the observed activity was best fitted when the speed of lateral connections within the mean-field was about 1 m/s, a propagation speed which is of the order of that measured for intra-cortical connections in the primary visual cortex (for a review, see Muller et al. 2018). A more functional (probabilistic) model also showed that the cortical suppressive wave allowed to disambiguate the stimulus by explaining away (i.e., suppressing) ambiguous alternatives. As a consequence, (1) lateral interactions are key to generate traveling waves on the surface of the cortex and (2) these waves help disambiguate the input stimulus. This corresponds to the implementation of a predictive process using an *a priori* knowledge of smoothly moving visual objects.

3.3. Summary

As a summary, we have seen that it is possible to extend predictive processing to topographic maps. In particular, the resulting computations are particularly adapted to vision. We have shown (see Figure 5.2) a model which represents (at any given present time) different variables (here "Source" and "Target"). In a more realistic model, neural activity is more likely to form intermediate representations between past, present, and also future representations (Glaser et al. 2018) and at different levels of adaptation as illustrated for the lrAM stimulus (Chemla et al. 2019). As a consequence, such processes are observed phenomenologically as the propagation of neural information tangentially to the cortical surface, modulating dynamically the feed-forward and feed-back streams. In particular it is an open question whether such neural computations could be implemented by traveling waves on the cortical surface (Muller et al. 2018).

4. Open Problems in the Science of Visual Predictive Processing

In section 2, we have studied the dynamics of predictive processing at the macroscopic scale, that is, by considering (cortical) areas as nodes of a dependency graph. In section 3, we have extended such models within such nodes as fields organized on the topography of each visual area. At an even finer scale than this intermediate mesoscopic scale is the microscopic scale of actual neural cells. To better understand the mechanisms of predictive processing, we will now finesse the granularity of the modeling to this scale. In particular, in addition to the asynchronous nature of the neural representation that we explored above, communication between neurons has the property of being event-based. Indeed, the vast majority of neural cells across the living kingdom communicate using prototypical, short pulses called action potentials or *spikes*. In this section, we will propose three open problems which are raised when modeling such spiking neural networks (SNNs) in the context of predictive processing.

4.1. The Challenges of Representing Visual Information in Spiking Neural Networks (SNNs)

Following the first generations of artificial neural networks (ANNs), present machine learning algorithms such as deep learning (DL) algorithms constitute a breakthrough which formed a second generation of ANNs. SNNs constitute a potential, third generation (Maass 1997). Indeed, event-based representations have many advantages which are a deadlock in DL. For instance, instead of repeating all computations for each layer, channel, and pixel of a hierarchical ANN, and for which energy-greedy GPUs are necessary, event-based computations need only to be performed for active units at the time of a spike. In particular, a fast developing area of research consists in developing dedicated hardware, such as neuromorphic chips, which would allow to scale the effective volume of computations beyond the last generations of classical semi-conductors (CPUs, GPUs) which attain the limits of Moore's Law.

Crucial in this new type of representation is on one hand the discrete nature of the addressing of neurons and on the other hand the analog nature of the timing of spikes. Notable results using such architectures have been made in real-time classification and sensor fusion (O'Connor et al. 2013) and in pattern recognition (Lagorce et al. 2017). Indeed, an important property of SNNs is the ability to dynamically encode a latent, internal variable (the membrane potential in neuro-physiology) and to emit a spike when (and only when) an internally defined threshold is reached. This defines each spiking neuron as an integrator (similarly to classical neurons), but also potentially as a synchrony detector (Perrinet 2002). This ability to modulate the processing based on the relative timing of presynaptic spikes constitutes a novel paradigm for neural computations (Paugam-Moisy and Bohte 2012). In particular, this shows that the balance in the flux of incoming excitatory and inhibitory spikes is crucial to maximize the efficiency of such SNNs (Hansel and Vreeswijk 2012).

4.2. The Role of Cortical Waves in Shaping the Dynamic Processing of Visual Information

Another crucial point in deciphering the predictive processing mechanisms is given by the functional anatomy. Indeed, in the primary visual cortex (V1) as in other cortical areas, the neural network is highly recurrent with a median number of 10,000 connections per neuron. Surprisingly, 95 percent of these connections occur within a 2-millimeter radius (macaque monkey) (Markov et al. 2013). This suggests that a majority of neural resources is devoted to intra-areal communications. One putative functional role of this dense network is to generate traveling waves which modulate the strength and dynamics of the incoming feed-forward neural activity (Muller et al. 2018). We have seen its potential role in disambiguating motion (Chemla et al. 2019) and it has also been shown to facilitate the progressive build-up of visual information (Bringuier et al. 1999). Previously, we have successfully modeled such a predictive process (Khoei et al. 2013, 2017, Perrinet and Masson 2012), and implemented it in an SNN (Kaplan et al. 2013).

One "holy grail" in that direction is to find canonical micro-circuits for predictive coding (Bastos et al. 2012). This follows from the observation that across species and areas, the cortex seems to follow some prototypical, layered structure. In the particular case of V1, while the thalamic input reaches mostly the (intermediate) granular layer, a feed-forward stream is mostly propagated to efferent layers through the supra-granular layers while feed-back is in majority mediated by infra-granular layers. This anatomical segregation could correspond to different types of signals in predictive coding, respectively expected states and prediction error (Bastos et al. 2012). Such basic micro-circuits have been applied to explain the response of V1 neurons to natural scenes (Kremkow et al. 2016) by using a push-pull mechanism. Still it is an open problem as to know how such a circuitry may emerge.

4.3. Integrative Properties of Cortical Areas: Toward Sparse, Efficient Representations

Another interesting perspective is the integrative nature of neural computations. While it was believed that neurons would represent the combination of visual features, this is in general not correct (Tring and Ringach 2018). Instead, it has been found that activity may become sharper as visual features are accumulated. For instance, Baudot et al. (2013) has shown that neurons in cat's area 17 respond more selectively when presenting natural images (which consist locally to a sum of edges) compared to a single edge. Recently, Ravello et al. (2019) has shown that a similar result may occur in rodents as soon as in the retina. Behaviorally, this fits also with the observation in humans that more complex textures are driving more robustly eye movements (Simoncini et al. 2012). Such phenomena are consistent with the predictive processing principle that by accumulating coherent information, the *a posteriori* probability (and hence the response of the system) gets more precise.

Strikingly, this translates in the neural activity by the fact that for a more coherent set of inputs, the neural activity of the population is more sparse (Baudot et al. 2013,

Vinje and Gallant 2002). This was already explained by the predictive coding model of Rao and Ballard (1999) and implemented in Kremkow et al. (2016) for instance. Importantly, the principle of sparse coding is itself sufficient to (1) explain in a principled fashion much of gain-control mechanisms (Heeger 2017) and (2) guide the learning of the connectivity within a population of neurons, such as in V1 (Olshausen and Field 1997, Perrinet 2010, 2015). This helps to solve an important problem, that is, that the system is self-organized and that the learning of the connectivity should be unsupervised. As such, the plasticity rules that should be developed in SNNs should use similar governing principles.

However, we still lack realistic models of such visual predictive processing. We have built a simplified model which is able to process static images (Boutin et al. 2019). It consists of a multi-layered neural network, where each layer includes both a recursive intra-cortical mechanism to generate sparse representations and also the ability for each layer to integrate (feedback) information from a higher-level layer. The main novelty of this network is that it allows for the unsupervised learning of the convolutional kernels within each layer. Compared to classical Convolutional Neural Networks such as commonly found in deep learning architectures, we found that the emerging kernels were more meaningful: For instance, when learning on a class of images from human faces, we observed in the second layer different neurons sensitive to face features such as eye, mouth, or nose. This is similar to what is found in the fusiform face area, but more simulations are needed to validate the emergence of this representation. Moreover, these simulations are computationally intensive and prohibit their use on conventional computer architectures. A translation of this algorithm into an SNN would therefore be highly beneficial and allow for its application to a dynamical stream of images.

5. Summary and Conclusions

As a summary, we have reviewed in this chapter different models of predictive coding applied to vision. We have seen at a macroscopic scale the role of dynamics using Active Inference (see section 2). Extending such model to a retinotopic map, we could describe a functional traveling wave to disambiguate visual stimuli (see section 3). However, we have also shown a limit of such models at the microscopic scale (see section 4). In particular, it is not yet understood at the single cell level how (1) information is represented in spiking activity, (2) what is the functional role of traveling waves on cortical surfaces, (3) if a common efficiency principle (such as sparse coding) could be used to guide the organization of such highly recurrent networks into a single universal circuit.

To further extend our knowledge of predictive processing in vision (see section 4), it thus seems necessary to be able to implement full-scale SNNs implementing complex visual processes. However, the three different anatomical scales that we have highlighted above (feed-forward, lateral, feedback) seem to be tightly coupled and can be difficult to be modeled separately. More generally, this is also true for the scales that we have defined, from the macroscopic, to the mesoscopic and microscopic. As such, it is highly difficult to produce models which are simple enough to be useful for our understanding of the underlying processing (Brette 2019, Varoquaux and Poldrack 2019). For instance, after deducing them from optimization principles, all the models that we have presented here are pre-connected: The hyper-parameters controlling the interconnection of neurons are fixed. Though we have provided with simulations showing the role of these hyper-parameters, it seems necessary for a better understanding to further explore their relative effects. In particular, we envision that such self-organized architectures could define time as an emerging variable synchronizing predictive processes at the multiple levels of visual processing.

Indeed, a normative theory for predictive processing should provide not only a possible solution (one given model with one set of hyper parameters) but with an exploration of *all possible solutions*. One first methodology is to have a complete understanding of the set of models using mathematical analysis. However, this becomes impossible for such complex systems and using simplifying assumptions often leads to a shallow complexity. Another venue is to develop adaptive strategies to explore the functional space of different models. This can be for instance developed using machine learning techniques such as the stochastic gradient descent commonly used in deep learning. Another promising solution is to explore bio-inspired adaptive strategies. Those exist at different time scales, from rapid adaption mechanisms, to a slower learning of connections, or to the long-term evolution of hyper-parameters. In particular, it is yet not completely understood how SNNs perform a spike-time dependent plasticity. This sets a future challenge in our understanding of the science of predictive processes in vision.

Acknowledgments

This work was supported by ANR project "Horizontal-V1" N°ANR-17-CE37-0006. The author would like to thank Berk Mirza, Hugo Ladret, and Manivannan Subramaniyan for careful reading and insightful remarks.

References

Adams, R. A., Perrinet, L. U. and Friston, K. J. (2012), "Smooth Pursuit and Visual Occlusion: Active Inference and Oculomotor Control in Schizophrenia," *PLoS ONE*, 7 (10): e47502+. doi.org/10.1371/journal.pone.0047502.

Atick, J. J. (1992), "Could Information Theory Provide an Ecological Theory of Sensory Processing?" *Network: Computation in Neural Systems*, 3 (2): 213–52.

Attneave, F. (1954), "Some Informational Aspects of Visual Perception," *Psychological Review*, 61 (3): 183–93.

Avila, M. T., Hong, L. E., Moates, A., Turano, K. A. and Thaker, G. K. (2006), "Role of Anticipation in Schizophrenia-Related Pursuit Initiation Deficits," *Journal of Neurophysiology*, 95 (2): 593–601. doi.org/10.1152/jn.00369.2005.

Barlow, H B. (1961), "Possible Principles Underlying the Transformation of Sensory Messages," *Sensory Communication*. doi.org/10.7551/mitpress/9780262518420.003.0013.

Barnes, G. R. and Asselman, T. (1991), "The Mechanism of Prediction in Human Smooth Pursuit Eye Movements," *The Journal of Physiology*, 439: 439–61.

Bastos, A. M., Martin, W. U., Adams, R. A., Mangun, G. R., Fries, P. and Friston, K. J. (2012), "Canonical Microcircuits for Predictive Coding," *Neuron*, 76 (4): 695–711. doi. org/10/f4gsgg.

Baudot, P., Levy, M., Marre, O., Monier, C., Pananceau, M. and Frégnac, Y. (2013), "Animation of Natural Scene by Virtual Eye-Movements Evokes High Precision and Low Noise in V1 Neurons," *Frontiers in Neural Circuits*, 7: 206. doi.org/10.3389/fncir.2013.00206.

Boutin, Victor, Franciosini, Angelo, Ruffier, Franck and Perrinet, Laurent U. (2020), "Effect of Top-down Connections in Hierarchical Sparse Coding," *Neural Computation*. https://arxiv.org/abs/2002.00892.

Brette, R. (2019), "Is Coding a Relevant Metaphor for the Brain?" *Behavioral and Brain Sciences*, February, 1–44. doi.org/10/gfvs6r.

Bringuier, V., Chavane, F., Glaeser, L. and Frégnac, Y. (1999), "Horizontal Propagation of Visual Activity in the Synaptic Integration Field of Area 17 Neurons," *Science*, 283 (5402): 695–99. doi.org/10/b9shf4.

Changizi, M., Hsieh, A., Nijhawan, R., Kanai, R. and Shimojo, S. (2008), "Perceiving the Present and a Systematization of Illusions," *Cognitive Science*, 32 (3): 459–503. doi. org/10.1080/03640210802035191.

Chemla, S., Reynaud, A., diVolo, M., Zerlaut, Y., Perrinet, L. U., Destexhe, A. and Chavane, F. (2019), "Suppressive Waves Disambiguate the Representation of Long-Range Apparent Motion in Awake Monkey V1," *Journal of Neuroscience*, 2792: 18. doi. org/10.1523/JNEUROSCI.2792-18.2019.

Damasse, J.-B., Perrinet, L. U., Madelain, L. and Montagnini, A. (2018), "Reinforcement Effects in Anticipatory Smooth Eye Movements," *Journal of Vision*, 18 (11): 1–18, 14. doi.org/10.1167/18.11.14.

D'Arcy Thompson, W. (1917), *On Growth and Form*, Cambridge: Cambridge University Press.

Friston, K. (2010) "The Free-Energy Principle: A Unified Brain Theory?," *Nature Reviews Neuroscience*, 11 (2): 127–38. doi.org/10.1038/nrn2787.

Friston, K. J., Adams, R. A., Perrinet, L. U. and Breakspear, M. (2012), "Perceptions as Hypotheses: Saccades as Experiments," *Frontiers in Psychology*, 3. doi.org/10.3389/fpsyg.2012.00151.

Friston, K., Klaas S., Li, B. and Daunizeau, J. (2010), "Generalised Filtering," *Mathematical Problems in Engineering*, 3: 1–34. doi.org/10.1155/2010/621670.

Glaser, J. I., Perich, M. G., Ramkumar, P., Lee, E. and Kording, K. P. (2018), "Population Coding of Conditional Probability Distributions in Dorsal Premotor Cortex," *Nature Communications*, 9 (1): 1788. doi.org/10/gdhvzr.

Gregory, R. L. (1980), "Perceptions as Hypotheses," *Philosophical Transactions of the Royal Society B: Biological Sciences*, 290 (1038): 181–97. doi.org/10/cgdwx9.

Hansel, D. and van Vreeswijk, C. (2012), "The Mechanism of Orientation Selectivity in Primary Visual Cortex without a Functional Map," *Journal of Neuroscience*, 32 (12): 4049–64.

Heeger, D. J. (2017), "Theory of Cortical Function," *Proceedings of the National Academy of Sciences of the United States of America*, 201619788. doi.org/10.1073/pnas.1619788114.

Jancke, D. and Erlhagen, W. (2010), "Bridging the Gap: A Model of Common Neural Mechanisms Underlying the Fröhlich Effect, the Flash-Lag Effect, and the Representational Momentum Effect," *Space and Time in Perception and Action*: 422–40. https://repositorium.sdum.uminho.pt/handle/1822/10949.

Kalman, R. E. (1960), "A New Approach to Linear Filtering and Prediction Problems," *Journal of Basic Engineering*, 82 (1): 35. doi.org/10.1115/1.3662552.

Kaplan, B. A., Lansner, A., Masson, G. S. and Perrinet, L. U. (2013), "Anisotropic Connectivity Implements Motion-Based Prediction in a Spiking Neural Network," *Frontiers in Computational Neuroscience*, 7 (112). doi.org/10.3389/fncom.2013.00112.

Karvelis, P., Seitz, A. R., Lawrie, S. M. and Seriès, P. (2018), "Autistic Traits, but Not Schizotypy, Predict Increased Weighting of Sensory Information in Bayesian Visual Integration," *eLife*, 7: e34115.

Kent, L., van Doorn, G., Hohwy, J. and Klein, B. (2019), "Bayes, Time Perception, and Relativity: The Central Role of Hopelessness," *Consciousness and Cognition*, 69: 70–80. doi.org/10/gft7b2.

Khoei, M. A., Masson, G. S. and Perrinet, L. U. (2013), "Motion-Based Prediction Explains the Role of Tracking in Motion Extrapolation," *Journal of Physiology-Paris*, 107 (5): 409–20. doi.org/10.1016/j.jphysparis.2013.08.001.

Khoei, M. A., Masson, G. S. and Perrinet, L. U. (2017), "The Flash-Lag Effect as a Motion-Based Predictive Shift," *PLoS Computational Biology*, 13 (1): e1005068. doi. org/10.1371/journal.pcbi.1005068.

Kirchner, H. and Thorpe, S. (2006), "Ultra-Rapid Object Detection with Saccadic Eye Movements: Visual Processing Speed Revisited," *Vision Research*, 46 (11): 1762–76. doi. org/10.1016/j.visres.2005.10.002.

Knill, D. C. and Pouget, A. (2004), "The Bayesian Brain: The Role of Uncertainty in Neural Coding and Computation," *Trends in Neurosciences*, 27 (12): 712–19. doi.org/10.1016/j. tins.2004.10.007.

Kowler, E., Aitkin, C. D., Ross, N. M., Santos, E. M. and Zhao, M. (2014), "Davida Teller Award Lecture 2013: The Importance of Prediction and Anticipation in the Control of Smooth Pursuit Eye Movements," *Journal of Vision*, 14 (5): 10, 1–16. doi. org/10.1167/14.5.10.

Kremkow, J., Perrinet, L. U., Monier, C., Alonso, J.-M., Aertsen, M., Frégnac, Y. and Masson, G. S. (2016), "Push-Pull Receptive Field Organization and Synaptic Depression: Mechanisms for Reliably Encoding Naturalistic Stimuli in V1," *Frontiers in Neural Circuits*, 10. doi.org/10.3389/fncir.2016.00037.

Lagorce, X., Orchard, G., Galluppi, F., Shi, B. E. and Benosman, R. B. (2017), "HOTS: A Hierarchy of Event-Based Time-Surfaces for Pattern Recognition," *IEEE Transactions on Pattern Analysis and Machine Intelligence*, 39 (7): 1346–59. doi.org/10.1109/ TPAMI.2016.2574707.

Lamme, V. A. and Roelfsema, P. R. (2000), "The Distinct Modes of Vision Offered by Feedforward and Recurrent Processing," *Trends in Neurosciences*, 23 (11): 571–79. doi. org/10/ccv3w2.

Linsker, R. (1990), "Perceptual Neural Organization: Some Approaches Based on Network Models and Information Theory," *Annual Review of Neuroscience*, 13 (1): 257–81.

Maass, W. (1997), "Networks of Spiking Neurons: The Third Generation of Neural Network Models," *Neural Networks*, 10 (9): 1659–71.

MacKay, D. M. (1958), "Perceptual Stability of a Stroboscopically Lit Visual Field Containing Self-Luminous Objects," *Nature*, 181 (4607): 507–8. doi. org/10.1038/181507a0.

Markov, N. T., Ercsey-Ravasz, M., Lamy, C., Ribeiro Gomes, A. R., Magrou, L., Misery, P., Giroud, P. et al. (2013), "The Role of Long-Range Connections on the Specificity of the Macaque Interareal Cortical Network," *Proceedings of the National Academy of Sciences*, 110 (13): 5187–92. doi.org/10.1073/PNAS.1218972110.

Marr, D. (1982). *Vision: A Computational Investigation into the Human Representation and Processing of Visual Information*, San Francisco, CA: W. H. Freeman.

Mirza, M. B., Adams, R. A., Mathys, C. and Friston, K. J. (2018), "Human Visual Exploration Reduces Uncertainty about the Sensed World," *PLOS ONE*, 13 (1): e0190429. doi.org/10.1371/journal.pone.0190429.

Muller, L., Chavane, F., Reynolds, J. and Sejnowski, T. J. (2018), "Cortical Travelling Waves: Mechanisms and Computational Principles," *Nature Reviews Neuroscience*, 19: 255–68. doi.org/10.1038/nrn.2018.20.

Nijhawan, R. (2002), "Neural Delays, Visual Motion and the Flash-Lag Effect," *Trends in Cognitive Sciences*, 6 (9): 387–93. doi.org/10.1016/s1364-6613(02)01963-0.

Nijhawan, R. and Wu, S. S. (2009), "Compensating Time Delays with Neural Predictions: Are Predictions Sensory or Motor?" *Philosophical Transactions of the Royal Society A: Mathematical, Physical and Engineering Sciences*, 367 (1891): 1063–78. doi.org/10.1098/rsta.2008.0270.

O'Connor, P., Neil, D., Liu, S.-C., Delbruck, T. and Pfeiffer, M. (2013), "Real-Time Classification and Sensor Fusion with a Spiking Deep Belief Network," *Frontiers in Neuroscience*, 7: 178. doi.org/10.3389/fnins.2013.00178.

Olshausen, B. A. and Field, D. J. (1997), "Sparse Coding with an Overcomplete Basis Set: A Strategy Employed by V1?," *Vision Research*, 37 (23): 3311–25.

Paugam-Moisy, H. and Bohte, S. (2012), "Computing with Spiking Neuron Networks" in Thomas Bäck and Grzegorz Rozenberg (eds.), *Handbook of Natural Computing*, Berlin: Springer.

Perrinet, L. U. (2002), "Coherence Detection in a Spiking Neuron via Hebbian Learning," *Neurocomputing*, 44–46: 133–39. doi.org/10.1016/s0925-2312(02)00374-0.

Perrinet, L. U. (2010), "Role of Homeostasis in Learning Sparse Representations," *Neural Computation*, 22 (7): 1812–36. doi.org/10.1162/neco.2010.05-08-795.

Perrinet, L. U. (2015), "Sparse Models for Computer Vision" in Gabriel Cristóbal, Laurent U. Perrinet and Matthias S. Keil (eds.), *Biologically Inspired Computer Vision*, Weinheim: Wiley-VCH Verlag GmbH & Co.

Perrinet, L. U., Adams, R. A. and Friston, K. J. (2014), "Active Inference, Eye Movements and Oculomotor Delays," *Biological Cybernetics*, 108 (6): 777–801. doi.org/10.1007/s00422-014-0620-8.

Perrinet, L. U. and Masson, G. S. (2012), "Motion-Based Prediction Is Sufficient to Solve the Aperture Problem," *Neural Computation*, 24 (10): 2726–50.

Rao, R. P. and Ballard, D. H. (1999), "Predictive Coding in the Visual Cortex: A Functional Interpretation of Some Extra-Classical Receptive-Field Effects," *Nature Neuroscience*, 2: 79–87. doi.org/10.1038/4580.

Ravello, C. U., Perrinet, L. U., Escobar, M.-J. and Palacios, A. G. (2019), "Speed-Selectivity in Retinal Ganglion Cells Is Sharpened by Broad Spatial Frequency, Naturalistic Stimuli," *Scientific Reports*, 9 (1). doi.org/10.1038/s41598-018-36861-8.

Simoncini, C., Perrinet, L. U., Montagnini, A., Mamassian, P. and Masson, G. S. (2012), "More Is Not Always Better: Dissociation between Perception and Action Explained by Adaptive Gain Control," *Nature Neuroscience*, 15: 1596–603. doi.org/doi:10.1038/nn.3229.

Statistical Parametric Mapping: The Analysis of Functional Brain Images—1st Edition. 2012. https://www.elsevier.com/books/statistical-parametric-mapping-the-analysis-of-functional-brain-images/penny/978-0-12-372560-8.

Tring, Elaine, and Ringach, Dario L. (2018), "On the Subspace Invariance of Population Responses," *arXiv preprint arXiv:1811.03251.*

Turkheimer, F. E., Hellyer, P., Kehagia, A. A., Expert, P., Lord, L.-D., Vohryzek, J., Dafflon, J., Brammer, M. and Leech, R. (2019), "Conflicting Emergences. Weak Vs. Strong Emergence for the Modelling of Brain Function," *Neuroscience & Biobehavioral Reviews*, 99: 3–10. doi.org/10/gft5mn.

Varoquaux, G. and Poldrack, R. (2019), "Predictive Models Avoid Excessive Reductionism in Cognitive Neuroimaging," *Current Opinion in Neurobiology*, 55: 1–6. doi.org/10.1016/j.conb.2018.11.002.

Vinje, W. E. and Gallant, J. L. (2002), "Natural Stimulation of the Nonclassical Receptive Field Increases Information Transmission Efficiency in V1," *Journal of Neuroscience*, 22 (7): 2904–15.

Von Helmholtz, H. (1867), *Handbuch Der Physiologischen Optik*, Vol. 9, Leipzig: Leopold Voss.

Wigner, E. P. (1990), "The Unreasonable Effectiveness of Mathematics in the Natural Sciences" in Ronald E. Mickens (ed.), *Mathematics and Science*, Singapura: World Scientific.

6

Predictive Processing and Consciousness: Prediction Fallacy and Its Spatiotemporal Resolution

Steven S. Gouveia
University of Minho

1. Predictive Processing: The Framework

Predictive Processing (PP) (also called "predictive coding theory of cognition") is a recent framework that brings together several ideas about the brain and the mind. The first of these is the refutation of what we can call the "traditional doctrine" of the brain (cf. Gouveia and Northoff 2019: 13–15). The brain is traditionally seen as a mere passive organ, whose activity is only determined by the external perception from the senses:

Traditional Doctrine of the Brain

Figure 6.1 Traditional doctrine of the brain.

More importantly, an active role of the brain is denied in this traditional doctrine: the only function that the brain has is the association of diverse stimuli with one another (e.g., Marr 1982). Despite being generally accepted, this model of the brain has been raising a lot of red flags for numerous reasons. The original idea of PP was initially exposed by psychologist Hermann von Helmholtz in the nineteenth century (Von Helmholtz 1867).

In contrast, the PP approach sees the brain as a prediction engine: the brain combines the sensory signals of reality with its prior expectations or beliefs about the way the world is to form its best guess of what caused those signals (cf. Clark 2013a, 2016). There are rough proposals of how PP can be implemented by the brain (see, for example, Bastos et al. 2012, Brodski et al. 2015, Engel and Singer 2001, Friston 2010, Wacongne et al. 2011), and here, it is assumed that the brain doesn't perceive sound or light: what we perceive is its best guess of what's out there in the world.

A few examples can be given to understand the elegance of this approach to explain the brain's activity in general. The first example is a perceptual illusion:

(a) WHAT I IF TOLD YOU
(b) YOU READ THE TOP LINE WRONG

What is happening between the reading of (a) and (b)?[1] The brain uses prior projections present into the circuits of specific part of it (e.g., the visual cortex). The perceived stimulus (a) hasn't changed: the sensory information is exactly the same. What changed then? According to the PP explanation, it was the brain's best guess of the causes of that sensory information, and how that influences what you consciously perceive.

The main general consequence of the PP view of perception is that, instead of perception depending on inputs from the world to the brain (traditional doctrine), the PP view reverses the directionality of the entire process: the perceptual predictions flow from the brain to the world (cf. Gregory 1980). In the PP framework, versus the traditional doctrine of the brain, it is assumed that human beings don't just passively perceive the world: quite the opposite, they actively generate it, as argued in one of the first studies on this approach:

> Classical theories of sensory processing view the brain as a passive, stimulus-driven device. By contrast, more recent approaches emphasize the constructive nature of perception, viewing it as an active and highly selective process. Indeed, there is ample evidence that the processing of stimuli is controlled by top-down influences that strongly shape the intrinsic dynamics of thalamocortical networks and constantly create predictions about forthcoming sensory events.
>
> (cf. Engel et al. 2001)

The PP framework is not just a specific account of perception, though. For some researchers, this theory can explain most (if not all) mechanisms of human cognition, including the self and consciousness.

Here is an example on the self[2]:

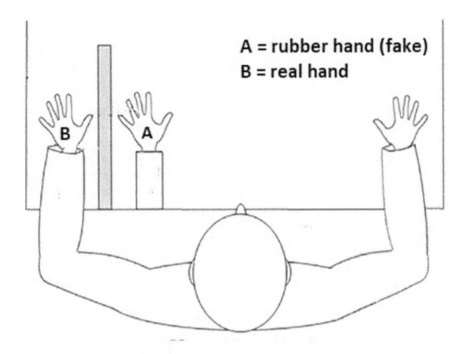

Figure 6.2 Example of the Rubber Hand Illusion.

The rubber hand illusion is more focused on the self than on perception *per se*. Anil Seth, for example, argues that the resemblance between the inputs of feeling a touch on one's hand (B) and seeing a touch on a fake hand (A) that is placed where the other (normal) hand (B) should be is sufficient for the human brain to create a model of the body where the fake hand (A) is actually part of that body (cf. Seth 2013).

In his view, rubber hand illusions (cf. Suzuki et al. 2013) show us that even experiences of what our body is are a kind of best guessing, a kind of "controlled hallucination" by the brain (cf. Horn 1980).

So, as much as human beings can be deceived in regards to how they perceive the world, they can also have mistaken perceptions of themselves. This main idea may create new insights in psychiatric research as its aim is not merely treating symptoms, but also in understanding the specific mechanisms related with disturbance of the self in conditions like schizophrenia or bipolar personality disorder (see the section of this volume on mental health).

Some (e.g., Seth 2013) have argued that it makes less sense for PP to be applied to the traditional senses that carry inputs from the world to the body and brain (what we call exteroception) but moreso to the sense of internal physiological conditions of the body (what we call interoception). The primary reason for that is the claim that has to do with the survival of an organism—it may be more vital to avoid bumping into unpredicted interoceptive states than to avoid encountering unpredicted exteroceptive states:

A level of blood oxygenation or blood sugar that is unexpected low is likely to be bad news for an organism, whereas unexpected exteroceptive sensations (like novel visual inputs) are less likely to be harmful and may in some cases be desirable.

(Seth 2017: 9)

Following the idea that brains are predictive machines, PP theorists usually claim that perception and action are mechanisms to minimize prediction error, that is, the discrepancy between sensory signals from the world (external) and the internally generated sensory predictions (internal). A result of this view is that the mechanism of the brain involves an interplay between top-down and bottom-up processing in cognition in general, against the traditional view (cf. Wanja and Metzinger 2017: 1).

The sophistication of this approach also lies in its formalization. Generally speaking, PP frameworks can be described as defending the following theses (cf. Ning 2019: 83–4): (1) Perception formation is inferential; (2) the unconscious inference is predictive; (3) the inference performed by the PP mind is (approximately) Bayesian; and (4) the goal of the brain is to minimize the prediction error. Let's see in more detail what each of these means:

(1) The inferentialist view is based on the idea that the input received is not perfectly captured: the brain has to combine the noisy information of the world (external) with the model of what caused that specific input (the internal). After comparing different models—different interpretations of what may cause that specific input—the brain infers then the "real" input (cf. Kiefer 2017);

(2) The predictivist proposal is derived from the assumption that the brain is anticipating the input that will be received from the external world. Contrary to the traditional explanation, the first step of the data's processing is not to receive a particular input from the outside world, but rather to generate a model (a prediction) that will be confirmed or disconfirmed by going to the world (cf. Anderson and Chemero 2013: 204, Clark 2013b: 236);

(3) The Bayesian Inference is a specific statistical method based on Bayes's theorem. The point is to update the probability of a particular hypothesis about the world as more information or input is processed by the system. The posterior probability $[P(H \mid E)]$ is calculated by the conjunction of the likelihood $[P(E \mid H)]$ with the prior probability $[P(H)]$ divided by marginal likelihood $[P(E)]$, where E stands for Evidence, that is, the new data from the external, and H stands for an Hypothesis, which probability may be influenced by E (cf. Wanja and Metzinger 2017);
Finally,

(4) The discrepancies between the predicted input and the actual input is not passively processed, but it is actively applied to update the information already formed in order to anticipate with more precision future external inputs. The main purpose of the updates is to minimize the prediction error resultant from the prior predictions made by the brain based on previous inputs (cf. Friston 2010: 129).

PP is, then, an empirical theory about how the brain operates and generates stimulus-induced or task-evoked activity, thereby presupposing a prediction model of brain:

Prediction model of the brain

Figure 6.3 Prediction model of the brain.

PP offers an interesting framework for the study of the brain and its mental features, in general. In that sense, there are two central questions with regard to consciousness:
    (5) Is PP sufficient for the selection of contents in consciousness?
    (6) Is PP sufficient to associate any given content with consciousness?
Grounded on empirical data on pre-stimulus prediction of subsequent conscious contents, we will claim that regarding (5), the prediction model of the brain can deal perfectly well with the selection of contents in consciousness. Nevertheless, PP may have more troubles regarding (6), namely, how any give content selected can be associated with consciousness (cf. Northoff 2018: 128). That will be the focus of the next section of this chapter.

2. Predictive Processing and the Prediction Fallacy (Negative Argument)

Is there a way to study the contents of consciousness? To explore this question, the group around Andreas Kleinschmidt (Hesselmann et al. 2008) used functional magnetic resonance imaging (fMRI) with human subjects that were experiencing the visual perception of the Rubin face-stimulus illusion:

Figure 6.4 Example of the Rubin face-stimulus illusion.

This kind of illusion has the following structure: the same stimulus (Figure 6.4) can be perceived as having two different contents, one as faces, and the other as a vase. In these cases, we have two discrete perceptual contents created by the same stimulus.

The perceptual phenomenon that describes changing contents in consciousness is called bistable or multistable perception. What lesson can we retrieve from this kind of bistable perception on the contents and their association with consciousness? The relevant thought that is important for our debate is the following: bistable perception shows that there is no direct and necessary relation between a particular input and a particular content in consciousness. As the example of the Rubin-face illusion shows us, the same specific stimuli can be interpreted in two different ways; that is, it can originate two different contents depending on specific neurobiological circumstances. What is happening in the brain during the different perceptual experience?

The empirical data (cf. Hesselmann et al. 2008) has shown that there are two main areas of the brain relevant to process of the visual input: (a) the prestimulus activity changes in fusiform face area (FFA) and (b) the prestimulus activity changes in the prefrontal cortex. Both (a) and (b) will directly impact which of the contents will be perceived in consciousness, showing that the resting state activity levels add something and can actually manipulate the input and its content (cf. Northoff 2018: 129). It is, then, in our view, empirically demonstrated that there is no direct and necessary relation between the contents of perception on the one hand, and the actual input's content on the other hand.

How can the prediction model of the brain account for what we just described? The group around Kleinschmidt (Sadaghiani et al. 2010) argues for a predictivist interpretation of the empirical findings: if the prestimulus activity level are high, the predicted input is strong and therefore cannot be overridden by the actual input, the stimulus, which results in a low prediction error (cf. Northoff 2018: 133). The following figure sums up what happens:

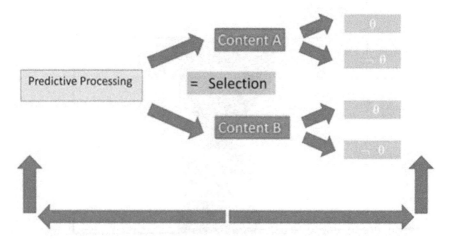

Figure 6.5 Selection of content account of the PP framework.

The only way to address that question on the basis of the prediction model of the brain is to commit what we can describe as the prediction fallacy (PF), wherein one infers from the processing of contents in terms of predicted and genuine input their actual association with consciousness (cf. Northoff 2018: 144). Despite this, it is our view that no empirical evidence supports the association of the contents related to predicted input or prediction error (predictive coding) with consciousness.

The prediction fallacy can be formulized in the following way:

$$(PF){:}x(\theta\lor\neg\theta) \text{ is conscious iff } x \in (a1, a2,...,an)$$

where θ = accurate and $\neg\theta$ = inaccurate and a1, a2, ..., an = content selected. The formalization can be problematic as it is, because it would be absurd to assume that every single selected content will be conscious: that would make no sense in terms of the way the brain economizes its energy. Perhaps some mental diseases present a scenario in which a strong version may be applied though: an abnormal brain may process too much information at the same time, ignoring the spatiotemporal dynamics of the world and its impact to balance the brain activity and, in consequence, the conscious experience. That interpretation happens if you do a strong reading of the PF. However, if you avoid the stronger interpretation, a weaker version will follow: for every selected content (a1, a2, ..., an), there is a possibility that some of those contents will be consciously active. With this weaker version of the principle, we can make sense of why the PF is useful to show the caveat that consciousness represents to the PP framework.

The PF suggests therefore that the cognitive model of stimulus-induced activity as presupposed on the basis of the prediction model of brain cannot be extended to consciousness. The main lesson to be learnt here is that a purely cognitive model of consciousness is insufficient (on both empirical and conceptual grounds) as a way to explain what happens in bistable perception. In a nutshell: consciousness does not come with the contents but extends beyond contents and our cognition of them (cf. Northoff 2018: 150).

Thus, we argue that there must be an additional factor that allows the association of contents with consciousness rather than having them remain purely unconscious (even when selected). This will require an argument for a non-cognitive model of consciousness as the "noncognitive consciousness" proposed by Cerullo (cf. Cerullo et al. 2015) that introduces an additional dimension and thereby extends beyond the cognitive model. We finish the chapter arguing that such an additional dimension can be found in the spatiotemporal dynamics of the brain. This leads us to argue for a spatiotemporal model of consciousness (cf. Northoff and Huang 2017).[3]

3. Predictive Processing and Spatiotemporal Dynamics (Positive Argument)

As we tried to show, the only way that PP can account for consciousness is by committing what we call the Prediction Fallacy (section 2). As Figure 6.5 shows, PP can well account with the selection of content. However, it is problematic regarding the association of consciousness with the specific content selected by the predictive machine as claimed by Northoff:

> The interoceptive contents themselves do not yet entail the association of contents with consciousness—they can well remain as unconscious (as is most often the case in daily life) irrespective of whether they are (judged and detected and become aware as) accurate or inaccurate.
>
> (Northoff 2018: 45)

We argue, then, that the distinction between accurate/inaccurate contents and consciousness of contents is empirically supported by data that demonstrates how interoceptive accuracy and awareness can be dissociated from interoceptive sensitivity (consciousness) (cf. Garfinkel et al. 2015). If that's the case, the selected content (accurate or inaccurate) can always remain unconscious: there is simply no way to give an account of how the selected content is associated with consciousness without adding an extra dimension.

This dissociation between selected contents and consciousness also occurs with exteroceptive contents. Again, those contents can be accurate or inaccurate regarding the way the world is, but without an extra dimension the selected ones will remain independent of any association with consciousness. This is also supported by several different empirical data sets (see Faivre and Koch 2014, Koch and Tsuchiya 2012, Koch et al. 2016, Lamme 2010, Northoff and Huang 2017, Tsuchiya et al. 2015).

Consequently, we can argue that the independence between selected contents and consciousness of contents is supported for both intero (body) and exteroceptive (world) contents. The predicted input in, for example, perception, or the prediction error minimization process, can always remain an unconscious element of the system. Neither entails, at least in a pure PP explanation, any association of the selected contents with consciousness.

Northoff offers us the following example to show how relevant is this idea:

> When we drive our car along familiar routes, much of our perception of the route including the landscape along it will remain an unconscious element. That changes once some unknown not yet encountered obstacle, such as a street blockade due to an accident, occurs. In such a case, we may suddenly perceive the houses along the route in a conscious way and become aware that, for instance, there are some beautiful mansions.
>
> (Northoff 2018: 147)

This example shows us two important ideas: First, there is a change in content as it changes from the first model of the "road" (based on your *priori* information that the brain collected from previous travels) to the update of that model, considering now the street blockade caused by the accident. That process can be well explained by PP framework as the predicted input changes in the two scenarios. That, in turn, entails changes in the prediction error and subsequently the content that is consciously perceived.

Second, the example shows two different states, an unconscious one and a conscious one, that are associated with the two distinct contents. This raises the question of why the latter content, unlike the first one, goes along with a change from unconscious to consciousness. That, in our view, cannot be explained by the PP framework without committing the PF.

The dynamic temporo-spatial approach argues that, in addition to the changes in the prediction error and its associated contents, there are more changes in the second scenario: these temporo-spatial changes (see (7), (8), (9), and (10)) are central in allowing to associate content with consciousness. Accordingly, taken together, we have two distinct changes: (i) a cognitive-based, as related to the contents, and (ii) a dynamic-based, as related to the difference between unconscious and conscious states. In this sense, the dynamic approach does not exclude PP, but complements it by accounting for the association of contents with consciousness and by embedding the PP machinery into the world while still considering the active role of the brain.

The main assumption, then, is to argue that, factually, we know that most of the elements of the environment remain unconscious in our perception and cognition in general. Similarly to driving along a familiar route, most of the time the contents from our body, such as our heartbeat, remain unconscious entities. The PF ignores the fact that some of the contents associated with both predicted input and prediction error can remain unconscious by our nervous system. If it is factual that some of the information processing happening in your brain is unconscious—what we can call "unconscious processing" (cf. de Ouden et al. 2009, Kok et al. 2013, Vetter et al. 2014, Wacongne et al. 2011)—then the only way to ignore this is to commit the PF.

The main lesson to take home is that PP and the prediction model of brain can adequately account for the distinction between accuracy and inaccuracy of contents: (5) the selection problem is not a real problem for a PP framework. However, it is our view that a PP framework cannot sufficiently account for why and how contents (accurate and inaccurate) can be associated with consciousness rather than remaining as unconscious contents: (6) the association problem is a real problem and needs a different solution. Figure 6.6 sums up our main ideas:

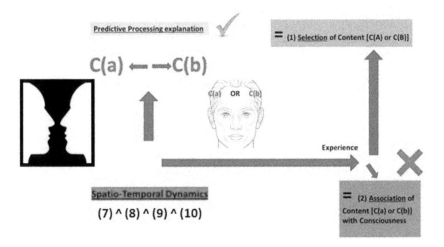

Figure 6.6 The selection and association problem in the PP framework.

Our hypothesis is then to defend that the PP framework needs to be embedded in a wider pre-predictive machinery framework that is based on the spatiotemporal dynamics of the world-body-brain relations.

The spatiotemporal theory of consciousness is based on the conjunction of four main concepts:

(7) Spatiotemporal nestedness (STN): the neuronal mechanism of STN accounts for the level or state of consciousness and it is related with the spontaneous activity of the brain that shows a multifaceted temporal organization of different temporal scales linked to each other. Experimentally, it can be tested with task-free/resting-state paradigms and it is associated with the neural predisposition of consciousness (NPC);

(8) Spatiotemporal alignment (STA): the neuronal mechanism of STA accounts for selecting the content and constituting the structure or form of consciousness and it is related with the prestimulus activity of the brain. Experimentally, it can be tested with prestimulus paradigms and it is associated with the neural prerequisite of consciousness (preNPC);

(9) Spatiotemporal expansion (STE): the neuronal mechanism of STE accounts for the phenomenal dimension of consciousness and it is related with the early stimulus-induced activity of the brain. Experimentally, it can be tested with poststimulus no-report paradigms and it is associated with the neural correlates of consciousness (NCC);

Finally,

(10) Spatiotemporal globalization (STG): the neuronal mechanism of STG accounts for the cognitive dimension of consciousness, the reporting of its contents, and it is related with the late stimulus-induced activity of the brain. Experimentally, it can be tested with poststimulus report paradigms and it is associated with the neural consequences of consciousness (NCCcon) (cf. Northoff 2018: 155).

As argued in section 2, consciousness goes beyond contents alone and needs additional dimensions or features. What might those be? In our view, they consist of the spatiotemporal mechanisms (7), (8), (9), and (10) that allow content (stimulus-based) to be associated with a phenomenal subjective experience (consciousness). Putting the PP machinery into the spatiotemporal dynamics of the relationship between the brain and the world, we do think we will have a better explanation to account for the conscious experience.[4]

4. Conclusion

We tried to show that consciousness cannot be solely determined by contents: it surpasses them. This is, in our view, empirically supported by showing that the neural mechanisms underlying these various cognitive functions do not sufficiently account for associating the cognitive functions and their contents with consciousness.

For that reason, any model of consciousness must extend beyond contents and cognition: that's the deflationary thesis proposed in this chapter that is independent from the positive argument. PP is a great first step against the traditional doctrine of the brain with a huge explanatory power. However, it may not be sufficient to handle the biggest problem of contemporary science: namely, to account for our subjective conscious experience. Toward that end, we proposed a positive argument based on the spatiotemporal dynamics of the brain.

We can, then, sum up both arguments as follows: The PP mechanisms are a necessary and eventually sufficient condition of the contents of consciousness; however, the PP mechanisms are not a sufficient condition for consciousness itself (negative argument). Therefore, a more spatiotemporal approach is needed that, in the gestalt of spatiotemporal dynamics, provides the sufficient condition of consciousness itself as distinct from its contents (positive argument).[5]

Notes

This work was generously funded by the Science and Technology Foundation (SFRH/BD/128863/2017). PhD Student at the University of Minho; visiting researcher at Minds, Brain Imaging and Neuroethics Unit, Royal Institute of Mental Health of the University of Minho; researcher of the Lisbon Mind & Reasoning Group (NOVA University of Lisbon); researcher of the Mind, Language and Action Group (University of Minho).

1   The idea of using this example is the following: when one first reads (a), (most) people don't notice that there is a mistake (the position of the "I" is in the wrong place in the sentence); after reading (b), one receives information about the fact that (a) is wrong, so in the second reading, your brain will notice the mistake and update the previous model of the sentence. In the first reading, you didn't really perceive the factual information in the world: your brain just guessed what could be there, based on prior information about English language and the assumptions that the author of the sentence knew English and wouldn't make a mistake. In the second reading, your brain had to go to the world to update its model in order to perceive the real sentence.

2   For a defense of the non-self view using the PP framework, see Letheby and Gerrans (2017). In the opposite direction, a defense of realism about the self can be found in Hohwy and Michael (2017).

3   One can accept the deflationary (negative) argument presented in the first part of the chapter (2. Predictive Processing and the Prediction Fallacy) without accepting the positive argumentation of the second part (3. Predictive Processing and Spatiotemporal Dynamics). Our main point is that we need an alternative model to account for consciousness. We will argue for a spatiotemporal model, but other models may be available.

4   Further detailed research will be done to specify how the spatiotemporal model of consciousness can account for the different world-brain relations (see, for example, Northoff et al. 2019).

5   I have presented preliminary versions of this chapter in different occasions: at the "Lisbon Mind & Reasoning Group Research in Progress Seminar," at the "Science of Consciousness Conference" (2019), at the "International Conference of Philosophy of Science—The Insides of Nature: Causalities, Causal Processes and Conceptions of Nature Borders," and at the "Seventh National Meeting in Analytic Philosophy." I would like to thank the audience whose questions significantly improved the chapter.

References

Anderson, M. L. and Chemero, T. (2013), "The Problem with Brain GUTs: Conflation of Different Senses of 'Prediction' Threatens Metaphysical Disaster," *Behavioral and Brain Sciences*, 36 (3): 204–5.

Bastos, A. M., Usrey, W. M., Adams, R. A., Mangun, G. R., Fries, P. and Friston, K. J. (2012), "Canonical Microcircuits for Predictive Coding," *Neuron*, 76 (4): 695–711.

Brodski, A., Paasch, G. F., Helbling, S. and Wibral, M. (2015), "The Faces of Predictive Coding," *The Journal of Neuroscience*, 35 (24): 8997–9006.

Cerullo, M. A., Metzinger, T. and Mangun, G. (2015), "The Problem with Phi: A Critique of Integrated Information Theory," *PLoS Computational Biology*, 11 (9): e1004286.

Clark, A. (2013a), "Whatever Next? Predictive Brains, Situated Agents, and the Future of Cognitive Science," *Behavioral and Brain Science*, 36: 181–253.

Clark, A. (2013b), "Are We Predictive Engines? Perils, Prospects, and the Puzzle of the Porous Perceiver," *Behavioral and Brain Sciences*, 36 (3): 233–53.

Clark, A. (2016), *Surfing Uncertainty: Prediction, Action and the Embodied Mind*, Oxford: Oxford University Press.

de Ouden, H. E., Friston, K. J., Daw, N. D., McIntosh, A. R. and Stephan, K. E. (2009), "A Dual Role for Prediction Error in Associative Learning," *Cerebral Cortex*, 19 (5): 175–1185.

Engel, A. K. and Singer, W. (2001), "Temporal Binding and the Neural Correlates of Sensory Awareness," *Trends in Cognitive Sciences*, 5 (1): 16–25.

Engel, A. K., Fries, P. and Singer, W. (2001), "Dynamic Predictions: Oscillations and Synchrony in Top-Down Processing," *Nature Reviews Neuroscience*, 2 (10): 704–16.

Faivre, N. and Koch, C. (2014), "Temporal Structure Coding with and without Awareness," *Cognition*, 131 (3): 404–14.

Friston, K. J. (2010), "The Free-Energy Principle: A Unified Brain Theory?" *Nature Reviews: Neuroscience*, 11: 127–38.

Garfinkel, S. N., Seth, A. K., Barrett, A. B., Suzuki, K. and Critchley, H. D. (2015), "Knowing Your Own Heart: Distinguishing Interoceptive Accuracy from Interoceptive Awareness," *Biological Psychology*, 104: 65–74.

Gregory, R. L. (1980), "Perceptions as Hypotheses," *Philosophical Transactions of the Royal Society of London. B, Biological Sciences*, 290 (1038): 181–97.

Gouveia, S. S. and Northoff, G. (2019), "A Neurophilosophical Approach to Perception" in D. Shottenkirk, M. Curado and S. Gouveia (eds.), *Perception, Cognition and Aesthetics*, New York: Routledge.

Hesselmann, G. et al. (2008), "Spontaneous Local Variations in Ongoing Neural Activity Bias Perceptual Decisions," *Proceedings of the National Academy of Sciences of USA*, 105 (31): 10984–9.

Hohwy, J. and Michael, J. (2017), "Why Should Any Body Have a Self?" in F. de Vignemont and A. J. T. Alsmith (eds.), *The Subject's Matter: Self-Consciousness and the Body*, Cambridge, MA: MIT Press.

Horn, B. K. P. (1980), "Derivation of Invariant Scene Characteristics From images," *Proceedings of the National Computer Conference*, 49: 371–6.

Kiefer, A. (2017), "Literal Perceptual Inference" in T. Metzinger and J. M. Windt (eds.), *Philosophy and Predictive Processing*, Frankfurt am Main: MIND Group.

Koch, C. and Tsuchiya, N. (2012), "Attention and Consciousness: Related yet Different," *Trends in Cognitive Sciences*, 16 (2): 103–5.

Koch, C. et al. (2016), "Neural Correlates of Consciousness: Progress and Problems," *Nature Reviews: Neuroscience*, 17 (5): 307–21.

Kok, P., Brouwer, G. J., van Gerven, M. A. and de Lange, F. P. (2013), "Prior Expectations Bias Sensory Representations in Visual Cortex," *Journal of Neuroscience*, 33 (41): 16275–16285.

Lamme, V. A. (2010), "How Neuroscience Will Change Our View on Consciousness," *Cognitive Neuroscience*, 1 (3): 204–20.

Letheby, C. and Gerrans, P. (2017), "Self Unbound: Ego Dissolution in Psychedelic Experience," *Neuroscience of Consciousness*, 2017 (1): nix016.

Marr, D. (1982), *Vision: A Computational Investigation into the Human Representation and Processing of Visual Information*, San Francisco, CA: W. H. Freeman.

Northoff, G. (2018), *The Spontaneous Brain*, Cambridge: MIT Press.

Northoff, G. and Huang, Z. (2017), "How Do the Brain's Time and Space Mediate Consciousness and Its Different Dimensions? Temporo-Spatial Theory of Consciousness (TTC)," *Neuroscience and Biobehavioral Reviews*, 80: 630–45.

Northoff, G., Wainio-Theberge, S. and Evers, C. (2019), "Is Temporo-spatial Dynamics the 'Common Currency' of Brain and Mind? In Quest of 'Spatiotemporal Neuroscience,'" *Physics Life Reviews*. doi.org/10.1016/j.plrev.2019.05.002.

Ning, Z. (2019), "Representing the World with Occam's Razor: An Informational Teleosemantics on the Basis Predictive Processing Paradigm" in S. Gouveia and M. Curado (eds.), *Automata's Inner Movie: Science and Philosophy of Mind*, Wilmington, DE: Vernon Press.

Sadaghiani, S. et al. (2010), "The Relation of Ongoing Brain Activity, Evoked Neural Responses, and Cognition," *Frontiers in Systems Neuroscience*, 4 (20): 1–14.

Seth, A. K. (2013), "Interoceptive Inference, Emotion, and the Embodied Self," *Trends in Cognitive Sciences*, 17 (11): 565–73.

Seth, A. K. (2017), "The Cybernetic Bayesian Brain: From Interoceptive Inference to Sensorimotor Contingencies" in T. Metzinger and J. M. Windt (eds.), *Philosophy and Predictive Processing*, Frankfurt am Main: MIND Group.

Suzuki, K., Garfinkel, S., Critchley, H. D. and Seth, A. K. (2013), "Multisensory Integration Across Exteroceptive and Interoceptive Domains Modulates Self-experience in the Rubber-hand Illusion," *Neuropsychologia*, 51 (13): 2909–17.

Tsuchiya, N., Block, N. and Koch, C. (2012), "Top-Down Attention and Consciousness: Comment on Cohen et al.," *Trends in Cognitive Sciences*, 16 (11): 527.

Tsuchiya, N., Wilke, M., Frässle, S. and Lamme, V. A. (2015), "No-report Paradigms: Extracting the True Neural Correlates of Consciousness," *Trends in Cognitive Sciences*, 19 (12): 757–70.

Vetter, P., Sanders, L. L. and Muckli, L. (2014), "Dissociation of Prediction from Conscious Perception," *Perception*, 43 (10): 1107–13.

Von Helmholtz, H. (1867), *Handbuch der physiologischen Optik*, Leipzig: Leopold Voss.

Wacongne, C. et al., (2011), "Evidence for a Hierarchy of Predictions and Prediction Errors in Human Cortex," *Proceedings of the National Academy of Sciences of the USA*, 108 (51): 20754–9.

Wanja, W. and Metzinger, T. (2017), "Vanilla PP for Philosophers: A Primer on Predictive Processing" in T. Metzinger and J. M. Windt (eds.), *Philosophy and Predictive Processing*, Frankfurt am Main: MIND Group.

7

The Many Faces of Attention: Why Precision Optimization Is Not Attention

Madeleine Ransom
Indiana University Bloomington, Department of Cognitive Science
Sina Fazelpour
Carnegie Mellon University, Department of Philosophy

1. Introduction

Predictive coding in its most general form is the view that a process reduces the amount of information that needs to be stored or transmitted by utilizing predictions. This reduction of information is often understood in terms of prediction error; the process represents only the difference between the predicted and actual input instead of representing the input directly.[1] It thus presupposes that the process employs a generative model: there must be a way to generate predictions so that they can be compared to incoming input, as well as a way to update these predictions in light of prediction error.

Predictive coding as it has been developed by Karl Friston (2008, 2009, 2010), and adopted by philosophers such as Andy Clark (2013a, 2015) and Jakob Hohwy (2012, 2013), is claimed to be a grand unifying theory of all cognitive functioning, though it has been most thoroughly developed as a theory of perception. Predictive coding combines the idea of transmitting only prediction error and using a generative model to make predictions with two other key concepts: Bayesian inference and a hierarchically structured model.[2] From here on, we shall refer to this combination of concepts as predictive coding (PC), and it is PC that our discussion and criticism here applies to.

The generative model as it is conceived of by PC is a model of the world—objects, forces and their interactions, people and their mental states. Possessing an internal generative model is key to addressing the problem our perceptual systems face: they must infer the distal causes (things out in the world) of sensory input, but there is not a one to one mapping between these two. The same sensory input could be caused by distinct objects, and a single object could produce different sensory inputs. A model generates hypotheses as to the potential distal causes of sensory input, and it also constrains the hypothesis space by limiting the sorts of hypotheses that can be generated.

Bayesian inference provides guidance on how to update hypotheses in light of new information. On Bayesian inference, the totality of the hypotheses produced by the generative model is the hypothesis space, with each hypothesis assigned a subjective prior probability. We also generate hypotheses of the likelihood of a given sensory input given certain worldly conditions. Upon receipt of sensory input, Bayesian conditionalization is used to update prior probabilities assigned to each hypothesis.

Due to computational intractability, the brain cannot implement a Bayesian model of the complexity needed to explain perceptual and mental processes. In light of this, PC holds that the brain instead approximates such inference by giving the generative model a hierarchical structure. The model is envisioned as being composed of distinct levels, each concerned with generating and updating predictions about the world. Higher-level hypotheses will tend to be more global predictions, which will then generate and constrain predictions at lower levels of the hierarchy. For example, a high-level prediction might be that there is a cat on a mat, and lower levels will concern the texture of the cat's fur, the color of the mat, and so on (Hohwy 2013: 27).

Putting all of these concepts together, the emerging picture (for perceptual inference) is as follows: We possess an internal model of the world that allows us to generate high-level hypotheses about the distal causes of sensory data, which in turn generate lower-level sub-hypotheses in a descending hierarchical fashion, with the more fine-grained perceptual details relegated to the bottom levels. These hypotheses are then compared to the incoming sensory data. When there is a mismatch, a prediction error is produced. These errors are the only feedforward or "bottom-up" signals propagated through the hierarchy—unresolved prediction error gets sent up to the next level, where the higher-level hypothesis is revised in a Bayesian fashion until prediction error is successfully minimized.[3] The hypotheses with the least prediction error are those selected to represent the world as we see it. This iterative process of hypothesis generation and prediction error minimization is taken to be a parsimonious and unified account of the functioning of all cognitive phenomena, including thought. Prediction error minimization is "all the brain ever does" (Hohwy 2013: 7).

A problem for PC as laid out thus far is that it must discern between noise and prediction error. When a model generates a predictive hypothesis, it isn't expected that it will fit the data exactly—there will always be some data points that don't behave according to the model's predictions. This is a problem because there are two ways data can fail to fit the hypothesis. The first is that the data is noise. In this case, the model should not be revised to accommodate these extra data points because this would lead to less accurate predictions and therefore less accurate representation of the external world. The second is that such data are legitimate prediction error. In this case, the model should be revised in light of this extra data because this will lead to more accurate predictions and so more accurate perceptual representations. The problem of uncertainty is how to discern between the two cases—when should the model be revised in light of the data, and when should it be ignored?

In order to address this problem, PC introduces second-order statistics into the model. While the measurement of prediction errors involves comparing the means of two probability distributions, expected precision is a measurement of the variance of the data about the mean. This is a measure of how reliable, or precise, we take the prediction error signal to be in a given context: how likely is it in a given situation that the incongruent data constitutes legitimate prediction error as opposed to noise? Noise in the world is context-dependent—in different contexts there will be more or less noise woven into signal. Listening to your friend's story in a deserted café is quite different from the experience of listening to her at a noisy party. However, one can begin to predict how much noise to expect in a given context on the basis of learned statistical regularities. In this way, we form precision expectations. We come to expect prediction error to be more or less precise in a given context, and so either trust it in revising the relevant hypothesis or discount it as noise and so refrain from revising the hypothesis.

Synaptic gain is thought to be the neural mechanism that encodes precision in the brain (Friston 2008). On PC, when prediction error is expected to be reliable this results in the gain on that prediction error being amplified, and so passed up the hierarchy to the level above it, where it is used to revise the hypothesis until it can successfully minimize the error, usually an iterative process. When a prediction error is expected to be unreliable, this results in the opposite effect—the prediction error is suppressed, or dampened. In this case the prediction error does not initiate revision of the hypothesis that generated it. Given that the total gain on prediction error must always sum to one, expected precisions drive selective processing by weighting some prediction errors over others (Hohwy 2012: 8). Such selectivity is often thought to be the functional role of attention, and so provides the basis for the PC theory of attention.

The PC theory of attention proposed by Friston (2009) and Feldman and Friston 2010) and defended by Hohwy (2012, 2013) and Clark (2013a, 2015) is that "attention is simply the process of optimizing precision during hierarchical inference" (Friston 2009: 299).

Given the goal of minimizing prediction error, the optimal way in which to revise perceptual hypotheses is on the basis of the prediction errors with the highest expected precisions. Expending effort on prediction errors likely containing high noise levels will lead to suboptimal perceptual results. Better to focus on the signals that are more likely to lead to improvements in the model—the reliable signals.

Attention then falls out directly from the PC account of perception. There is no machinery involved in the process over and above that which is needed to account for perceptual inference. On this picture attention has the functional role of guiding perceptual inference by directing processing resources toward the prediction errors with the higher expected precisions given a context. Again, this results in the minimization of prediction error, though attention is concerned only with expected precision of prediction error and not directly with the accuracy of hypotheses. However, because the estimation of expected precisions is a fundamental aspect of perceptual inference, then so is attention.

While there are overarching theories of attention that provide a unitary explanation of the phenomenon in terms of cognitive unison (Mole 2011), selection for action (Wu 2014), or some type of prioritizing activity (Watzl 2017), there are nevertheless important differences between different varieties of attention. There is a phenomenological difference between having your attention grabbed by a loud explosion on the street, and deciding to attend to the words on this page. Empirical researchers have also identified substantive behavioral and neural differences between different kinds of attention, such as time course and involved brain regions (Carrasco 2011, Posner 2011). In order for the PC claim that attention is the optimization of precision expectations to go through, then it must be able to accommodate all varieties of attentional phenomena. Here we review those varieties that have been given the most thorough treatment in the PC literature. The primary focus of PC has been on explaining both sides of a canonical division of attention into endogenous and exogenous processes (Posner 1980).

Exogenous attention is an automatic orienting response to environmental stimuli. Intuitively, it is when attention is captured by some object or state of affairs that the agent was not already previously searching for. It can thus be described in terms of task relevance: while the object in question is irrelevant to the task the agent is currently performing, it nevertheless captures her attention. This is thought to occur sometimes due to contextually mediated perceptual salience—whether something is salient or not will depend upon the context it is presented in. A neon pink circle against a white backdrop catches the eye; against a neon pink backdrop it does not.

The PC account of exogenous attention is as follows. First, one's generative model must formulate a hypothesis about a region of space or an object that one is not currently attending to (or that is not the main focus of attention). Note that because attention sets the gain on prediction error, there will therefore be a low gain on the prediction error generated for unattended or peripherally attended regions or objects. Second, the presentation of a stimulus such as a sudden noise, light, or movement results in an abrupt and large prediction error. Third, the gain on this prediction error will be amplified. This is because of a learned statistical regularity (precision expectation) that in our sort of environment any change in variability due to noise is rather slow and small, so the abrupt onset of the signal itself is taken as an indication of its high precision (Hobson and Friston 2012: 92, Hohwy 2013: 197). Given this precision expectation, the gain or amplitude of the already large prediction error will be enhanced; this amounts to paying attention to the stimulus. Fourth, attention will then cause the hypothesis to be revised preferentially in light of this prediction error.

In endogenous attention, the object or spatial region of attention is to some degree directed by the agent, usually according to a purpose or task. Empirical studies of attention, including those conducted within PC, tend to operationalize endogenous attention as task relevance (Chennu et al. 2013, Jiang et al. 2013, Kok et al. 2011). PC explains endogenous attention by positing that we have learned precision expectations that guide such endogenous shifts. Consider the classic Posner paradigm (Posner 1980), which is a cueing task that investigates how covert attention can facilitate stimulus detection. In one common version of the task an arrow provides a spatial cue as to where the stimulus will likely appear. Through repeated trials the subject learns that when an arrow is shown pointing to a given area on a computer screen, an object will likely appear in that area. This learned statistical regularity is a contextually mediated precision expectation: when there is an arrow pointing toward a given location, the prediction error that will subsequently be produced by the appearance of the object in that location is expected to be precise, or reliable. When an arrow appears on the screen, pointing to the bottom right corner, this causes the gain from the prediction error issuing from this region to be increased (this is tantamount to saying that one pays attention to the bottom right corner). As a consequence, when the stimulus appears it is perceived more rapidly.

With these explanations of exogenous and endogenous attention on the table, we can begin to build our criticism. In section 2 we argue that the weighting of prediction error based on expected precisions is too narrow a phenomenon to be identified with attention, because it cannot accommodate the full range of attentional phenomena. We review criticisms that PC cannot account for volitional attention and affect-biased attention, and we propose that it also cannot account for intellectual attention and feature-based attention. In section 3 we argue that the precision weighting of prediction error is too broad a phenomenon to be identified with attention because such weighting plays a central role in multimodal integration.

2. PC Theory of Attention Is too Narrow

The varieties of attentional phenomena are richer than a simple bipartite division into endogenous and exogenous attention. Indeed, the very usefulness of this dichotomy in the face of empirical research has come under question (Awh et al. 2012, Todd and Manaligod 2018). Even operating with the division in place, however, further distinctions can be made between spatial, object, and feature-based attention, as well as overt and covert attention, among others (Carrasco 2011, Mole 2011, Wu 2014). In what follows, we don't cover the full range of divisions that have been made, but instead focus on those that have been flagged as problematic for PC—affect-biased attention and volitional attention—and then propose that intellectual attention and feature-based attention are also problematic.

2.1 Affect-biased Attention

Affect-biased attention is attention to stimuli that are affectively salient in virtue of their association with reward or punishment (Markovic et al. 2014, Mather and Sutherland 2011, Rolls 2000, Todd and Manaligod 2018, Vuilleumier 2015). As Ransom et al. (2020) point out, it is not straightforwardly categorized as exogenous attention because affectively salient objects can succeed in capturing attention in spite of a lack of physical salience (Anderson et al. 2011, 2012, Anderson 2013, Anderson and Yantis 2013, Della Libera and Chelazzi 2009, Hickey Chelazzi and Theeuwes 2010, Niu et al. 2012, Shomstein and Johnson 2013). Neither does it sit comfortably in the category of endogenous attention, given that affectively salient objects also capture attention when they are not task relevant (Awh et al. 2012, Todd et al. 2012).

The principle criticism that Ransom et al. (2020) raise, however, is that precision expectations and affective salience are dissociable. There will be occasions upon which we will have low-precision expectations for prediction errors generated by a given hypothesis, but where the potential rewards or punishment is significant enough that we ought nevertheless to attend. For example, if you are hiking in the Pacific

Northwest, a rustle in the bush is most likely caused by wind or a bird, but there is a small chance it could be a large predator such as a cougar or bobcat. In such cases, the cost of getting it wrong is so high that one ought to attend, regardless of the fact that prediction error generated by the movement in the grass is likely best dismissed as noise. Examples such as these suggest that it is not just the expected precision of the prediction error, but also the value or affective salience of the object that ought to drive attention. Affective salience thus constitutes an independent source of influence, one that is not assimilable to precision expectations (see also Colombo and Wright 2017, Gershman and Daw 2012).

2.2. Volitional Attention

While endogenous attention is driven by learned statistical regularities pertaining to the external environment, sometimes we attend to things out of will or whimsy. If I make up my mind to pay attention to the tree outside my window, or the bare wall of my office, then I am generally able to do so. This ability isn't well captured by the above account of endogenous attention, where the top-down cueing is still relatively automatic, and is based on an external prompt. One pays attention to the spatial region indicated by the arrow without deciding to do so in any substantive, volitional sense. In order to account for volitional attention, Hohwy invokes active inference (2013: 197–9).

Active inference is meant to explain how and why it is that we perform intentional actions, using the explanatory tools of PC. Rather than mere passive perceivers, we move through our environment and act so as to change it. On PC, this is the result of generating a counterfactual hypothesis (where the content is the desired state of the organism), and then acting in the world to bring about the desired state and so minimize prediction error with respect to the hypothesis. While both perceptual and active inference have the goal of minimizing predictive error, in perceptual inference the hypothesis is revised on the basis of the prediction error, and in active inference the hypothesis is held fixed and the agent's position in the world is altered such that the resulting incoming sensory data aligns with the hypothesis. This prediction error will be in part proprioceptive—it will pertain to one's sense of one's body position in space.

For example, suppose you are currently sitting in your armchair and, given your desire to go look out the window, you generate the counterfactual hypothesis that you are standing at the window. This generates a large prediction error—you are in fact presently sitting, not standing. The way in which you will minimize prediction error is then by plotting a course of action, again using a generative hierarchical model to formulate hypotheses about the best route to take and to monitor the movement process such that prediction error with respect to course is also minimized. So you implicitly plan to take the direct path to the window by putting one foot in front of the other, and should you run into an unexpected obstacle, such as a computer extension cord, you can avoid it (minimize prediction error with respect to your plan of action) by lifting your foot higher than normal to step over it. Finally, after countless Bayesian calculations, you arrive at your goal of looking out the window. This results in a minimization of the prediction error with respect to the counterfactual hypothesis— you are now in the location you desired to be in.

Active inference is well suited to explain volitional endogenous attention because this involves a decision or desire on the part of the agent to act, though it is "a slightly unusual instance of action because the way we change our relation to the world is to increase the sensory gain in one region of space" (Hohwy 2013: 198). However, if a unitary explanation of attention is to be offered, and active inference constitutes some cases of attention, then it too must be explicable in terms of expected precisions.

The PC account of volitional attention is as follows: when we make the decision to attend to a certain spatial region, this decision functions much like the arrow cue in the Posner case—our decision causes us to expect a high-precision stimulus to occur in the relevant spatial region. This is so in virtue of a learned statistical regularity: when we choose to attend to a given region, high-precision stimuli are often detected there. Just as in the Posner case, gain from this region is then enhanced, which is tantamount to attending to it. This speeds subsequent detection of any object at the location.

Against this proposal, Ransom et al. (2017) have argued that volitional attention is not satisfactorily accommodated by PC theory of attention. This is because this same type of regularity holds for *any* stimulus whatsoever. If I decide to attend to the wall of my office, I enhance the precision of prediction errors associated with the wall. If I decide to attend to the tiny bit of lint stuck to my sweater, I get a similar result. Indeed, it is a trivial observation, and one which is taken as a datum by any account of attention: more often than not, attending to a stimulus results in enhanced precision of the signal arriving from that stimulus. The precision enhancement of such an act is a "self-fulfilling prophecy" for just about anything we decide to look at. With this in mind, precision expectations cannot be what drive attention in such cases because we will have equivalent precision expectations for all objects regardless of whether we desire to shift our attention to them. Thus, in instances such as this the optimization of precision expectations cannot be identified with attention. What really seems to be driving our attention in this case is our antecedent desire to attend, not the precision expectation.

Clark (2017) has responded to this criticism, arguing that it can be addressed through a proper appreciation of PC's recasting of desires as beliefs. This assimilation is an endorsement of what Clark has termed elsewhere "desert landscape" theories of PC (Clark 2013a). It is required in order to make good on the claim that PC is a unified theory of all cognitive functioning. On this theory, desires are understood using the PC account of active inference, as explained briefly above. They are hypotheses that are currently false of the world, but can be made true through action (Friston et al. 2011). In this sense, all (realizable) desires are self-fulfilling prophecies on PC. On this account the sorts of desires involved in volitional attention are just more of the same, and so not problematic. While there is no alteration of precision estimations out in the world, the formulation of the desire (hypothesis) together, perhaps, with changes in interoceptive context (Clark 2017: 118) are sufficient to alter the precision expectations for that hypothesis.

However, this response does not address the point that mental actions are importantly different from physical actions in that they are not resolved by minimizing proprioceptive prediction error (see Ransom et al. 2017: 109). The problem can be made clearer by considering covert attention. Covert attention is attending to a stimulus without saccading toward it. Covert attention can be voluntary. This is easy to experience: simply keep your gaze fixated on a point in front of you, and shift only your attention to some object off to the side—a lamp or a door perhaps. It stands in contrast to overt attention, which involves shifting one's gaze and saccading to the thing or area one is interested in. Lest covert attention seem like a fringe form of attention, it has been found to precede and guide the eye movements involved in overt attention in a variety of everyday tasks—the phenomenon is ubiquitous (Carrasco 2011).

Endogenous or volitional covert attention is a pure mental adjustment of attention; it does not involve changes in the physical position of the body. This makes it unlike other cases of desire fulfillment, because there is no proprioceptive prediction error. When I desire to drink a cup of tea, a proprioceptive and perceptual prediction error is generated because I am not in fact doing so. When I desire to attend to the lamp at the periphery of my vision, keeping my eyes locked on the page in front of me, there is no corresponding proprioceptive prediction error.

It is also not clear that there are perceptual prediction errors in some cases of covert attentional shifts. If I am attending to the words on the page but desire to attend to the lamp on the corner of my desk that is still in the periphery of my vision, then the (counterfactual) perceptual hypothesis will be something like "I am looking at my lamp." But it's already true that I perceive the lamp; it's in my field of vision. So the hypothesis is more adequately described as "I am attending to the lamp." This is false, and so "desire-like" in the sense required to initiate active inference, but it's unclear both whether this hypothesis is perceptual (because we are already perceiving the lamp), and what it would mean to expect the prediction error generated by this hypothesis to be precise (because it seems to be a first-order attentional hypothesis, and so it is bizarre to think we have precision expectations for attention).

In summary, if PC analyzes volitional attention in terms of active inference, then precision expectations will pertain in part to proprioceptive prediction errors. However, in the case of covert voluntary attention there are no such prediction errors, and it is not clear whether there are perceptual prediction errors in all such cases.

Clark also responds to Ransom, Fazelpour, and Mole's criticism by suggesting that the attentional shifts involved in mental action are no more mysterious than how desires are produced in the first place.

> Whatever set of personal and environmental circumstances might conspire to install or suddenly foreground a desire (for example, the desire to attend to a [particular object]), those same circumstances are now called upon to install or suddenly foreground the behaviorally-equivalent belief.
>
> (Clark 2017: 118)

So, if other models of volitional attention have a preferred explanation that cites the relevant set of personal and environmental circumstances, the PC theorist can simply re-formulate that explanation in terms of a precision-concerning belief. And if the alternative accounts lack such an explanation, then surely we cannot view the lack of an explanation as a shortcoming of the PC account in particular.

However, claiming that there can be a post-hoc reformulation of every explanation into the formalism of PC framework is one thing. Demonstrating that a satisfactory model of attention—capable of yielding novel predictions and explanations—emerges from the PC framework using only the explanatory tools of PC is quite another thing. Given the generality of PC's formalism, the first claim is rather trivial. The challenge for the PC theorists, therefore, is to provide evidence for the second claim. This challenge is not addressed by Clark's response to Ransom, Fazelpour, and Mole's criticism.

2.3. Intellectual Attention

We have complex inner lives made up of deliberations, ruminations, mind-wanderings, memories, and imaginings, and we often attend to what goes on within. Here we will call attention to thought, broadly construed "intellectual attention" (Fortney, forthcoming). Intellectual attention can occur simultaneously with perception—one needn't close one's eyes in order to pay attention to one's thoughts. The picture is rendered more complicated insofar as sometimes these shifts are exogenous and sometimes they are endogenous—sometimes we decide to pay attention to our thoughts and sometimes our attention is drawn involuntarily inwards. A complete theory of attention should be able to account for these shifts between our inner and outer lives, as well as the shifts between different sorts of mental activities, such as when task-directed thought morphs into rumination. The PC theory of attention has had little to say so far about intellectual attention, but extrapolating from their treatment of perceptual attention, the proposal would be that we pay attention to our thoughts, imaginings, or memories when we expect them to be precise. This might take the form of a large abrupt prediction error, as in the case of exogenous attention. Perhaps the sudden thought that one has left the stove on at home is like this. Or, we may turn our attention relatively deliberately to our thoughts after an external prompt we have learned to reliably associate with our own mental activity, as with endogenous attention. A friend asks, "*What was the name of the author of Don Quixote?*" Searching for the answer to this question is accompanied by a phenomenal shift inwards—we expect to retrieve the name from memory, if anywhere.[4]

Here the challenge for the PC theory is to explain the attentional shifts in terms of precision expectations—it must provide an explanation of what sorts of regularities drive the formation of precision expectations for thoughts. This project will rest on providing an adequate theory of how thoughts—the objects of intellectual attention—are generated in the first place. This is no small task. Recall the fundamental role that sensory feedback systems play in hypothesis revision for perceptual and active inference. In the case of perception, the world serves as the hidden cause of the sensory effects that drive perceptual hypothesis revision. Perceptions are predictions of the sensory effects of the world, prediction errors tell us when our predictions are off, and precision expectations tell us whether we should alter our predictions to resolve the prediction error or not. Without a hidden cause that produces the sensory effects that provide feedback to the model, the hypothesis generation process stands uncorrected, and the model becomes "top-heavy," producing ever-wilder hypotheses without revisions. In the perceptual case, this results in visual hallucinations. What then—if anything—serves as the hidden cause in the case of the mental, constraining our thoughts and preventing them from being anything other than pure fantastical fabrications?

While some of our stranger thoughts and imaginings might be well explained by the relative lack of bottom-up prediction error, we also create other more "grounded" thoughts that stay on track, or have some relatively stable connection with the world. PC may be able to explain some of these more grounded thoughts and imaginings in terms of offline proprioceptive simulations that have been used to account for long-term planning. Clark (2013b) follows Friston et al. (2011) in suggesting that precision weighting may play a role in allowing us to run simulations of future actions without actually carrying them out. By assigning a low weighting to the prediction error from lower levels of the motor system, one can simulate carrying out some action without actually bringing it about.

The precision weighting of prediction error will also likely play a role in explaining how it is that we shift between different kinds of mental activities. Clark (2013b: 5–6) follows Daw et al. (2005) in employing precision-weighted prediction error to explain how we switch from model-based to model-free decision strategies (roughly, strategies that directly involve drawing on the resources of the generative model posited by PC to problem-solve and those that involve only learning action-value pairings directly). When we are confronted with a given problem, there may be multiple competing neural resources that are employed to formulate different action plans. Which of these plans is selected will be determined by which has the highest expected precisions.

Perhaps a similar story can be told for other varieties of thought: for example, we may come to trust the deliverances of memory over imagining in some contexts. This picture would need to explain how it is that our thoughts are sometimes derailed by other systems in a given context. For example, goal-directed thought, such as trying to understand the point an author is making in a philosophical paper, may devolve into mind-wandering over time (Christoff 2012).

At this point, intellectual attention and understanding our mental lives more generally in terms of PC constitute not so much a problem for PC but rather an unexplored frontier. Whether PC theory can accommodate intellectual attention, and the full range of mental phenomena, will depend on details that have yet to be specified. However, the role that affective salience likely plays in directing our attention inwards suggests that the same issue that was raised for perceptual attention in section 2.1 will recur here. Consider again the thought that you may have left the stove on. Supposing that you are not in general a forgetful person, then it's unlikely that this is the case. But the consequences of having left the stove on are potentially dire, and so it seems that the thought ought to capture our attention regardless of low associated precision expectations. If this is right, then intellectual attention may also be driven by affective salience independently of precision expectations.

2.4. Feature-based Attention

Within the category of endogenous attention, several theorists make a further distinction between spatial attention and feature-based attention (Carrasco 2011, Egner et al. 2008, Rossi and Paradiso 1995). We can attend to a given spatial region due to some learned regularity such as that an arrow cue predicts that something will appear in a given location. Or, we can attend to a given feature of an object because we have learned that it provides relevant information, such as when we attend to the eyes and mouth areas of a person in order to assess their emotional state. Feature-based attention guides visual search, such as when while waiting for a friend we look for particular features that may distinguish her from the crowd (e.g., her height, the color of her jacket, and so on).

In the Posner paradigm described above, the arrow cue does not predict which object with what type of features will appear (unless a hypothesis has been formed for this as well via conditioning, such as that dots are likely to appear after arrow cues). However, Hohwy claims that the same sort of explanation given for spatial endogenous attention can be applied to feature-based endogenous attention (2013: 196). In such cases, we can focus our attention on particular features of an object in a scene. Supposing we are looking to identify all the red apples in a barrel, or all the people with red and white striped shirts in a crowd. Feature-based endogenous attention allows us to do so quickly and efficiently, even if the spatial location of these features is not well predicted. How might this work? It is crucial that it do so, as many cases of endogenous attention are those involving searches for certain features or objects over others. However, it is unclear how the account is supposed to go, given that attention must be driven by expected precisions.

To illustrate the problem that arises for the PC account, take the case of searching for one's keys. What are the relevant precision expectations driving attention? They cannot be spatial—one doesn't have high expected precision for any particular spatial region (beyond a few general expectations, such as that one's lost keys typically won't be found hanging from the ceiling). They are also not happily described as proprioceptive prediction errors—while it is true that some cases of endogenous attention are well described in terms of active inference, feature-based attention needn't involve any physical action on the part of the agent. Feature-based attention operates independently of spatial attention, and can "highlight" a given feature regardless of where it appears in the visual field (Carrasco 2011: 1507).

The relevant precision expectations must then be for perceptual prediction errors. In accordance with this, Hohwy (2015) explains feature-based attention as follows: "When the system endogenously attends to an as yet unseen feature, the precision of prediction error for that feature is expected to be high, which causes increased gain for that prediction error."

However, the issue in this case is that the visual system must first locate the relevant feature in order to apply the perceptual hypothesis, and only then can the gain be enhanced for that prediction error. One cannot enhance the gain on a prediction error that has not yet been generated, and the way to generate prediction error is to test one's hypothesis against the incoming sensory data. Moreover, the perceptual hypothesis must be applied selectively to the scene, because applying it indiscriminately to all objects would result in larger prediction errors being generated for all items that are not those items one is looking for, and as a consequence would result in an attentional pattern that is the inverse of what is seen in feature-based attention.

Bowman et al. (2013) raise a related worry for the PC account of endogenous attention:

What makes attention so adaptive is that it can guide towards an object at an unpredictable location—simply on the basis of features. For example, we could ask the reader to find the nearest word printed in bold. Attention will typically shift to one of the headers, and indeed momentarily increase precision there, improving reading. But this makes precision weighting a *consequence* of attending. At least as interesting is the mechanism *enabling* stimulus selection in the first place. The brain has to first deploy attention before a precision advantage can be realized for that deployment.

(207, emphasis original)

This criticism rests in part on a failure to appreciate the difference between precision expectations and the consequent precision weighting of prediction error. The former will determine the latter, and so high-precision expectations for the relevant feature are what guide attention to it. Nevertheless, there is still a question as to how precision expectations can guide attention when the spatial location of the object is not known. Contrasting this with spatial endogenous attention is instructive. In such cases precision expectations drive us to look in the right place, and so speed stimulus detection. Expecting precise prediction error from a perceptual hypothesis that has not yet been applied to a scene is different. In itself it does nothing to help select the relevant features. It is useful to consider Clark's response to Bowman et al.'s worry in detail. He writes, employing the example of looking for a four-leaf clover:

The resolution of this puzzle lies, I suggest, in the potential assignment of precision-weighting at many different levels of the processing hierarchy. Feature-based attention corresponds, intuitively, to increasing the gain on the prediction error units associated with the identity or configuration of a stimulus (e.g. increasing the gain on units responding to the distinctive geometric pattern of a four-leaf clover). Boosting that response (by giving added weight to the relevant kind of sensory prediction error) should enhance detection of that featural cue. Once the cue is provisionally detected, the subject can fixate the right spatial region, now under conditions of "four-leaf-clover-there" expectation. Residual error is then amplified for that feature at that location, and high confidence in the presence of the four-leaf clover can (if you are lucky!) be obtained.

(Clark 2013a: 238)

While this addresses the problem insofar as one accepts that "provisional detection" can guide attention, it raises the issue of how provisional detection is accomplished in PC. It too must function according to the same process of top-down hypothesis generation and revision, if PC is to be explanatorily complete. Perhaps provisional detection can be understood along the lines of "gist perception" (see Clark 2015: 163–4, Hohwy 2012: 2). Bar (2003) holds that perception is facilitated by the ability to first generate a prediction of the "gist" of the scene or object using low spatial frequency visual information that results in a basic-level categorization of the object's likely identity (see also Bar et al. 2001, Barrett and Bar 2009, Oliva and Torralba 2001, Schyns and Oliva 1994, Torralba and Oliva 2003). This then allows for the more fine-grained details to be filled in using the basic-level categorization as a guide. The idea here is that such basic-level categorization could guide selective application of the clover hypothesis, ensuring that it be applied only to objects that have the coarse-grained features of four-leaf clovers. This would then guide attention to the relevant spatial locations, privileging perceptual processing of these areas.

To be sure, the range of visual features that can be provisionally detected with this sort of gist perception is limited to what can be extracted from low spatial frequency information, namely, shapes and configurations (and so will exclude features like colors). Even with respect to these types of features, however, such a proposal is only a solution if the basic-level categorization itself is the result of PC, and here it is unclear as to whether the "gist" is constructed using the PC hierarchical framework. It certainly does not rely on high-level hypotheses such as "clover." Constructing the gist of a scene or object would rather be reliant on lower-level properties such as shape. It is then a further question whether such properties are detected in a feedforward model inconsistent with PC, or predicted in a feedback model consistent with PC. For example, rather than construing gist perception as an essential component of object recognition, Bar (2003) takes it to merely facilitate the process. Gist perception only reduces the time it takes to categorize an object, except perhaps in cases where the object is highly occluded or camouflaged. Bar (2003: 7) points to studies of patients with frontal cortex lesions as support for the ability of recognition to take place in a wholly bottom-up manner. Given Bar's own commitment to bottom-up processing it remains to be seen whether or not gist perception provides a solution to the problem at hand.

We can make the same point by examining more closely some other ways of modeling the top-down influence of expectations on visual search.[5] A central notion in many accounts of visual search is that of topographically organized "feature maps," which consist of neurons that respond to the same feature at different locations across the visual field (Humphreys and Mavritsaki 2012: 59). Activity in a given feature map indicates the presence of that feature at a particular location in the visual field. The activity of different feature maps is subsequently integrated in a central location map.

Given this setup, expectations about what some desired target looks like can guide the search by modulating the activity of different feature maps. In Wolfe's (1994) Guided Search model, for example, expectation for the particular features possessed by a target (e.g., its particular shape and color) pre-activates the corresponding feature maps. Thanks to this selective boosting, when the activity of various feature maps are integrated together in the central location map, spatial locations occupied by stimuli possessing the sought-after features exhibit heightened activity. This allows the spatial locations to be ordered in terms of their salience to the search, thus enabling an effective means for selecting the location of the desired target. In addition to this type of *target pre-activation*, there is evidence that similar effects are achieved by means of *non-target suppression*, where the activity of the feature maps associated with non-targets are selectively inhibited (Watson and Humphreys 1997).

On the face of it, the PC model of feature-based attention seems to fit neatly with the above account of visual search. In the case of the PC model, the expectation for features of the target is formulated in terms of an expectation that the precision of the prediction errors for those features is going to be high. What is more, preferentially increasing the gain on that prediction error leads to a "pre-emptive down-weighting of ... prediction errors [associated with other non-target features]" (Hohwy 2015). It appears then that the PC model provides an economical way of capturing target pre-activation as well as non-target suppression.

However, in the Guided Search model sketched above, the feedforward information relayed from a given feature map contains information about the presence or absence of the feature at different locations across the visual field; the information does *not* merely consist of an "error response" to a prior prediction. Consequently, proponents of PC may be required to go beyond the talk of increasing the gain on the signals regarding the target features; they should explain the prior predictions that generate the signals (now seen as prediction error), the particular type of prediction error at issue, and so on.[6] Otherwise, PC must provide a clear explanation of feature-based attention without the assistance of tools that rely on a conception of bottom-up signals that extend beyond prediction errors.

3. The Precision Weighting of Prediction Error Is too Broad

Though postsynaptic gain is ubiquitous in the brain, attention is not synonymous with all such gain. It manifests only in the gain on prediction error, and not, for instance, with respect to gain on top-down predictions. Thus, it avoids the criticism that it is too broad a phenomenon to account for attention's selective functional role (Feldman and Friston 2010: 18). However, even with this constraint in place, the precision weighting of prediction error may be too broad to be synonymous with attention. The precision weighting of prediction error has been assigned a dizzying number of roles. Along with explaining how we switch between model-based and model-free cognitive strategies, and its potential role in planning for the future (see section 2.3), it has also been invoked to explain our sense of agency, and how we understand the actions of others (Clark 2013b). To understand the actions of others, we observe a person's behavior and then simulate it as if we were the ones performing the action, generating hypotheses as to the intention behind the behavior. By assigning an extremely low (imprecise) weight to proprioceptive prediction errors generated by lower levels of the hierarchy, we prevent ourselves from actually performing the actions of our mental simulations. Our sense of agency arises in cases where proprioceptive prediction error is highly weighted but resolved by our top-down predictions.

In all such instances PC holds that shifts in precision weighting of prediction errors are constitutive of attentional shifts. Therefore, in each case we may ask whether the hypothesized attentional patterns correspond to our actual attentional behavior. Here we will focus on the case of multimodal integration, which involves the integration of information from the different sensory modalities—sight, sound, smell, taste, touch, and the sense of one's body in space (proprioception)—to form a coherent and unified percept. We perceive the smell as coming from the lillies and the surf of the ocean, the sound as being produced by the seagull, the flavor as deriving from the mango we are eating. Our expected precisions for these modalities may differ according to context—in dim lighting we may weight our auditory prediction errors more heavily, and in a noisy crowd we may be more confident in the deliverances of our visual prediction errors. We also may have more stable differential precision weightings, such as expecting visual information to provide more reliable fine-grained locational information than sound.

Differential precision weighting plays a central role in explaining crossmodal illusions that result from multimodal integration, such as the McGurk effect (McGurk and MacDonald 1976). In this illusion, participants watch a video of a person's lips moving as if making a certain sound together with audio of a different sound. Participants usually report hearing a third sound that can be understood as a sort of "compromise" between the visual and auditory information. For example, when the auditory information is "ba" and the visual information is "ga" then participants report hearing "da." This can be explained on PC by positing that we expect visual information pertaining to lip movements to be relatively precise in comparison to auditory information, all else equal, and so this information "overrides" the auditory signal to some degree in order to produce the illusion (e.g., Miller and Clark 2018: 2566–7). This precision expectation can also shift with context—when the auditory information is degraded, then the illusion is more pronounced (Massaro and Cohen 2000). On PC this would be explained by a lower relative precision weighting of auditory prediction error over visual prediction error in this context.

With a basic understanding of the account, we can turn to the question of whether the precision weighting of modality-specific information can be identified with attention. We argue that it cannot. This is most evident in the case of crossmodal illusions such as the McGurk effect. On PC, a lower precision weighting of the prediction error generated by audition should correspond to decreased auditory attention. But the illusion is not accompanied by a decrease in the apparent volume of the speaker. Instead we mishear the sound, at its original volume. Precision weighting of prediction error in this case seems to work not by shifting our attention away from the relevant sensory modality, but rather by causing us to alter the content of that modality.

Other crossmodal illusions pose the same challenge. In the case of the rubber hand illusion (Botvinick and Cohen 1998), the participant's arm is kept out of view and a rubber arm is placed on the table in front of her, in the same place her own hand might reasonably be located given her position. An experimenter then touches, tickles, or pokes the rubber arm, while also simultaneously performing the same actions on the participant's hidden arm. The result is usually that the participant begins to experience an illusion that the rubber arm is her own, and will respond to threats to the rubber hand in the same way as she responds to threats to her real hand (Ehrssen et al. 2007).

PC provides an explanation of the illusion in terms of the higher relative precision weighting of visual and tactile prediction errors over proprioceptive prediction errors (Hohwy 2013: 107).[7] Though we initially begin with the sense of our arm as being situated in its actual location, out of sight, the visual information of the rubber arm being manipulated, along with the sensations in our own arm or hand, causes us to shift our sense of where our arm is located in space. Again, this illusion is impervious to our knowledge that the arm is not really our own, but made of rubber. This sort of illusion is also problematic insofar as the incongruous visual and proprioceptive hypotheses are resolved not by diminishing our attention to where our arm is located in space, but by changing our sense of location. In fact, we may pay more attention than ever to our sense of bodily location just because the illusion is so bizarre.

But perhaps there is a PC story here about how, even though proprioceptive prediction error is assigned a smaller precision weight at lower levels of the hierarchy, attention is only allocated at higher levels of the hierarchy, to multimodal hypotheses. This is consistent with PC's proposal of how our perceptual systems solve the problem of binding inputs from disparate sensory modalities to form a unified percept—they propose that instead of trying to bind together disparate sensory inputs, the top-down hypotheses generated on PC already presuppose that the inputs are bound (see Hohwy 2013: ch. 5). They are already multimodal.

While this seems a reasonable solution, note that the precision weighting of prediction error is no longer synonymous with attention at lower levels of the hierarchy. The solution does not address our criticism that the precision weighting of prediction error is broader than attentional phenomena. The examples provided here suggest that, at least at lower levels of the generative model's hierarchy, precision-weighted prediction error cannot be identified with attention.

4. Conclusion

In this chapter we have argued that attention cannot be straightforwardly equated with the optimization of expected precisions, as some PC theorists have suggested. It is simultaneously too narrow and too broad a concept. The optimization of precision expectations is too narrow in that it may fail to account for a variety of attentional phenomena. Affect-biased attention suggests that attention to affectively salient objects can occur even in the absence of prediction error that is expected to be precise. PC faces difficulties in explaining voluntary attention because while arbitrary decisions to attend to things do result in an increase in precision, such decisions cannot meaningfully said to be driven by precision expectations; it is equally true of all possible objects of attention that precision will be enhanced by deciding to attend. Whether or not PC can explain intellectual attention will depend on the details of the account, but we suspect that shifts in intellectual attention are also sometimes affectively driven, and so also not fully accommodated by precision expectations. Feature-based attention may not be accounted for by PC because it appears to rely in part on bottom-up processes not explainable in terms of prediction error.

Finally, we have argued that the optimization of precision expectations is too broad a phenomenon to be identified with attention because such optimization is crucially involved in multimodal integration. PC theory explains crossmodal illusions in terms of differential precision weightings, but this does not translate into attentional phenomena as one would expect on PC.

As a whole the criticisms we have provided here suggest that PC needs to go beyond the precision weighting of prediction error to accommodate the full range of attentional phenomena, thus hampering its claims to completeness. At minimum, the challenges we have raised here are an opportunity for PC theorists to clarify important details of their account.[8]

Notes

1   For a review of different PC algorithms, see Spratling (2017).
2   See Aitchison and Lengyel (2017) for discussion of how these concepts come apart. PC is also often combined with the free energy principle. Free energy is an information-theoretic measure; it bounds the evidence for our internal generative models of sensory data (MacKay 1995). The free energy principle is that all adaptive changes in the brain will minimize free energy, where such changes range from those that occur on evolutionary time scales to those happening in real-time (Friston 2009). Under some simplifying assumptions, to minimize free energy is to minimize prediction error (Friston 2010).
3   See Rauss and Pourtois (2013) for discussion of how to understand "top-down" and "bottom-up" in PC.
4   We might retrieve the answer "Cervantes" or "Pierre Menard," depending on one's view of the ontological status of literary works.
5   See Humphreys and Mavritsaki (2012) for an informative summary of different models of visual search.
6   For instance, neurophysiological studies often distinguish between two types of prediction errors pertaining to a feature or an object: positive prediction error corresponds to the occurrence of an unexpected instance of that feature or object. Negative prediction error pertains to the unexpected omission of that feature or object (Egner et al. 2010). Clearly, it makes a difference whether the type of prediction error generated during the search is due to occurrence or omission of the feature and very different consequences would follow from increasing the gain on each of these types.
7   For an understanding of how interoceptive inference might also play a role in the illusion, see Suzuki et al. (2013).
8   Thanks to Jakob Hohwy, Carolyn Dicey-Jennings, and David Barack for their comments on earlier versions of this chapter, as well as the audience at the 2015 Society for Philosophy and Psychology annual conference and at the 2015 Minds Online conference. We would also like to acknowledge the financial support of the Summer Seminar for Neuroscience and Philosophy at Duke University, through which a portion of this research was conducted.

References

Anderson, B. A. (2013), "A Value-Driven Mechanism of Attentional Selection," *Journal of Vision*, 13 (3): 1–16.

Anderson, B. A. and Yantis, S. (2013), "Persistence of Value-driven Attentional Capture," *Journal of Experimental Psychology: Human Perception and Performance*, 39 (1): 6.

Anderson, B. A., Laurent, P. A. and Yantis, S. (2011), "Learned Value Magnifies Salience-Based Attentional Capture," *PloS one*, 6 (11): e27926.

Anderson, B. A., Laurent, P. A. and Yantis, S. (2012), "Generalization of Value-based Attentional Priority," *Visual Cognition*, 20 (6): 647–58.

Anderson, B. A., Laurent, P. A. and Yantis, S. (2013), "Reward Predictions Bias Attentional Selection," *Frontiers in Human Neuroscience*, 7: 262.

Aitchison, L. and Lengyel, M. (2017), "With or Without You: Predictive Coding and Bayesian Inference in the Brain," *Current Opinion in Neurobiology*, 46: 219–27.

Awh, E., Belopolsky, A. V. and Theeuwes, J. (2012), "Top-Down versus Bottom-Up Attentional Control: A Failed Theoretical Dichotomy," *Trends in Cognitive Sciences*, 16 (8): 437–43.

Bar, M. (2003), "A Cortical Mechanism for Triggering Top-Down Facilitation in Visual Object Recognition," *Journal of Cognitive Neuroscience*, 15 (4): 600–9.

Bar, M., Tootell, R., Schacter, D. L., Doug, G. N., Fischl, B., Mendola, J. D., Rosen, B. R. and Dale, A. M. (2001), "Cortical Mechanisms Specific to Explicit Visual Object Recognition," *Neuron*, 29 (2): 529–35.

Barrett, L. F. and Bar, M. (2009), "See It with Feeling: Affective Predictions during Object Perception," *Philosophical Transactions of the Royal Society B: Biological Sciences*, 364 (1521): 1325–34.

Botvinick, M. and Cohen, J. (1998), "Rubber Hands 'Feel' Touch That Eyes See," *Nature*, 391 (6669): 756.

Bowman, H., Filetti, M., Wyble, B. and Olivers, C. (2013), "Attention Is More than Prediction Precision," *The Behavioral and Brain Sciences*, 36 (3): 206–8.

Carrasco, M. (2011), "Visual Attention: The Past 25 Years," *Vision Research*, 51 (13): 1484–525.

Chennu, S., Noreika, V., Gueorguiev, D., Blenkmann, A., Kochen, S., Ibánez, A., Owen, A. M. and Bekinschtein, T. A. (2013), "Expectation and Attention in Hierarchical Auditory Prediction," *Journal of Neuroscience*, 33 (27): 11194–205.

Christoff, K. (2012), "Undirected Thought: Neural Determinants and Correlates," *Brain Research*, 1428: 51–9.

Clark, A. (2013a), "Whatever Next? Predictive Brains, Situated Agents, and the Future of Cognitive Science," *Behavioral and Brain Sciences*, 36 (3): 181–204.

Clark, A. (2013b), "The Many Faces of Precision (Replies to Commentaries on 'Whatever Next? Neural Prediction, Situated Agents, and the Future of Cognitive Science')," *Frontiers in Psychology*, 4: 270.

Clark, A. (2015), *Surfing Uncertainty: Prediction, Action, and the Embodied Mind*, New York: Oxford University Press.

Clark, A. (2017), "Predictions, Precision, and Agentive Attention," *Consciousness and cognition*, 56: 115–19.

Colombo, M. and Wright, C. (2017), "Explanatory Pluralism: An Unrewarding Prediction Error for Free Energy Theorists," *Brain and Cognition*, 112: 3–12.

Daw, N. D., Niv, Y. and Dayan, P. (2005), "Uncertainty-based Competition between Prefrontal and Dorsolateral Striatal Systems for Behavioral Control," *Nature Neuroscience*, 8 (12): 1704.

Della Libera, C. and Chelazzi, L. (2009), "Learning to Attend and to Ignore Is a Matter of Gains and Losses," *Psychological Science*, 20 (6): 778–84.

Egner, T., Monti, J. M. and Summerfield, C. (2010), "Expectation and Surprise Determine Neural Population Responses in the Ventral Visual Stream," *Journal of Neuroscience*, 30 (49): 16601–16608.

Egner, T., Monti, J., Trittschuh, E. H., Wieneke, C. A., Hirsch, J. and Mesulam, M.-M. (2008), "Neural Integration of Top-Down Spatial and Feature-based Information in Visual Search," *Journal of Neuroscience*, 28 (24): 6141–51.

Ehrsson, H. H., Wiech, K., Weiskopf, N., Dolan, R. J. and Passingham, R. E. (2007), "Threatening a Rubber Hand That You Feel Is Yours Elicits a Cortical Anxiety Response," *Proceedings of the National Academy of Sciences*, 104 (23): 9828–33.

Feldman, H. and Friston, K. J. (2010), "Attention, Uncertainty, and Free-energy," *Frontiers in Human Neuroscience*, 4: 215.

Fortney, M. (2019), "Conceptualizing Intellectual Attention," *Theory & Psychology*, 29 (6): 775–88.

Friston, K., Mattout, J. and Kilner, J. (2011), "Action Understanding and Active Inference," *Biological Cybernetic*, 104 (1–2): 137–60.

Friston, K. J. (2008), "Hierarchical Models in the Brain," *PLoS Computational Biology*, 4 (11): e1000211.

Friston, K. J. (2009), "The Free-Energy Principle: A Rough Guide to the Brain?," *Trends in Cognitive Sciences*, 13 (7): 293–301.

Friston, K. J. (2010), "The Free-Energy Principle: A Unified Brain Theory?," *Nature Reviews Neuroscience*, 11 (2): 127.

Friston, K. J., Daunizeau, J., Kilner, J. and Kiebel, S. J. (2010), "Action and Behavior: A Free-Energy Formulation," *Biological Cybernetics*, 102 (3): 227–60.

Gershman, S. J. and Daw, N. D. (2012), "Perception, Action and Utility: The Tangled Skein," *Principles of Brain Dynamics: Global State Interactions*: 293–312. doi. org/10.7551/mitpress/9108.003.0015.

Helmholtz, H. V. (2005), *Treatise on Physiological Optics*, Mineola: Dover.

Hickey, C., Chelazzi, L. and Theeuwes, J. (2010), "Reward Changes Salience in Human Vision Via the Anterior Cingulate," *Journal of Neuroscience*, 30 (33): 11096–11103.

Hobson, J. A. and Friston, K. J. (2012), "Waking and Dreaming Consciousness: Neurobiological and Functional Considerations," *Progress in Neurobiology*, 98 (1): 82–98.

Hohwy, J. (2012), "Attention and Conscious Perception in the Hypothesis Testing Brain," *Frontiers in Psychology*, 3: 96.

Hohwy, J. (2013), *The Predictive Mind*, New York: Oxford University Press.

Hohwy, J. (2015), "Comments on Ransom and Fazelpour's Three Problems for the Predictive Coding Theory of Attention," *Minds Online*. http://mindsonline. philosophyofbrains.com/2015/session4/three-problems-for-the-predictive-coding-theory-of-attention/#comment-284.

Hohwy, J., Roepstorff, A. and Friston, K. J. (2008), "Predictive Coding Explains Binocular Rivalry: An Epistemological Review," *Cognition*, 108 (3): 687–701.

Huang, Y. and Rao, R. (2011), "Predictive Coding," *Wiley Interdisciplinary Reviews: Cognitive Science*, 2 (5): 580–93.

Humphreys, G. W. and Mavritsaki, E. (2012), "Models of Visual Search: From Abstract Function to Biological Constraint" in Michael I. Posner (ed.), *Cognitive Neuroscience of Attention*, New York: The Guilford Press.

Jiang, J., Summerfield, C. and Egner, T. (2013.), "Attention Sharpens the Distinction Between Expected and Unexpected Percepts in the Visual Brain," *Journal of Neuroscience*, 33 (47): 18438–47.

Kok, P., Rahnev, D., Jehee, J., Lau, H. C. and De Lange, F. P. (2011), "Attention Reverses the Effect of Prediction in Silencing Sensory Signals," *Cerebral Cortex*, 22 (9): 2197–206.

Körding, K. P. and Wolpert, Daniel M. (2006), "Bayesian Decision Theory in Sensorimotor Control," *Trends in Cognitive Sciences*, 10 (7): 319–26.

MacKay, D. J. (1995), "Free Energy Minimisation Algorithm for Decoding and Cryptanalysis," *Electronics Letters*, 31 (6): 446–7.

Markovic, J., Anderson, A. K. and Todd, R. M. (2014), "Tuning to the Significant: Neural and Genetic Processes Underlying Affective Enhancement of Visual Perception and Memory," *Behavioural Brain Research*, 259: 229–41.

Massaro, D. W. and Cohen, M. M. (2000), "Tests of Auditory–Visual Integration Efficiency within the Framework of the Fuzzy Logical Model of Perception," *The Journal of the Acoustical Society of America*, 108 (2): 784–9.

Mather, M. and Sutherland, M. R. (2011), "Arousal-biased Competition in Perception and Memory," *Perspectives on Psychological Science*, 6 (2): 114–33.

McGurk, H. and MacDonald, J. (1976), "Hearing Lips and Seeing Voices," *Nature*, 264 (5588): 746.

Miller, M. and Clark, A. (2018), "Happily Entangled: Prediction, Emotion, and the Embodied Mind," *Synthese*, 195 (6): 2559–75.

Mole, C. (2011), *Attention Is Cognitive Unison: An Essay in Philosophical* Psychology, New York: Oxford University Press.

Niu, Y., Todd, R. and Anderson, A. K. (2012), "Affective Salience Can Reverse the Effects of Stimulus-Driven Salience on Eye Movements in Complex Scenes," *Frontiers in Psychology*, 3: 336.

Oliva, A. and Torralba, A. (2001), "Modeling the Shape of the Scene: A Holistic Representation of the Spatial Envelope," *International Journal of Computer Vision*, 42 (3): 145–75.

Posner, M. I. (1980), "Orienting of Attention," *Quarterly Journal of Experimental Psychology*, 32 (1): 3–25.

Posner, M. I. (ed.) (2011), *Cognitive Neuroscience of Attention*, New York: Guilford Press.

Ransom, M., Fazelpour, S. and Mole, C. (2017), "Attention in the Predictive Mind," *Consciousness and Cognition*, 47: 99–112.

Ransom, M., Fazelpour, S., Markovic, J., Kryklywy, J., Thompson, E. T. and Todd, R. M. (2020), "Affect-Biased Attention and Predictive Processing," *Cognition*, 203: 104370.

Rao, R. and Ballard, D. H. (2005), "Probabilistic Models of Attention Based on Iconic Representations and Predictive Coding" in Laurent Itti and Geraint Rees (eds.), *Neurobiology of Attention*, Cambridge: Academic Press.

Rauss, K. and Pourtois, G. (2013), "What Is Bottom-up and What Is Top-Down in Predictive Coding?," *Frontiers in Psychology*, 4: 276.

Rolls, E. T. (2000), "On the Brain and Emotion," *Behavioral and Brain Sciences*, 23 (2): 219–28.

Rossi, A. F. and Paradiso, M. A. (1995), "Feature-specific Effects of Selective Visual Attention," *Vision Research*, 35 (5): 621–34.

Schyns, P. G. and Oliva, A. (1994), "From Blobs to Boundary Edges: Evidence for Time- and Spatial-Scale-Dependent Scene Recognition," *Psychological Science*, 5 (4): 195–200.

Seth, A. K. and Critchley, H. D. (2013), "Extending Predictive Processing to the Body: Emotion as Interoceptive Inference," *Behavioral and Brain Science*, 36 (3): 227–8.

Seth, A. K., Suzuki, K. and Critchley, H. D. (2012), "An Interoceptive Predictive Coding Model of Conscious Presence," *Frontiers in Psychology*, 2: 395.

Shomstein, S. and Johnson, J. (2013), "Shaping Attention with Reward: Effects of Reward on Space-and Object-based Selection," *Psychological* Science, 24 (12): 2369–78.

Spratling, M. W. (2008), "Predictive Coding as a Model of Biased Competition in Visual Attention," *Vision Research*, 48 (12): 1391–408.

Spratling, M. W. (2017), "A Review of Predictive Coding Algorithms," *Brain and Cognition*, 112: 92–7.

Srinivasan, M. V., Laughlin, S. B. and Dubs, A. (1982), "Predictive Coding: A Fresh View of Inhibition in the Retina," *Proceedings of the Royal Society of London. Series B. Biological Sciences*, 216 (1205): 427–59.

Summerfield, C. and Egner, T. (2009), "Expectation (and Attention) in Visual Cognition," *Trends in Cognitive Sciences*, 13 (9): 403–9.

Suzuki, K., Garfinkel, S. N., Critchley, H. D. and Seth, A. K. (2013), "Multisensory Integration Across Exteroceptive and Interoceptive Domains Modulates Self-experience in the Rubber-hand Illusion," *Neuropsychologia*, 51 (13): 2909–17.

Todd, R., Cunningham, W. A., Anderson, A. K. and Thompson, E. (2012), "Affect-biased Attention as Emotion Regulation," *Trends in Cognitive Sciences*, 16 (7): 365–72.

Todd, R. M. and Manaligod, M. (2018), "Implicit Guidance of Attention: The Priority State Space Framework," *Cortex*, 102: 121–38.

Torralba, A. and Oliva, A. (2003), "Statistics of Natural Image Categories," *Network: Computation in Neural Systems*, 14 (3): 391–412.

Vuilleumier, P. (2015), "Affective and Motivational Control of Vision," *Current Opinion in Neurology*, 28 (1): 29–35.

Watson, D. G. and Humphreys, G. W. (1997), "Visual Marking: Prioritizing Selection for New Objects by Top-Down Attentional Inhibition of Old Objects," *Psychological Review*, 104 (1): 90.

Watzl, S. (2017), *Structuring Mind: The Nature of Attention and How It Shapes Consciousness*, New York: Oxford University Press.

Wilkinson, S. (2014), "Accounting for the Phenomenology and Varieties of Auditory Verbal Hallucination within a Predictive Processing Framework," *Consciousness and Cognition*, 30: 142–55.

Wolfe, J. M. (1994), "Guided Search 2.0: A Revised Model of Visual Search," *Psychonomic Bulletin & Review*, 1 (2): 202–38.

Wu, W. (2014), *Attention*, London: Routledge.

8

Predictive Processing: Does It Compute?

Chris Thornton

Centre for Research in Cognitive Science, University of Sussex

1. Introduction

There is mounting enthusiasm for what Clark calls "the emerging unifying vision of the brain as an organ of prediction using a hierarchy of generative models" (Clark 2013: 185). Part of a long tradition emphasizing the role of prediction in perception (James 1890/1950, Lashley 1951, Mackay 1956, Tolman 1948, von Helmholtz 1867), this approach is now advancing on a broad range of fronts (Brown et al. 2011, Clark 2016, Friston 2005, 2010, Hohwy et al. 2008, Huang and Rao 2011, Jehee and Ballard 2009, Knill and Pouget 2004, Lee and Mumford 2003, Rao and Ballard 1999, 2004, Williams 2018, Yon et al. 2019). Given the principle that "the best ways of interpreting incoming information via perception, are deeply the same as the best ways of controlling outgoing information via motor action" (Eliasmith 2007: 7), the proposal can also be seen as a way of unifying interpretive and behavioral functionality (Brown et al. 2011, Friston et al. 2009). The implication then becomes that "perceiving and acting are but two different ways of doing the same thing" (Hohwy 2013: 76).

Clark's proposal (Clark 2013, 2016) characterizes function organized in this way as predictive processing (PP). In his view, the brain is an inner engine of probabilistic prediction that is "constantly trying to guess at the structure and shape of the incoming sensory array" (Clark 2016: 3). Each layer of the engine is seen to express a generative model, in an arrangement that involves higher layers sending predictions to lower layers, and lower layers passing prediction errors upward. Minimizing these errors, it is presumed, will turn the structure into a largely veridical model of the world.

The proposal continues to gain support (Williams 2018, Yon et al. 2019). But there are questions about what is implied computationally. The operations involved are not generally specified in precise detail, as Clark acknowledges. He describes his own characterization of PP (Clark 2016) as "relatively abstract" (2016: 298), and no more than a "mid-level organizational sketch" (2016: 2). But with the fine details left open in this way, questions of functionality inevitably arise. By means of what calculations do higher layers send predictions downward? How are the prediction errors computed? What is the mechanism for transmitting these upward through the hierarchy?

A key question relates to layer coordination. In Clark's description of the scheme, individual layers in the hierarchy are considered to be largely independent. Each layer is seen to predict "the response profiles at the layer below" (Clark 2016: 93), while also reducing any error reported back. Predictions make up the downward flow of information within the hierarchy, while error signals make up the upward flow. There is no other mechanism of communication or coordination between layers. As Clark emphasizes, it is a distinctive characteristic of the proposal that "it depicts the forward flow of information as solely conveying error, and the backward flow as solely conveying predictions" (Clark 2016: 38).

The difficulty is to see how this arrangement would have the effect of improving prediction of sensory input overall. The onus on each layer is to reduce its error in predicting the state of the layer below.[1] But it is only the state at the lowest layer of the hierarchy which represents sensory data. Without layers being coordinated in some way, there is no reason why prediction at the sensory layer should be improved by reducing error higher in the hierarchy. Representational coordination of layers would seem to be pre-requisite. In the case of data compression by predictive coding, often cited as an inspiration for PP, coordination of predictive sources is ensured by specification of the algorithm (e.g., Kobayashi 1974, Pensiri and Auwatanamongkol 2012).

The lack of specificity about critical computational details is also problematic. The calculations that are assumed to convey the upward and downward flows of information are not precisely specified and, as will be seen, it is not always obvious what is implied. There is a need to develop a specification that resolves these ambiguities. This is the initial aim of the present chapter. The intention is to establish what PP involves at a detailed, computational level of description.

The calculations that mediate upward and downward flows in PP are potentially defined in terms of the inferential operations of Bayesian probability theory (Berger 1985, Howson and Urbach 1989, Jaynes 2003). Use of the framework of information theory (Shannon 1948, Shannon and Weaver 1949) is also a possibility. Which of these two approaches leads to a more coherent computational implementation will be carefully examined. The degree to which adopting a specific implementation addresses the question of layer coordination will also be assessed.

The chapter is divided into four main sections. Sections 2 and 3 examine contrasting implementations of PP. Section 2 evaluates an implementation based on use of Bayesian calculations; section 3 examines an implementation based on use of information-theoretic calculations. The degree to which the approach addresses the requirement for layer coordination is explored. Section 4 then presents a general discussion and some concluding comments.

2. An Inferential Implementation

Although the calculations that mediate PP are not generally specified in detail, it is often assumed they must be Bayesian in nature (Hohwy 2013). They are typically taken to be acts of probabilistic inference. This acknowledges the degree to which the framework is founded in the Bayesian brain hypothesis, which proposes that "the brain codes and computes weighted probabilities" (Clark 2016: 41), and the general assumption that neural processing can be understood as a form of Bayesian inference (cf. Doya et al. 2007, Pouget et al. 2013).

There are two ways in which an inferential implementation of PP can be developed, however. A Bayesian probability linking two outcomes allows an unconditional probability to be inferred for either the conditioning outcome, or the conditioned outcome. There are two forms of inference available—one forward, one backward—for mediating the flows of information, and two forms of flow—upward and downward— to be implemented. A particular implementation can be arrived at by mapping inferential forms to flows in a particular way, therefore.

A convenient approach links the downward flow to forward inference. This has the unfortunate consequence of creating a terminological clash, as the downward flow is termed "backward" neurologically. The advantage is that it has the effect of placing conditioned outcomes (i.e., Bayesian evidence) below conditioning outcomes (i.e., hypotheses) in the hierarchy. Outcomes representing sensory evidence are also placed in the lowest layer. Mediation of the upward flow is then by means of Bayes's rule—that is, by derivation of posterior probability. This general scheme is recognized by Clark as one way of realizing PP in a specifically Bayesian way (Clark 2016: 172–5).

A simple illustration appears in the upper panel of Figure 8.1. This shows a single Bayesian hierarchy involving the outcomes T, U, V, W, X, Y, Z. The hierarchy is drawn

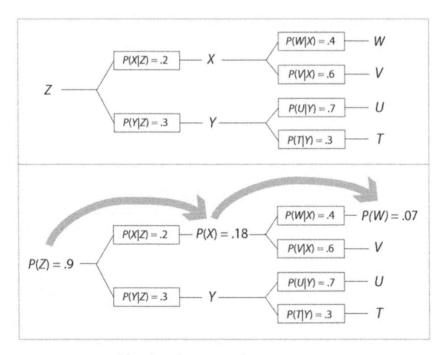

Figure 8.1 Downward flow through Bayesian inference.

on its side, with the root on the left. Each between-layer connection is defined by a likelihood, as shown. This states the conditional probability of an outcome in the layer below, given an outcome in the layer above. For example, $P(X|Z) = .2$ defines the top-left connection. (Here and elsewhere, probabilities are approximate.) Outcomes at the lowest layer are considered to be sensory in nature. Outcomes W, V, U, and T are sensory, then, while outcomes X, Y, and Z are internal.

The lower panel of Figure 8.1 illustrates processing involved in the downward flow. The sequence is initiated by the assertion of an unconditional (i.e., prior) probability for the root outcome Z. With $P(Z)$ given the value .9, unconditional probabilities can then be inferred for outcomes at lower layers. $P(X) = P(X|Z) P(Z) \approx .18$ can be derived, followed by $P(W) = P(W|X) P(X) \approx .07$. The probability given to Z eventually yields a probability for W in this way.

Under the depicted arrangement, priors at higher layers of the hierarchy are seen to "cascade downwards" by probabilistic expectation. A point in favor of this scheme is that it echoes the way theorists have assumed the downward flow must operate. Both Clark (2013) and Hohwy (2013) describe the downward flow in just these terms. Hohwy refers to the importance of what he calls the "pulling down" of priors (Hohwy 2013: 33). Clark sees downward flow as the way in which a system can "infer its own priors (the prior beliefs essential to the guessing routines) as it goes along" (Clark 2013: 3). The proposed implementation, in which the downward flow is exclusively in this form, may go beyond what these theorists intend, however. The role played by lateral (within layer) connectivity is also particularly emphasized in Clark (2016), for example.[2]

Figure 8.2 illustrates the upward flow. The upper panel shows the (approximate) posterior probabilities that can be inferred for X and Z, after W is awarded an unconditional probability of .5. All outcomes are considered to have a default prior of 1, and each inferential step represents an application of Bayes's rule. X's probability, for example, is the posterior:

$$P(X|W) = \frac{P(W|X)P(X)}{P(W)} \approx .8$$

The lower panel shows the upward flow after all the sensory outcomes are awarded unconditional probabilities, and posteriors are combined appropriately. As will be seen, X comes to acquire an (approximate) unconditional probability of .6 rather than .8, due to the influence of $P(V|X) = .6$ and $P(V) = .8$.

The results achieved by implementing the upward flow in this inferential way are less satisfactory. What is then conveyed upward is posterior probability, whereas what should be conveyed upward is prediction error. The two quantities are related, so it is not unreasonable to ask whether one might represent the other. It is certainly the case that the posterior probability of an outcome increases with the degree to which it is predicted by the relevant likelihood and conditional prior. Treating posterior probability as an inverse measure of prediction error might be considered an option on this basis.

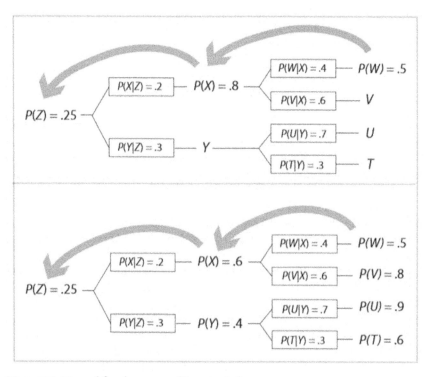

Figure 8.2 Upward flow by means of Bayesian inference.

In practice, this arrangement fails. It can be shown that posteriors cannot represent prediction errors in certain cases. Imagine a situation in which the predicted probability of an outcome exceeds its observed probability. Rain might be observed to have a probability of .5, say, but be predicted on theoretical grounds to have a probability of .9. (This situation, in which the predicted probability of an outcome exceeds its observed probability, is typical for a weather forecast.) The prediction potentially gives rise to a prediction error. But an error of this kind cannot be dealt with by derivation of posteriors, even in principle.

Given the predicted probability derives from a likelihood of .9 and a prior of 1, the posterior probability of rain cannot be derived. The numerator in the Bayesian calculation is then greater than the denominator, implying an invalid posterior. Within the terms of Bayesian theory, the posterior has to be considered undefined.[3] Posteriors cannot represent prediction errors in general, then. Implementing the upward flow in this way is ruled out.[4]

The general conclusion is that attempting to operationalize PP in a strictly Bayesian way, using inferential calculations to mediate information flows, fails to produce a satisfactory result. Arguably, the effect is simply to beg further questions. If the upward flow of posteriors cannot serve to convey prediction error, how does it fit into the processing otherwise performed? If transfer of error involves information flow that progresses up the hierarchy in some way, how does this interact with the upward flow that reflects ordinary Bayesian inference? Do the two flows proceed in parallel? Are they integrated in some way? The attempt to develop a strictly Bayesian implementation of PP begs a number of questions.

3. In Informational Implementation

The information flows in PP can also be calculated using operations drawn from the framework of information theory (Shannon 1948, Shannon and Weaver 1949). Like the Bayesian framework, this deals with assignments of probability. But whereas the Bayesian framework is concerned with how probabilities can be updated from relevant priors and likelihoods, information theory focuses on what happens when an outcome of given probability occurs. A way of quantifying the information that is then generated is the framework's key contribution. Being focused on outcomes in this way, information theory is well-suited to deal with prediction of outcomes, and hence with PP.

Key to information theory is the principle that an outcome has an informational value that is inversely related to its probability (Shannon 1948, Shannon and Weaver 1949). Specifically, the informational value of some outcome W is defined as $-\log_2 P(W)$ bits.[5] If $P(W) = .5$, for example, the informational value of W is $-\log_{2.5} = 1$ bit. This quantity is termed the outcome's surprisal (Tribus 1961). For present purposes, it is prediction of outcomes that is of interest, and this is naturally modeled in terms of conditional probability. Consider $P(W|X)$. This denotes the conditional probability of outcome W given outcome X. Equivalently, it can be seen to denote the probability of outcome W that outcome X predicts. The assertion $P(W|X) = .3$ can be considered to assert that outcome X predicts outcome W with probability .3, for example.

A relatively simple PP implementation can then be envisaged, which is essentially a direct translation of the Bayesian implementation. In it, the conditional probabilities which define the structure of the model are considered to express predictions. Upward and downward flows are progressed by probabilistic expectation as before, but with the values derived now being quantities of information rather than probabilities. Figure 8.3 illustrates the processing then obtained. The upper panel depicts the downward flow commencing from the assignment $P(Z) = .25$. This yields a surprisal value—here denoted as inf(Z)—of 2 bits. The lower panel depicts the upward flow commencing from the assignment by $P(W) = .5$. This yields an information value of .2 bits for outcome Z.

Unfortunately, this direct translation of the Bayesian implementation lacks generality. It accommodates the various ways in which outcomes can be predicted, but not the possibility that they might not occur. This needs to be taken into account. The informational value of an outcome is its surprisal, but only if the outcome occurs. A predicted outcome has the potential not to occur. The outcome may be mispredicted. Where there is prediction of an outcome that fails to occur, how is the expected value of the predicting outcome to be derived? To obtain a fully general specification for the upward flow, this issue needs to be resolved.

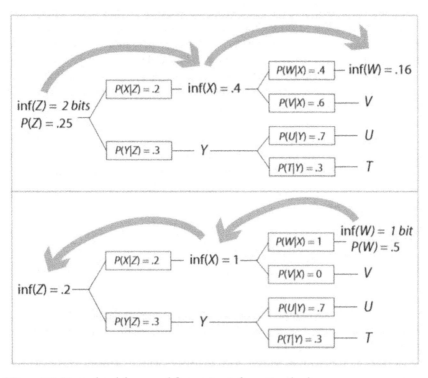

Figure 8.3 Upward and downward flows using informational values.

Shannon's framework (Shannon 1948, Shannon and Weaver 1949) does not explicitly address the case of non-occurring outcomes. It can be deduced that a prediction of a non-occurring outcome must always have a negative value in this context, however. This is best demonstrated using a concrete example. Imagine a weather forecast that gives a 100 percent chance of rain during the day. This prediction can be modeled as the assertion $P(W|X) = 1$, where W is occurrence of rain, and X represent whatever cue(s) the forecast derives from. Assuming rain is observed to occur on 50 percent of all days, we have $P(W) = .5$, and hence $\inf(W) = \log_{2.5} = 1$ bit. Given these assignments, what is the informational value of the prediction of rain?

If the rain occurs, the evaluation is straightforwardly derived. The forecast has the effect of bringing forward the outcome in question, supplying its information content in advance. Acceptance of the forecast increases possession of information by the value of the outcome predicted. The value of the forecast is 1 bit. If the rain does not occur, the forecast is then a misprediction and, as we might expect, the evaluation turns negative. To see this, consider a forecast that gives a 50 percent chance of rain. Implicitly, this also gives a 50 percent chance of no rain—it gives the two possible outcomes equal probability. The forecast is completely neutral then and, given the observed probability of rain is itself .5, entirely without value.

On this basis, the evaluation of the original forecast in the case of the rain failing to occur can be deduced. Assuming the value of a successful prediction must be positive, it follows that the value of its unsuccessful counterpart must be correspondingly negative. This is what the zero evaluation of the neutral forecast entails. With correct and incorrect predictions given equal probability, the forecast's zero evaluation requires that the positive value of the correct prediction is precisely offset by the negative value of the incorrect prediction part. The evaluations of the prediction and misprediction must be equal and opposite.

Combining this with the observation that the value of a correct prediction is the surprisal of the outcome predicted, the value of a misprediction can then be defined as the negative of the outcome's surprisal. This has the effect of ensuring that a misprediction is exactly as costly as its counterpart is beneficial. The relationship can be stated formally as

$$I_P(e) = \begin{cases} -\log_2 P(e) & \text{if } e = e' \\ \\ \log_2 P(e) & \text{if } e \neq e' \end{cases} \tag{1}$$

where $P(e)$ is outcome e's observed probability and e' is the outcome that occurs. $IP(e)$ is then the informational value of predicting outcome e. (Notice that the upper value is positive, and the lower negative.)

As outcomes may be predicted with any probability in general, this should be allowed for. The overall evaluation then becomes a weighted average of the gains and losses produced by the individual parts of the forecast. It is the expected informational revenue of the predicted distribution. Let $Q(e)$ be the probability with which outcome e is predicted.[6] The informational value of the predictions expressed by distribution Q is then the average:

$$I_{Q:P} = \sum_e Q(e) I_P(e) \tag{2}$$

The measure can also be generalized for situations involving more than two outcomes. This requires use of a normalization. With more than two outcomes, we have more than one incorrect outcome and, consequently, more than one negative value in the summation of Equation 2. To ensure commensurability between positive and negative contributions, the latter must be discounted by $n-1$, where n is the number of outcomes. The modified equation then becomes

$$I_P(e) = \begin{cases} -\log_2 P(e) & \text{if } e = e' \\ \\ \dfrac{\log_2 P(e)}{n-1} & \text{if } e \neq e' \end{cases} \tag{3}$$

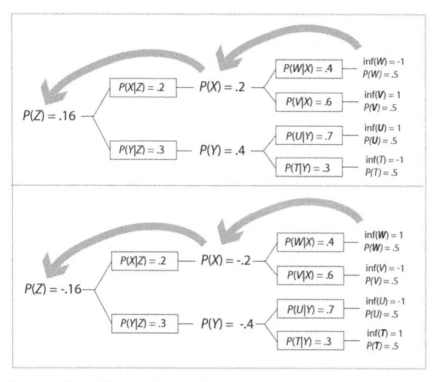

Figure 8.4 Upward flow by information-theoretic calculation.

Situations involving any number of outcomes can then be dealt with. The informational value of a prediction, assessed in this way, is termed its predictive payoff (Thornton 2017).[7]

How the upward flow is to be implemented in the face of outcomes that may or may not occur can then be resolved. The evaluation that any higher outcome obtains should be its predictive payoff with respect to the outcomes that it conditionally awards probability to. Upward flow should be progressed by derivation of predictive payoff, in other words. The upper and lower panels of Figure 8.4 illustrate the patterns of processing that are obtained on this basis.

The upward flow of information to X, and from X to Z, is depicted in two different scenarios. The upper panel deals with the case where the sensory outcomes predicted by X with greatest probability (i.e., V and U) both occur. The lower panel deals with the case where they fail to occur. (Notice occurring outcomes are set in bold.) The upward flow is mediated by derivations of predictive payoff in all cases. Outcome X acquires a value of approximately .2 bits due to its attribution of probability to W and V, and their informational values. The payoff is

$$-1 \times .4 + 1 \times .6 \approx .2 \text{ bits}$$

An important feature of the upward flow, when implemented in this way, is the degree to which it both expresses prediction error and brings about its reduction. This effect can be explained in terms of Figure 8.4. In the situation depicted in the upper panel, there are no mispredictions. All predictions are correct in the sense that occurring outcomes are given greater probability (e.g., $P(V|X) > P(W|X)$). Predictive payoff to both X and Y (and hence Z) is positive. In the situation depicted by the lower panel, the occurring outcome is T rather than U. This is now mispredicted. U is given greater probability than T, and the derived value of Y changes its sign in result. The prediction error leads to Y having a negative value.

The prediction error, in this case, leads to Y having a negative evaluation, and this then comes to serve as a kind of error signal. No particular significance attaches to the evaluation's sign. Its capacity to serve as a prediction error depends purely on its relational properties. The strength with which a model in this form expresses a particular prediction depends on the informational value of the outcome from which it derives. The effect produced by the upward flow is to concentrate predictive strength at outcomes that better predict. Information flows toward sources of prediction, then, and in proportion to their predictive efficacy. Information congregates as prediction originates. On this basis, better predictions are then naturally forthcoming. Prediction error that is implicitly conveyed upward is also implicitly reduced. The system predicts, and reduces error at the same time, without requiring any extraneous mechanism of error reduction.

Unlike its predecessor, this informational implementation meets all requirements of the PP scheme, then. Both information flows are handled appropriately. Error is conveyed upward in a way that ensures it is reduced at each layer. Predictions are conveyed downward in a way that meets the requirement for the model to be "generative in nature" (cf. Clark 2016: 93). An additional attraction is that the implementation respects Clark's description of error derivation. This requires the upward flow to originate in measurements of surprisal, specifically.[8] Upward flow in the proposed implementation originates in exactly this way. One drawback of the implementation, however, is that it fails to separate encodings of prediction and prediction error in the way that Clark (2016: 39) emphasizes is important. Under the proposed implementation, they are fully integrated.

4. Discussion

Regardless of how useful the PP framework may be for explaining functionalities of the brain, there is a need to determine whether it makes sense computationally—whether it hangs together as a system of calculation. This is the main aim of the present chapter. The result of the study is largely positive. It has been shown that a computationally precise interpretation of the scheme can be assembled. There are various reservations to be noted, however.

Layer coordination is a prominent concern. The original scheme envisages a hierarchical structure in which higher layers send predictions to lower layers, and lower layers pass prediction errors upward. On the proviso that each layer predicts the state at the layer below (and the lowest layer predicts sensory input),[9] it is assumed that minimizing error at any layer will have the effect of improving prediction of sensory input overall. This is problematic. If it is assumed that the task of each layer is to predict the state at the layer below, there is no reason why this effect should occur. Improving prediction of a state that itself predicts badly cannot be a way to make it predict better. The effect might easily be the reverse.

Designing the hierarchy in a way that allows each layer to predict sensory input directly would appear to resolve this difficulty. Any error passed upward is then the residual of a single quantity. It is what remains after lower-layer predictions have been taken into account. Minimizing errors of this kind can only improve prediction of sensory input overall. Unfortunately, an arrangement of this kind only solves the problem in a degenerate way. If the error reported by every layer of the hierarchy is a residual in this way, all layers are then functionally linked together, and the attribution of hierarchical structure is called into question. Viewing the structure as a single, non-hierarchical model would seem equally justified.

Implementations of PP would seem to face an inherent dilemma, then. Without coordination of layers, there is no reason why error reduction at higher layers should improve prediction of sensory input. With coordination of layers, the model's hierarchical structure is cast into doubt. The hierarchical structure identified seems to be essentially a projection. How this predicament can be resolved is not obvious. Working computational incarnations of PP do exist, however. The predictive coding model of Rao and Ballard (1999) is often cited as a demonstration. If the scheme faces an irresolvable dilemma, how do we explain systems such as this, which seem to demonstrate its feasibility?

It is worth looking at the system described by Rao and Ballard in more detail. It is key to the design of this that predictions apply to sensory input directly. Layers are then representationally coordinated in the desired way. An error passed upward is always a residual error, on which basis reducing error at any layer of the hierarchy improves prediction of sensory data. In principle, this arrangement calls into question the hierarchical structure of the model, as noted. But in the Rao and Ballard system, the model's hierarchical structure has a validity that is seen to exist independently.

It is part of the system's design that the presentation of sensory input is itself hierarchically organized. Sensory data derives from the responses of visual receptive fields, as seen in Figure 8.5. Higher layers make reference to receptive fields that are hierarchically composed out of those referenced by lower layers. An error passed upward is then a residual error in a spatial sense. It refers to effects that extend beyond the limits of receptive fields for the current layer, but which remain within the composite fields referenced by the higher layer. Reducing error at any layer of the hierarchy then has the effect of tuning the model to the hierarchical structure of the input stream. The system is then seen to "learn a hierarchical internal model of its natural image inputs" (Rao and Ballard 1999: 80).

The Rao and Ballard system is of great interest, but there is a risk of over-interpreting it. The temptation is to assume that its derivation of a specifically hierarchical model is a consequence of the PP it carries out. This potentially leads to PP being viewed as a general, data-driven method for learning hierarchically structured models.[10] A

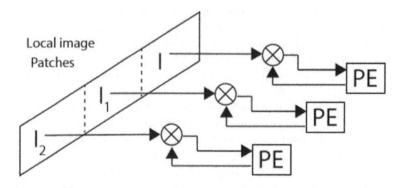

Figure 8.5 Detail from part C of Fig. 1, Rao and Ballard (1999) showing an initial stage in the hierarchical organization of sensory data. The "PE" units are predictive estimators. Higher-level predictive estimators' reference receptive fields that are hierarchically composed from fields referenced by lower-level estimators.

computational assessment of the situation suggests the method's capabilities fall short of this, and that it can be applied only to models whose hierarchical structure is pre-given and in some way externally validated.

At a more fine-grained level of detail, it is questions of calculation that become the main concern. What kinds of calculation should be used to progress the upward and downward flows that PP requires? Given the scheme's links to the Bayesian brain hypothesis, the expectation is that inferential calculations will suffice. As seen above, this is not what is found. A purely Bayesian way of implementing the downward flow can be identified—this is simply the process of "pulling down" priors which theorists such as Hohwy (2013) and Clark (2013) have long viewed as integral to the scheme. Implementation of the upward flow is more problematic, however.

The PP scheme envisages an upward flow in the form of prediction errors that are passed from layer to layer. The problem is that a hierarchical Bayesian model naturally gives rise to an upward flow in a different form. Derivations of posterior probability (i.e., applications of Bayes's rule) are also constitutive of an upward flow. The computational relationship between the two flows is then difficult to reconcile. The assumption that they proceed in parallel faces difficulties, as does the assumption that they are integrated. One possibility is to assume the inferential flow mediates the transmission of prediction error. The difficulty then faced is that there are meaningful predictive scenarios in which posterior probabilities cannot be derived.

Attempting to implement PP in a Bayesian/inferential way faces serious obstacles, then. Arguably, this is due to the incapacity of the Bayesian framework to deal satisfactorily with the phenomenon of prediction. Cases of prediction that cannot be conceptualized in Bayesian terms are easily identified. Any outcome may be predicted to have a probability that exceeds its observed probability. In some contexts, this is the norm. Rain that is observed to have a probability of .4 may be predicted—on evidential or theoretical grounds—to occur with probability .7. A car observed to break down with probability .2 may be predicted to break down with probability .8. A student observed to attend seminars with probability.6 may be predicted to attend one with probability.9, and so on. These predictions are in no way abnormal; all may turn out to yield errors in the usual way. From the Bayesian point of view, however, they are all intractable.

It is not that the Bayesian apparatus cannot be applied. A predicted probability can be expressed as the product of a likelihood and a hypothesis prior in the usual way. An observed probability can be expressed as the corresponding evidential prior. The difficulty is that the posterior probability of the hypothesis is then compromised. If the numerator in Bayes's rule exceeds the denominator, as it does in the cases above, what is obtained is a value greater than one. This cannot be a probability. An inferential approach to situations such as those above always fails in this way. It is arguable that the Bayesian framework is fundamentally ill-suited to deal with the phenomenon of prediction for this reason. The difficulty of obtaining a Bayesian implementation of PP may well be a reflection of this.

The main finding of the present inquiry is that information theory is of more use for clarifying the computational details of PP. In this respect, the analysis follows in the footsteps of Friston and colleagues (Friston 2005, 2010, 2013, Friston et al. 2012, 2017) and the informational conception of prediction that they advocate. This emphasizes the degree to which prediction and prediction error are intimately related to uncertainty and information. Successful prediction must reduce uncertainty, and reduction of uncertainty accomplishes information gain (Mackay 2003). Optimizing prediction of sensory input is equivalent to maximizing information gain in this sense. The objective of PP can then be viewed as the task of minimizing the average surprisal (informational uncertainty) of sensory data. The conceptual perspective that this leads to is well summarized by Friston's dictum that "Predictive coding is a consequence of surprise minimization" (Friston 2013: 32).[11]

With PP reconceptualized in this way, the proposal's scientific implications change to some degree. The idea that emerges is less that of a Bayesian brain and more that of an *infotropic* brain. Bayes's rule is seen to be replaced by information gain, as the underlying principle that guides processing (cf. Thornton 2014, 2017).[12] For present purposes, however, it is the practical benefits of the informational approach that are mainly of interest. The framework of information theory is found to provide all that is required for a computationally precise interpretation of PP.

Improving prediction of a state that itself predicts badly will not generally have the effect of improving the state's own predictive performance. A critical element of the PP scheme is thus the requirement for representational coordination of layers. The problem, as noted above, is that this cannot be met without effectively eliminating the all-important hierarchical structure of the referenced model.

Under the informational implementation, this catch-22 is dealt with to some degree. What is conveyed upward in this arrangement is not prediction error as such. It is informational quantities that are derived from those which define the sensory data. The upward flow consists of a series of abstractions of (derivations from) the sensory data in this sense. Predictions at higher layers then do refer to the sensory data, but at differing removes. There is then no reason to doubt the efficacy of the processing scheme. Reducing error higher in the hierarchy can have the effect of reducing it at the lowest layer as well. Equally, there is no reason to doubt the hierarchical structure of the model.

Notes

1   See Clark's assertion that each layer must be "capable of predicting the response profiles at the layer below" (Clark 2016: 93); see also Williams's observation that "the data for every level of the hierarchy—with the exception of the first—consists of representations at the level below" (Williams 2018: 151).

2   Clark notes that "in the standard implementation of PP higher level 'representation units' send predictive signals laterally (within level) and downwards (to the next level down) thus providing priors on activity at the subordinate level" (Clark 2016: 143).

3   Neutral predictions are problematic for the same reason. Imagine the predicted probability of rain is .5. Given the observed probability of rain is also .5, this prediction is entirely neutral. It is completely without value and, in that sense, maximally in error. The derived posterior, on the other hand, is now maximized, implying minimal prediction error.

4   An additional problem with this implementation is that it fails to respect the stipulated architectural requirements. It is seen as a key part of the scheme that there should be a "functional separation between encodings of prediction and prediction error" (Clark 2016: 39).

5   The quantity is expressed in bits just in case logs are taken to base 2.

6   We might have $Q(rain) = .3$ and $Q(no\ rain) = .7$, for example.

7   The formulation presented in (Thornton 2017) differs in the way it discounts disrewards in the case of there being more than one non-occurring outcome.

8   Clark states that prediction error should reflect "the 'surprise' induced by a mismatch between the sensory signals encountered and those predicted. More formally—and to distinguish it from surprise in the normal, experientially loaded sense—this is known as surprisal" (Clark 2016: 25).

9   In Williams's (2018) description, "the data for every level of the hierarchy—with the exception of the first—consists of representations at the level below" (Williams 2018: 151).

10   Consider, for example, Lupyan and Clark (2015) who suggest that a "remarkable consequence of this [predictive processing] arrangement is that seeking to reduce the overall prediction error produces representations at multiple levels of abstraction, flexibly incorporating whatever sources of knowledge help to reduce the overall prediction error" (Lupyan and Clark 2015: 279).

11   Friston's position is that surprisal must be minimized indirectly, via a bound termed free energy; the ground proposition is termed the free energy principle accordingly. The identified connection with surprisal remains unaffected, however. As Wiese and Metzinger note, "free energy constitutes a tight bound on the surprisal of sensory signals. Hence, minimizing free energy by changing sensory signals will, implicitly, minimize surprisal" (Wiese and Metzinger 2017: 12). Furthermore, free energy "on most PP accounts would amount to the long-term average of prediction error" (Wiese and Metzinger 2017: 18).

12   It also suggests neural signals convey information encoded in a positive or negative (i.e., bidirectional) form. Potentially relevant to this is the observation that neural signals in the dopaminergic system can be modulated in a bidirectional way (Keller and Mrsic-Flogel 2018: 425). Spratling (2017), however, takes the view that positive and negative firing rates are "biologically implausible" (Spratling 2017: 94).

References

Berger, J. O. (1985), *Statistical Decision Theory and Bayesian Analysis*, 2nd ed., Berlin: Springer-Verlag.

Brown, H., Friston, K. and Bestamnn, S. (2011), "Active Inference, Attention and Motor Preparation," *Frontiers in Psychology*, 2: 218.

Clark, A. (2013), "Whatever Next? Predictive Brains, Situated Agents, and the Future of Cognitive Science," *Behavioral and Brain Sciences*, 36: 181–253.

Clark, A. (2016), *Surfing Uncertainty: Prediction, Action, and the Embodied Mind*, Oxford: Oxford University Press.

Doya, K., Ishii, S., Rao, R. P. N. and Pouget, A. (eds.) (2007), *The Bayesian Brain: Probabilistic Approaches to Neural Coding*, Cambridge: MIT Press.

Eliasmith, C. (2007), "How to Build a Brain: From Function to Implementation," *Synthese*, 159: 373–88.

Friston, K. (2005), "A Theory of Cortical Responses," *Philosophical Transactions of the Royal Society of London B: Biological Sciences*, 360 (1456): 815–36.

Friston, K. (2013), "Active Inference and Free Energy," *Behavioral and Brain Sciences*, 36: 212–13.

Friston, K., Thornton, C. and Clark, A. (2012), "Free-energy Minimization and the Dark Room Problem," *Frontiers in Perception Science*, 3: 130.

Friston, K., Rigoli, F., Schwartenbeck, P. and Pezzulo, G. (2017), "Active Inference: A Process Theory," *Neural Computation*, 29 (1): 1–49.

Friston, K. J. (2010), "The Free-energy Principle: A Unified Brain Theory?" *Nature Reviews Neuroscience*, 11 (2): 127–38.

Friston, K. J., Daunizeau, J. and Kiebel, S. J. (2009), "Reinforcement Learning or Active Inference," *PLoS One*, 4 (7): 1–13.

Hohwy, J. (2013), *The Predictive Mind*, Oxford: Oxford University Press.

Hohwy, J., Roepstorff, A. and Friston, K. (2008), "Predictive Coding Explains Binocular Rivalry: An Epistemological Review," *Cognition*, 108 (3): 687–701.

Howson, C. and Urbach, P. (1989), *Scientific Reasoning: The Bayesian Approach*, Chicago: Open Court Publishing Co.

Huang, Y. and Rao, R. (2011), "Predictive Coding," *Wiley Interdisciplinary Reviews: Cognitive Science*, 2: 580–93.

James, W. (1890/1950), *The Principles of Psychology*, Vol. 1, New York: Dover.

Jaynes, E. T. (2003), *Probability Theory: The Logic of Science*, Cambridge, UK: Cambridge University Press.

Jehee, J. F. M. and Ballard, D. H. (2009), "Predictive Feedback Can Account for Biphasic Responses in the Lateral Geniculate Nucleus," *PLoS (Public Library of Science) Computational Biology*, 5 (5): e1000373.

Keller, G. B. and Mrsic-Flogel, T. D. (2018), "Predictive Processing: A Canonical Cortical Computation," *Neuron*, 100 (2): 424–35.

Knill, D. C. and Pouget, A. (2004), "The Bayesian Brain: The Role of Uncertainty in Neural Coding and Computation," *Trends in Neuroscience*, 27 (12): 712–19.

Kobayashi, H. (1974), "Image Data Compression by Predictive Coding I: Prediction Algorithms," *Journal of Research and Development*, 18 (2): 164–71.

Lashley, K. S. (1951), "The Problem of Serial Order in Behavior" in Jeffries (ed.), *Cerebral Mechanisms in Behavior*, New York: John Wiley & Sons.

Lee, T. S. and Mumford, D. (2003), "Hierarchical Bayesian Inference in the Visual Cortex," *Journal of Optical Society of America*, A, 20 (7): 1434–48.

Lupyan, G. and Clark, A. (2015), "Words and the World: Predictive Coding and the Language-Perception-Cognition Interface," *Current Directions in Psychological Science*, 24 (4): 279–84.

Mackay, D. (1956), "Towards an Information-flow Model of Human Behaviour," *British Journal of Psychology*, 43: 30–43.

Mackay, D. J. C. (2003), *Information Theory, Inference, and Learning Algorithms*, Cambridge: Cambridge University Press.

Pensiri, F. and Auwatanamongkol, S. (2012), "A Lossless Image Compression Algorithm Using Predictive Coding Based on Quantized Colors," *WSEAS Trans- Actions on Signal Processing*, 8 (2): 43–53.

Pouget, A., Beck, J., Ma, W. J. and Latham, P. (2013), "Probabilistic Brains: Knowns and Unknowns," *Nature Neuroscience*, 16 (9): 1170–8.

Rao, R. P. N. and Ballard, D. H. (1999), "Predictive Coding in the Visual Cortex: A Functional Interpretation of Some Extra-classical Receptive-field Effects," *Nature Neuroscience*, 2 (1): 79–87.

Rao, R. P. N. and Ballard, D. H. (2004), "Probabilistic Models of Attention Based on Iconic Representations and Predictive Coding" in Itti, Rees and Tsotsos (eds.), *Neurobiology of Attention*, Cambridge: Academic Press.

Shannon, C. and Weaver, W. (1949), *The Mathematical Theory of Communication*, Urbana: University of Illinois Press.

Shannon, C. E. (1948), "A Mathematical Theory of Communication," *Bell System Technical Journal*, 27: 379–423 & 623–56.

Spratling, M. V. (2017), "A Review of Predictive Coding Algorithms," *Brain and Cognition*, 112: 92–7.

Thornton, C. (2014), "Infotropism as the Underlying Principle of Perceptual Organization," *Journal of Mathematical Psychology*, 61: 38–44.

Thornton, C. (2017), "Predictive Processing Simplified: The Infotropic Machine," *Brain & Cognition*, 112: 13–24.

Tolman, E. C. (1948), "Cognitive Maps in Rats and Men," *Psychological Review*, 55: 189–208.

Tribus, M. (1961), *Thermostatics and Thermodynamics*, Princeton, NJ: D. Van Nostrand.

Von Helmholtz, H. (1867), *Handbuch der physiologischen Optik*, Leipzig: Leopold Voss.

Wiese, W. and Metzinger, T. (2017), "Vanilla PP for Philosophers: A Primer on Predictive Processing" in Metzinger and Wiese (eds.), *Philosophy and Predictive Processing*, Frankfurt am Main: MIND Group.

Williams, D. (2018), "Predictive Processing and the Representation Wars," *Minds & Machines*, 28: 141–72.

Yon, D., de Lange, F. P. and Press, C. (2019), "The Predictive Brain as a Stubborn Scientist," *Trends in Cognitive Sciences*, 23 (1): 6–8.

Part Three

Predictive Processing: Mental Health

9

The Predictive Brain, Conscious Experience, and Brain-related Conditions

Lorena Chanes

Department of Clinical and Health Psychology-Serra Húnter Programme, Universitat Autònoma de Barcelona, Catalunya, Spain

Lisa Feldman Barrett

Department of Psychology, Northeastern University, Boston, United States & Department of Psychiatry and the Athinoula A. Martinos Center for Biomedical Imaging, Massachusetts General Hospital, Charlestown, United States

An Architecture for Predictive Processing in the Cerebral Cortex

Predictive processing has emerged over the past decades as an integrative framework to understand perception and action (for recent reviews, see, for example, Clark 2013, Friston 2010, Hohwy 2013). According to these approaches, the brain works as a hypothesis tester, constantly generating predictions to explain the input it receives through the different peripheral sensors (retina, cochlea, etc.). Predictions are generated using an internal model based on past experience and are contrasted with actual sensory evidence leading to updating the internal model if needed, in a constant interplay that results in our unique experience of the world. In recent years, an increasing number of works have proposed predictive processing perspectives for a myriad aspects of brain function including multiple perceptual phenomena (e.g., Rao and Ballard 1999), speech (Hickok 2012), attention (Hohwy 2012, Kok et al. 2012), pain (e.g., Roy et al. 2014), emotion (Barrett 2017, Hoemann et al. 2017, Seth 2013, Seth and Critchley 2013), sociality (Atzil et al. 2018, Chanes et al. 2018), self-recognition (Apps and Tsakiris 2014), and allostasis (Sterling 2012). In the clinical domain, predictive processing models have been proposed to understand different brain-related conditions, including autism spectrum disorders (Lawson et al. 2014, Pellicano and Burr 2012, Sinha et al. 2014, Van de Cruys et al. 2014), depression (Bar 2009, Barrett et al. 2016), schizophrenia (Fletcher and Frith 2009, Fogelson et al. 2014), and psychosis (Sterzer et al. 2018). All these proposals have importantly contributed to the emergent picture that the brain works predictively, and that mental illness may be understood as disruptions of this predictive organization. However, these models often build on the core idea of predictive processing, leaving relatively open the computational details, the formalization of which can be complex (see, for example, Friston 2005, 2010), as well as the specific underlying neuroanatomical substrate of the circuits involved. An integration of predictive processing notions within a general anatomical model of how the cortex is structurally and functionally organized across systems may lead to novel insights on our understanding of brain function in health and disease. Such efforts often require integrating knowledge from different fields of study that have traditionally remained apart and are still relatively rare (although see, for example, Bastos et al. 2012, Chanes and Barrett 2016, Mesulam 2012).

Within the cerebral cortex, the notion of a hypothesis testing scheme in which predictions are contrasted with sensory evidence is understood within a hierarchy (Mumford 1992). At each level of such hierarchy, predictions cascading from the immediately higher level are compared with the sensory input left to be explained at the immediately lower level. The difference, called prediction error, is relayed up the hierarchy. Moreover, the idea that the cortex is hierarchically organized is also present in the neuroanatomical literature studying sensory pathways (e.g., Jones and Powell 1970, Mesulam 1998). In these studies, cortico-cortical connections have been typically described according to the direction of information flow, as feedback (backward or descending; predictions, in predictive processing terms) when they connect higher to lower areas, or feedforward (forward or ascending; prediction errors, in predictive processing terms) when they move away from primary sensory cortices (for reviews see Barbas and Rempel-Clower 1997, Felleman and Van Essen 1991, for recent reviews see Barbas 2015, Pandya et al. 2015). Feedback and feedforward connections present a specific laminar structure, differing in the cortical layers that they predominantly originate and terminate in (for a review, see Felleman and Van Essen 1991). This breadth of knowledge informed neural implementations of predictive processing, leading to the proposal that predictions originate predominantly in deep layers, being conveyed primarily to the superficial layers of a lower level (feedback), whereas prediction errors originate predominantly in superficial layers, being conveyed primarily to the deep layers of a higher level (feedforward) (Bastos et al. 2012, Friston 2005, 2010). Moving one step further in the neuroanatomical literature, the structural model of cortico-cortical connections proposed that the direction of information flow, that is, whether the connection is feedback or feedforward, is predicted by the laminar structure of the connected cortical areas (Barbas and Rempel-Clower 1997, for recent reviews see Barbas 2015, García-Cabezas et al. 2019). According to the structural model, feedback connections originate in cortical areas with a lower degree of laminar differentiation than the cortical areas they terminate in, whereas feedforward connections follow the opposite pattern, originating in cortical areas that are better laminated than the ones they terminate in (Barbas and Rempel-Clower 1997). Thus, feedback connections parallel the progressively increasing degree of laminar differentiation of the cortex (from less to more laminated areas), whereas feedforward connections follow the opposite direction. An implication of implementing predictive coding within the structural model of cortico-cortical connections is that predictions originate in less laminated cortical areas, flowing to better-laminated areas, whereas prediction errors originate in better-laminated areas and flow to less laminated ones (Barrett 2017, Barrett and

Simmons 2015, Chanes and Barrett 2016). It has to be noted that it remains unclear whether or how this implementation may be extended beyond the neocortex to include allocortical and/or subcortical structures, as it is not well understood whether or how the structural model of cortico-cortical connections itself holds beyond neocortical areas. Moreover, the structural model describes a systematic organization of connections that applies beyond sensory systems (Barbas 2015), extending the notion of "feedback" and "feedforward" and providing a general architecture for how predictive signals flow across the whole cerebral cortex (Chanes and Barrett 2016).

Cortical Limbic Areas: At the Core of the Cortical Architecture for Prediction

A direct implication of predictions flowing (following feedback connections) from less to more laminated areas is that the position of a given cortical area in the predictive hierarchy is determined by its laminar structure. Thus, areas with a low degree of laminar differentiation occupy top levels of the cortical hierarchy, issuing predictions that cascade to the rest of the cortex (Chanes and Barrett 2016); these are agranular (no layer IV) and dysgranular (rudimentary layer IV) areas, adjacent to the allocortex, and are known together as cortical limbic areas (Barbas 2015).[1] Moreover, representations at high levels in the hierarchy are highly abstract, while information representations become progressively more concrete at lower levels, which correspond to more specialized areas (Mesulam 1998, Mumford 1992). This spatial organization is paralleled by a suitable temporal structure, so that higher levels, representing more abstract, integrated, stable information, would be associated to slower rhythms than lower levels needing to sample the environment in real time (Kiebel et al. 2008, Murray et al. 2014). Thus, predictions issued by cortical limbic areas are highly abstract and involve longer periods of time, becoming more specific and tracking faster events as they reach progressively lower-level better-laminated areas (e.g., eulaminate I, eulaminate II in structure following the terminology used in Barbas 2015). Given their high level of abstraction, cortical limbic areas are shared across cortical systems, whereas lower levels in the hierarchy, such as unimodal association areas and primary sensory cortices, relate primarily to a specific cortical system (e.g., visual, auditory). Sensory evidence from the different sensory modalities reaches the cortex primarily at the lowest level of the different cortical sensory systems (primary sensory cortices), it is compared with predictions at that level, and the resulting prediction error (difference) is relayed to upper levels to be used to update the model and subsequent predictions if needed. It has to be noted that there are differences across sensory modalities regarding the cortical structure of the lowest level of the predictive hierarchy, that is, the level at which sensory input from a specific sensory modality reaches the cerebral cortex (primary sensory cortices). Whereas for some systems (visual, auditory, somatosensory) sensory input reaches the cortex at koniocortical areas, that is, areas exhibiting well-differentiated six layers, including a prominent layer IV, in other systems (gustatory, interoceptive) sensory input reaches the cortex at comparatively less laminated areas. The implications of a varying degree of laminar differentiation across primary sensory cortices would need to be assessed in the future (for a brief discussion, see Chanes and Barrett 2016). Moreover, this general scheme of cortical organization may be extended beyond sensory systems (see, for example, the notion of active inference Friston et al. 2011). For example, the motor system also involves areas with different degrees of laminar differentiation, with the primary motor cortex presenting the better-laminated structure, including a layer IV (Barbas and Garcia-Cabezas 2015, Morecraft et al. 2012). All these cortical systems would be structured following a gradient of laminar differentiation, higher levels corresponding to less laminated areas. Although cortical limbic areas would be shared across cortical systems, similarly to multimodal areas at the immediately lower level, some degree of functional specialization is likely to exist among them and remains to be better understood.

Within this general cortical organization, cortical limbic areas occupy a privileged position, as predictions generated in these areas can reach the rest of the cerebral cortex by cascading down the predictive hierarchy to reach the lowest level of each cortical system. Moreover, these areas are strongly interconnected and hold intense connections to allocortical and subcortical structures such as the amygdala and the hypothalamus (for a brief review see Chanes and Barrett 2016). Taken together, such organization enables highly integrated abstract representations in limbic cortices, including important information related to current state and needs of the organism, to be readily accessible by virtually the whole brain (Chanes and Barrett 2016). Being at the core of the brain's architecture for prediction, holding highly abstract representations, with privileged connections to reach the whole brain, led to the proposal that limbic cortices may play a relevant role in conscious experience (Chanes and Barrett 2016). Moreover, limbic cortices have been recently shown to exhibit a "high-level connector" connectivity profile, integrating already highly integrated information across systems (Zhang et al. 2019). A role of these areas in conscious experience is further supported by multiple observations that disruptions at the level of cortical limbic areas lead to important, core, disruptions of the person's experience in/of the world, as outlined below.

Predictive Cortical Architecture Disruptions in Mental Disorders, Focal Brain Damage, and Neurodegenerative Diseases

Mental disorders, focal lesions, and neurodegenerative diseases are likely to alter the general principles of cortical organization described above, disrupting the flow of predictive signals in the brain. Mental disorders typically involve the disruption of fundamental aspects of a person's affective, cognitive, and behavioral functioning, rather than specific aspects within a single functional domain. The neural bases of these disorders have been shown to be largely distributed, with a potential neurodevelopmental component for at least some of the disorders (e.g., Christensen and Bilder 2000). In line with this notion, within the predictive processing framework, the models proposed for different mental disorders typically describe general disruptions of predictive signals, rather than disturbances within specific systems. The cortical architecture for prediction described above provides a basis for hypotheses about potential neural implementations for these models. For example, autism spectrum disorders have been described as involving altered, and particularly "attenuated," predictions, which would lead to a perception of the world that is "more accurate" (less influenced by priors) (Pellicano and Burr 2012) but that may seem "magical," as it may be difficult to infer the causes of experience (Sinha et al. 2014). The cortical organization described above suggests that this could result from impairments at high levels in the hierarchy, responsible for highly abstract predictions, notably cortical limbic areas issuing predictions to lower-level areas with a higher degree of laminar differentiation. Neuroanatomical data supports this hypothesis, as axons leaving cortical limbic areas (anterior cingulate and posterior orbitofrontal cortices) have been shown to be more affected in individuals diagnosed with autism spectrum disorders than axons leaving lower-level multimodal areas, such as the dorsolateral prefrontal cortex (Trutzer et al. 2019, Zikopoulos and Barbas 2010, 2013, Zikopoulos et al. 2018). This would lead to deficits of predictions at high, general, levels of the hierarchy, making abstraction difficult. Another example is depression, as predictive processing approaches have proposed that this disorder may be related to a "locked in" brain (relatively insensitive to prediction error) (Barrett et al. 2016) functioning in a way that may not be efficient (Bar 2009, Barrett et al. 2016). Indeed, in individuals diagnosed with depression, the subgenual anterior cingulate cortex, a cortical limbic area, has been shown to be hyperactive (Mayberg et al. 1999), and downregulation of axons leaving this area using deep brain stimulation can help individuals with treatment-resistant disease (Mayberg et al. 2005). These observations possibly reflect a cortical organization "dominated" by predictions issued by limbic cortices, as well as an amelioration of symptoms through the "rebalancing" of predictive signals along the predictive hierarchy. In line with a dominance of high-level predictions at the cortical limbic level, the dorsolateral prefrontal cortex, at the immediately lower (better-laminated) level, appears to be hypoactive in these individuals, and noninvasive brain stimulation of this area has been shown to improve symptoms (for a review, see, for example, Koenigs and Grafman 2009), possibly as a result of rebalancing predictive signals to counteract limbic prediction dominance. A whole-cortex theoretical approach to brain organization and function, anchored on solid neuroanatomical knowledge, can contribute to better understand why different treatments may work for the same condition and, moreover, may guide the identification of novel targets (for a discussion on the interest of network approaches see Fox et al. 2013, 2014). Although mental disorders are likely to alter cortical organization across multiple levels, disrupting the flow of predictive signals in the brain, disruptions of cortical limbic areas seem to be commonly observed. Because of their key position in the predictive hierarchy, disruptions at that level are more likely to yield significant disruptions of the whole cortical architecture than are disruptions to better-laminated areas, which occupy lower more specialized levels. This, together with the notion that higher levels represent highly abstract information (Mesulam 1998, Mumford 1992) at slower temporal scales (Kiebel et al. 2008, Murray et al. 2014), suggests that cortical limbic disruptions may crucially contribute to the general, fundamental, cognitive-affective-behavioral disturbances observed across mental disorders. Indeed, a recent meta-analysis of 193 structural neuroimaging studies across multiple mental disorder diagnoses (schizophrenia, bipolar disorder, depression, addiction, obsessive-compulsive disorder, and anxiety) found that gray matter loss converged in three regions, the dorsal anterior cingulate, the left and the right insula (Goodkind et al. 2015), all of which are limbic in structure.

A similar picture emerges from the study of focal lesions. Within the frontal cortex, syndromes arising from focal lesions to less laminated areas, including cortical limbic areas, involve profound, fundamental disruptions in motility and motivation, as observed in the abulic hypokinetic syndrome and the disinhibited hyperkinetic syndrome, respectively (Giaccio 2006). In contrast, more subtle impairments of motility and volition are observed when the damaged areas are better laminated, as observed in the dysexecutive syndrome and environmental dependency syndrome, respectively (Giaccio 2006). Thus, lesions at higher levels in the cortical hierarchy seem to lead to disturbances of core aspects of the person's experience of/in the world.

Moreover, the important involvement of cortical limbic areas in brain damage and disorders can also be observed in neurodegenerative diseases. In Alzheimer's and Parkinson's disease, the two most prevalent neurodegenerative diseases (Erkkinen et al. 2018), problematic aggregation of proteins tau and α-synuclein, respectively, follows a specific topographical spreading pattern, propagating from limbic to progressively better-laminated areas (Arnold et al. 1991, Braak et al. 2006, for a review see Brettschneider et al. 2015). This pattern of progression overlaps with the degree of laminar differentiation so that the more laminated an area is the later in the progression of illness it will be affected, suggesting particular vulnerability of cortical limbic areas for pathology related to neuropsychiatric disease. Cortical limbic vulnerability is also suggested by recent evidence that the expression of markers of stability and plasticity vary along the systematic variation of cortical structure (García-Cabezas et al. 2017). Such evidence indicates that cortical limbic areas show enhanced plasticity but also low stability, which may make them vulnerable to disease (García-Cabezas et al. 2017). Along the same lines, neuroimaging evidence from postnatal development has shown that cortico-cortical connectivity between cortical limbic, allocortical, and association areas is significantly stronger at later stages of development (childhood vs. adulthood) (Supekar et al. 2009) and during network maturation (particularly regarding the default mode network) limbic cortices (specifically the posterior and pregenual anterior cingulate cortex) are the ones primarily undergoing changes (Supekar et al. 2010). During early development, a hierarchical brain organization have been shown to emerge, converging in high-level areas, including cortical limbic areas (Pendl et al. 2017).

Together, evidence from brain-related conditions indicates that a neural implementation of predictive processing within a solid neuroanatomical model valid across cortical systems may provide an integrative framework to better understand brain organization and function in health and disease. It is also in line with the notion that limbic cortices occupy high levels in the cortical hierarchy, holding representations and yielding predictions that can reach the whole brain, with fundamental consequences for a person's experience of/in the world when these areas are disrupted either as a result of macroscopic focal damage or because of brain-related diseases.

Note

1   For related ideas of a hierarchical cortical processing organization in which cortical limbic areas, sometimes called paralimbic, occupy high levels, see Mesulam (1998, 2012).

References

Apps, M. A. and Tsakiris, M. (2014), "The Free-Energy Self: A Predictive Coding Account of Self-Recognition," *Neuroscience & Biobehavioral Reviews*, 41: 85–97. doi. org/10.1016/j.neubiorev.2013.01.029.

Arnold, S. E., Hyman, B. T., Flory, J., Damasio, A. R. and Van Hoesen, G. W. (1991), "The Topographical and Neuroanatomical Distribution of Neurofibrillary Tangles and Neuritic Plaques in the Cerebral Cortex of Patients with Alzheimer's Disease," *Cerebral Cortex*, 1 (1): 103–16. doi.org/10.1093/cercor/1.1.103.

Atzil, S., Gao, W., Fradkin, I. and Barrett, L. F. (2018), "Growing a Social Brain," *Nature Human Behaviour*, 2: 624–36. doi.org/10.1038/s41562-018-0384-6.

Bar, M. (2009), "A Cognitive Neuroscience Hypothesis of Mood and Depression," *Trends in Cognitive Sciences*, 13 (11): 456–63. doi.org/10.1016/j.tics.2009.08.009.

Barbas, H. (2015), "General Cortical and Special Prefrontal Connections: Principles from Structure to Function," *Annual Review of Neuroscience*, 38: 269–89. doi.org/10.1146/ annurev-neuro-071714-033936.

Barbas, H. and Garcia-Cabezas, M. A. (2015), "Motor Cortex Layer 4: Less Is More," *Trends in Neurosciences*, 38 (5): 259–61. doi.org/10.1016/j.tins.2015.03.005.

Barbas, H. and Rempel-Clower, N. (1997), "Cortical Structure Predicts the Pattern of Corticocortical Connections," *Cerebral Cortex*, 7 (7): 635–46.

Barrett, L. F. (2017), *How Emotions Are Made*, Boston: Houghton Mifflin Harcourt.

Barrett, L. F. and Simmons, W. K. (2015), "Interoceptive Predictions in the Brain," *Nature Reviews Neuroscience*, 16 (7): 419–29. doi.org/10.1038/nrn3950.

Barrett, L. F., Quigley, K. and Hamilton, P. (2016), "An Active Inference Theory of Allostasis and Interoception in Depression," *Philosophical Transactions of the Royal Society of London. Series B*, 371 (1708): 20160011. doi.org/10.1098/rstb.2016.0011.

Bastos, A. M., Usrey, W. M., Adams, R. A., Mangun, G. R., Fries, P. and Friston, K. J. (2012), "Canonical Microcircuits for Predictive Coding," *Neuron*, 76 (4): 695–711. doi. org/10.1016/j.neuron.2012.10.038.

Braak, H., Bohl, J. R., Müller, C. M., Rüb, Udo, de, V., Rob, A.I. and Del Tredici, K. (2006), "Stanley Fahn Lecture 2005: The Staging Procedure for the Inclusion Body Pathology Associated with Sporadic Parkinson's Disease Reconsidered," *Movement Disorders*, 21 (12): 2042–51. doi.org/10.1002/mds.21065.

Brettschneider, J., Del Tredici, K., Lee, V. M. Y. and Trojanowski, J. Q. (2015), "Spreading of Pathology in Neurodegenerative Diseases: A Focus on Human Studies," *Nature Reviews Neuroscience*, 16 (2): 109–20. doi.org/10.1038/nrn3887.

Chanes, L. and Barrett, L. F. (2016), "Redefining the Role of Limbic Areas in Cortical Processing," *Trends in Cognitive Sciences*, 20 (2): 96–106. doi.org/10.1016/j. tics.2015.11.005.

Chanes, L., Wormwood, J. B., Betz, N. and Barrett, L. F. (2018), "Facial Expression Predictions as Drivers of Social Perception," *Journal of Personality and Social Psychology*, 114 (3): 380–96. doi.org/10.1037/pspa0000108.

Christensen, B. K. and Bilder, R. M. (2000), "Dual Cytoarchitectonic Trends: An Evolutionary Model of Frontal Lobe Functioning and Its Application to Psychopathology," *Canadian Journal of Psychiatry*, 45 (3): 247–56. doi. org/10.1177/070674370004500303.

Clark, A. (2013), "Whatever Next? Predictive Brains, Situated Agents, and the Future of Cognitive Science," *Behavioral and Brain Sciences*, 36 (3): 181–204. dx.doi.org/10.1017/ S0140525X12000477.

Van de Cruys, S., Evers, K., Hallen, R., Eylen, L., Boets, B., De-Wit, L. and Wagemans, J. (2014), "Precise Minds in Uncertain Worlds: Predictive Coding in Autism," *Psychological Review*, 121 (4): 649–75. doi.org/10.1037/a0037665.

Erkkinen, M. G., Kim, M.-O. and Geschwind, M. D. (2018), "Clinical Neurology and Epidemiology of the Major Neurodegenerative Diseases," *Cold Spring Harbor Perspectives in Biology*, 10 (4): a033118. doi.org/10.1101/cshperspect.a033118.

Felleman, D. J. and Van Essen, D. C. (1991), "Distributed Hierarchical Processing in the Primate Cerebral Cortex," *Cerebral Cortex*, 1 (1): 1–47.

Fletcher, P. C. and Frith, C. D. (2009), "Perceiving Is Believing: A Bayesian Approach to Explaining the Positive Symptoms of Schizophrenia," *Nature Reviews Neuroscience*, 10 (1): 48–58. doi.org/10.1038/nrn2536.

Fogelson, N., Litvak, V., Peled, A., Fernandez-del-Olmo, M. and Friston, K. (2014), "The Functional Anatomy of Schizophrenia: A Dynamic Causal Modeling Study of Predictive Coding," *Schizophrenia Research*, 158 (1–3): 204–12. doi.org/10.1016/j. schres.2014.06.011.

Fox, M. D., Liu, H. and Pascual-Leone, A. (2013), "Identification of Reproducible Individualized Targets for Treatment of Depression with TMS Based on Intrinsic Connectivity," *NeuroImage*, 66: 151–60. doi.org/10.1016/j.neuroimage.2012.10.082.

Fox, M. D., Buckner, R. L., Liu, H., Chakravarty, M., Lozano, A. M. and Pascual-Leone, A. (2014), "Resting-State Networks Link Invasive and Noninvasive Brain Stimulation across Diverse Psychiatric and Neurological Diseases," *Proceedings of the National Academy of Sciences*, 111 (41): E4367–75. doi.org/10.1073/PNAS.1405003111.

Friston, K. (2005), "A Theory of Cortical Responses," *Philosophical Transactions of the Royal Society B: Biological Sciences*, 360 (1456): 815–36. doi.org/10.1098/ rstb.2005.1622.

Friston, K. (2010), "The Free-Energy Principle: A Unified Brain Theory?" *Nature Reviews Neuroscience*, 11 (2): 127–38. doi.org/10.1038/nrn2787.

Friston, K., Mattout, J. and Kilner, J. (2011), "Action Understanding and Active Inference," *Biological Cybernetics*, 104 (1–2): 137–60. doi.org/10.1007/s00422-011-0424-z.

García-Cabezas, Á., Zikopoulos, M. B. and Barbas, H. (2019), "The Structural Model: A Theory Linking Connections, Plasticity, Pathology, Development and Evolution of the Cerebral Cortex," *Brain Structure and Function*, 224 (3): 985–1008. doi.org/10.1007/ s00429-019-01841-9.

García-Cabezas, M., Joyce, M. K. P., John, Y. J., Zikopoulos, B. and Barbas, H. (2017), "Mirror Trends of Plasticity and Stability Indicators in Primate Prefrontal Cortex," *European Journal of Neuroscience*, 46 (8): 2392–405. doi.org/10.1111/ejn.13706.

Giaccio, R. G. (2006), "The Dual Origin Hypothesis: An Evolutionary Brain-Behavior Framework for Analyzing Psychiatric Disorders," *Neuroscience and Biobehavioral Reviews*, 30 (4): 526–50. doi.org/10.1016/j.neubiorev.2005.04.021.

Goodkind, M., Eickhoff, S. B., Oathes, D. J., Jiang, Y., Chang, A., Jones-hagata, L. B., Ortega, B. N. et al. (2015), "Identification of a Common Neurobiological Substrate for Mental Illness," *JAMA Psychiatry*, 5797 (4): 305–15. doi.org/10.1001/jamapsychiatry.2014.2206.

Hickok, G. (2012), "The Cortical Organization of Speech Processing: Feedback Control and Predictive Coding the Context of a Dual-Stream Model," *Journal of Communication Disorders*, 45 (6): 393–402. doi.org/10.1016/j.jcomdis.2012.06.004.

Hoemann, K., Gendron, M. and Barrett, L. F. (2017), "Mixed Emotions in the Predictive Brain," *Current Opinion in Behavioral Sciences*, 15: 51–7. doi.org/10.1016/j.cobeha.2017.05.013.

Hohwy, J. (2012), "Attention and Conscious Perception in the Hypothesis Testing Brain," *Frontiers in Psychology*, 3: 96. doi.org/10.3389/fpsyg.2012.00096.

Hohwy, J. (2013), *The Predictive Mind*, New York: Oxford University Press.

Jones, E. G. and Powell, T. P. (1970), "An Anatomical Study of Converging Sensory Pathways within the Cerebral Cortex of the Monkey," *Brain*, 93 (4): 793–820.

Kiebel, S. J., Daunizeau, J. and Friston, K. J. (2008), "A Hierarchy of Time-Scales and the Brain," *PLoS Computational Biology*, 4 (11): e1000209. doi.org/10.1371/journal.pcbi.1000209.

Koenigs, M. and Grafman, J. (2009), "The Functional Neuroanatomy of Depression: Distinct Roles for Ventromedial and Dorsolateral Prefrontal Cortex," *Behavioural Brain Research*, 201: 239–43.

Kok, P., Rahnev, D., Jehee, J. F. M., Lau, H. C. and De Lange, F. P. (2012), "Attention Reverses the Effect of Prediction in Silencing Sensory Signals," *Cerebral Cortex*, 22 (9): 2197–206. doi.org/10.1093/cercor/bhr310.

Lawson, R. P., Rees, G. and Friston, K. J. (2014), "An Aberrant Precision Account of Autism," *Frontiers in Human Neuroscience*, 8: 302. doi.org/10.3389/fnhum.2014.00302.

Mayberg, H. S., Liotti, M., Brannan, S. K., McGinnis, S., Mahurin, R. K., Jerabek, P. A., Silva, J. A. et al. (1999), "Reciprocal Limbic-Cortical Function and Negative Mood: Converging PET Findings in Depression and Normal Sadness," *American Journal of Psychiatry*, 156 (5): 675–82. doi.org/10.1176/ajp.156.5.675.

Mayberg, H. S., Lozano, A. M., Voon, V., McNeely, H. E., Seminowicz, D., Hamani, C., Schwalb, J. M. and Kennedy, S. H. (2005), "Deep Brain Stimulation for Treatment-Resistant Depression," *Neuron*, 45 (5): 651–60. doi.org/10.1016/j.neuron.2005.02.014.

Mesulam, M. M. (1998), "From Sensation to Cognition," *Brain*, 121 (Pt6): 1013–52.

Mesulam, M. M. (2012), "The Evolving Landscape of Human Cortical Connectivity: Facts and Inferences," *Neuroimage*, 62 (4): 2182–9. doi.org/10.1016/j.neuroimage.2011.12.033.

Morecraft, R. J., Stilwell-Morecraft, K. S., Cipolloni, P. B., Ge, J., McNeal, D. W. and Pandya, D. N. (2012), "Cytoarchitecture and Cortical Connections of the Anterior Cingulate and Adjacent Somatomotor Fields in the Rhesus Monkey," *Brain Research Bulletin*, 87 (4–5): 457–97. doi.org/10.1016/j.brainresbull.2011.12.005.

Mumford, D. (1992), "On the Computational Architecture of the Neocortex. II. The Role of Cortico-Cortical Loops," *Biological Cybernetics*, 66 (3): 241–51.

Murray, J. D., Bernacchia, A., Freedman, D. J., Romo, R., Wallis, J. D., Cai, X., Padoa-Schioppa, C. et al. (2014), "A Hierarchy of Intrinsic Timescales across Primate Cortex," *Nature Neuroscience*, 17 (12): 1661–3. doi.org/10.1038/nn.3862.

Pandya, D. N., Petrides, M., Seltzer, B. and Cipolloni, P. B. (2015), *Cerebral Cortex: Architecture, Connections, and the Dual Origin Concept*, New York: Oxford University Press.

Pellicano, E. and Burr, D. (2012), "When the World Becomes 'Too Real': A Bayesian Explanation of Autistic Perception," *Trends in Cognitive Sciences*, 16 (10): 504–10.

Pendl, S. L., Salzwedel, A. P., Goldman, B. D., Barrett, L. F., Lin, W., Gilmore, J. H. and Gao, W. (2017), "Emergence of a Hierarchical Brain during Infancy Reflected by Stepwise Functional Connectivity," *Human Brain Mapping*, 38 (5): 2666–82. doi. org/10.1002/hbm.23552.

Rao, R. P. and Ballard, D. H. (1999), "Predictive Coding in the Visual Cortex: A Functional Interpretation of Some Extra-Classical Receptive-Field Effects," *Nature Neuroscience*, 2 (1): 79–87. doi.org/10.1038/4580.

Roy, M., Shohamy, D., Daw, N., Jepma, M., Wimmer, G. E. and Wager, T. D. (2014), "Representation of Aversive Prediction Errors in the Human Periaqueductal Gray," *Nature Neuroscience*, 17 (11): 1607–12. doi.org/10.1038/nn.3832.

Seth, A. K. (2013), "Interoceptive Inference, Emotion, and the Embodied Self," *Trends in Cognitive Sciences*, 17 (11): 565–73. doi.org/10.1016/j.tics.2013.09.007.

Seth, A. K. and Critchley, H. D. (2013), "Extending Predictive Processing to the Body: Emotion as Interoceptive Inference," *Behavioral and Brain Sciences*, 36 (3): 227–8. doi. org/10.1017/S0140525X12002270.

Sinha, P., Kjelgaard, M. M., Gandhi, T. K., Tsourides, K., Cardinaux, A. L., Pantazis, D., Diamond, S. P. and Held, R. M. (2014), "Autism as a Disorder of Prediction," *Proceedings of the National Academy of Sciences of the United States of America*, 111 (42): 15220–5. doi.org/10.1073/pnas.1416797111.

Sterling, P. (2012), "Allostasis: A Model of Predictive Regulation," *Physiology & Behavior*, 106 (1): 5–15. doi.org/10.1016/j.physbeh.2011.06.004.

Sterzer, P., Adams, R. A., Fletcher, P., Frith, C., Lawrie, S. M., Muckli, L., Petrovic, P., Uhlhaas, P., Voss, M. and Corlett, P. R. (2018), "The Predictive Coding Account of Psychosis," *Biological Psychiatry*, 84 (9): 634–43.

Supekar, K., Musen, M. and Menon, V. (2009), "Development of Large-Scale Functional Brain Networks in Children," *PLoS Biology*, 7 (7): e1000157. doi.org/10.1371/journal. pbio.1000157.

Supekar, K., Uddin, L. Q., Prater, K., Amin, H., Greicius, M. D. and Menon, V. (2010), "Development of Functional and Structural Connectivity within the Default Mode Network in Young Children," *NeuroImage*, 52 (1): 290–301. doi.org/10.1016/j. neuroimage.2010.04.009.

Trutzer, I. M., García-Cabezas, M. Á. and Zikopoulos, B. (2019), "Postnatal Development and Maturation of Layer 1 in the Lateral Prefrontal Cortex and Its Disruption in Autism," *Acta Neuropathologica Communications*, 7 (1): 40. doi.org/10.1186/s40478-019-0684-8.

Zhang, J., Scholtens, L. H., Wei, Y., van den Heuvel, M. P., Chanes, L. and Barrett, L. F. (2019), "Topography Impacts Topology: Anatomically Central Areas Exhibit a 'High-Level Connector' Profile in the Human Cortex," *Cerebral Cortex*, bhz171. doi. org/10.1093/cercor/bhz171.

Zikopoulos, B. and Barbas, H. (2010), "Changes in Prefrontal Axons May Disrupt the Network in Autism," *The Journal of Neuroscience: The Official Journal of the Society for Neuroscience*, 30 (44): 14595–14609. doi.org/10.1523/JNEUROSCI.2257-10.2010.

Zikopoulos, B. and Barbas, H. (2013), "Altered Neural Connectivity in Excitatory and Inhibitory Cortical Circuits in Autism," *Frontiers in Human Neuroscience*, 7: 609. doi. org/10.3389/fnhum.2013.00609.

Zikopoulos, B., García-Cabezas, M. Á. and Barbas, H. (2018), "Parallel Trends in Cortical Gray and White Matter Architecture and Connections in Primates Allow Fine Study of Pathways in Humans and Reveal Network Disruptions in Autism," *PLoS Biology*, 16 (2): e200455. doi.org/10.1371/journal.pbio.2004559.

10

Disconnection and Diaschisis: Active Inference in Neuropsychology

Thomas Parr

Wellcome Centre for Human Neuroimaging, Institute of Neurology, University College London, WC1N 3BG, UK

Karl J. Friston

Wellcome Centre for Human Neuroimaging, Institute of Neurology, University College London, WC1N 3BG, UK

Introduction

Active inference is a formal (mathematical) approach that frames behavior as a process of inference (Friston et al. 2010). It is based upon the idea that we use internal (generative) models of the world (Von Helmholtz 1867) to explain our sensations. This has been successfully applied across a range of disciplines, ranging from morphogenesis (Friston 2013) to ecology (Bruineberg et al. 2018) and neuroscience (Shipp 2016). In this chapter, we offer an overview of recent work that uses active inference to address the computational deficits that characterize neuropsychological disorders (Parr et al. 2018). In doing so, we explore important aspects of the generative models that underwrite active inference, and the consequences of their disruption. By focusing on the form of these generative models one can recover two important concepts that arise from clinical neurological research. These are the notions of disconnection (Catani and Ffytche 2005, Geschwind 1965) and diaschisis (von Monakow 1914). The former refers to the loss of influence of one population of neurons over another, and may be due to a structural disconnection (i.e., cutting of the axons connecting two regions) or a functional disconnection resulting from synaptic pathology (Friston et al. 2016). A diaschisis is a network-level pathology, in which a focal lesion has wide-ranging consequences throughout the brain (literally, shocked throughout). While originally used to describe the depression of neural activity following disconnection of excitatory connections from another region (Finger et al. 2004) (cf. "crossed cerebellar diaschisis" (Pantano et al. 1986)), this idea has been generalized to include a wide spectrum of functional changes that manifest in the activity of distributed networks in the brain (Carrera and Tononi 2014, Fornito et al. 2015, Price et al. 2001).

The concepts of disconnection and diaschisis are central to the field of neuropsychology, which tries to account for the relationship between brain systems and the psychological processes that arise from their interaction (Luria 1992, 2012). They are also used to account for disorders of (active) perceptual processing, including visual neglect and Lewy body dementia. Visual neglect is a classic disorder of active inferential processing, characterized by a failure to engage with stimuli on (typically) the left side of space (Halligan and Marshall 1998), and has been described as a frontoparietal disconnection syndrome (Ciaraffa et al. 2013, He et al. 2007). Lewy body dementia is a synucleinopathy that involves pathological changes in certain anatomical locations whose consequences are measurable in distant regions, including attenuated responses to visual stimuli (Harding et al. 2002, McKeith et al. 2004). This functional disconnection from the sensorium leads to visual hallucinations (Collerton et al. 2005)—inferences that are not appropriately constrained by the sensorium.

Active inference offers a useful framework in which to understand the relationship between pathological lesions and the changes in computation that they evince. Technically, this relationship rests upon the complete class theorems (Wald 1947) that state that any behavior, no matter how apparently pathological, is Bayes optimal under the right set of prior beliefs (Daunizeau et al. 2010). As active inference frames behavior as a consequence of employing a particular generative model, it is well suited to the investigation of abnormal behaviors in terms of the priors that cause them. In other words, it is, in principle, possible to explain any behavior in terms of active inference if one can find the appropriate priors that constitute a generative model. The problem for computational neuropsychology can then be seen as the challenge of finding the set of prior beliefs that would render a pathological behavior Bayes optimal (Parr et al. 2018). The anatomical process theories (Friston, FitzGerald et al. 2017, Parr and Friston 2018) associated with active inference then furnish a useful vehicle to understand how structural lesions change these priors. This is a complex problem to solve, as the conditional dependencies between variables in a generative model (of the sort employed by the brain) ensure that local changes (i.e., beliefs about a specific variable) do not remain local. Another way of saying this is the (possibly trivial) statement that no brain system operates in isolation.

This chapter illustrates the utility of appealing to active inference in asking how pathological changes in the brain give rise to psychological consequences. More broadly, this may be seen as an example of the use of active inference in formalizing established scientific concepts (for an example of this in cognitive psychology, please see Parr and Friston 2017d). This affords the opportunity to use quantitative simulations to illustrate the face validity of these concepts in relation to measurable behavior, and to perform model comparisons using empirical data (Mirza et al. 2018, Schwartenbeck and Friston 2016). In brief, active inference facilitates the formal articulation, validation, and evaluation of hypotheses derived from a range of established disciplines. In the following, we begin with a formal overview of active inference, and describe a general form for a (Markov Decision Process) generative model. We then present two illustrative examples applied to neuropsychology; specifically, the inferential disconnections and diaschisis seen in visual neglect (Parr and Friston 2017b) and hallucinatory disorders as exemplified by Lewy body dementia (Parr et al. 2018).

Active Inference

Central to modern physiology is the concept of homeostasis (Cannon 1929); the idea that living organisms must act to maintain their physiological state (e.g., blood pressure, temperature, etc.) within a preferred distribution. This implies a set of interactions between the variables that make up this state, sensors that measure deviations in these quantities, and effectors that correct these deviations. This may be formalized by defining a distribution (P) of allowable sensor values, or observations (o), and stating that actions (effectors) (u) must change states (s) to maximize the probability of observations under the preferred distribution (or, equivalently, its log):

$$u = \arg \max_u \ln P(o(u))$$

$$P(o) = \sum_s P(o, s) \qquad (1)$$

This is sufficient for dealing with simple reflexive actions. However, when the relationship between states and observations becomes more complex, it may be impossible to perform the summation in Equation 1 in an efficient and timely way. A solution to this (that we suppose has been discovered by evolution) is to appeal to variational methods (Beal 2003, Dayan et al. 1995, Feynman 1998) that convert this summation into an optimization. In place of maximizing the log probability, we instead minimize a quantity called variational free energy. This uses beliefs (Q) about states of the world to contextualize the selection of actions:

$$u = \arg \min_u F[Q, o(u)]$$

$$F[Q, o(u)] = E_Q[\ln Q(s) - \ln P(o, s)]$$

$$\approx - \ln P(o) \Leftrightarrow \qquad (2)$$

$$Q(s) = \arg \min_Q F[Q, o(u)]$$

$$\approx P(s \mid o)$$

These equations summarize the idea that underwrites active inference. This is a generalization of the concept of homeostasis, appealing to beliefs[1] about the world in order to optimize sensory observations through action. These may be interoceptive observations (as in classical homeostasis), but could be proprioceptive or exteroceptive. Equation 2 says that actions minimize variational free energy, which is (roughly) equivalent to maximizing some desired distribution over observations (Equation 1) when beliefs (Q) minimize free energy through approximating the posterior probability of states given observations. Minimizing free energy is then a common imperative for action and perception. In the context of neuroscience, the need to compute posterior probabilities resonates with the idea of "the Bayesian brain" (Knill and Pouget 2004, O'Reilly et al. 2012), but puts this in the service of selecting the best actions.

Equation 2 additionally emphasizes that, to compute the free energy, we need to know the form of the joint probability distribution over states and outcomes (i.e., the generative model). For this, we use a (partially observed) Markov Decision Process (MDP), as illustrated in Figure 10.1. This describes a sequence of states through time, where the probability of each state depends upon the state at the previous time. Each state gives rise to an observation. The sequence of states depends upon which sequence of actions are selected. Transitions from one state to the next therefore depend upon alternative action sequences, or policies (π). To incorporate policies into the model, we must specify a prior belief about the most probable policies. Given that we are dealing with a free energy minimizing agent, a self-consistent prior is that the most probable policies are those that would lead to the lowest expected free energy:

$$
\begin{aligned}
\ln P(\pi) &= -G(\pi) \\
G(\pi) &= E_{\hat{Q}}[\ln Q(s \mid \pi) - \ln P(o,s)] \\
\hat{Q}(o,s \mid \pi) &= P(o \mid s)Q(s \mid \pi)
\end{aligned}
\tag{3}
$$

The expected free energy for a policy has the same form as the free energy (Equation 2) but includes an expectation over observations. This ensures that it can be evaluated for future times, where no observation has yet been made. The expected free energy may be rearranged to give:

$$
G(\pi) = \underbrace{E_{\hat{Q}}[ln\, Q\,(s|\pi) - ln\, P\,(s|o)]}_{\text{(negative) salience}} - \underbrace{E_{\hat{Q}}[ln\, P\,(o)]}_{\text{expected utility}}
\tag{4}
$$

This decomposition emphasizes the dual behavioral imperatives toward exploration (salience) and exploitation (expected utility) (Friston et al. 2015). Expected utility is the extent to which a policy coheres with prior preferences. Salience is the information gain afforded by a policy (Parr and Friston 2019) and is formally equivalent to accounts of optimal experimental design (Lindley 1956). While information gain in this context refers to optimization of beliefs about states of the world, this may be generalized to include beliefs about the parameters of a generative model through addition of an additional (novelty) term (Friston, Lin et al. 2017):

$$
G(\pi) = \underbrace{E_{\hat{Q}}[\ln Q(s \mid \pi) - \ln P(s \mid o)]}_{\text{(negative) salience}} - \underbrace{E_{\hat{Q}}[\ln P(o)]}_{\text{expected utility}}
$$
$$
+ \underbrace{E_{\hat{Q}}[\ln Q(A \mid \pi) - \ln P(A \mid o)]}_{\text{(negative) novelty}}
\tag{5}
$$

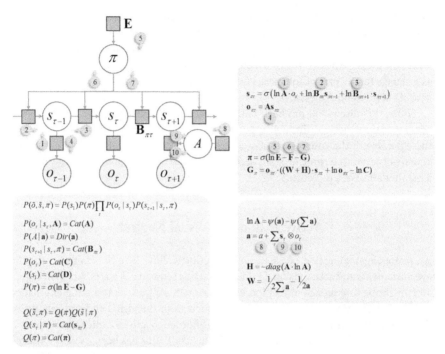

Figure 10.1 Generative models and message passing. The left of this figure shows the form of a Markov Decision Process model, while the right shows the message passing scheme that minimizes free energy. The generative model expresses the dependencies between different sorts of variable. Arrows from one variable (circle) to another (via square "factor" nodes) indicate that the second variable depends upon the first. With this in mind, the graph can be read as saying that states depend upon states at the previous time, and upon the policy selected. Outcomes depend upon the state that occurs at the same time. The probability distributions associated with these dependencies are specified in the blue panel, where "~" indicates a trajectory over time, "Cat" means a categorical distribution, ψ is a digamma function, and "Dir" indicates a Dirichlet distribution. The pink panels on the right show the Bayesian belief updating equations that underwrite inference about this generative model. While these look a little complicated, they are just the gradients of the free energy written out explicitly in terms of the sufficient statistics of a generative model, and approximate posterior beliefs. The form of these gradients licenses an interpretation in terms of inferential message passing—using locally derived information to update beliefs about each variable in the generative model. This is highly consistent with the form of (local) synaptic communication in the brain. Details of these equations may be found in Friston, FitzGerald et al. (2017).

Equation 5 says that optimal policies are those associated with large changes in beliefs about states (inference) and parameters (learning), and that fulfill prior preferences. This prior completes the specification of a generative model. With this in place, we can then find the beliefs that minimize variational free energy to comply with Equation 2. Figure 10.1 shows how this may be done through passing messages across the factors in a generative model (Dauwels 2007, Yedidia et al. 2005). Combining local messages allows the computation of posterior beliefs about states, policies, and parameters. Crucially, this approach to inference lends itself to the notion of a disconnection, where the message passed across a factor fails to elicit belief updating, and a diaschisis, as a change to any part of the model influences all other parts of the model through a cascade of inferential messages.

So far, this discussion has been fairly abstract. In the next sections, we attempt to concretize these notions through appeals to two examples from neurology. The first of these deals with the consequences of a sensorimotor disconnection when evaluating courses of action (i.e., policies). The second illustrates how disconnection may itself be a manifestation of a diaschisis.

Active Vision and Visual Neglect

An interesting application of the principles outlined above is in the realm of saccadic eye movements and active vision. In this context, the sequence of states shown in Figure 10.1 might be a sequence of fixation locations, with policies representing alternative saccades. Each state then has sensory consequences in the visual and proprioceptive domains. In this setting, salience is something afforded to any saccadic target expected to yield informative sensory data (Itti and Baldi 2006). This has been used to illustrate the sorts of saccadic searches required for the categorization of visual scenes (Mirza et al. 2016), and to account for phenomena like "inhibition of return" and the "streetlight effect" (Parr and Friston 2017c). These depend upon the fidelity (or precision) of the mapping from hidden states (fixation locations) to sensory data. If this precision is low for a given location, saccades to this location will be poor perceptual "experiments," as they will fail to disambiguate between alternative causes for that scene. Figure 10.1 illustrates the way in which this arises through active inference. Ambiguity is represented by H, and makes a positive contribution to the expected free energy (G). For beliefs about policies (π) to minimize the expected free energy, those policies associated with a higher expected ambiguity must be less probable.

Sometimes, particularly when dealing with high-dimensional representations of the visual world, it is more efficient to encode relationships between "where I could look" and "what I would see there," as opposed to representing what is present at every point in visual space. Intuitively, if we consider a simple visual world (Parr and Friston 2017a) comprising an 8×8 grid that contains only three types of object, we could represent this in one of two ways. First, we could represent whether objects 1, 2, and 3 are present at each of the 64 locations in space, requiring 192 (64×3) representational units (e.g., neurons). Alternatively, we could represent the same world by storing this information in the conditional probability of seeing one of the three objects given a fixation location. This means we only need represent 64 locations, and 3 possible outcomes (67 units), and optimize beliefs about the probabilistic relationship between the two. This could be simplified further by factorizing the coordinate system to 8 horizontal and 8 vertical positions, leaving us with 19 units (8 + 8 + 3). The minimal complexity in this sort of visual map supports (via Occam's razor) an enactive take on visual perception (Bruineberg et al. 2016, Kiverstein 2018, Zimmermann and Lappe 2016), in which we optimize a motor map of visual space (or beliefs about "what I would see if I looked there"), and treat sensations as consequences of actions.

Figure 10.1 (lower right panel) specifies how optimization of these mappings occurs for a free energy minimizing agent. This involves accumulating counts (**a**) for each combination of fixation location (**s**) and visual consequence (*o*) whenever this combination is observed (messages 9 and 10). This incremental process resembles Hebbian plasticity (Hebb 1949), in the sense that the co-occurrence of the two strengthens their coupling. These counts are then normalized such that they sum to one, giving a probability distribution (**A**) that expresses the probability of an observation conditioned upon a state. An important consequence of this is that, when the counts are already high, a new observation causes little change in beliefs about this mapping. However, when counts are low, new observations cause a substantial change in the normalized probability distribution.[2] This means that saccadic targets associated with low values of **a** afford good opportunities to resolve uncertainty about parameters of the generative model. This is the idea that underwrites novelty and can be seen explicitly in Figure 10.1. **W** is more negative when **a** is small, leading to a lower value of **G**, and a higher value for the corresponding element of **π**. The upper part of Figure 10.2 illustrates the way in which this drives saccadic exploration under normal conditions. This rests upon the fact that locations that have never been fixated will always have fewer counts than previously visited locations.

With this in mind, we are now able to consider how a disconnection may be articulated in formal terms, and to think about its consequences throughout a network. The upper part of Figure 10.2 illustrates this through appealing to visual neglect, a syndrome associated with disconnection of frontoparietal pathways (Bartolomeo et al. 2012) that manifests in impaired visual scene construction (Fruhmann Berger et al. 2008). Typically, lesions to white matter tracts in the right parietal lobe result in impoverished attentional sampling of the left side of space. This is shown in the (synthetic) eye-tracking trace in the upper right of Figure 10.2. The upper left and central parts of the figure show an interpretation of the frontoparietal disconnection in terms of a change in a generative model (Parr and Friston 2017b), associating the connection between frontal and parietal regions with the likelihood mapping from fixation to its sensory consequences.

Disconnection means that this mapping can no longer be optimized following a new fixation, implying the counts (**a**) associated with this are so large that any increment to them is negligible for the normalized probability distribution. In this sense, disconnection may be thought of as inducing an inappropriately confident prior belief about the probabilistic structure of the world, such that new sensory evidence causes no change in this belief. Returning to Figure 10.1, we see that large **a** parameters lead to a small value for **W**. This means a relatively large **G**, and consequently a small probability (**π**), associated with saccades to the side of space associated with this disconnection. Intuitively, if new data cannot drive optimization of a model, because the neurons comprising that model are no longer connected, there is no point seeking these data; in other words, there is nothing to be learned and there is no novelty or allure in "looking there." This serves to illustrate the cascade of changes that occur following a focal lesion to one part of a generative model. Ultimately, this diaschisis becomes apparent through the selection of eye movements, such that the consequences of cerebral damage can be measured through observing behavior.

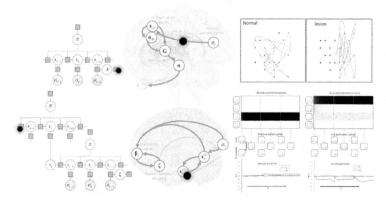

Figure 10.2 Disconnections and diaschisis. This figure illustrates the two cardinal computational pathologies showcased in the main text. The upper panels show the disconnection implicated in visual neglect, and the behavioral (saccadic) manifestation of the ensuing diaschisis. The lower parts of the figure show the consequences of temporal lobe neuropathology in Lewy body dementia, and the functional disconnection it induces earlier in the ventral visual stream (through cholinergic mechanisms). On the left, we show the form of the Markov Decision Processes used for the generative models. The visual neglect model is a single-level MDP incorporating beliefs about the parameters of the A-matrix. The states here are current fixation locations, with outcomes representing the visual consequences of these fixations. The lesion that induces a neglect syndrome targets the (Dirichlet) prior over the parameters of A. The model for Lewy body induced hallucinations is hierarchical. This means that the states at the lower level (objects in the visual scene) are themselves generated by beliefs about the scene category at the higher level. The likelihood mapping at the low level here is parameterized in terms of a Gibbs distribution, using an inverse temperature parameter (ζ) to optimize the precision. The lesion induced here is at the higher level, altering the prior probability of different scene categories. The computational anatomy implied by these generative models is plotted next to each of them, highlighting the location of the lesion in anatomical terms. For visual neglect, the lesion here is in the white matter tract connecting the frontal and parietal cortices. For Lewy body dementia, we focus upon the temporal lobe pathology associated with hallucinations, and its propagation through the ventral visual stream. This causes a mismatch between low-level states and visual data, which is accounted for by reducing signaling from the basal forebrain nucleus to the early visual pathway. The plots on the right illustrate numerical simulations of these deficits. The upper plot shows a saccadic cancellation task, and the bias toward rightward saccades induced by a lesion. The lower plot shows inferences about first- and second-level beliefs with (right) and without (left) induction of pathology at the second level. This pathology leads to down-weighting of precision and hallucination of an object in the lower left quadrant (as seen in the plots labeled "posterior"). These images are reproduced from Parr and Friston (2017b) and Parr et al. (2018), where more detailed descriptions can be found.

Neuromodulation and Hallucinations

The example of visual neglect outlined above illustrates how the events resulting from a disconnection may propagate throughout the brain, eventually influencing behavior. It is also important to note that disconnection itself may be a manifestation of a diaschisis. This makes the point that disconnections need not be structural lesions of white matter tracts but could be due to synaptic dysfunction (cf. The disconnection hypothesis of schizophrenia (Friston et al. 2016)). This may be due to primary synaptic pathologies (e.g., channelopathies or autoantibodies (Rosch et al. 2018, Vincent et al. 2006)) but could be due to disruptions of neuromodulation following damage to another part of the brain. An interesting example of this is the set of pathological changes that surround the development of visual hallucinations in synuclein disorders. These involve the pathological accumulation of abnormal proteins, known as Lewy bodies, and include Parkinson's disease and Lewy body dementia (McCann et al. 2014, Tsuboi and Dickson 2005). The latter is associated with visual hallucinations, accompanied by occipital hypometabolism (Heitz et al. 2015, Lobotesis et al. 2001), cholinergic dysfunction (Perry et al. 1991), and attenuated visually evoked potentials. Interestingly, the site of the synuclein pathology most linked to visual changes is in the temporal lobe (Harding et al. 2002), anatomically distant from these measured changes.

To understand this, it is worth thinking about the form of the generative model required to make inferences about objects, and about the scene in which they are embedded, based upon visual input. This problem requires a hierarchical model, as the objects in a scene are conditionally dependent upon the context of the scene. We can think of this in terms of a generative model that describes a slowly changing context (scene) that provides empirical prior beliefs about the objects in that scene at a lower hierarchical level (Friston, Rosch et al. 2017, Parr et al. 2018). Beliefs about these objects then entail predictions about the sort of visual data they will generate. This is shown in the lower left of Figure 10.2, by stacking the generative model of Figure 10.1. The lower level model here is subtly different to that of the previous section, as it is equipped with beliefs about the precision (ζ) of sensory data. For those unfamiliar with precision, it is the inverse variance associated with a given probability distribution. In the present context, it can be interpreted as the fidelity with which objects generate visual data. This is important, in that data believed to be highly precise is very informative (Feldman and Friston 2010). Increases in precision then drive a greater rate of belief updating, and consequently a greater amplitude of evoked responses to visual data. One can see immediately why people associate increases in precision with attentional selection, in the sense that affording sensory data greater precision effectively increases its influence on belief updating and perceptual synthesis.

Underestimation of precision releases inference from the constraints of sensory data (Benrimoh et al. 2018, O'Callaghan et al. 2017), favoring internally generated perceptual content. This appears a good mechanism to account for the functional changes in posterior cortices combined with visual hallucinations (inferences unconstrained by the sensorium). In addition, synucleinopathies are associated with impaired cholinergic signaling to the cortex (Perry et al. 1994, Tiraboschi et al. 2000)—associated with control of precision (Marshall et al. 2016, Moran et al. 2013,

Parr and Friston 2017c, Vossel et al. 2014, Yu and Dayan 2002). However, the problem remains as to how to account for the link between temporal lobe pathology and these changes. Figure 10.2 illustrates one solution to this by considering how precision may be optimized. The image in the center of the lower row expresses the idea that beliefs about more abstract visual states (superscript 2) contextualize beliefs about more elemental states (superscript 1) that are themselves directly answerable to visual data. Discrepancies (or congruencies) between beliefs about the latter states and the data they would predict imply precision should be attenuated (or augmented). The inferential processes underwriting this are depicted as connections from beliefs about states and observations to the prefrontal cortex, which itself projects to the basal nucleus of Meynert (Zaborszky et al. 1997), altering the cholinergic modulation of the forward connections from early to later visual areas.

The lower right plots show how this hierarchical inference process unfolds in the presence or absence of a simulated lesion to the temporal lobes, disrupting priors about the overall scene. When there is no lesion (left), the second-level beliefs settle upon the scene that was used to generate the data. This sets up an empirical prior at the lower (object) level that is consistent with incoming sensory data. The consistency between beliefs and data leads to an increased estimation of the precision of the likelihood distribution. On introducing a synthetic temporal lobe (Lewy body) lesion, by setting the prior probability of the correct scene to zero, the empirical prior induced at the lower level is incompatible with the stimuli. This inconsistency leads to an attenuation of the sensory precision, releasing the inference process from the constraints of data, resulting in false positive inferences that can be seen in the posterior probability images. Comparing these with the true states, we see a hallucinated object in the lower left quadrant. Note that the attenuation of precision (cholinergic dysfunction) and the resulting functional disconnection in early visual processing are secondary to a single primary lesion in a distant part of the brain. As such, these phenomena may be thought of as manifestations of a diaschisis that leads to a pernicious form of attentional deficit—and subsequent false perceptual inference.

Conclusion

In the above, we have outlined two recent examples of the application of active inference to understand the computational mechanisms that underwrite neuropsychological syndromes. These examples highlight two important motifs in inferential pathology. The first is the notion of a disconnection, in which variables that normally reside within each other's Markov blankets—i.e., are conditionally dependent upon one another—no longer interact. In our examples above, this could be a failure to optimize beliefs about the relationship between two variables, or a failure to alter beliefs about one of the two variables when presented with information about the other. The second pathological process is the functional diaschisis that inevitably results from damage to one part of a network. As outlined above, this could manifest in behavior, perception, or measurements of brain physiology.

While a neuropsychological setting illustrates these changes in a concrete way, the same principles could be generalized to any system that engages in active inference.

At small scales, this includes the disconnection induced by the loss of an enzyme in a biochemical pathway, or the diaschisis that this induces through widespread regulatory processes that result from this. At much larger scales, disruptions in communication between parts of a social network represent an analogous disconnection that will inevitably cause a diaschisis measurable in other parts of this system. In other words, these may represent canonical computational pathologies that apply to any system whose dynamics can be described as optimizing a generative model. For example, applications in fields as diverse as cellular self-organization and ecological niche construction (see Bruineberg et al. 2018, Friston 2013, Kirchhoff et al. 2018).

This chapter has explored the utility of predictive processing in understanding the behavior of systems with complex dynamics—like a brain—in response to disruption of that system. The framework of active inference facilitates the articulation of key concepts, including disconnection and diaschisis, in a formal and crisp way. The generality of this formalism means that, while these ideas can be usefully applied in neuropsychology, their mathematical expression could apply to any system. These methods can be applied to simulate such systems, affording the opportunity to assess the face validity of theoretical constructs. They can then be used to assess the evidence in favor of these constructs through fitting to empirical data. In the context of neuropsychology and medicine, active inference can be used to compare alternative diagnoses framed in computational terms, to phenotype patients according to their most probable inferential pathology, and ultimately to inform decisions about treatment in individual patients.

Acknowledgments

TP is supported by the Rosetrees Trust (Award Number 173346). KJF is a Wellcome Principal Research Fellow (Ref: 088130/Z/09/Z).

Notes

1   These are typically sub-personal beliefs, used in the technical sense of "Bayesian belief updating." Formally, they are approximate posterior probabilities (i.e., the probability of some state given what I have observed).

2   Intuitively, three heads in a row might lead us to infer that a coin is unfairly weighted toward heads. However, 3 heads in a row following 100 coin flips with an equal number of heads and tails would do little to change our beliefs about the coin's fairness.

References

Bartolomeo, P., de Schotten, M. T. and Chica, A. B. (2012), "Brain Networks of Visuospatial Attention and Their Disruption in Visual Neglect," *Frontiers in Human Neuroscience*, 6: 110. doi.org/10.3389/fnhum.2012.00110.

Beal, M. J. (2003), *Variational Algorithms for Approximate Bayesian Inference*, London: University of London, United Kingdom.

Benrimoh, D., Parr, T., Vincent, P., Adams, R. A. and Friston, K. (2018), "Active Inference and Auditory Hallucinations," *Computational Psychiatry*, 2: 183–204. doi.org/10.1162/cpsy_a_00022.

Bruineberg, J., Kiverstein, J. and Rietveld, E. (2016), "The Anticipating Brain Is Not a Scientist: The Free-energy Principle from an Ecological-enactive Perspective," *Synthese*, 1–28. doi.org/10.1007/s11229-016-1239-1.

Bruineberg, J., Rietveld, E., Parr, T., van Maanen, L. and Friston, K. J. (2018), "Free-energy Minimization in Joint Agent-environment Systems: A Niche Construction Perspective," *Journal of Theoretical Biology*, 455: 161–78. doi.org/10.1016/j.jtbi.2018.07.002.

Cannon, W. B. (1929), "Organization for Physiological Homeostasis," *Physiological Reviews*, 9 (3): 399–431. doi.org/10.1152/physrev.1929.9.3.399.

Carrera, E. and Tononi, G. (2014), "Diaschisis: Past, Present, Future," *Brain*, 137 (9): 2408–22. doi.org/10.1093/brain/awu101.

Catani, M. and Ffytche, D. H. (2005), "The Rises and Falls of Disconnection Syndromes," *Brain*, 128 (10): 2224–39. doi.org/10.1093/brain/awh622.

Ciaraffa, F., Castelli, G., Parati, E. A., Bartolomeo, P. and Bizzi, A. (2013), "Visual Neglect as a Disconnection Syndrome? A Confirmatory Case Report," *Neurocase*, 19 (4): 351–9.

Collerton, D., Perry, E. and McKeith, I. (2005), "Why People See Things That Are Not There: A Novel Perception and Attention Deficit Model for Recurrent Complex Visual Hallucinations," *Behavioral and Brain Sciences*, 28 (6): 737–57. doi.org/10.1017/S0140525X05000130.

Daunizeau, J., den Ouden, H. E. M., Pessiglione, M., Kiebel, S. J., Stephan, K. E. and Friston, K. J. (2010), "Observing the Observer (I): Meta-Bayesian Models of Learning and Decision-Making," *PLOS ONE*, 5 (12): e15554. doi.org/10.1371/journal.pone.0015554.

Dauwels, J. (2007), "On Variational Message Passing on Factor Graphs," *IEEE International Symposium on Information Theory, ISIT*.

Dayan, P., Hinton, G. E., Neal, R. M. and Zemel, R. S. (1995), "The Helmholtz Machine," *Neural Computation*, 7 (5):889–904.

Feldman, H. and Friston, K. J. (2010), "Attention, Uncertainty, and Free-Energy," *Frontiers in Human Neuroscience*, 4 (215). doi.org/10.3389/fnhum.2010.00215.

Feynman, R. P. (1998), *Statistical Mechanics: A Set of Lectures*, New York: Avalon Publishing.

Finger, S., Koehler, P. J. and Jagella, C. (2004), "The Monakow Concept of Diaschisis: Origins and Perspectives," *Archives of Neurology*, 61 (2): 283–8.

Fornito, A., Zalesky, A. and Breakspear, M. (2015), "The Connectomics of Brain Disorders," *Nature Reviews Neuroscience*, 16 (3): 159–72. doi.org/10.1038/nrn3901.

Friston, K. (2013), "Life as We Know It," *Journal of The Royal Society Interface*, 10 (86): 20130475.

Friston, K. J., Daunizeau, J., Kilner, J. and Kiebel, S. J. (2010), "Action and Behavior: A Free-energy Formulation," *Biological Cybernetics*, 102 (3): 227–60. doi.org/10.1007/s00422-010-0364-z.

Friston, K., Brown, H. R., Siemerkus, J. and Stephan, K. E. (2016), "The Dysconnection Hypothesis," *Schizophrenia Research*, 176 (2): 83–94. doi.org/10.1016/j.schres.2016.07.014.

Friston, K., FitzGerald, T., Rigoli, F., Schwartenbeck, P. and Pezzulo, G. (2017), "Active Inference: A Process Theory," *Neural Computation*, 29 (1): 1–49. doi.org/10.1162/NECO_a_00912.

Friston, K. J., Rosch, R., Parr, T., Price, C. and Bowman, H. (2017), "Deep Temporal Models and Active Inference," *Neuroscience & Biobehavioral Reviews*, 77: 388–402. doi.org/10.1016/j.neubiorev.2017.04.009.

Friston, K., Rigoli, F., Ognibene, D., Mathys, C., Fitzgerald, T. and Pezzulo, G. (2015), "Active Inference and Epistemic Value," *Cognitive Neuroscience*, 6 (4): 187–214. doi.org/10.1080/17588928.2015.1020053.

Friston, K. J., Lin, M., Frith, C. D., Pezzulo, G., Hobson, J. A. and Ondobaka, S. (2017), "Active Inference, Curiosity and Insight," *Neural Computation*, 29 (10): 2633–83.

Fruhmann Berger, M., Johannsen, L. and Karnath, H.-O. (2008), "Time Course of Eye and Head Deviation in Spatial Neglect," *Neuropsychology*, 22 (6): 697–702. doi.org/10.1037/a0013351.

Geschwind, N. (1965), "Disconnexion Sydromes in Animals and Man," *Brain*, 88 (2): 237–94. doi.org/10.1093/brain/88.2.237.

Halligan, P. W. and Marshall, J. C. (1998), "Neglect of Awareness," *Consciousness and Cognition*, 7 (3): 356–80. doi.org/10.1006/ccog.1998.0362.

Harding, A. J., Broe, G. A. and Halliday, G. M. (2002), "Visual Hallucinations in Lewy Body Disease Relate to Lewy Bodies in the Temporal Lobe," *Brain*, 125 (2): 391–403. doi.org/10.1093/brain/awf033.

He, B. J., Snyder, A. Z., Vincent, J. L., Epstein, A., Shulman, G. L. and Corbetta, M. (2007), "Breakdown of Functional Connectivity in Frontoparietal Networks Underlies Behavioral Deficits in Spatial Neglect," *Neuron*, 53 (6): 905–18. doi.org/10.1016/j.neuron.2007.02.013.

Hebb, D. O. (1949), "The First Stage of Perception: Growth of the Assembly," *The Organization of Behavior*, 1: 60–78.

Heitz, C., Noblet, Vincent, C., Benjamin, P., Nathalie, K., Laurent, S., Mélanie, H., Fabrice, A., Namer, I. and Blanc, F. (2015), "Neural Correlates of Visual Hallucinations in Dementia with Lewy Bodies," *Alzheimer's Research & Therapy*, 7 (1): 6. doi.org/10.1186/s13195-014-0091-0.

Itti, L. and Baldi, P. (2006), "Bayesian Surprise Attracts Human Attention," *Advances in Neural Information Processing Systems*, 18: 547.

Kirchhoff, M., Parr, T., Palacios, E., Friston, K. and Kiverstein, J. (2018), "The Markov Blankets of Life: Autonomy, Active Inference and the Free Energy Principle," *Journal of The Royal Society Interface*, 15 (138): 20170792.

Kiverstein, J. (2018), "Free Energy and the Self: An Ecological–Enactive Interpretation," *Topoi*. doi.org/10.1007/s11245-018-9561-5.

Knill, D. C. and Pouget, A. (2004), "The Bayesian Brain: The Role of Uncertainty in Neural Coding and Computation," *TRENDS in Neurosciences*, 27 (12): 712–19.

Lindley, D. V. (1956), "On a Measure of the Information Provided by an Experiment," *Annals of Mathematical Statistics*, 27 (4): 986–1005. doi.org/10.1214/aoms/1177728069.

Lobotesis, K., Fenwick, J. D., Phipps, A., Ryman, A., Swann, A., Ballard, C., McKeith, I. G. and O'Brien, J. T. (2001), "Occipital Hypoperfusion on SPECT in Dementia with Lewy Bodies but not AD," *Neurology*, 56 (5): 643–9. doi.org/10.1212/wnl.56.5.643.

Luria, A. R. (1992), "Neuropsychology: Its Sources, Principles, and Prospects" in Frederic G. Worden, Judith P. Swazey and George Adelman (eds.), *The Neurosciences: Paths of Discovery, I*, Boston: Birkhäuser Boston.

Luria, A. R. (2012), *Higher Cortical Functions in Man*, Berlin: Springer Science & Business Media.

Marshall, L., Mathys, C., Ruge, D., de Berker, A. O., Dayan, P., Stephan, K. E. and Bestmann, S. (2016), "Pharmacological Fingerprints of Contextual Uncertainty," *PLOS Biology*, 14 (11): e1002575. doi.org/10.1371/journal.pbio.1002575.

McCann, H., Stevens, C. H., Cartwright, H. and Halliday, G. M. (2014), "α-Synucleinopathy Phenotypes," *Parkinsonism & Related Disorders*, 20 (Supplement 1): S62–7. doi.org/10.1016/S1353-8020(13)70017-8.

McKeith, I., Mintzer, J., Aarsland, D., Burn, D. et al. (2004), "Dementia with Lewy Bodies," *The Lancet Neurology*, 3 (1): 19–28. doi.org/10.1016/S1474-4422(03)00619-7.

Mirza, M. B., Adams, R. A., Mathys, C. and Friston, K. J. (2018), "Human Visual Exploration Reduces Uncertainty about the Sensed World," *PLOS ONE*, 13 (1): e0190429. doi.org/10.1371/journal.pone.0190429.

Mirza, M. B., Adams, R. A., Mathys, C. D. and Friston, K. J. (2016), "Scene Construction, Visual Foraging, and Active Inference," *Frontiers in Computational Neuroscience*, 10 (56). doi.org/10.3389/fncom.2016.00056.

Moran, R. J., Campo, P., Symmonds, M., Stephan, K. E., Dolan, R. J. and Friston, K. J. (2013), "Free Energy, Precision and Learning: The Role of Cholinergic Neuromodulation," *The Journal of Neuroscience: The Official Journal of the Society for Neuroscience*, 33 (19): 8227–36. doi.org/10.1523/JNEUROSCI.4255-12.2013.

O'Callaghan, C., Hall, J. M., Tomassini, A., Muller, A. J., Walpola, I. C., Moustafa, A. A., Shine, J. M. and Lewis, S. J. G. (2017), "Visual Hallucinations Are Characterized by Impaired Sensory Evidence Accumulation: Insights from Hierarchical Drift Diffusion Modeling in Parkinson's Disease," *Biological Psychiatry: Cognitive Neuroscience and Neuroimaging*, 2 (8): 680–8. doi.org/10.1016/j.bpsc.2017.04.007.

O'Reilly, J. X., Jbabdi, S. and Behrens, T. E. J. (2012), "How Can a Bayesian Approach Inform Neuroscience?" *European Journal of Neuroscience*, 35 (7): 1169–79. doi.org/10.1111/j.1460-9568.2012.08010.x.

Pantano, P., Baron, J. C., Samson, Y., Bousser, M. G., Derouesne, C. and Comar, D. (1986), "Crossed Cerebellae Diaschisis. Further Studies," *Brain*, 109 (4): 677–94. doi.org/10.1093/brain/109.4.677.

Parr, T. and Friston, K. J. (2017a), "The Active Construction of the Visual World," *Neuropsychologia*, 104: 92–101. doi.org/10.1016/j.neuropsychologia.2017.08.003.

Parr, T. and Friston, K. J. (2017b), "The Computational Anatomy of Visual Neglect," *Cerebral Cortex*, 1–14. doi.org/10.1093/cercor/bhx316.

Parr, T. and Friston, K. J. (2017c), "Uncertainty, Epistemics and Active Inference," *Journal of The Royal Society Interface*, 14 (136): 1–10.

Parr, T. and Friston, K. J. (2017d), "Working Memory, Attention, and Salience in Active Inference," *Scientific Reports*, 7 (1): 14678. doi.org/10.1038/s41598-017-15249-0.

Parr, T. and Friston, K. J. (2018), "The Anatomy of Inference: Generative Models and Brain Structure," *Frontiers in Computational Neuroscience*, 12 (90). doi.org/10.3389/fncom.2018.00090.

Parr, T. and Friston, K. J. (2019), "Attention or Salience?" *Current Opinion in Psychology*, 29: 1–5. doi.org/10.1016/j.copsyc.2018.10.006.

Parr, T., Rees, G. and Friston, K. J. (2018), "Computational Neuropsychology and Bayesian Inference," *Frontiers in Human Neuroscience*, 12 (61). doi.org/10.3389/fnhum.2018.00061.

Parr, T., Benrimoh, D., Vincent, P. and Friston, K. (2018), "Precision and False Perceptual Inference," *Frontiers in Integrative Neuroscience*, 12 (39). doi.org/10.3389/fnint.2018.00039.

Perry, E. K., McKeith, I., Thompson, P., Marshall, E., Kerwin, J., Jabeen, S., Edwardson, J. A., Ince, P., Blessed, G., Irving, D. and Perry, R. H. (1991), "Topography, Extent, and Clinical Relevance of Neurochemical Deficits in Dementia of Lewy Body Type, Parkinson's Disease, and Alzheimer's Disease," *Annals of the New York Academy of Sciences*, 640 (1): 197–202. doi.org/10.1111/j.1749-6632.1991.tb00217.x.

Perry, E. K., Haroutunian, V., Davis, K. L., Levy, R., Lantos, P., Eagger, S., Honavar, M., Dean, A., Griffiths, M. and McKeith, I. G. (1994), "Neocortical Cholinergic Activities Differentiate Lewy Body Dementia from Classical Alzheimer's Disease," *Neuroreport*, 5 (7): 747–9.

Price, C. J., Warburton, E. A., Moore, C. J., Frackowiak, R. S. J. and Friston, K. J. (2001), "Dynamic Diaschisis: Anatomically Remote and Context-sensitive Human Brain Lesions," *Journal of Cognitive Neuroscience*, 13 (4): 419–29.

Rosch, R. E., Wright, S., Cooray, G., Papadopoulou, M., Goyal, S., Lim, M., Vincent, A., Upton, A. L., Baldeweg, T. and Friston, K. J. (2018), "NMDA-receptor Antibodies Alter Cortical Microcircuit Dynamics," *Proceedings of the National Academy of Sciences*, 115 (42): E9916. doi.org/10.1073/pnas.1804846115.

Schwartenbeck, P. and Friston, K. J. (2016), "Computational Phenotyping in Psychiatry: A Worked Example," *eNeuro*, 3 (4): ENEURO.0049-16.2016. doi.org/10.1523/ENEURO.0049-16.2016.

Shipp, S. (2016), "Neural Elements for Predictive Coding," *Frontiers in Psychology*, 7: 1792. doi.org/10.3389/fpsyg.2016.01792.

Tiraboschi, P., Hansen, L. A., Alford, M., Sabbagh, M. N., Schoos, B., Masliah, E., Thal, L. J. and Corey-Bloom, J. (2000), "Cholinergic Dysfunction in Diseases with Lewy Bodies," *Neurology*, 54 (2): 407–10. doi.org/10.1212/wnl.54.2.407.

Tsuboi, Y. and Dickson, D. W. (2005), "Dementia with Lewy Bodies and Parkinson's Disease with Dementia: Are They Different?" *Parkinsonism & Related Disorders*, 11 (Supplement 1): S47–51. doi.org/10.1016/j.parkreldis.2004.10.014.

Vincent, A., Lang, B. and Kleopa, K. A. (2006), "Autoimmune Channelopathies and Related Neurological Disorders," *Neuron*, 52 (1): 123–38. doi.org/10.1016/j.neuron.2006.09.024.

Von Helmholtz, H. (1867), *Handbuch der physiologischen Optik*, Vol. 9, Leipzig: Voss.

von Monakow, C. (1914), *Die Lokalisation im Grosshirn und der Abbau der Funktion durch kortikale Herde*, Wiesbaden: J.F. Bergmann.

Vossel, S., Bauer, M., Mathys, C., Adams, R. A., Dolan, R. J., Stephan, K. E. and Friston, K. J. (2014), "Cholinergic Stimulation Enhances Bayesian Belief Updating in the Deployment of Spatial Attention," *The Journal of Neuroscience*, 34 (47): 15735.

Wald, A. (1947), "An Essentially Complete Class of Admissible Decision Functions," *The Annals of Mathematical Statistics*, 549–55. doi.org/10.1214/aoms/1177730345.

Yedidia, J. S., Freeman, W. T. and Weiss, Y. (2005), "Constructing Free-energy Approximations and Generalized Belief Propagation Algorithms," *IEEE Transactions on Information Theory*, 51 (7): 2282–312.

Yu, A. J. and Dayan, P. (2002), "Acetylcholine in Cortical Inference," *Neural Networks*, 15 (4): 719–30.

Zaborszky, L., Gaykema, R. P., Swanson, D. J. and Cullinan, W. E. (1997), "Cortical Input to the Basal Forebrain," *Neuroscience*, 79 (4): 1051–78. doi.org/10.1016/S0306-4522(97)00049-3.

Zimmermann, E. and Lappe, M. (2016), "Visual Space Constructed by Saccade Motor Maps," *Frontiers in Human Neuroscience*, 10 (225). doi.org/10.3389/fnhum.2016.00225.

11

The Phenomenology and Predictive Processing of Time in Depression

Zachariah A. Neemeh

Department of Philosophy, University of Memphis, United States & Institute for Intelligent Systems, University of Memphis, United States

Shaun Gallagher

Department of Philosophy, University of Memphis, United States & Faculty of Law, Humanities and the Arts, University of Wollongong, Australia

Introduction

Predictive processing has been characterized as an "intermediate-level model" that at once abstracts from neural architecture while remaining below the level of conscious awareness (Spratling 2013). It is the "Bayesian brain" that performs predictive processing—or, in less neurocentric formulations, it is the Bayesian brain together with its body that engages with its world according to predictive processing principles (Clark 2013, 2016, Gallagher and Allen 2018). Whatever brains and bodies are doing in this regard, there is a correlatively rich phenomenology, understood not just as a phenomenal "what it is like," but as phenomenologists in the tradition of Edmund Husserl describe, as a dynamically structured flow of intentional experience. Phenomenology describes not the phenomenal surface, but rather the stable and relatively invariant structures that allow for the orderliness of experience. Rather than being a swirling, fluxional chaos of sense data, the stream of consciousness is ordered by regularities.

In this chapter, we focus on time, or, more precisely, on the intrinsic temporality of consciousness. Although the ticking of the clock or the decay of radioactive isotopes occurs in a regular and invariable sequence, the experience of time is variable. It can appear to slow down, as in periods of boredom. It can seem to speed up, as when we are engrossed in an activity or caught up in playing a game. In the early twentieth century, Harry L. Hollingworth (1910) noted that stimuli of longer and shorter durations tend to be judged as equal around the central mean of their distributions—the "central tendency effect" (see Shi and Burr 2016). That is, phenomena shorter in duration than is typical of phenomena of that type tend to be judged as longer than they are; phenomena longer in duration than is typical tend to be judged as shorter than they really are. Even earlier, at the beginning of psychophysical research into time perception, Karl von Vierordt (1863) noted a similar effect. Known as "Vierordt's law," subjects tend to perceive shorter intervals as longer and longer intervals as shorter. These effects are only some of many factors that alter the perception of time. Different sensory modalities, processing in different neural circuits, process at faster or slower temporal velocities. Audition reaches early sensory areas quicker than vision. Activation of primary visual cortex (V1) is usually assumed to occur 45–55 milliseconds after stimulus; auditory input reaches the cortex in less than half the time (9 to 15 milliseconds) (Clark et al. 1995, Foxe and Simpson 2002, Vaughan and Arezzo 1988, Vaughan et al. 1980). These are not differences that we experience; experientially, however, auditory phenomena are often perceived as longer in duration from equally long visual phenomena (Shi and Burr 2016, Wearden et al. 2006). Time perception varies by age, for example, and the perception of calendric time tends to speed up in older persons (Friedman 1990). Time perception can also vary across cultures and may be markedly different in those not dominated by the regime of the clock (Telban 2017; for an early iteration of this idea, see Whorf 1956[1]).

Husserl (1991), influenced by his reading of James, analyzed the intrinsic subjective temporal flow of experience in terms of formal, transcendental structures of consciousness related to intentionality: retention, primal impression, protention. He sought to capture not only the perception of time but also the genesis of the specious present—the aspect of the experience of present time as nonpunctual that includes a past and future temporal extension (James 1890)—and experience itself *as* temporal. Recent analyses in predictive processing complement the phenomenological approach to time. In the hierarchical arrangement of predictive processing, different regularities are processed across multiple timescales (fast and more detailed vs. slow and more abstract) (Hohwy 2013: 27). Changes in such processes can modulate the relations of retention-primal impression-protention and generate different experiences of time. These phenomenological and empirical approaches to the structure of intrinsic temporality can help us understand experiences such as time dilation (the experiential deceleration of time), time contraction (the experiential acceleration of time), and other disturbances of the flow of time—especially as they manifest in depression.

In this chapter we first elucidate the subjective flow of time particularly as developed by Husserl. We next discuss time and timescales in predictive processing. We then consider how the phenomenological analysis of time can be naturalized within a predictive processing framework. In the final section, we develop an analysis of the temporal disturbances characteristic of depression using the resources of both phenomenology and predictive processing.

The Phenomenology of Intrinsic Temporality

Time holds a very privileged place in phenomenological thought. For the phenomenologist, rather than being a mere succession of instants, all experiences are permeated and structured by temporality. Spatial perception, for example, is typically explained in relatively static terms in the empirical literature. Merleau-Ponty, by contrast, discusses spatiality and depth perception as *temporal* phenomena, without denying the empirical lawlike relatedness of size to distance (Favela and Chemero 2016). Even phenomena that seem purely spatial in nature have a fundamentally temporal structure, as does human existence more generally (see Heidegger 2010). Merleau-Ponty summarizes this phenomenological view: "Time must be understood as a subject, and the subject must be understood as time" (1968: 445). Merleau-Ponty develops an understanding of temporality as an auto-affection that unfolds or generates both subjectivity and the world. Both Heidegger and Merleau-Ponty attempt to think of time as something nonrepresentational—not as a spatialized dimension, as in physics, but an originary unfolding of subjectivity and being (Heidegger 1972, 2012). In this regard, they follow the lead of Husserl, who defined subjective and intentional relations in terms of an originary temporalization. In this section, we review Husserl's original exposition of the temporality of subjectivity and intentionality and his notions of active and passive syntheses. In the following sections, we relate these syntheses to the integration of multiple timescales in predictive processing.

Objective time is sometimes conceived of as a container, line, or series of momentary points. Husserl (1991) is keen to differentiate his phenomenological investigation of temporality from objective, numerical, or spatialized conceptions of time. He does not seek to ascertain how many seconds or milliseconds the perceived present or the "now" encompasses—which is generally recognized among psychologists as nonpunctual and in some theories extending up to 30 seconds (Baddeley 2007, James 1890, Wearden 2016). It is not that chronometric time is irrelevant—"it does interest us that data 'in objective time' are *meant* in these experiences" (Husserl 1991: 10). By bracketing objective time, however, he thinks we are able to reveal a more originary intrinsic temporal structure in subjectivity—a "time-constituting consciousness" (ibid., 28)—which helps to explain how it is even possible to experience meant objects that extend in objective time.

Naïve reflection or introspection may operate on a preconception that the subject is living in a punctiform present, with this point moving along a metaphorical line with a past receding backwards and a future yet to come (see Figure 11.1). Time is centered upon the present or the now, and the past and future are, respectively, presents that are no longer and presents that are yet to come. The past nows are representations of the presents they once were, and these representations can be more or less vivid or dull.

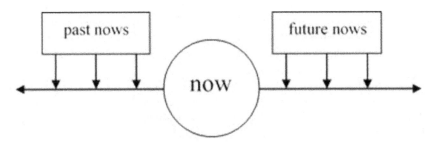

Figure 11.1 The naïve or pre-phenomenological conception of subjective time.

The naïve subject who reports her experience of time to the psychophysicist already conceives of her experience of time in terms of an objective linearity. The chronometric time of psychophysical experimentation is itself a refinement of the folk concept (Heidegger 2012, Husserl 1991). Phenomenology calls for a different way of thinking of temporality rather than a refinement of the folk concept. The phenomenology of time is not merely a careful reflection on the sequence, duration, or timing of our experiences framed in terms of this folk concept; it is not simply a careful description and analysis of the subjective flow of time. Rather, Husserl reconceives of temporality as a structuring or genesis of the movement of the modes of intentionality. As Merleau-Ponty says, "Time is not a line, but rather a network of intentionalities" (2012: 440). It's a processual network structured by three temporal aspects: retention, primal impression, and protention. In regard to this structure, Husserl distinguishes between processes of active and passive syntheses. Both types of synthesis have the same basic retentional-impressional-protentional form. Active synthesis is manifest in the embodied activities of the subject. Passive synthesis occurs in the background processes outside of and surrounding the active focus of the subject. Husserl calls this structure a "passive synthesis" because it is not actively undertaken by the subject or by a homuncular controller.[2]

Husserl initially conceived of the primal impression as an originary awareness of the occurrent moment of the perceived object, which then slips into retention as that moment passes. In the later *Bernau Manuscripts*, the primal impression is reconceived as the intersection of retention and protention (Gallagher 2017a, Gallagher and Zahavi 2014). That is, retention and protention together interlace and constitute the immediate "living present" experience, which means that the primal impression is never given raw without protentional and retentional mediation. Husserl continually returns to the example of listening to musical notes. When a note is heard, the immediately palpable and visceral sounding occurs and registers in primal impression. However, a mere series of such nows cannot be all there is since there would be no connection between them; a note would appear and disappear followed by another note that would do the same; this would be a succession of experiences that would not be an experience of succession. Rather, as the note runs off it is modified by the retentional process, and it is maintained in the living present, but with the intentional sense *as just past*. "The tone itself is the same, but the tone 'in the manner in which' it appears is continually different" (Husserl 1991: 27). If the note is sounded for 1 second, the note qua intentional object perdures throughout the duration of this second and then stops. The intentional sense of this note continues to perdure in retention even after the physical vibrations and psychophysical sensations have died down. As Merleau-Ponty writes, "For every moment that arrives, the previous moment suffers a modification: I still hold it in hand, it is still there, and yet it already sinks back, it descends beneath the line of presents" (2012: 439).

The retention of just past notes allows me to hear the melody as such. Retention in this sense is part of the structure of the perception of the melody; it's not an act of memory that is added to perception to provide a representation of something in the past, but rather the continuation in the present of the trajectory of the intentional object—in this case, the note. "It is [perceptual] consciousness *of what has just been*" (Husserl 1991: 34). Protention is a pre-reflective anticipation of the imminent transformations to occur in the perceived object. When I hear a note within a melody, I have some anticipations of what is about to come next—anticipations that may be more or less vague. I may not know exactly what will come, but I will be surprised if a completely unexpected sound appears next. Even in the middle of a piece by Philip Glass, I may not know exactly what will come next, but I do have a sense that it will be a typical Philip Glass move, and I would be surprised to hear some conventionally ordered composition.

For Husserl and Merleau-Ponty, the possibility of hearing a melody as an extended object, not simply one note in an isolated instant followed by a further note, is evidence that the experienced or lived present is constituted by a temporal structure that includes the impression integrated with retentional and protentional moments. This interweaving of just-past, now-present, and just-about-to-be in the intentionality structure of awareness is effected in an ongoing process of passive synthesis, and this constitutes the intrinsic temporality of consciousness. When I listen to you utter a sentence, the only objectively present phenomenon is the occurrent word (or part thereof) that you are currently speaking. However, for me to hear you utter that word as part of a sentence, I have to hold or retain the previous part of the sentence as you continue to finish it. In addition, as I listen to you speak, I anticipate where your sentence is heading. If, for example, you start to utter the sentence "Mary had a little lamb ...," at the point where you say "little," I hear that word (in the now extant primal impression [pi]) within the context of a fuller grouping constituted by a train of retention (r) and a projection of protention (p).

The threefold structuring process of intrinsic temporality is relational, and it is only through the interrelation of its component processes that pre-reflective consciousness is generated (Fuchs 2013b). None of its three moments is separable from the other. Retention and protention work together to shape the primal impression, and vice versa, forming a synthesis. This process of passive synthesis (that Husserl sometimes calls "auto-affection") importantly has a conative aspect. Fuchs (2013b: 78) calls this "the

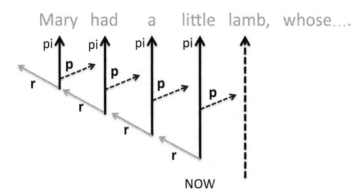

Figure 11.2 Intrinsic temporal structure.

basic 'energetic' momentum of mental life which can be expressed with such concepts as drive, striving, and urge or affection" (see Husserl 2001: 280, Minkowski 1970). That is, the temporal movement of cognition is driven in part by affective salience. Passive synthesis structures most elements of experience and forms a background condition on which some object or set of objects may be thematized based on what may be the most affectively salient features for the subject. Husserl (2001: 280) writes: "Already within passivity, affection is a specific modality of objectivation for the ego. The ego is aroused in a special way here, although it does not yet orient itself actively."

Affectivity can draw the interest of the active subject. When an event or object has a high-enough affective salience, it becomes thematized as the explicit focus of active consciousness or attentional focus. Husserl calls this the movement from passive to active synthesis. Passive syntheses, however, constantly have an affective component; it is only when that affectivity becomes salient enough that a specific region is attentionally focused upon. This drives a bodily "I can" or mode of will based in the basic affective moment of the syntheses of time:

> The will is not a separate mode of consciousness, but rather a special and higher form of activity that can appear everywhere under certain essential conditions that lie in presupposed objectivations and intentionality of feelings.
>
> (ibid., 282–83)

The retention-primal impression-protention structure of intrinsic temporality characterizes not only the intentionality of consciousness but also the dynamical organization of intentional movement and action (Gallagher 2011); insofar as it is implicated in the "I can," intrinsic temporality is enactive or action-oriented (Gallagher and Zahavi 2014). Like affect, practical interests and doings also have an effect on our temporal experience. Intrinsic temporality, together with the affective and embodied action-oriented aspects of existence, together "form the intentional arc of attention, perception and action" (Fuchs 2013b: 79).

This is an important part of the analysis of intrinsic temporality that allows us to address the subjective variations in experience. The phenomenon of intentional binding shows that an agent's experience of time between initiation of action and action effect is modulated by intention (Moore and Obhi 2012). The appraisal of the relevance of a goal, or of a potential reward, has been shown to lengthen the perceived duration of an event (Fung et al. 2017, Uusberg et al. 2018). The perception of danger likewise can slow down the perception of time (Friedman 1990: 20). Negative emotions like anger can have the opposite effect, shortening the perceived duration of an event (Gable et al. 2016). Intense exercise and mindfulness meditation can both provoke a sense of time speeding up (Edwards and McCormick 2017, Thönes and Wittmann 2016). Certain psychopathologies can also alter the perception of time and the duration of events. While time perception is typically highly context-sensitive (Van Hedger et al. 2017), some psychopathologies are associated with *chronic* alterations in time perception. In PTSD, the past continues to erupt into the present. In depression, phenomenological psychiatrists have charted the different ways in which time perception becomes static and hollowed out, no longer feeling like a dynamic movement (Fuchs 2001, 2013a, 2013b, Jaspers 1997, Minkowski 1970, Ratcliffe 2012, 2015, Straus 1947).

Time in Predictive Processing

As with phenomenology, time holds a privileged position within predictive processing. Predictive processing models cognition as a Bayesian process of prediction error minimization (PEM) (Friston 2005, Friston and Kiebel 2009). Whereas classical computational frameworks for understanding perception, such as that of David Marr (2010), model perception as a largely bottom-up process, predictive processing emphasizes top-down and lateral mechanisms of inference.[3] Instead of passively representing the world based on afferent signals, the cognitive system *actively* creates a series of predictions about the state of the world and its contents. On a more minute scale, neuronal activity in the hierarchically arranged perceptual system predict the cause of the incoming sensory signals. These predictions attempt to chart the most probable external state of the world based on prior learning and experience (Doya et al. 2007). While predictions at a cortically lower level may seek to interpret the immediate perceptual datum at hand, higher-level predictions operate at longer timescales and anticipate subsequent states of the object or the world. In the PEM process predictions are continually updated against incoming information. It's likely that the incoming information will not exactly match the prior prediction. This mismatch between prior prediction (also called beliefs, priors, or hypotheses) and the actual state of affairs as perceived generates a prediction error. The surprise generated by the prediction error leads to the formation of a new prediction recalibrated for greater accuracy resulting in an updated posterior probability. The next time around, or at most after some number of learning trials, the prior will be more accurate than it was before. Still, the world will inevitably trump expectations, and the cycle of error production and prior recalibration will continue.

The notion of inference is an ambiguous one in predictive processing models. In PEM the concept of inference is not a personal-level operation undertaken by the agent; it's a subpersonal process that perhaps is only metaphorically inferential (see Hatfield 2002). Helmholtz (1962: 430) originally suggested that the processes of perception "are *like* inferences" (emphasis added).[4] Hohwy indicates something similar. The causal inference conducted by the brain is "*analogous* in many respects to our everyday reasoning about cause and effect, and to scientific methods of causal inference" (emphasis added). He continues:

> There is a sense in which, in spite of being Bayesian, [PEM] is more mechanical than it is inferential … The 'neuronal hardware' of the mechanism itself is not literally inferential: neuronal populations are just trying to generate activity that anticipates their input.
>
> (Hohwy 2013: 13, 55)

In this respect, one might think of the processes described in perceptual PEM as a kind of passive synthesis rather than an inference. Passive synthesis is informed by an association from past experience (what predictive models call a prior), which shapes "actual and possible expectations" (Husserl 2001: 119). Passive synthesis thus involves a process involving a horizon of expectations about the world, each with varying degrees of probability.

In order for these predictions to operate, there must be relatively stable regularities in the world. These regularities operate at different timescales. The Bayesian system (on some accounts, the brain or the brain-body with its environment) hierarchically processes these regularities according to their respective timescales. Long-term regularities are the highest level and most abstract in the hierarchy. On the opposite end of the hierarchical scale are short-term regularities. The rapid, online predictions at short, elementary timescales of milliseconds facilitate the immediate perception of objects in the world. Within the brain, neuronal assemblies gear up to predict their imminent states. These short-term regularities and predictions are hierarchically ordered by coarser-grained predictions operating on slower/longer timescales. Predictions cascade downwards from slower timescales to faster timescales in a top-down fashion. This is "a dynamic, self-organizing system in which the inner (and outer) flow of information is constantly reconfigured" (Clark 2016: 3).

During action, predictions *project* the desired subsequent state onto the world. In this process, called active inference, the system physically modifies its environment in order to get a match between priors and posteriors. Perception, it must be noted, is equally as active as action itself. Whereas classical cognitive models view the mind as a passive machine developing representations of its input, predictive processing posits an active mind that generates its world (Clark 2016, Hutto 2018).

PEM, on a standard interpretation, moves through inferences to update hypotheses, hierarchically structured on varying timescales. Hohwy et al. (2016) use this PEM framework to explain the specious present. They then apply it to Husserl's phenomenological and Grush's (2008) computational accounts of the specious present. They present the phenomenological account as a temporal formalism of retention-primal impression-protention. They use this formal division to temporally distinguish the elements in Grush's (2007, 2008) theory,[5] which they reformulate in terms of predictive processing. Retention is a smoothing or posterior updating. Primal impression is a filtering or prior updating.[6] Protention is then the prediction such that "at *t*, the state estimate simultaneously has retention, via smoothing, primary impression, via filtering, and protention, via prediction" (Hohwy et al. 2016: 328).

They explain the movement of the temporal window, the flow or the perception of the passage of time by proposing that predictions' likelihood weightings rapidly drop, even while they continue to hold true. They refer to this instability metaphorically as a "distrust of the present."

> The sense of flow arises as the system gives up one hypothesis and settles on a new one due to its propensity for distrusting the present. The current prior decreases [in likelihood] and this makes it seem like we are inexorably being pushed forward. The window of the specious present moves forward because the system expects change and therefore down-regulates the current input.
>
> (ibid., 330)

The movement of the specious present is driven by a kind of meta-prediction that current hypotheses will rapidly be disproven as a result of imminent change. Protention is never perfectly fulfilled (there is always some degree of prediction error) and this drives the system to continue its processing. This explains phenomena such as the bistability of the Necker cube, where perception fails to settle on one single interpretation and instead shifts between two alternate predictions. The changes in the perception of the Necker cube are driven by the meta-prediction that current hypotheses will rapidly be replaced by new ones, although the input remains constant.

Hohwy, Paton, and Palmer's discussion of the specious present remains relatively abstract and disembodied, however. This is consistent with their internalism, as clearly expressed by Hohwy:

> PEM should make us resist conceptions of [a mind-world] relation on which the mind is in some fundamental way open or porous to the world, or on which it is in some strong sense embodied, extended or enactive. Instead, PEM reveals the mind to be inferentially secluded from the world, it seems to be more neurocentrically skull-bound than embodied or extended, and action itself is more an inferential process on sensory input than an enactive coupling with the environment.
>
> (Hohwy 2016: 259)

As we've noted, however, temporal experience can have significant *affective* and *embodied* components that modify the formal inferential structure of the specious present. These many affective and embodied temporal effects are significant for the phenomenology of intrinsic temporality. The specious present is not a phenomenon with constant dimensions but is subject to alteration under affective conditions. Husserl (2001: 280) and other phenomenologists allow for this and insist that, in addition to the formal temporal structure of retention-primal impression-protention, temporal consciousness is fundamentally driven forward by affectivity. Furthermore, this temporal structure is often realized within an embodied "I can" and its sensorimotor intentionalities. These more embodied and affective aspects can be integrated into a predictive processing account of the specious present by taking into account active inference, which includes exteroceptive, interoceptive, and proprioceptive aspects.

Predictive Engagement and Affectivity in Intrinsic Temporality

We propose a revised predictive processing account of intrinsic temporality enhanced by integrating affective and embodied elements of Husserl's phenomenological analyses and by emphasizing the dynamical integration of timescales. Time in predictive processing is ordered according to a hierarchical series of timescales, from the rapid/shorter timescales of neural assemblies to the slower/longer timescales of goal-oriented behavior. The relations among different timescales are significant for understanding the phenomenology of intrinsic temporality. Francisco Varela (1999) provides a theoretical connection by introducing three timescales relevant to Husserlian intrinsic time: the *elementary scale* of neuronal processes (the 1/10 scale measured in milliseconds), the *integrative scale* of pre-reflective consciousness—the specious or living present (the 1 scale measured in seconds), and the *narrative scale* of projects and discourse (the 10 scale of longer time measures) (see Gallagher 2016, 2017a, 2017b, 2018).

The elementary scale includes processes such as "the intrinsic cellular rhythms of neuronal discharges, and … the temporal summation capacities of synaptic integration. These events fall within a range of 10 milliseconds (e.g., the rhythms of bursting interneurons) to 100 msec (e.g., the duration of an EPSP/IPSP sequence in a cortical pyramidal neuron)" (Varela 1999: 117). The integrative timescale is the time of the flow of pre-reflective consciousness in the living present—the scale of a simple conscious act, a basic bodily action, or attention shift,[7] operating from .5 to 3 seconds. It is called "integrative" because the cell assemblies firing at the elementary scale are synchronized and integrated at this level into larger-scale assemblies in ways that are coupled with (aligned with, attuned to) bodily and environmental processes (Varela 1999, Gallagher 2016). The narrative timescale is the time of reflective consciousness, long-term memory, expectations, discourse, and explicit goal-seeking behavior.

Elementary, integrative, and narrative timescales are dynamically nonlinear; accordingly, cognitive processes are not straightforwardly contemporaneous across levels. They are not simply diachronic if we think of diachronicity as involving mere succession, and they are not necessarily additive or sequential across different timescales. For example, auditory and visual signals are processed at different rates at the elementary timescale, and yet they are experientially bound together at the integrative timescale. Thus, Varela suggests that these timescales are recursively and hierarchically structured to compose unified wholes. The explication of these time scales "addresses the question of how something temporally extended can show up as present but also reach far into my temporal horizon" (1999: 116–17). Specifically, Varela suggests that neuronal activations at the elementary level become coupled through dynamically instable phase-locking syntheses that manifest through retentional processes as conscious, behavioral, or action moments on the integrational level. The instability of phase-locked synchrony that transitions into relaxation states and phase transition generates the flow of experience.

> In brief, we have neuronal-level constitutive events, which have a duration on the 1/10 scale, forming aggregates that manifest as incompressible but complete cognitive acts on the 1 scale. This completion time is dynamically dependent on a number of dispersed assemblies and not a fixed integration period; in other words it is the basis of the origin of duration without an external or internally ticking clock …. The integration-relaxation processes at the 1 scale are strict correlates of present-time consciousness.
>
> (1999: 118–19)

Importantly, these timescales characterize processes in the brain and throughout the body (West 2012), across synchronized human bodies (Fuchs 2001), and in coupling with the environment.

While predictive processing is generally presented as an internalist model, as we see in Hohwy (2013) and Hohwy et al. (2016), it has also been proposed as a model that can integrate embodied and environmental aspects. Andy Clark, for example, suggests that predictive processing provides "the perfect neuro-computational partner for recent work on the embodied mind—work that stresses the constant engagement of the world by cycles of perceptual-motor activity" (2016: 1). In effect, Clark (ibid., 133), in contrast to Hohwy, emphasizes active inference—active, embodied engagement that manipulates the environment in order to reduce prediction errors. "The predictive brain, if this is correct, is not an insulated inference engine so much as an action-oriented engagement machine" (ibid., 1).

Thinking of cognitive and action-related processes in terms of predictive engagement means, on a phenomenologically informed enactive reading, thinking of these processes in terms of dynamical adjustments "in which the brain, *as part of and along with the larger organism*, actively responds in ways that allow for the right kind of ongoing attunement with the environment—an environment that is physical but also social and cultural" (Gallagher and Allen 2018: 2634). On this view, active inference is a dynamic engagement with the world that integrates exteroceptive, interoceptive, and proprioceptive factors (see Seth 2013, Seth and Friston 2016). It is not something that is simply computable within the brain but requires an embodied agent embedded within an environment.

The recursivity that Varela describes in terms of the nonlinear dynamics across different timescales is described by Clark as processes of "rolling cycles" that involve action and perception, so that "what we perceive is constantly conditioned by what we do," and vice versa. In an ongoing reciprocal causal fashion, top-down predictions entrain actions that "help sculpt the sensory flows that recruit new high-level predictions (and so on, in a rolling cycle of expectation, sensory stimulation and action)" (2016: 176). In predictive engagement, where brain, body, and environment are dynamically integrated across different timescales, both affective (interoceptive) processes and agentive practical interests drive the process. According to Clark, these processes are "pragmatic" insofar as "they are adapted to produce good control" for a set of possible actions "constantly conditioned by our own 'action repertoire' … in interaction with our needs, projects, and opportunities" (2016: 180).

Varela also links affectivity to the ongoing processes of intrinsic temporality. Specifically, protention "is always suffused with affect and emotional tone that accompanies the flow" (1999: 131). Protention is not an abstract, merely formal or dis-interested prediction. In predictive processing terms, the prior that shapes the protention is affectively suffused and practically interested. Varela cites Husserl's unpublished C-manuscript, to indicate that the agent "follows affect, or still it is attracted, held, taken in by that which affects it" (Ms. CIII/1, Varela 1999: 131). In this regard, affect has an impact on the structure of intrinsic temporality. Here he quotes Natalie Depraz's insight into Husserl's analysis: "Affect is there before being there for me in full consciousness: I am affected before knowing that I am affected. It is in that sense that affect can be said to be primordial" (Depraz 1994: 75).

This idea is clearly captured in predictive processing models. For example, Barrett and Bar (see also Barrett and Simmons 2015, Chanes and Barrett 2016) show that in regard to perception, "responses signaling an object's salience, relevance or value do not occur as a separate step after the object is identified. Instead, affective responses support vision from the very moment that visual stimulation begins" (2009: 1325). On the elemental timescale, activation of the visual cortex generates a train of muscular and hormonal changes throughout the body, generating interoceptive sensations from bodily organs, muscles, and joints associated with prior experience. Perception is formed in an integration (a passive synthesis) of interoception with current exteroceptive sensory information. On the integrative timescale, the organism as a whole responds and contributes to shaping subsequent actions. This ongoing integration of "sensory information from the external world with that from the body indicates that conscious percepts are indeed intrinsically infused with affective value, so that the affective salience or significance of an object is not computed after the fact." Accordingly, "the predictions generated during object perception carry affective value as a necessary and normal part of visual experience" (Barrett and Bar 2009: 1328). As Gallagher and Allen (2018) suggest, priors, which include affect, are not just in the brain but involve whole body dispositions and adjustments.

The specious present and modulations in our experience of time can be understood within a predictive processing model by taking into account the affective and embodied processes involved in the temporal flow of experience. If protention is in some sense prediction, retention the updating of posteriors, and primal impression the updating of priors (Hohwy et al. 2016: 328), these elements are interlaced by different timescales operating across the brain, body, and environment. This dynamic interrelation of timescales across brain, body, and environment composes a predictive engagement with the world. At the narrative timescale, goal-oriented behavior hierarchically modifies passive and active synthesizing processes at the integrative and elementary timescales. Affective salience drives the dynamic interaction of timescales at all levels. When affective salience is modified, we can expect that temporal phenomenology will correlatively undergo a modification. In the following section, we trace one such modification in depression.

Predictive Engagement and Depression

According to Erwin Straus (1947: 255), the *entire* symptomatology of depression involves anomalies in temporal experience. Minkowski (1970) too suggests that the generative disorder in depression involves temporality. More generally, phenomenologically informed approaches to psychopathology have described the temporality of depression as involving modifications of embodiment (Boss 1983: 113–14) and affectivity (Fuchs 2001, 2013b, 2018, Gallagher 2012, Jaspers 1997). The phenomenology of depression is marked by feelings of time slowing down, running out, or even feelings of detachment from time (Fuchs 2013b, Ratcliffe 2012, 2015).

> Reality is felt purely as a temporal immediacy; or, to put it another way, we feel as if nothing were timelessly there ... "It feels as if it is always the same moment, it is like a timeless void."
>
> (Jaspers 1997: 84)

According to Jaspers, this may be accompanied by a sense of disappearance of the future. The experience of time becomes something ossified. This corresponds to a flattening of affect and a sense of hopelessness or "the feeling of having lost feeling" (ibid., 111). Hopelessness is a nonspecific feeling of the emptiness of existence and not a lack of hope for any particular future state. It is related to the closing off of the future insofar as hope is fundamentally a prospective anticipation of nascent possibilities in the world (Ratcliffe 2015: 110). Hopelessness is indicative of a general closing-off of one's possibilities for engagement with the world. In this respect, and at the extreme, the protentional moment of intrinsic time is modified and no longer opens toward future possibilities.

In the DSM-5 and ICD-10 symptomatology, classical depression or Major Depressive Disorder (MDD) incorporates affective, bodily, and cognitive (call them ABC) symptoms.

A. Disturbances of affect in MDD include persistent depressed mood (sadness, emptiness, hopelessness), and diminished interest in daily activities, feelings of worthlessness or guilt, but also loss of empathic resonance with others, loneliness, self-loathing or low self-esteem, pervasive sense of dread, unaccountable fears, feeling that one's experience is absolutely private and absolutely isolating, despair, feeling of being excluded, not understood, underappreciated, self-alienation.
B. Significant bodily disturbances include weight loss or gain, insomnia or hypersomnia, psychomotor agitation, and fatigue, lack of appetite, slowness of movement.
C. Disturbances in cognition include attenuation of concentration, excessive rumination, toxic thought processes, mind fog, nihilism, persistent thoughts of death, recurrent suicidal ideation. Also, as noted above, difficulty in imagining a different future, changed time perception, time experienced as passing very slowly, closure of the future. (American Psychological Association 2013: 160–1, Gallagher and Daly 2018)

These affective, bodily, and cognitive symptoms (involving interoception, proprioception, and exteroception) operate across different timescales, from the elementary to the narrative. Although not every subject with depression manifests all of these symptoms, some number of these symptoms will form a pattern, a "complete form of existence" (Merleau-Ponty 2012: 110) or "an organized and vital unity" (Minkowski 1970: 223) that defines depression.

From the perspective of both phenomenology and predictive engagement, the flattening of affect, sense of hopelessness, and feeling of the ossification of time and the loss of the future must be understood at multiple timescales. Varela (1999), for example, suggests a correlation between the three time scales (elementary, integrative, and narrative) and different forms of affect: emotional tonality (which plays into the dynamics of flow), experiential affect, and mood, respectively. At the elementary timescale, the activation of neural assemblies, embodied affective, and sensorimotor control processes undergo modification. Short-term patterns of neural activation may eventually result in long-term plastic changes including hypo- and hyperconnectivity between different regions (Kaiser et al. 2015). Altered sensorimotor control manifests as slower gait speeds (Sanders et al. 2012), lesser degrees of arm swinging in movement, reduced head movements (Michalak et al. 2009), and slouching or poor posture

(Canales et al. 2017) and decreased sensory attenuation (Badcock et al. 2017). Hand movements, which are rapid but normally fractal when looked at in slower timescales (minutes to hours), smooth out toward Brownian noise in depressed persons (Aybek et al. 2012). This is consistent with a broader trend in illness of the breakdown of fractal patterns into noise (West 2012).

Changes in bodily (sensorimotor) and affective processes change the way the subject perceives the world. At the integrative timescale, as the body slouches, gait speed slows, and arm and head movements are reduced, there is a correlative affective flattening of affordances as objects lose their affective salience (de Haan et al. 2013, 2015). The body's active engagement with the world itself slows down. Fewer objects and events in the world affectively draw the person to action. The depressed person becomes less active, or if they maintain their level of activity, it is with a sense of futility, emptiness, and non-fulfillment. As high-level predictions of lack of affective salience develop, they reciprocally affect neural and sensorimotor processes.

Since affect contributes to the phenomenology of intrinsic time, an affective disturbance creates a disturbance in the intentional structure of experience. As we already noted, Varela thinks of protention as "always suffused with affect and emotional tone that accompanies the flow" (1999: 131, also Gallagher and Varela 2003, Varela and Depraz 2005). On this view, protention is constitutionally involved with an affective tone or tension or, from a different perspective, a readiness for action. In the case of depression, instead of the "not yet" always being suffused with an "I can," it is rather constrained by an "I cannot" or perhaps an "I'm not interested."

Not only actions but other bodily processes at narrative timescales also undergo modification. These include mood and sleep disturbances (Lee et al. 2017, Whalen et al. 2017, Wiebe et al. 2012).[8] As the world consistently begins to afford fewer opportunities for action at the integrative timescale, narratives and goals at slower/ longer timescales are affected. Metanarratives about the hopelessness of existence may develop, along with a preoccupation with thoughts of death or suicidal ideation. "All that remains of the future is the increasing proximity of one's unavoidable extinction" (Ratcliffe 2015: 189–90). This feeling of hopelessness and of the hollowing out of time reflects the diminished affective salience of objects and events in the world at the integrative scale. Nevertheless, hopelessness and emptiness, as narratives structuring behavior, themselves become predictions modifying processes at elementary and integrative timescales.

The loss of affective salience at the integrative timescale and the flattening of the field of affordances may generate a higher-order prediction of general emptiness and hopelessness at the narrative timescale. This prediction, in turn, cascades into a further closing-off of the affective salience of objects in the world and reduces active inferential engagement with the world. The persistent attenuation of affordances is mirrored in the attenuation of motricity and bodily energy. There is little for the body to do or engage with, and it mirrors this lack with its own retardation and de-energization. The symptom of indecisiveness also is directly related to the flattened field of affordances. If everything is more or less irrelevant and lacking in affective salience, objects lose their ability to sway decisions either way. Quite simply, they do not afford any actions, so there is nothing to decide or to take action upon. The perception of an ossification or emptying of time, or a feeling of being cut-off from the future, is a direct reflection of the loss of possibilities for action in the world (Ratcliffe 2015: 110). As I adapt to the seeming inevitabilities of hopelessness and emptiness, objects and events further lose affective salience. The more I ruminate on these beliefs and the more real they become for me, the more trapped I become in the vicious cycle of depression. As the field of affordances flattens, I gain a sense of hopelessness and may even begin to imagine death or suicide as a way out. These integrative scale priors sediment in the subject and generate narrative-scale predictions (integrative → narrative). But likewise, the field of affordances becomes further flattened as my experiences of hopelessness and beliefs about death become stronger, and I begin to predict and even actively infer a situation of hopelessness (narrative → integrative). The protentional movement of prediction retroacts on the sedimentations and retentions (posterior updating), bringing them further in line with the subject's active inferential processes.

In a word, I begin to expect that everything will be hopeless, and my expectation becomes something of a self-fulfilling prophecy with repercussions at multiple timescales across brain, body, and environment. The narrative-scale predictions of hopelessness and emptiness are not cases of passive synthesis or passive inference that the agent comes to by examination of disruptions at elemental or integrative timescales. They are cases of active synthesis, part of an active inference that the agent enacts, albeit often unwittingly and unwillingly within the frame of impoverished action. Although the DSM-5 and ICD-10 symptomatology of MDD isolates individual symptoms, they are deeply connected across timescales and regions. A vital unity (Minkowski 1970: 223) or complete form of existence (Merleau-Ponty 2012: 110) forms as emergent patterns of neural activation, plastic reshaping of neural interconnectivity, sensorimotor engagements, overt behaviors, and narratives mutually implicate one another. As rapid, low-level regularities shape slower, high-level predictions, these predictions in turn hierarchically affect the rapid predictions involved in sensorimotor and neural processes. The feeling of the hollowing out and emptying of time and hope is only the most vivid of the multiple changes occurring at all levels of the embodied agent.

Conclusion

While we agree that a predictive processing approach can enlighten the nature of the temporal flow (Hohwy et al. 2016), we have argued that the phenomenology of temporal consciousness is ultimately affective and embodied. Active inference must be understood as embodied action, beyond mere neural inferences. Perceptual processes in the specious present likewise have affective and embodied components pivotal to their structure. To understand the predictive aspect of predictive processing in terms of protention means that it is subjected to affective salience. Significant alterations in affective salience can lead to modifications in the felt passage of time in the specious present. This leads to experiences such as time apparently speeding up while deeply engrossed in an activity or slowing down in periods of boredom (where little has affective grip).

We can see how one such modified temporal phenomenology arises in depression by noting the typical affective, bodily, and cognitive changes undergone by depressed persons. Expanding upon phenomenological analyses of depression through the lens of predictive engagement, we proposed that simultaneous bottom-up and top-down processes, from low-level perception and action to high-level, narrative-scale engagement with the world, explain this modified phenomenology. Ultimately, depression becomes a vicious circle where narrative-scale predictions and active syntheses modify elementary and integrative processes, and vice versa.

Acknowledgments

We would like to thank Kevin J. Ryan for helpful comments. Z.A.N. would like to thank the Institute of Intelligent Systems for a travel grant to present an earlier version of this paper at the XXIV World Congress of Philosophy.

Notes

1   "I find it gratuitous to assume that a Hopi who knows only the Hopi language and the cultural ideas of his own society has the same notions, often supposed to be intuitions, of time and space that we have, and that are generally assumed to be universal" (Whorf 1956: 56).

2   "A 'passive synthesis' would be contradictory if synthesis means composition, and if passivity consists in receiving a multiplicity rather than composing it. We meant, in speaking of a passive synthesis, that the multiple is penetrated by us, and that, nevertheless, we are not the ones who perform the synthesis" (Merleau-Ponty 2012: 451).

3   Error minimization is simultaneously a minimization of free energy (Friston and Kiebel 2009). Predictive processing is a hierarchical framework, with "each level providing constraints on the level below" (Friston 2005: 822). The hierarchical structure of predictive layers emulates the hierarchical causal structure of the world (Hohwy 2013, Rao 2007). Higher cortical levels predict input at lower levels. This allows for multisensory and cross-modal priors to integrate in order to produce the best possible predictions.

4   "Using the term 'inference' to describe such a process may seem to be somewhat metaphorical and thus to undercut the force of the claim that perception works by unconscious inference. But, as we said at the outset, unconscious inference must be at least somewhat metaphorical, since normal inference is quite clearly slow, laborious, and conscious, whereas perception is fast, easy, and unconscious. The important point for present purposes is that perception relies on processes that can be usefully viewed as inferences that require heuristic assumptions" (Palmer 1999: 83).

5   Grush's original model is based on the Kalman filter, not on predictive error minimization.

6   This accords with Husserl's later understanding of the primal impression in the *Bernau Manuscripts*, where primal impression no longer has an original content in itself but is instead woven from protentions and retentions.

7 Cognitive processes are the result of dynamical, nonlinear integration across these time scales. Accordingly some processes are not neatly confined to one time scale, for example, working memory, which for some types of information can last up to 30 seconds (Baddeley 2007). Another example is referred to as "preparatory set," which includes proactive control processes, such as anticipations, which prepare for imminent events (Ruge et al. 2013). It is "a rapid, largely subcortical response; although it is not fully unconscious it is distinct from the conscious rational appraisal and voluntary decision-making processes" (Payne and Crane-Godreau 2015: 2).

8 These are sometime accompanied by changes in temperature, melatonin levels, and cortisol circadian rhythms (Ehlers et al. 1988, Grandin et al. 2006), as well as plastic alterations in the connectivity between neuronal regions (Kaiser et al. 2015).

References

American Psychiatric Association (2013), *Diagnostic and Statistical Manual of Mental Disorders*, 5th ed., Arlington, VA: American Psychiatric Association.

Aybek, S., Ionescu, A., Berney, A., Chocron, O., Aminian, K. and Vingerhoets, F. G. (2012), "Fractal Temporal Organisation of Motricity Is Altered in Major Depression," *Psychiatry Research*, 200: 288–93. doi.org/10.1016/j.psychres.2012.03.047.

Badcock, P. B., Davey, Christopher G., Whittle, Sarah, Allen, Nicholas B. and Friston, Karl J. (2017), "The Depressed Brain: An Evolutionary Systems Theory," *Trends in Cognitive Sciences*, 21 (3): 182–94. doi.org/10.1016/j.tics.2017.01.005.

Barrett, L. F. and Bar, M. (2009), "See It with Feeling: Affective Predictions during Object Perception," *Philosophical Transactions of the Royal Society B: Biological Sciences*, 364: 1325–34. doi.org/10.1098/rstb.2008.0312.

Barrett, L. F. and Simmons, W. K. (2015), "Interoceptive Predictions in the Brain," *Nature Reviews Neuroscience*, 16 (7): 419–29. doi.org/10.1038/nrn3950.

Baddeley, A. (2007), *Working Memory, Thought, and Action*, Oxford: Oxford University Press.

Boss, M. (1983), *Existential Foundations of Medicine and Psychology*, Translated by Stephen Conway and Anne Cleaves, New York: Jason Aronson.

Canales, J. Z., Fiquer, J. T., Campos, R. N., Soeiro-de-Souza, M. G. T and Moreno, R. A. (2017), "Investigation of Associations between Recurrence of Major Depressive Disorder and Spinal Posture Alignment: A Quantitative Cross-Sectional Study," *Gait & Posture*, 52: 258–64. doi.org/10.1016/j.gaitpost.2016.12.011.

Chanes, L. and Barrett, L. F. (2016), "Redefining the Role of Limbic Areas in Cortical Processing," *Trends in Cognitive Science*, 20 (2): 96–106. doi.org/10.1016/j.tics.2015.11.005.

Clark, A. (2013), "Whatever Next? Predictive Brains, Situated Agents, and the Future of Cognitive Science," *Behavioral and Brain Sciences*, 36: 181–204. doi.org/10.1017/S0140525X12000477.

Clark, A. (2016), *Surfing Uncertainty: Prediction, Action, and the Embodied Mind*, Oxford: Oxford University Press.

Clark, V. P., Fan, S. and Hillyard, S. A. (1995), "Identification of Early Visual Cortex by Crossmodal Spatial Attention," *Human Brain Mapping*, 2: 170–87.

De Haan, S., Rietveld, E., Stokhof, M. and Denys, D. (2013), "The Phenomenology of Deep Brain Stimulation-Induced Changes in OCD: An Enactive Affordance-Based Model," *Frontiers in Human Neuroscience*, 7: 653. doi.org/10.3389/fnhum.2013.00653.

De Haan, S., Rietveld, E., Stokhof, M. and Denys, D. (2015), "Effects of Deep Brain Stimulation on the Lived Experience of Obsessive-Compulsive Disorder Patients: In-Depth Interviews with 18 Patients," *PLoS One*, 10 (8): 1–29. doi.org/10.1371/journal.pone.0135524.

Depraz, N. (1994), "Temporalité et affection dans les manuscrits tardifs sur la temporalité (1929–1935) de Husserl," *Alter*, 2: 63–86.

Doya, K., Ishii, S., Pouget, A. and Rao, R. P. N. (eds.) (2007), *Bayesian Brain: Probabilistic Approaches to Neural Coding*, Cambridge: MIT Press.

Edwards, A. M. and McCormick, A. (2017), "Time Perception, Pacing and Exercise Intensity: Maximal Exercise Distorts the Perception of Time," *Physiology & Behavior*, 180: 98–102. doi.org/10.1016/j.physbeh.2017.08.009.

Ehlers, C. L., Frank, E. and Kupfer, D. J. (1988), "Social Zeitgebers and Biological Rhythms: A Unified Approach to Understanding the Etiology of Depression," *Archives of General Psychiatry*, 45 (10): 948–52. doi.org/10.1001/archpsyc.1988.01800340076012.

Favela, L. H. and Chemero, A. (2016), "The Animal-Environment System" in Yann Coello and Martin H. Fischer (eds.), *Foundations of Embodied Cognition: Perceptual and Emotional Embodiment*, New York: Routledge, pp. 59–74.

Foxe, J. J. and Simpson, G. V. (2002), "Flow of Activation from V1 to Frontal Cortex in Humans," *Experimental Brain Research*, 142 (1): 139–50. doi.org/10.1007/s00221-001-0906-7.

Friedman, W. J. (1990), *About Time: Inventing the Fourth Dimension*, Cambridge: MIT Press.

Friston, K. (2005), "A Theory of Cortical Responses," *Philosophical Transactions of the Royal Society B*, 360: 815–36. doi.org/10.1098/rstb.2005.1622.

Friston, K. and Kiebel, S. (2009), "Predictive Coding under the Free-Energy Principle," *Philosophical Transactions of the Royal Society B: Biological Sciences*, 364: 1211–21. doi.org/10.1098/rstb.2008.0300.

Fuchs, T. (2001), "Melancholia as a Desynchronization: Towards a Psychopathology of Interpersonal Time," *Psychopathology*, 34: 179–86. doi.org/10.1159/000049304.

Fuchs, T. (2013a), "Depression, Intercorporeality, and Interaffectivity," *Journal of Consciousness Studies*, 20 (7–8): 219–38.

Fuchs, T. (2013b), "Temporality and Psychopathology," *Phenomenology and Cognitive Science*, 12: 75–104. doi.org/10.1007/s11097-010-9189-4.

Fuchs, T. (2018), *Ecology of the Brain: The Phenomenology and Biology of the Embodied Mind*, Oxford: Oxford University Press.

Fung, B. J., Murawski, C. and Bode, S. (2017), "Caloric Primary Rewards Systematically Alter Time Perception," *Journal of Experimental Psychology: Human Perception and Performance*, 43 (11): 1925–36. doi.org/10.1037/xhp0000418.

Gable, P. A., Neal, L. B. and Poole, B. D. (2016), "Sadness Speeds and Disgust Drags: Influence of Motivational Direction on Time Perception in Negative Affect," *Motivation Science*, 2 (4): 238–55. doi.org/10.1037/mot0000044.

Gallagher, S. (2011), "Time in Action" in C. Callender (ed.), *Oxford Handbook on Time*, Oxford: Oxford University Press, pp. 419–37.

Gallagher, S. (2012), "Time, Emotion, and Depression," *Emotion Review*, 4 (2): 127–32. doi.org/10.1177/1754073911430142.

Gallagher, S. (2016), "Timing Is Not Everything: The Intrinsic Temporality of Action" in Roman Altshuler and Michael J. Sigrist (eds.), *Time and the Philosophy of Action*, New York: Routledge.

Gallagher, S. (2017a), *Enactivist Interventions: Rethinking the Mind*, Oxford: Oxford University Press.

Gallagher, S. (2017b), "The Past, Present and Future of Time-Consciousness: From Husserl to Varela and Beyond," *Constructivist Foundations*, 13 (1): 91–7.

Gallagher, S. (2018), "New Mechanisms and the Enactivist Concept of Constitution" in M. P. Guta (ed.), *Consciousness and the Ontology of Properties*, London: Routledge, pp. 207–20. doi.org/10.4324/9781315104706.

Gallagher, S. and Allen, M. (2018), "Active Inference, Enactivism and the Hermeneutics of Social Cognition," *Synthese*, 195 (6): 2627–48. doi.org/10.1007/s11229-016-1269-8.

Gallagher, S. and Daly, A. (2018), "Dynamical Relations in the Self-Pattern," *Frontiers in Psychology*, 9: 664. doi.org/10.3389/fpsyg.2018.00664.

Gallagher, S. and Varela, F. J. (2003), "Redrawing the Map and Resetting the Time: Phenomenology and the Cognitive Sciences," *Canadian Journal of Philosophy*, 29: 93–132. doi.org/10.1080/00455091.2003.10717596.

Gallagher, S. and Zahavi, D. (2014), "Primal Impression and Enactive Perception" in Valtteri Arstila and Dan Lloyd (eds.), *Subjective Time: The Philosophy, Psychology, and Neuroscience of Temporality*, Cambridge: MIT Press.

Grandin, L. D., Alloy, L. B. and Abramson, L. Y. (2006), "The Social Zeitgeber Theory, Circadian Rhythms, and Mood Disorders: Review and Evaluation," *Clinical Psychological Review*, 26: 679–94. doi.org/10.1016/j.cpr.2006.07.001.

Grush, R. (2007), "Skill Theory 2.0: Dispositions, Emulation, and Spatial Perception," *Synthese*, 159: 389–416. doi.org/10.1007/s11229-007-9236-z.

Grush, R. (2008), "Temporal Representation and Dynamics," *New Ideas in Psychology*, 26: 146–57. doi.org/10.1016/j.newideapsych.2007.07.017.

Hatfield, G. (2002), "Perception as Unconscious Inference" in D. Heyer (ed.), *Perception and the Physical World: Psychological and Philosophical Issues in Perception*, Chichester: John Wiley & Sons, pp. 113–43.

Heidegger, M. (1972), *On Time and Being*, Translated by Joan Stambaugh, New York: Harper & Row.

Heidegger, M. (2010), *Being and Time*, rev. ed., Translated by Joan Stambaugh, Albany: State University of New York Press.

Heidegger, M. (2012), *Contributions to Philosophy (of the Event)*, Translated by Richard Rojcewicz and Daniela Vallega-Neu, Bloomington: Indiana University Press.

Helmholtz, H. V. (1962), *Treatise on Physiological Optics, Volume III*, 3rd ed., Translated by James P. C. Southall, New York: Dover.

Hohwy, J. (2013), *The Predictive Mind*, Oxford: Oxford University Press.

Hohwy, J. (2016), "The Self-Evidencing Brain," *Noûs*, 50 (2): 259–85. doi.org/10.1111/nous.12062.

Hohwy, J., Patton, B. and Palmer, C. (2016), "Distrusting the Present," *Phenomenology and the Cognitive Sciences*, 15: 315–35. doi.org/10.1007/s11097-015-9439-6.

Hollingworth, H. L. (1910), "The Central Tendency of Judgment," *The Journal of Philosophy, Psychology and Scientific Methods*, 7 (17): 461–9. doi.org/10.2307/2012819.

Husserl, E. (1991), *On the Phenomenology of the Consciousness of Internal Time*, Translated by John B. Brough, Dordrecht: Kluwer Academic.

Husserl, E. (2001), *Analyses Concerning Passive and Active Synthesis: Lectures on Transcendental Logic*, Translated by Anthony J. Steinbock, Dordrecht: Kluwer Academic.

Hutto, D. (2018), "Getting into Predictive Processing's Great Guessing Game: Bootstrap Heaven or Hell?" *Synthese*, 195: 2445–58. doi.org/10.1007/s11229-017-1385-0.

James, W. (1890), *The Principles of Psychology*, New York: Henry Holt and Co.

Jaspers, K. (1997), *General Psychopathology, Volume 1*, Translated by J. Hoenig and Marian W. Hamilton, Baltimore, MD: Johns Hopkins University Press.

Kaiser, R. H., Andrews-Hanna, J., Wagner, T. and Pizzagalli, D. A. (2015), "Large-Scale Network Dysfunction in Major Depressive Disorder: A Meta-analysis of Resting-State Functional Connectivity," *JAMA Psychiatry*, 72 (6): 603–11. doi.org/10.1001/jamapsychiatry.2015.0071.

Lee, J. E., Park, S., Nam, J.-Y., Young, J. J., and Park, E.-C. (2017), "Effect of Changes in Sleep Quantity and Quality on Depressive Symptoms among Korean Children," *The Journal of School Nursing*, 33 (4): 299–306. doi.org/10.1177/1059840516660015.

Marr, D. (2010), *Vision: A Computational Investigation into the Human Representation and Processing of Visual Information*, Cambridge: MIT Press.

Merleau-Ponty, M. (1968), *The Visible and the Invisible*, Translated by Alphonso Lingis, Evanston, IL: Northwestern University Press.

Merleau-Ponty, M. (2012), *Phenomenology of Perception*, Translated by Donald A. Landes, New York: Routledge.

Michalak, J., Troje, N. F., Fischer, J., Vollmar, P., Heidenreich, T. and Schulte, D. (2009), "Embodiment of Sadness and Depression—Gait Patterns Associated with Dysphoric Mood," *Psychosomatic Medicine*, 71: 580–7. doi.org/10.1097/PSY.0b013e3181a2515c.

Minkowski, E. (1970), *Lived Time: Phenomenological and Psychopathological Studies*, Translated by Nancy Metzel, Evanston, IL: Northwestern University Press.

Moore, J. W. and Obhi, S. S. (2012), "Intentional Binding and the Sense of Agency: A Review," *Consciousness and Cognition*, 21 (1): 546–61. doi.org/10.1016/j.concog.2011.12.002.

Palmer, S. E. (1999), *Vision Science: Photons to Phenomenology*, Cambridge, MA: MIT Press.

Payne, P. and Crane-Godreau, M. A. (2015), "The Preparatory Set: A Novel Approach to Understanding Stress, Trauma, and the Bodymind Therapies," *Frontiers in Human Neuroscience*, 9: 1–22. doi.org/10.3389/fnhum.2015.00178.

Rao, R. P. N. (2007), "Neural Models of Bayesian Belief Propagation" in Kenji Doya, Shin Ishii, Alexandre Pouget, and Rajesh P. N. Rao (eds.), *Bayesian Brain: Probabilistic Approaches to Neural Coding*, Cambridge: MIT Press.

Ratcliffe, M. (2012), "Variety of Temporal Experience in Depression," *Journal of Medical Philosophy*, 37 (2): 114–38. doi.org/10.1093/jmp/jhs010.

Ratcliffe, M. (2015), *Experiences of Depression: A Study in Phenomenology*, Oxford: Oxford University Press.

Ruge, H., Jamadar, S., Zimmermann, U. and Karayanidis, F. (2013), "The Many Faces of Preparatory Control in Task Switching: Reviewing a Decade of fMRI Research," *Human Brain Mapping*, 34: 12–35. doi.org/10.1002/hbm.21420.

Sanders, J. B., Bremmer, M. A., Deeg, D., Beekman J. H. and Aartjan, T. F. (2012), "Do Depressive Symptoms and Gait Speed Impairment Predict Each Other's Incidence? A 16-Year Prospective Study in the Community," *Journal of the American Geriatrics Society*, 60 (9): 1673–80. doi.org/10.1111/j.1532-5415.2012.04114.x.

Seth, A. K. (2013), "Interoceptive Inference, Emotion, and the Embodied Self," *Trends in Cognitive Sciences*, 17 (11): 565–73. doi.org/10.1016/j.tics.2013.09.007.

Seth, A. K. and Friston, K. J. (2016), "Active Interoceptive Inference and the Emotional Brain," *Philosophical Transactions of the Royal Society B*, 371 (1708): 1–10. doi.org/10.1098/rstb.2016.0007.

Shi, Z. and Burr, D. (2016), "Predictive Coding of Multisensory Timing," *Current Opinion in Behavioral Sciences*, 8: 200–6. doi.org/10.1016/j.cobeha.2016.02.014.

Spratling, M. W. (2013), "Distinguishing Theory from Implementation in Predictive Coding Accounts of Brain Function," *Behavioral and Brain Sciences*, 36 (3): 231–2. doi.org/10.1017/S0140525X12002178.

Straus, E. (1947), "Disorders of Personal Time in Depressive States," *Southern Medical Journal*, 40 (3): 254–9.

Telban, B. (2017), "Seeing and Holding Time: Karawari Perceptions of Temporalities, Calendars and Clocks," *Time & Society*, 26 (2): 182–202. doi.org/10.1177/096146 3X15577273.

Thönes, S. and Wittmann, M. (2016), "Time Perception in Yogic Mindfulness Meditation—Effects on Retrospective Duration Judgments and Time Passage," *Psychology of Consciousness: Theory, Research, and Practice*, 3 (4): 316–25. doi.org/10.1037/cns0000088.

Uusberg, A., Naar, R., Tamm, M., Kreegipuu, K. and Gross, J. J. (2018), "Bending Time: The Role of Affective Appraisal in Time Perception," *Emotion* 18 (8): 1174–88. doi.org/10.1037/emo0000397.

Van Hedger, K., Necka, E. A., Barakzai, A. K. and Norman, G. J. (2017), "The Influence of Social Stress on Time Perception and Psychophysiological Reactivity," *Psychophysiology*, 54: 706–12. doi.org/10.1111/psyp.12836.

Varela, F. J. (1999), "The Specious Present: A Neurophenomenology of Time Consciousness" in Jean Petitot, Francisco J. Varela, Bernard Pachoud, and Jean-Michel Roy (eds.), *Naturalizing Phenomenology: Issues in Contemporary Phenomenology and Cognitive Science*, Stanford: Stanford University Press.

Varela, F. J. and Depraz, N. (2005), "At the Source of Time: Valence and the Constitutional Dynamics of Affect," *Journal of Consciousness Studies*, 12 (8–10): 61–81.

Vaughan, H. G. and Arezzo, J. C. (1988), "The Neural Basis of Event-Related Potentials" in T. W. Picton (ed.), *Human Event-Related Potentials. Handbook of Electroencephalography and Clinical Neurophysiology*. Revised Series, Vol. 3, Amsterdam: Elsevier, pp. 45–96.

Vaughan, H. G., Ritter, W. and Simson, R. (1980), "Topographic Analysis of Auditory Event-Related Potentials." *Progress in Brain Research*, 54: 279–85. doi.org/10.1016/S0079-6123(08)61635-0.

Wearden, J. (2016), *The Psychology of Time Perception*, London: Palgrave Macmillan.

Wearden, J. H., Todd, N. P. M. and Jones, L. A. (2006), "When Do Auditory/Visual Differences in Duration Judgments Occur?" *The Quarterly Journal of Experimental Psychology*, 59 (10): 1709–24. doi.org/10.1080/17470210500314729.

West, B. J. (2012), *Fractal Physiology and Chaos in Medicine*, 2nd ed., Singapore: World Scientific.

Whalen, D. J., Gilbert, Kirsten E., Barch, Deanna M., Luby, Joan L. and Belden, Andy C. (2017), "Variation in Common Preschool Sleep Problems as an Early Predictor for Depression and Anxiety Symptom Severity across Time," *The Journal of Child Psychology and Psychiatry*, 58 (2): 151–9. doi.org/10.1111/jcpp.12639.

Whorf, B. L. (1956), *Language, Thought, and Reality: Selected Writings of Benjamin Lee Whorf*, edited by John B. Carroll, Cambridge: MIT Press.

Wiebe, S. T., Cassoff, J. and Gruber, R. (2012), "Sleep Patterns and the Risk for Unipolar Depression: A Review," *Nature and the Science of Sleep*, 4: 63–71. doi.org/10.2147/NSS.S23490.

12

Why Use Predictive Processing to Explain Psychopathology? The Case of *Anorexia Nervosa*

Stephen Gadsby

Cognition & Philosophy Lab, Department of Philosophy, Monash University

Jakob Hohwy

Cognition & Philosophy Lab, Department of Philosophy, Monash University

1. Introduction

Predictive processing (PP) is a framework for explaining mental function, which is gaining increasing influence in cognitive science (Hohwy 2013, Clark 2016). PP accounts are increasingly called upon to explain mental disorder. It seems an attractive explanatory framework because the core idea of prediction error minimization can be applied to simultaneously account for several perceptual, attentional, and reasoning deficits.

However, it can seem unclear how much is truly gained by such accounts: the proffered explanations appear to have several weaknesses such as being (i) too liberal, since PP is a framework for approximating Bayesian inference and any behavior can be fitted to some prior and likelihood function or cost function, (ii) too shallow, since PP accounts often merely subsume or re-describe existing theories or explanations, or (iii) too wedded to formal notions of statistical learning, in the sense that psychopathology reduces to failures of absorbing statistical information, rather than to biologically based illness.

Here, we first focus on the often unrecognized variety of explanatory tools under the PP framework and discuss how they can be employed to provide substantial explanations. We then apply the framework to anorexia nervosa (AN), an eating disorder characterized by a complex set of perceptual, reasoning, and decision-making problems. We conclude that the PP framework is a valuable type of explanation for psychopathology. It provides advances in understanding because it can make new distinctions within existing approaches to AN and provide new understanding of some key problems for these approaches, such as the resistance of patients' pathological beliefs to counterevidence. The key contribution is that, under PP, the only imperative for an agent is to minimize prediction error in the long-term average, by any tools available; often those tools are quite abstract priors about model selection, simplicity, and types of policies for action over different time scales, about which it is difficult to be confident. This predicts individual differences in different contexts, some of which can be associated with mental illness.

2. Predictive Processing and Psychopathology

Predictive processing approaches to mind and cognition belong to a broad tradition of views centered on internal generative models of the causes of sensory input, or, more heuristically, perceptual inference. In its contemporary shape, PP posits that internal models are used to generate predictions of the sensory input that would occur if the environment (including the agent) is as the model describes. Predictions are then tested against the actual sensory input such that evidence for the model is maximized for accurate and precise predictions. The initial upshot of such PP is veridical perception of the causes of sensory input. The basic framework is reviewed extensively elsewhere (see Hohwy 2013, Clark 2016; for introduction to the mathematical and computational background see Bogacz 2017, Buckley et al. 2017). Here, we discuss several more intricate properties of PP, in particular associated with the active inference approaches to PP, associated with the free energy principle and process theories under this principle (Friston 2010). This discussion then sets the scene for discussion of PP approaches to psychopathology, in particular our test case: anorexia nervosa.

Perceptual inference is inference of the causes of sensory input. Under PP (in particular when implemented with predictive coding as the process theory), this is not merely a matter of matching predictions directly with input. The difference between predictions and input is the prediction error, which functions as a learning signal in the revision of the internal model. The amount of learning accrued from prediction error can be conceived as the learning rate (cf. Bayesian inference). The learning rate is governed by the ratio of the likelihood precision (i.e., the precision of the prediction error) and the prior precision (i.e., the degree of existing evidence for the model generating the prediction). The learning rate is variable, under contextually guided expectations for the volatility of the sensory input (i.e., unexpected changes in the mean and precision of the input). This ensures that the perceptual system in question can engage adaptively within a dynamically changing environment, characterized by uncertainty and nonlinearities in the sensory input. The range of inferred causes is broad, encompassing both the external environment and the internal environment of bodily states (i.e., proprioception, interoception).

Perceptual inference through predictive coding is hierarchical, which reflects both the interaction of contextual precision beliefs with the precision gain set on sensory input, and the deep causal structure of the sensorium; thus, many different levels of the perceptual hierarchy contribute to everyday perception of bodies, houses, cars, trees, and the other objects and states in and around us. One organizing principle for the hierarchy is spatiotemporal scale, where higher levels have wider receptive fields and process causal regularities occurring over longer time scales. In this perspective, different psychopathologies can be phenotyped in terms of different constellations of priors (Montague et al. 2012, Friston et al. 2017). For example, autism has been hypothesized to relate to a strong prior expectation for the precision of sensory input (Van de Cruys et al. 2014) or a strong prior belief in low volatility of sensory input (Palmer et al. 2017); psychotic symptoms associated with schizophrenia, such as hallucinations, have been linked with different volatility beliefs as well (Sterzer et al. 2018, Corlett et al. 2019).

Just as perception is inferential, so is action. Most fundamentally, adaptive agents need to select optimal policies (conceived as sequences of control states leading to concrete behaviors) to achieve their desired (expected) states, a task that is made difficult in a dynamic environment where there can be no one-one relation between policies and outcomes. This therefore presents a forward-looking inference problem: which policy should the agent infer is its own? Inference of policies then leads to action as the inferred policy induces prediction error that is minimized by selectively sampling sensory input expected under that policy. This is known as *active inference*.

As with perceptual inference, precisions are crucial for active inference; under an expectation that the agent occupies states with efficient prediction error minimization, high-precision policies are favored (i.e., policies that have high-fidelity mapping from actions to observed outcomes). Policies are thus ranked on their precision, which captures how confident the agent can be that they will produce states that are not far removed from the expected states of the agent (i.e., the (Kullbach-Leibler) divergence between the state that the policy can be expected to achieve and the expected state). Active inference comes in two flavors: there is action for utility, which is the common notion that we act to reap rewards, and then there is action for epistemic value, which is the less common idea that we act to reduce uncertainty about our model of the world (e.g., looking closer to see if that dark, moving object is really a spider). Thus, sometimes one must act to reduce uncertainty about the world in order to get oneself into a position where one can act to reap rewards (Friston et al. 2015, 2016).

Across perceptual and active inference, PP is subject to one critical imperative, namely that prediction error should be minimized over the *long-term average*. That is, PP is not a simple rule that only the current prediction error is minimized. If that were the case, then shutting down all systems and sitting in a dark room would be the most efficient strategy. But, of course, we don't do that, precisely because that strategy would lead to increased deviation from our expected states in the longer term, as we get hungry and dirty, as we don't get paid because we don't turn up to work, and so on. Rather, we operate within expected boundaries of prediction error, allowing us to maintain ourselves within our expected states in the long term. This is reflected in our inference of policies, as some actions will be, for example, aimed at exploring the current state, even if that might temporarily increase prediction error.

The models on which perceptual and active inference are based should be neither too *simple* nor too *complex*. Overly simple models cannot accommodate future contingencies, produced by interactions among hidden causes, and overly complex models are fitted to noise that does not repeat—thus in both cases the models will generate more prediction error than they would if their complexity had been optimized. Model complexity is non-trivial to get right, and depends on longer-term learning of levels of irreducible noise and of patterns of state-dependent noise in different contexts.

It is common to consider issues of complexity for perceptual inference, but it is critical for active inference too. The expected prediction error under a policy depends on the complexity of the underlying model, such that execution of an overly cumbersome policy in a messy environment may be less productive than a simpler policy, even if the former would give an excellent outcome were it to succeed. This in turn speaks to beliefs about the controllability of the (volatile) environment as well as issues around the time scale over which policies are relevant.

Simplicity and complexity relate to (Bayesian) *model selection* in a wider sense, where simplicity may be a factor alongside context-dependence considerations. Model selection can be considered a discrete process, where a given model is prioritized (e.g., this is a dice game rather than a coin throwing game) and prediction error then minimized under that model. Selection of a model is revisited if there is unexpected accumulation of prediction error under the model, forcing selection of a new model. This process is however sensitive to the prior probability of competing models; in principle, if no alternative model has significant model evidence (e.g., competing models are overly complex), then the system in question may need to tolerate quite high levels of accumulated prediction error and thus sub-optimal inference.

Beliefs, thoughts, and conscious perceptions are the upshots of the underlying perceptual and active predictive processes. Bayesian priors are sometimes labeled "belief" but should not be confused with explicit, propositional belief. Exactly why belief, thought, and perceptions have the phenomenology that they do is not strongly determined by accounts of PP. However, it does seem likely that the structure of experience is somehow determined by the process of prediction error minimization. For example, in the well-known rubber hand illusion, touch sensation and sense of ownership are felt for a visible but fake hand when the real, hidden hand is touched synchronously with the fake hand. The mislocation of touch may be driven by weighting of expected precisions in the sensory input, and favoring of the illusory hypothesis may be facilitated by complexity considerations, as the veridical hypothesis (namely that the experimenter is the hidden cause of both the seen touch and the unseen touch on the real hand) has a more complex causal structure (Hohwy 2013: Chs. 5–6). It is not commonly observed that similar false inference can occur in the domain of active inference too. Thus, we should expect that, in some circumstances, expectations of precision conspire with particular contexts and complexities to lead to false inference of policies.

Overall, the PP framework provides a picture of perceptual and cognitive processes that goes substantially beyond the initial idea of just a meeting of predictions and input. There are many interlocking predictive processes that prepare the ground for, and execute, successful long-term average prediction error minimization. Since no environment is ever learned completely, priors about precisions, complexities, volatilities, and irreducible noise will be fraught with uncertainty. This predicts that there will be individual differences in how these processes are balanced against each other. More abstractly, under a variational inference scheme, there is approximation to exact inference as the different parameters of the recognition model are optimized; this means the inference will spend time deviating from the optimal, exact inference, which will manifest as more or less transitory or entrenched false inference.

The richness of the PP toolbox mitigates somewhat against several perceived weaknesses of its use to account for mental disorder. We briefly consider three of these perceived weaknesses. PP is often considered too liberal because *any* behavior can be "explained" in Bayesian terms by picking appropriate priors and likelihoods (Jones and Love 2011). However, under the complete class theorem (Wald 1947), which guarantees this situation, this is now conceived as a strength. This is implicit in the comment above, to the effect that psychopathologies can be phenotyped down to an individual level according to their priors, derived from the behavior. This yields a principled, unifying nosology expressed in PP terms. Admittedly, this leads to a second perceived weakness, namely that now explanations are too shallow. The worry is that even though psychopathology can be phenotyped mathematically through their priors, there is no guarantee as to how these priors are expressed in terms of real, underlying neuronal mechanisms. Explaining psychopathology in terms of priors seems merely descriptive. However, this weakness can be overcome by identifying anatomically informed models, which locate the offending priors and the associated message passing along neuronal pathways, subject to specific neurotransmitter processes appropriate to the different computational roles needed for PP (Marshall et al. 2016, Parr and Friston 2018).

Finally, by phrasing everything in terms of probabilistic inference, it may appear that PP is too wedded to *statistical learning*, in the sense that every intractable mental disorder appears to be a mere failure of absorbing the right statistical regularities, and subject to correction through education on statistical regularities. However, explaining psychopathologies in terms of errors in statistical learning highlights the possibility that departures from optimal perceptual and active inference can fail to correct themselves *over time*, as they lead to cascading and increasingly ensconced malfunctions; this may capture the crucial developmental aspect of many disorders. Beyond this, anatomically informed models show how intractable (chronic) malfunction is reflected in the computational roles necessary for the various aspects of optimal PP. Given these models, biological malfunction can be seen as the underlying cause of failures in statistical learning.

The PP framework thus appears potentially resourceful as a general approach to psychopathology, though there remain several unresolved questions. In the remainder of this chapter, we consider anorexia nervosa under the PP framework. This will both yield a new take on this disorder and serve as a test case for the explanatory worth of PP in psychopathology.

3. The Empiricist Model of Anorexia Nervosa

While predictive coding's explanatory toolkit has been applied to a host of psychopathologies, here we consider its application to a further disorder: anorexia nervosa (AN). We focus first on a centrally relevant feature of the disorder: the false beliefs patients hold about their own body size. Despite their dangerously low weight, AN patients regularly profess to being overweight, or at least not being excessively thin (Gadsby 2017a). A first step in understanding how the PP framework might illuminate the cause of such beliefs is in reviewing explanations that have already been provided.

Recently, an *empiricist* model of these beliefs has been offered (Gadsby 2017a, 2017b). The guiding insight of empiricist models—commonly associated with Maher's (1974) treatment of delusions—is that the proximal cause of delusional beliefs are particularly unusual experiences that patients suffer from. The empiricist model of false body size beliefs in anorexia thus specifies a number of abnormal experiences of body size that patients may suffer from. Here, we focus on two of the abnormal experiences of body size posited by this model (for more discussion, see Gadsby 2018).

One proposal rests on evidence suggesting that AN patients suffer from what is known as *recurrent spontaneous mental imagery*. Most commonly associated with social anxiety disorder, this phenomenon involves individuals experiencing conscious, invasive, recurrent mental imagery representing their fears (i.e., having an overweight body) (Kadriu et al. 2019). One eating-disordered patient describes the content of one such imagery experience, "In the image I see myself obese, with very fat thighs and a fat stomach" (ibid., 8). In the case of social anxiety disorders, patients are known to interpret this imagery as veridical, coming to believe that the content of these image episodes accurately reflects reality. The empiricist model of anorexia suggests that if a similar interpretational bias is present in AN, then these episodes of spontaneous imagery may be the cause of the relevant false body size beliefs (Gadsby 2018).

A second proposal for a form of abnormal experience of body size relates to the process of *self-other comparison*. Specifically, it has been suggested that due to a distorted mental representation of their own bodies (the "perceptual body image"), patients engage in dysfunctional self-other body comparison (Gadsby 2017a). When assessing whether other seen bodies are either larger or smaller than themselves, they perceptually *misjudge*, such that bodies which are in fact larger are judged to be smaller. These consistent misjudgments—i.e., "my body is bigger than hers"—are proposed to ground the relevant false body size beliefs.

How might the PP framework help to illuminate and contribute to this explanatory model? In keeping with the PP account of delusional beliefs as arising in response to aberrant prediction error (Fletcher and Frith 2009), we might posit that the relevant false beliefs about body size emerge through an attempt to "explain away" ongoing aberrant prediction error concerning body size. However, it is not immediately clear that the PP framework in itself brings any explanatory benefit, above and beyond the standard empiricist model—whether we use the term "abnormal experience" or "aberrant prediction error" apparently makes little difference to the mechanistic details of the model itself.

Building on the outline of PP in the previous section, we do believe there can be positive explanatory advantage to redescribing the empiricist approach in PP terms. The framework can point to a mapping of empiricist or folk psychological idioms onto the parts and processes of a neural message-passing mechanism. For example, if one relies on expectations of precisions as well as of means, then PP can illuminate their interaction in Bayesian as well as mechanistic terms, as there must be distinct neuronal pathways for the message passing of both precisions and means. This is not anticipated on the standard empiricist approach, and could help explain, for example, more subtle aspects of AN experience relating to multisensory integration (Case et al. 2012, Zopf et al. 2016). In addition, once we consider the PP mechanism, new explanatory avenues become apparent, for example, relating to the level of the hierarchy at which deficits arise or cascade to, and to ways in which cognitive or pharmacological interventions may be expected to work (e.g., a cognitive learning task that engages volatility learning may be more appropriate than a task that engages learning of means) (Parr et al. 2018, Tulver et al. 2019).

The PP account can also generate new conceptual and mechanistic distinctions among the proposed types of experience of body size in the empiricist account. For example, imagery concerns the upshot of perceptual inference, under conditions where the bottom-up signal is weighted low; low weighting of bottom-up signals would relate to precision optimization, which can be either exogenous (driven by the precision of the bottom-up prediction error signal) or endogenous (volitional reduction of expected precision of sensory input, cf. attention) (for a relevant PP account, see Aru et al. 2018). Spontaneous imagery of body size would then arise through perceptual inference that is poorly controlled by the bottom-up prediction error signal, possibly partly driven exogenously by poor precision of the interoceptive prediction error signals in AN.

While faulty self-other comparison is presumed to stem from the misrepresentation of bodily dimensions (Gadsby 2017c), PP may illuminate how this misrepresentation arises. A key insight of the PP framework is that misrepresentation (i.e., inaccurate means) can arise due to suboptimal estimates of prediction error precision (Fletcher and Frith 2009). Perhaps the imprecision of bodily signals in AN (Herbet and Pollatos 2018) is responsible for the misrepresentation of bodily dimensions which, in turn, causes the evident dysfunctional self-other body comparisons.

It is worth noting that though these two potential analyses of the empiricist approach are distinct, they both refer to differences in precision optimization for body size in AN. This may serve to unify the otherwise distinct accounts in one proposal, namely that imprecision is involved in some of the unusual experiences of body size cited in the empiricist account. One possible hypothesis would then be that the primary processing problem is not in the unusual experiences themselves, and the misrepresentation of bodily dimensions they suggest, but in precision optimization. This hypothesis would be aligned with PP accounts of other disorders, which also revolve around precision optimization (e.g., schizophrenia and autism).

4. Sensory Contexts

Not only can the process of recapitulating folk psychology into PP terms open up new explanatory avenues, the PP framework can be used to illuminate possible solutions to problems with current models. For example, a main issue with the aforementioned empiricist model is known as the *maintenance problem* (Gadsby 2018). The starting point for this problem is the consideration that patients are exposed to significant evidence that contradicts their pathological beliefs. For example, family and caregivers repeatedly emphasizing the patients' extreme thinness. Answering the maintenance problem involves explaining why patients maintain their false beliefs in the face of this disconfirmatory evidence.

One answer to this problem emerging from the PP literature on delusions pertains to the epistemic contexts in which such beliefs arise. Hohwy and Rosenberg (2005) suggest that delusions arise in contexts whereby—given the kind of content of the delusional belief—reality testing via some channels of evidence is rendered exceedingly difficult. For example, delusions with a basic emotional or interoceptive content happen to be relatively private and therefore amenable only to relatively limited, private reality testing—other people's views about your own emotions and body states are mostly considered inconsequential. Similarly, theoretical background theories about the nature of emotions and body states are unlikely to dislodge the way an individual experiences them—you may know that emotions are tied to autonomous arousal but that seems inconsequential to the way you feel emotions. Perhaps then this idea can be fruitfully applied to the case of AN, helping to solve the maintenance issue in this context.

The question at hand then is whether body size is the kind of realm that is inaccessible to reality testing. First, there are a number of sources of contradictory evidence regarding body size that we believe are unlikely to sway the patients' beliefs: theoretical belief and other people's belief. Conflicting information regarding body size that arises from other people's beliefs seems unlikely to efficiently counteract patients' experience of their own body size, as the types of abnormal body size evidence posited by the basic empiricist model all plausibly include sources that are hard to address and correct on the basis of other's evidence (Gadsby 2018). Similarly so for contradictory background beliefs. For example, patients might believe that someone who weighs only 35 kilograms, or wears a certain size clothes should not be "overweight"—indeed clinical testimony speaks to the surprise patients experience when shopping for clothes or viewing their weight on scales (Casper et al. 1979: 60; Espeset et al. 2011). Yet, such forms of indirect evidence regarding body size, we posit, will be unlikely to dislodge belief which patients have more constant and direct experiential evidence for via interoceptive sensory channels.

AN beliefs about body size may thus be relatively evidentially insulated from external contradictory types of evidence, which may play some role in maintaining them. However, body size beliefs seem less obviously insulated than more typical delusional beliefs, which are often more exclusively and clearly based on relatively private emotional and interoceptive experience (e.g., made emotions, or delusions of alien control). Further, in the case of AN there does seem to be an available avenue for *intermodal* reality testing by the patients themselves. Intermodal reality testing occurs, for example, when one feels something that can also be seen (or vice versa). AN patients have the possibility of reality testing regarding their own body size, not through mental imagery, or self-other judgments, but rather through visual perception: they may simply look at and measure their own bodies to test if indeed they are overweight or not. This form of reality testing bears on a significant issue within the AN literature: the issue of whether patients' visual experience of their bodies is veridical or not, an issue we turn to in the next section (see section 5).

The maintenance problem can also be addressed in terms of model selection, rather than direct reality testing. A belief that one is overweight may encounter plenty of contradicting evidence, but if no other equally consistent model presents itself, then the patient may be "stuck" with the false belief. This raises the question of why alternative models would have low Bayesian model evidence? One possibility has to do with complexity cost: alternative models would have to explain away the contradictory evidence and the initial evidence in support of the false belief. If these sets of data pull in different directions then the underlying model of latent causes (e.g., true weight, size, visual configuration) could be explained away only by a fairly complex model representing many interactions among causes. As such, the *complexity* of alternative models may partly contribute to the maintenance of false (but simple) overweight beliefs (see section 6 for further appeal to complexity).

5. Visual Perception and Cognitive Penetrability

The following quotes, from three different patients, touch on a long-standing tension within the literature pertaining to the direct visual experience patients have of their own bodies:

> … when I was younger I think I saw myself bigger in the mirror than I actually was in reality …
> With my eyes I actually saw myself as big …
> … when I look at myself in the mirror I really can't understand where I have anorexia. It's nowhere!
>
> (Espeset et al. 2011: 182, 184, 185)

While many patients (like the above) claim to genuinely *see* themselves as overweight (Smeets and Panhyusen 1995), it has been argued that this cannot be a genuine case of mis*perception* (Gadsby, 2017c: 27). Complicating matters further is the worry that positing false visual body size perception entails a kind of *cognitive penetrability*, whereby higher-order beliefs influence lower-level (visual) perception. There is ongoing discussion about the extent to which cognitive penetrability describes a real phenomenon or not (Firestone and Scholl 2013).

It seems then that the standard empiricist model is faced with a dilemma: if patients visually perceive their body size veridically, then why does this veridical perception fail to dislodge the relevant false beliefs? Alternatively, if patients *see* themselves as overweight, then what accounts for this distorted perception (presuming cognitive penetration is unavailable as an explanation)? Here, we would note that this dilemma is forced upon us by folk psychology's firm distinction between "perception" and "belief." Such a distinction forces researchers into an explanation which refers to *either* perceptual *or* propositional belief formation processes. However, the PP framework softens the strict division between perception and belief and thereby opens the door to further explanatory resources in terms of more subtle and cyclical influences on belief formation and perceptual inference, consistent with relatively mild and uncontentious aspects of cognitive penetrability (Hohwy 2013: Ch. 6).

One important insight from the PP literature pertains to the conditions under which top-down modulation of perceptual experience occurs. In the rubber hand illusion mentioned above, and many other illusions, priors modulate the incoming sensory input, giving rise to the relevant illusory percepts. What is important to note about these illusions are the conditions that facilitate top-down influence. In many illusions, perceptual conditions are relatively uncertain due to sensory noise, as when we see illusory patterns in visual noise, or due to cue ambiguity, as when congruent visuo-tactile signals conflict with proprioception in the rubber hand illusion. Uncertainty can also stem from constrained action for epistemic value, as when we cannot measure the length of lines in the Müller-Lyer illusion, or move the real hand in the rubber hand illusion. As discussed, uncertain sensory domains result in low precision estimation of the incoming prediction error and underconfident policy inference. When prediction error has low precision, priors hold more (relative) weight and are thus given greater influence in sculpting the relevant perceptual representation or shape of policies selected.

Such underlying uncertainty may also be at play in instances of self-viewing in AN. After all, as stipulated, patients are exposed to significantly noisy and ambiguous evidence regarding their own body size: some input (emanating from the experiences posited by the standard empiricist model) suggests they are overweight, while other sources (e.g., visual, testimonial) suggest they are underweight. More generally, as we speculated in section 3, the PP framework seems to suggest that there is expected imprecision for prediction error pertaining to body size, leading to down-weighting of signals in this domain. In contexts where the expected precision of incoming prediction error is low, our perceptual representations are more highly weighted by our priors. In instances of self-viewing, then, it might be the case that for those patients far along in the disorder, the expected precision of the incoming prediction error will be low, causing them to form a visual representation of themselves that is more highly weighed toward their priors. If we assume that patients predict they will see an overweight body (consistent with their now well-established beliefs about being overweight), then the visual percept may be weighted toward this expectation. The PP explanation here appeals to the hierarchically bound mixture of priors and prediction errors that is fundamental to perceptual inference but in the context of the cascading dynamics of consecutive Bayesian inference.

This account coheres with anecdotal reports that, for some patients, brief perception of their own bodies as underweight often occurs in contexts where patients aren't expecting to see their own bodies, that is, where the context has not primed the relevant overweight priors. For example,

> I remember one occasion, I was passing an open door and saw myself in the mirror, but actually, I didn't know that I saw myself. I just saw the image of a person in the mirror and thought; "Oh gosh, she is thin!" But then, when I understood that it was actually me, I didn't see me as thin anymore. But then I actually saw a glimpse of it.
>
> (Espeset et al. 2011: 183)

Beyond the claim that, in low-precision sensory contexts, perceptual content can be biased by priors, there is another explanatory avenue offered by the PP framework, which seems to cohere with evidence from the AN literature. Consider the situation of a patient with AN viewing themselves in a mirror. Such an experience will likely generate prediction error, arising from the mismatch between the incoming (thin-looking) input and the patient's expectations of their own bodies as being overweight. Agents have a number of minimization strategies available when faced with prediction error. One common way is to simply update one's priors, adjusting them such that they cohere with the incoming prediction error. If this strategy was adopted, then the patients' pathological beliefs would resolve.

However, AN patients might enact other *prima facie* reasonable strategies, such as action for epistemic value, in order to minimize prediction error but which transform the ordinary process of self-viewing in a mirror to one of false belief reinforcement: they might turn their visual attention away from the mirror, avoid the image altogether, or they might specifically attend to the parts of their body they judge to be unattractive (i.e., overweight). There is evidence to suggest that, when self-viewing, AN patients do visually attend toward body parts which they believe are unattractive (i.e., overweight) and that many patients avoid self-viewing altogether (Gadsby 2018). Such strategies would enable patients to maintain their beliefs about being overweight, in the face of contradictory visual input but they would nevertheless cause the prediction error to cease. As such, the PP toolbox does offer some potential explanations for why direct visual experience of one's body size does not constitute a useful form of inter-modal reality testing: alternative ways of minimizing visually produced body size prediction error may instead come into play.

If such explanations of AN were to be on the right track, PP can begin to furnish genuine explanatory advances because the *only* imperative of the perceptual and cognitive system is to minimize (long-term average) prediction error, and the description of the full PP mechanism sets out several different ways this can happen. There is no independently accessible check available for the agent to the system for whether its efforts at prediction error minimization are efficient, or good for aiming at veridical beliefs. Which route to prediction error minimization is chosen is determined by the relative precisions of the different beliefs (about body size, precisions, etc.) together with beliefs about what shape of model and policies may lead to the best prediction error minimization in the long term. On an individual basis, the exact route to prediction error minimization reveals differences in priors about means and precisions, including expectations for long-term prediction error trajectories (Parr et al. 2018). Given there can be multiple different sources of evidence feeding the overweight beliefs, it is likely that there will be quite different landscapes of priors as well, associated with different trajectories for prediction error minimization and thus different presentations of AN.

Accordingly, there is evidence of considerable individual difference both in the contents of the reported body size experiences and in the tenacity with which they are maintained. In AN, as in other mental disorders like schizophrenia, there are both between-patient differences in reported experience of body size as well as within-patient differences, as many profess to a *fluctuating* experience of body size.

> But I really can't see any anorexia on myself. I've never had any such experiences as "maybe I'm a bit thin." Never! I always see that I'm fat. (Frida);

I've always seen that I'm thin. And that's quite unusual. I have always realized that I have a problem. (Louisa);
One day I see myself as too thin, and the next day too fat, and it can also vary from hour to hour. (Irene)

(Espeset et al. 2011: 181)

Similarly for the characteristics of the relevant beliefs about body size. Using semi-structured interview techniques, researchers have discovered significant between-patient differences in belief characteristics such as conviction and incorrigibility (Phillipou et al. 2017).

Such diversity among patients may reflect diversity in the prediction error minimization strategies, including the aforementioned strategies—the sculpting of noisy prediction error by expectation (leading to visual perception of one's body as larger than reality) and the avoidance of the visual input altogether. The PP framework provides a mechanism sketch by which these different strategies can be accounted for, allowing us to account for the diversity among patients and understand symptom etiology at the level of the individual. This explanation of diversity is then tied together by the hypothesis of initial problems with precision optimization of signals normally associated with body size experience.[1]

6. Model Selection and Simplicity

While we have seen that the PP approach affords some genuine explanatory advances, the accounts we have considered do not quite close off the reasonable challenge that it is unclear *why*, at least in the longer run, patients adopt the aforementioned strategies for prediction error minimization rather than simply updating the priors pertaining to their own body size? That is, in spite of the various types of explanations PP may be able to offer, why don't patients over time construct an alternative hypothesis and slowly begin to unlearn their suboptimal inference about their body size? This question relates to the type of process that PP always returns to, which is *statistical learning*: the internal model is shaped through prediction error learning that should correct false inferences such that the model eventually comes to recapitulate the causal structure of the world, including the true body size of the agent themselves.

One possible answer refers to an extended history of sociocultural influence, a theme that often recurs in AN debates. Patients are consistently exposed, through adolescence and via multiple sociocultural channels, to unrealistic body size standards. This plausibly results in prioritizing the belief that one is overweight. In the spirit of social constructivism, one might here argue that the patients are recapitulating the causal structure of the world they live in because they are picking up and inferring a powerful ideal, meshed deeply with peer behavior, social discourse, media empires, and fashion industries. However, there is an issue with this hypothesis, in terms of the kinds of representational content socioculturally derived priors would exhibit. It is not that patients simply believe that they are "overweight"—i.e., an evaluative claim—rather, the *physical dimensions* of their body are misrepresented (Gadsby 2017a, 2018).

And while sociocultural influence may be to blame for agents believing they are overweight, it does not convey information about one's own bodily dimensions.

With PP, a relatively straightforward link can be attempted between the socio-culturally driven overweight model and the experience of body size. As the selected model, it determines the parameters for subsequent prediction error minimization. So, if the model is that one is overweight, this will generate prediction error which is sought to be minimized under that model. However, this explanation does not stick very deep, as it immediately leads to new questions: why is it that the model is not eventually de-selected once prediction error accumulates over the long term, as body weight in fact plummets? If the explanation is on the right track, then there must be something about the selected overweight model that inoculates it against being de-selected, in spite of accumulating prediction error.

We suggest a hypothesis that is uniquely consistent with the PP account of cognition. Patients may persistently settle on the overweight model due to a *bias toward simplicity*. Consider for a moment the two competing models: one whereby the agent is overweight and one whereby the agent is underweight. As stated, these models will drive minimization of distinct forms of prediction error: one minimizes prediction error suggesting the agent is underweight, the other minimizes prediction error suggesting the agent is overweight. Assuming that both are more or less equal in minimizing the ongoing prediction error for body size, we must look to what other prediction error minimization advantages might be gained through adopting the (in fact false) overweight hypothesis.

First, recall that, according to the PP account, systems do not exclusively strive to minimize *occurrent* prediction error, but also long-term *expected* prediction error. This means, as mentioned earlier, that the agent considers simplicity and complexity of the competing models. This implies that there may be a preference for simpler models than more complex models even if the former are worse at relatively short-term prediction error minimization.

Following this reasoning, it may be that for patients, the overweight hypothesis is *simpler* than the underweight hypothesis. In assessing models' simplicity, we must consider not only the agent's model of her own body, but also her model of the causal regularities of the entire environment, including aspects of her own agency. In discussing the model selection problem—that is, why patients choose the overweight, rather than underweight hypothesis—the AN researcher Anouk Keizer (personal communication) suggested that if patients were to accept that they had achieved their ideal size, though many of the problems in their life remain, then this would entail accepting that these perceived problems were not simply side effects of not being thin enough. In other words, patients' current model of the world exhibits significant simplicity: the achievement of ideal body size is a (single parameter) solution to a variety of psychological and social issues.

This idea—that AN patients adopt a model of the world whereby a diverse and complex set of personal problem are reduced to simply being about the patient's body size—has been touted regularly within the literature. For example, in reviewing a number of cognitive models of anorexia nervosa (and bulimia nervosa), Vitousek and Hollon write:

These theories differ along a number of dimensions, but hold one important set of premises in common: that anorexics and bulimics endow weight with rich connotations, equate their personal value with the shape of their bodies, and use the regulation of weight to subserve numerous functions in their lives.

(1990: 192)[2]

There are two important features of model simplicity emphasized in this quote. The first is the equation of personal value (a vastly complex multidimensional property) with a single feature (body shape). The second notion of simplicity highlighted pertains to action policies: the policy not to eat may be inferred at least partly because not eating is a simple policy, at least over some medium-length time scale, compared to the very non-obvious and extremely complex policy one would have to single out, which could improve self-esteem and social worth. As discussed earlier, active inference implies inference of high-precision policies understood as high fidelity in the mappings from actions to expected outcomes. The difference between policies can be borne out partly in terms of simplicity: the no-eat policy is much simpler than the utterly complex policies needed to change the way the world looks upon one and the way one feels about oneself. And of course, in the initial phases of acting on the no-eat policy, there may well be positive reinforcement from the environment, which can further anchor the policy. This dual aspect of model simplicity is evident throughout Vitousek and Hollon's discussion, as the simpler model not only "provides clear templates for evaluating daily experience," but also "prescribes a simple set of rules for seeking safety and avoiding danger [and] reduces the complexity of formulating attributions about the past and expectations for the future" (1990: 193).

While there is a general propensity for simplicity for all PP processing, there will also be individual differences. Our proposal is then that it may emerge as a bias in AN. If so, we would expect such a bias to be evident in other domains too. In fact, there seems to be some evidence for this pattern. A significant body of evidence now suggests that AN patients have a higher sensitivity to the rubber hand illusion (e.g., Eshkevari et al. 2012, Keizer et al. 2014, Zopf et al. 2016). That is, when faced with the multi-modal conflict presented by the paradigm, they have a tendency to opt for the simpler model "the touch sensation and visual movement are co-located, caused by one latent cause, and the rubber hand is mine" over the more complex "the touch sensation and visual movement are distinctly located, caused by different latent causes, and the hand is not mine." Further, susceptibility to the illusion is positively correlated with measures of eating disorder psychopathology (Eshkevari et al. 2012). This hypothesis opens the doorway to further experimentation, verifying that AN patients' model selection exhibits a greater tendency toward simplicity than neurotypical participants.

7. Conclusion

We have discussed the PP framework and how it may explain psychopathology. Initial applications of PP appear to mainly re-describe known theories and phenomena in different terms. However, once the full and varied PP toolbox is brought to bear on psychopathological conditions, then genuine explanatory advances emerge. Here, we have focused on AN, and shown how analysis of prominent approaches (in particular, the empiricist approach) can be distinctively refined through PP, which points to the potential existence of an underlying deficit in precision optimization, which may be implicated in unusual body size experiences. This provides a ground for a PP account addressing how the unusual beliefs about body size are maintained against counterevidence, with appeal to considerations about top-down influences across hierarchical inference, issues of model selection and model simplicity, and an attempt to understand the role of social influences on AN.

These are all explanations that become available when applying PP under the idea that agents are blind slaves to the objective function of minimizing prediction error in the long-term average by whatever tools available in the full PP toolbox. Often agents have be guided by quite abstract priors about which tools will best ensure long-term average prediction error minimization; agents might appeal to difficult-to-confirm priors about the efficiency of simplicity over complexity in a given type of context, or what signals to trust in spite of imprecision, or how to maintain the right balance between perceptual and active inference, and so on. This gives leeway for individual differences and pathological perceptual and active inference in the sense that inference becomes driven by unusual priors about, for example, the usefulness of simplicity in policy inference, the expected precision of body size experience, and the reality of ideals promulgated in social media.

Here we come up against the last charge of triviality of the PP framework, namely that it in fact does not really allow false, Bayes suboptimal inference. Rather, it allows divergent priors which explain optimal inference that *appears* suboptimal. This does in a sense trivialize the account of psychopathology, including AN, but can be considered a strength of PP, since it allows precise phenotyping of disorder in terms of underlying priors, making a virtue out of what is normally considered a vice of Bayesian approaches, that is, any behavior can be modeled with appropriate priors.

In this perspective, the case of AN is in fact rather perplexing for the PP framework (especially as founded on the free energy principle (Friston 2010)): PP essentially says that organisms withstand destruction of their bodily boundaries and thereby death and dispersion, by minimizing their long-term average of prediction error (or free energy) given a model of their expected states, which are usually conceived in terms of their homeostatic set points (heart rate, body temperature, glucose levels, etc.). AN seems to rather directly lead patients to insult their homeostatic set points, in virtue of the high-fidelity mapping between the action of not eating and outcomes that are in fact life-threatening—they seem to act such as to unequivocally increase probabilistic surprisal in the short and long term. The only available PP response to this is that AN patients have inferred a model of their basic homeostatic state that deviates dramatically from the expectations defining the typical human phenotype. It is however not easy to accept that our basic (homeostatic) model, against which all surprise is eventually assessed, can change as dramatically as this. This may be some kind of ultimate limitation on PP explanations.

Notes

1 This furnishes a more general advantage of PP in explaining delusions (as opposed to simply the false body size beliefs of AN patients). Though often overlooked, there is significant diversity among patients with delusions. While some hold their beliefs with enough conviction to act on them (often with disastrous consequences), others profess to incredulity at their own belief, and within-patient vacillation (between belief and non-belief) is also evident (Coltheart 2007).

2 Speaking to the ubiquity of this feature of the disorder among patients (not just models), Vitousek & Hollon also write:

> In the course of preparing the present paper, a number of current and former eating-disordered women were interviewed about their perceptions of the "cognitive essence" of their symptomatology; although each nominated some contributing factors not shared by the group as a whole, every one implicated the "simplification of life" as a major component of her disorder.
>
> (1990: 206)

References

Aru, J. et al. (2018), "It's All in Your Head: Expectations Create Illusory Perception in a Dual-task Setup," *Consciousness and Cognition*, 65: 197–208.

Bogacz, R. (2017), "A Tutorial on the Free-energy Framework for Modelling Perception and Learning," *Journal of Mathematical Psychology*, 76, Part B: 198–211.

Buckley, C. L., Kim, C. S., McGregor, S. and Seth, A. K. (2017), "The Free Energy Principle for Action and Perception: A Mathematical Review," *Journal of Mathematical Psychology*, 81: 55–79.

Case, L. K., Wilson, R. C. and Ramachandran, V. S. (2012), "Diminished Size–Weight Illusion in Anorexia Nervosa: Evidence for Visuo-proprioceptive Integration Deficit," *Experimental Brain Research*, 217 (1): 79–87.

Casper, R., Halmi, K., Goldberg, S., Eckert, E. and Davis, J. (1979), "Disturbances in Body Image Estimation as Related to Other Characteristics and Outcome in Anorexia Nervosa," *The British Journal of Psychiatry: The Journal of Mental Science*, 134: 60–6.

Clark, A. (2016), *Surfing Uncertainty: Prediction, Action, and the Embodied Mind*, Oxford University Press.

Coltheart, M. (2007), "The 33rd Sir Frederick Bartlett Lecture: Cognitive Neuropsychiatry and Delusional Belief," *The Quarterly Journal of Experimental Psychology*, 60 (8): 1041–62. https://doi.org/10.1080/17470210701338071.

Corlett, P. R., Horga, G., Fletcher, P. C., Alderson-Day, B., Schmack, K. and Powers, A. R. (2019), "Hallucinations and Strong Priors," *Trends in Cognitive Sciences*, 23 (2): 114–27.

Eshkevari, E., Rieger, E., Longo, M., Haggard, R. and Treasure, J. (2012), "Increased Plasticity of the Bodily Self in Eating Disorders," *Psychological Medicine*, 42 (4): 819–28.

Espeset, E. M., Nordbø, R. H., Gulliksen, K. S., Skårderud, F., Geller, J. and Holte, A. (2011), "The Concept of Body image Disturbance in Anorexia Nervosa: An Empirical Inquiry Utilizing Patients' Subjective Experiences," *Eating Disorders*, 19 (2): 175–93.

Firestone, C. and Scholl, B. (2013), "'Top-Down' Effects Where None Should Be Found: The El Greco Fallacy in Perception Research," *Journal of Vision*, 13 (9): 780.

Fletcher, P. C. and Frith, C. D. (2009), "Perceiving Is Believing: A Bayesian Approach to Explaining the Positive Symptoms of Schizophrenia," *Nature Reviews Neuroscience*, 10 (1): 48–58.

Friston, K. (2010), "The Free-energy Principle: A Unified Brain Theory?," *Nature Reviews Neuroscience*, 11: 127–38.

Friston, K., Rigoli, F., Ognibene, D., Mathys, C., Fitzgerald, T. and Pezzulo, G. (2015), "Active Inference and Epistemic Value," *Cognitive Neuroscience*, 6 (4): 187–214.

Friston, K., FitzGerald, T., Rigoli, F., Schwartenbeck, P., O'Doherty J. and Pezzulo, G. (2016), "Active Inference and Learning," *Neuroscience & Biobehavioral Reviews*, 68: 862–79.

Friston, K. J., Redish, A. D. and Gordon, J. A. (2017), "Computational Nosology and Precision Psychiatry," *Computational Psychiatry*, 1: 2–23.

Gadsby, S. (2017a), "Explaining Body Size Beliefs in Anorexia," *Cognitive Neuropsychiatry*, 22 (6): 495–507.

Gadsby, S. (2017b), 'Anorexia Nervosa and Oversized Experiences," *Philosophical Psychology*, 30 (5): 594–615.

Gadsby, S. (2017c), "Distorted Body Representations in Anorexia Nervosa," *Consciousness and Cognition*, 51: 17–33.

Gadsby, S. (2018), "Self-Deception and the Second Factor: How Desire Causes Delusion in Anorexia Nervosa," *Erkenntnis*, 85: 1–18.

Herbert, B. M. and Pollatos, O. (2018), "The Relevance of Interoception for Eating Behaviour and Eating Disorders" in Manos Tsakiris and Helena De Preester (eds.), *The Interoceptive Basis of the Mind*, New York: Oxford University Press

Hohwy, J. (2013), *The Predictive Mind*, Oxford: Oxford University Press.

Hohwy, J. and Rosenberg, R. (2005), "Unusual Experiences, Reality Testing, and Delusions of Control," *Mind & Language*, 20 (2): 141–62.

Jones, M. and Love, B. C. (2011), "Bayesian Fundamentalism or Enlightenment? On the Explanatory Status and Theoretical Contributions of Bayesian Models of Cognition," *Behavioral and Brain Sciences*, 34 (4): 169–88.

Kadriu, F., Claes, L., Witteman, C., Norré, J., Vrieze, E. and Krans, J. (2019), "Characteristics and Content of Intrusive Images in Patients with Eating Disorders," *European Eating Disorders Review*. doi.org/10.1002/erv.2671.

Keizer, A., Smeets, M. A., Postma, A., van Elburg, A. and Dijkerman, H. C. (2014), "Does the Experience of Ownership over a Rubber Hand Change Body Size Perception in Anorexia Nervosa Patients?," *Neuropsychologia*, 62: 26–37.

Maher, B. A. (1974), "Delusional Thinking and Perceptual Disorder," *Journal of Individual Psychology*, 30: 98–113.

Marshall, L., Mathys, C., Ruge, D., Berker, A. O. de Dayan, P., Stephan, K. E. and Bestmann, S. (2016), "Pharmacological Fingerprints of Contextual Uncertainty," *PLOS Biology*, 14 (11): e1002575.

Montague, P. R., Dolan, R. J., Friston, K. J. and Dayan, P. (2012), "Computational Psychiatry," *Trends in Cognitive Sciences*, 16 (1): 72–80.

Palmer, C. J., Lawson, R. P. and Hohwy, J. (2017), "Bayesian Approaches to Autism: Towards Volatility, Action, and Behavior," *Psychological Bulletin*, 143 (5): 521–42.

Parr, T. and Friston, K. J. (2018), "The Anatomy of Inference: Generative Models and Brain Structure," *Frontiers in Computational Neuroscience*, 12 (90). doi.org/10.3389/fncom.2018.00090.

Parr, T., Rees, G. and Friston, K. J. (2018), "Computational Neuropsychology and Bayesian Inference," *Frontiers in Human Neuroscience*, 12 (61). doi.org/10.3389/fnhum.2018.00061.

Parr, T., Benrimoh, D., Vincent, P. and Friston, K. (2018), "Precision and False Perceptual Inference," *Frontiers in Integrative Neuroscience*, 12: 39. doi.org/10.3389/fnint.2018.00039.

Phillipou, A., Mountjoy, R. L. and Rossell, S. L. (2017), "Overvalued Ideas or Delusions in Anorexia Nervosa?," *Australian & New Zealand Journal of Psychiatry*, 51 (6): 563–4.

Smeets, M. and Panhuysen, G. (1995), "What Can Be Learned from Body Size Estimation? It All Depends on Your Theory," *Eating Disorders*, 3 (2): 101–14.

Sterzer, P., Adams, R. A., Fletcher, P., Frith, C., Lawrie, S. M., Muckli, L., Petrovic, P., Uhlhaas, P., Voss, M. and Corlett, P. R. (2018), "The Predictive Coding Account of Psychosis," *Biological Psychiatry*, 84 (9): 634–43.

Tulver, K. et al. (2019), "Individual Differences in the Effects of Priors on Perception: A Multi-paradigm Approach," *Cognition*, 187: 167–77.

Van de Cruys, S., Evers, K., Van der Hallen, R., Van Eylen, L., Boets, B., Lee De-wit, L. and Wagemans, J. (2014), "Precise Minds in Uncertain Worlds: Predictive Coding in Autism," *Psychological Review*, 121 (4): 649–75.

Vitousek, K. B. and Hollon, S. D. (1990), "The Investigation of Schematic Content and Processing in Eating Disorders," *Cognitive Therapy and Research*, 14 (2): 191–214.

Wald, A. (1947), "An Essentially Complete Class of Admissible Decision Functions," *The Annals of Mathematical Statistics*, 18 (4): 549–55.

Zopf, R., Contini, E., Fowler, C., Mondraty, N. and Williams, M. A. (2016), "Body Distortions in Anorexia Nervosa: Evidence for Changed Processing of Multisensory Bodily Signals," *Psychiatry Research*, 245: 473–81.

Index

Ingram Content Group UK Ltd.
Milton Keynes UK
UKHW021028040423
419614UK00005B/166